HONG KONG

19TH EDITION

Where to Stay and Eat
for All Budgets

Must-See Sights
and Local Secrets

Ratings You Can Trust

Fodor's Travel Publications   New York, Toronto, London, Sydney, Auckland
www.fodors.com

FODOR'S HONG KONG
Editor: Douglas Stallings

Editorial Production: Tom Holton
Editorial Contributors: Collin Campbell, Tracey Furniss, Eva Chui Loiterton, Tim Metcalfe, Sofia A. Suárez
Maps: David Lindroth, *cartographer*; Bob Blake and Rebecca Baer, *map editors*
Design: Fabrizio La Rocca, *creative director*; Guido Caroti, *art director*; Moon Sun Kim, *cover designer*; Melanie Marin, *senior picture editor*
Production/Manufacturing: Angela L. McLean
Cover Photo (Dragon dance, Central Plaza): © Picture Finders Ltd./eStockPhoto

COPYRIGHT
Copyright © 2005 by Fodors LLC

Fodor's is a registered trademark of Random House, Inc.

All rights reserved under International and Pan-American Copyright Conventions. Published in the United States by Fodor's Travel Publications, a unit of Fodors LLC, a subsidiary of Random House, Inc., and simultaneously in Canada by Random House of Canada Limited, Toronto. Distributed by Random House, Inc., New York.

No maps, illustrations, or other portions of this book may be reproduced in any form without written permission from the publisher.

Nineteenth Edition

ISBN 1–4000–1442–5

ISSN 1070–6887

SPECIAL SALES
This book is available for special discounts for bulk purchases for sales promotions or premiums. Special editions, including personalized covers, excerpts of existing books, and corporate imprints, can be created in large quantities for special needs. For more information, write to Special Markets/Premium Sales, 1745 Broadway, MD 6-2, New York, New York 10019, or e-mail specialmarkets@ randomhouse.com.

AN IMPORTANT TIP & AN INVITATION
Although all prices, opening times, and other details in this book are based on information supplied to us at press time, changes occur all the time in the travel world, and Fodor's cannot accept responsibility for facts that become outdated or for inadvertent errors or omissions. So **always confirm information when it matters,** especially if you're making a detour to visit a specific place. Your experiences—positive and negative—matter to us. If we have missed or misstated something, **please write to us.** We follow up on all suggestions. Contact the Hong Kong editor at editors@fodors.com or c/o Fodor's at 1745 Broadway, New York, NY 10019.

PRINTED IN THE UNITED STATES OF AMERICA

10 9 8 7 6 5 4 3 2 1

DESTINATION: HONG KONG

Hong Kong is constantly in the process of reinventing itself. Once a British colonial outpost, this dynamic city is now known as a Special Administrative Region (SAR) of China. The soul of Hong Kong is pure energy, from the frenetic street markets and luxury shopping malls, to a wild nightlife underlining the city's "work hard, play hard" lifestyle. And for all the ups and downs of recent years, from the so-called "Asian Meltdown" to the SARS crisis in 2003, Hong Kong has a habit of bouncing back—just a little bit stronger than before. You can't help being impressed by the sheer efficiency and speed of everyday life here, a fusion of eastern and western cultures where incense-filled temples and glass-and-steel skyscrapers live side by side. Time waits for no one in this distinctly Asian parallel universe— and your best bet is simply to ride with it and enjoy. Just don't expect to get too much sleep! Have a great trip!

Tim Jarrell, Publisher

CONTENTS

ABOUT THIS BOOK

The best source for travel advice is a like-minded friend who's just been where you're headed. But with or without that friend, you'll be in great shape to find your way around your destination once you learn to find your way around your Fodor's guide.

SELECTION

You can go on the assumption that everything in this book is recommended wholeheartedly by our writers and editors. Flip to On the Road with Fodor's to learn more about who they are. It goes without saying that no property pays to be included.

RATINGS

Orange stars ★ denote sights and properties that our editors and writers consider the very best in the area covered by the entire book. These, the best of the best, are listed in the Fodor's Choice section in the front of the book. Black stars ★ highlight the sights and properties we deem Highly Recommended, the don't-miss sights within any region. In cities, sights pinpointed with numbered map bullets ❻ in the margins tend to be more important than those without bullets.

SPECIAL SPOTS

Pleasures & Pastimes and text on chapter title pages focus on experiences that reveal the spirit of the destination. Also watch for Off the Beaten Path sights. Some are out of the way, some are quirky, and all are worth while. When the munchies hit, look for Need a Break? suggestions.

TIME IT RIGHT

Check On the Calendar up front and chapters' Timing sections for weather and crowd overviews and best days and times to visit.

SEE IT ALL

Use Fodor's exclusive Great Itineraries as a model for your trip. Good Walks guide you to important sights in each neighborhood; ☞ indicates the starting points of walks and itineraries in the text and on the map.

BUDGET WELL

Hotel and restaurant price categories from ¢ to $$$$ are defined in the opening pages of each relevant chapter—expect to find a balanced selection for every budget. For attractions, we always give standard adult admission fees; reductions are usually available for children, students, and senior citizens.

BASIC INFO

Smart Travel Tips lists travel essentials for the entire area covered by the book; city- and region-specific basics end the side-trips chapters. To find the best way to get around, see the transportation section; see individual modes of travel ("Car Travel," "Train Travel") for details.

ON THE MAPS

Maps throughout the book show you what's where and help you find your way around. Black and orange numbered bullets ❻ ❻ in the text correlate to bullets on maps.

BACKGROUND

We give background information within the chapters in the course of explaining sights as well as in the CloseUp boxes and in Understanding Hong Kong at the end of the book. To get in the mood, review Books & Movies.

FIND IT FAST

In the Exploring Hong Kong chapter, sights are organized based on whether they are on Hong Kong Island, in Kowloon, or in the New Territories and Outer Islands, and they are further divided by neighborhood or, in Chapter 8, by town or island. Where to Eat and Where to Stay are also organized by neighborhood—Where to Eat is further divided by cuisine type. The Nightlife & the Arts and Sports & the Outdoors chapters are arranged alphabetically by type of entertainment or by sport. Within Shopping, descriptions of the city's main shopping districts, shopping centers, and markets are followed by a list of specialty shops grouped according to their focus. The Side Trip to Macau chapter explores the nearby territory of Macau. The Side Trips to South China chapter is subdivided by town, and the towns are covered in logical geographical order. Heads at the top of each page help you find what you need within a chapter.

DON'T FORGET

Restaurants are open for lunch and dinner daily unless we state otherwise; we mention dress only when there's a specific requirement and reservations only when they're essential or not accepted— it's always best to book ahead. Hotels have private baths, phones, TVs, and air-conditioning and operate on the European Plan (a.k.a. EP, meaning without meals). We always list facilities but not whether you'll be charged extra to use them, so when pricing accommodations, find out what's included.

SYMBOLS

Many Listings

★	Fodor's Choice
★	Highly recommended
⊠	Physical address
✢	Directions
⬚	Mailing address
☎	Telephone
🖷	Fax
⊕	On the Web
✎	E-mail
🖭	Admission fee
☉	Open/closed times
►	Start of walk/itinerary
Ⓜ	Metro stations
▭	Credit cards

Outdoors

⅄	Golf
⚠	Camping

Hotels & Restaurants

🏨	Hotel
⇋	Number of rooms
♨	Facilities
ⅤⅪ	Meal plans
✕	Restaurant
⚑	Reservations
🏛	Dress code
↘	Smoking
🍺	BYOB
✕🏨	Hotel with restaurant that warrants a visit

Other

♨	Family-friendly
🛈	Contact information
⇨	See also
⊠	Branch address
☞	Take note

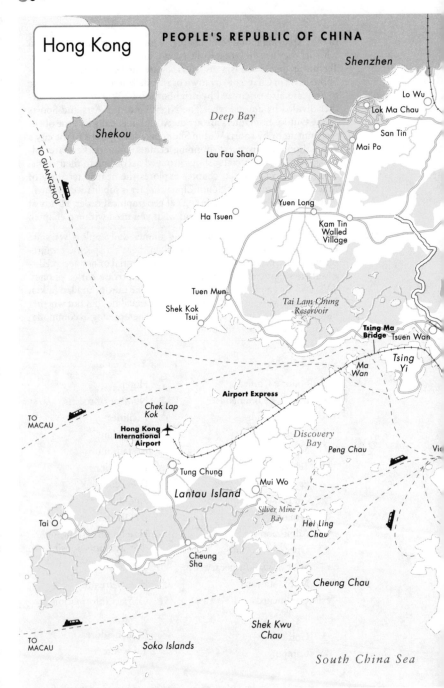

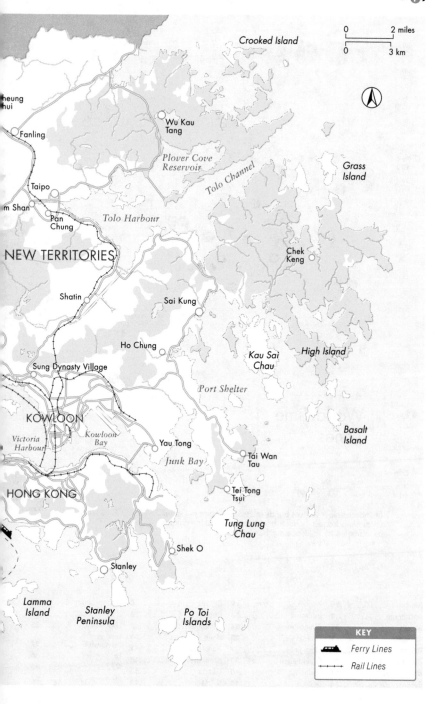

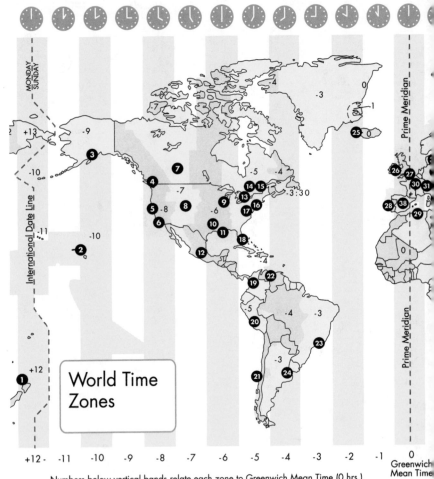

World Time Zones

Numbers below vertical bands relate each zone to Greenwich Mean Time (0 hrs.).
Local times frequently differ from these general indications,
as indicated by light-face numbers on map.

+12 · -11 -10 -9 -8 -7 -6 -5 -4 -3 -2 -1 0 Greenwich Mean Time

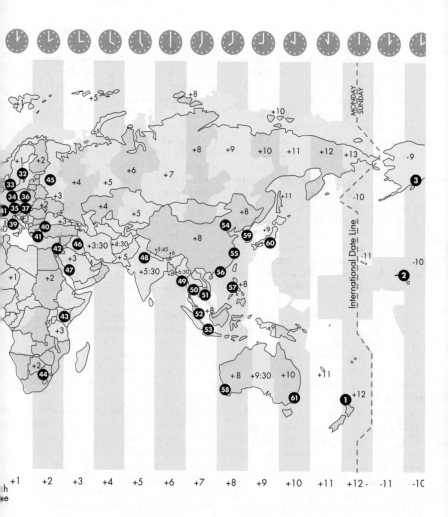

ON THE ROAD WITH FODOR'S

A trip takes you out of yourself. Concerns of life at home completely disappear, driven away by more immediate thoughts—about, say, what marvels will beguile the next day, or where you'll have dinner. That's where Fodor's comes in. We make sure that you know all your options, so that you don't miss something that's around the next bend just because you didn't know it was there. Because the best memories of your trip might well have nothing to do with what you came to Hong Kong to see, we guide you to sights large and small all over the region. You might set out to take in the view from atop Victoria Peak, but back at home you find yourself unable to forget your dolphin-spotting trip or high tea at the Mandarin Oriental Hotel. With Fodor's at your side, serendipitous discoveries are never far away.

Our success in showing you every corner of Hong Kong is a credit to our extraordinary writers. Although there's no substitute for travel advice from a good friend who knows your style, our contributors are the next best thing—the kind of people you would poll for travel advice if you knew them.

Born in Hong Kong and raised in Australia, Eva Chui Loiterton returned to her birthplace in 1995. For two years she reported on the city's arts and popular-culture scenes as the entertainment editor for *HK* magazine, a weekly finger on Hong Kong's pulse. Moving to broadcast media, she then spent three years as a producer for Channel V, Asia's No. 1 music-TV station. Currently, she divides her time between writing and working in the television and film industries in Hong Kong. For this edition, she updated several chapters, including Exploring, Nightlife & the Arts, and the Side Trip to Macau.

Tracey Furniss, who updated the Where to Stay and Shopping chapters for this edition, has lived in Southeast Asia and Hong Kong for more than 20 years. She started out writing for various magazines in Hong Kong, then went on to work in radio and television, including six years at CNN. She now editor for *The Parents' Journal* in Hong Kong and writes for the *South China Morning Post,* as well as covering what's new in Hong Kong for various magazines in the United Kingdom and United States.

Tim Metcalfe has been writing, editing, and dining his way around Hong Kong since 1988. The globe-trotting English journalist initially joined the *South China Morning Post* on arrival in the former British colony, and was subsequently assistant editor of the *Hong Kong Standard* for five years. Since 1995 he has freelanced for countless publications, syndication agencies, and organizations in Hong Kong and around the world, specializing in travel, food, and wine. He updated Where to Eat and Sports & the Outdoors for this edition, as well as sections at the front of the book.

Sofia A. Suárez runs her communications company, Fiorini Bassi, in Hong Kong, where she was born and raised. After studying in the U.S. and Italy, the Italian-Filipina moved to New York to work for Fairchild Publications. Sofia now contributes to various newspapers and magazines around the world including the *South China Morning Post,* for whom she writes weekly style and art columns, and *The Peninsula Magazine.* She updated Smart Travel Tips and the Side Trips to Southern China chapters for this edition.

Hong Kong Island

Central & Lan Kwai Fong. The nerve center of the city is on the go around the clock. Luxury shopping malls and alleyway markets around the legendary Mandarin Oriental and Ritz-Carlton hotels make it a hive of activity by day. At night, the entertainment district of Lan Kwai Fong never sleeps.

Admiralty. Next door to Central, this area is home to a cluster of five-star hotels, including the massive Marriott, Conrad, and Island Shangri-La, and the upmarket Pacific Place shopping mall.

Wanchai. East of Central, the former "World of Suzie Wong," just at the next stop of the antiquated but charming tram line down the harbor front, remains a haven for denizens of the night—but it is also at the center of international business these days with its Convention and Exhibition Centre, which includes the Grand Hyatt and Renaissance Harbour View hotels.

Causeway Bay. Serious shoppers head to this area, which is convenient to the Excelsior, Regal Hongkong, and Park Lane hotels. It is also within walking distance of the legendary Happy Valley Racetrack and the Hong Kong Stadium, venue for most major sporting events.

North Point & Quarry Bay. Beyond Causeway Bay, these emerging business districts are of little interest to tourists, but you will find some of the cheapest hotels on the north side of Hong Kong Island here if you are willing to accept the distance from the major sights.

Midlevels & SoHo. Rising above Central, this is the area where much of wealthy Hong Kong sleeps in high-rise luxury apartment blocks soaring straight out of the tropical bush. SoHo is an emerging neighborhood of restaurants and nightspots, accessed from the long Midlevels Escalator.

The Peak. The exclusive residential area of Victoria Peak is the highest (at 1,805 feet) of a small group of hills in the middle of the island, high above Midlevels. Reached via the Peak Tram or zigzagging roads, its lookout station is on every itinerary.

Western & Sheung Wan. Stretching from the western end of Central to the Macau Ferry Terminal, these two neighborhoods are a glimpse of the "old" Hong Kong, brimming with medicine shops and ethnic produce markets, not to mention the restored Western Market.

South Side. On the south side of Hong Kong Island, **Aberdeen** is a bustling fishing port, and **Apleichau** island is just a sampan ride away; the port is most famous for its spectacular, garish floating restaurants— an essential experience when visiting Hong Kong—as well as Ocean Park, the island's principal theme park until Disneyland Hong Kong comes along. Beyond Aberdeen are beachfront suburbs for the rich and famous. **Repulse Bay** is the island's most popular beach; **Stanley** has Hong Kong's most popular street market; and remote **Shek O** is a laid-back beach haven.

Kowloon

Tsim Sha Tsui. Bustling Kowloon occupies the tip of the peninsula across from Hong Kong Island. Tsim Sha Tsui, at the bottom of the peninsula, is at the start of the so-called "Golden Mile" of Nathan Road—not to mention home to such renowned hotels as the Peninsula, InterContinental Hong Kong (formerly the Regent), the Langham Hotel Hong Kong (formerly the Great Eagle), Holiday Inn Golden Mile, New World Renaissance, and various Marco Polo hotels.

Tsim Sha Tsui East. A stroll away in Tsim Sha Tsui East, the location of Hong Kong's fascinating new Museum of History, which explains the evolution of the city from prehistoric times to today, are the Kowloon Shangri-La, Intercontinental Grand Stanford, and Hotel Nikko.

Jordan, Mong Kok & Yau Ma Tei. Up the Golden Mile are the neighborhoods, noted for the Temple Street Night Market, Bird Market, Jade Market, Flower Market, and Knutsford Terrace nightlife center. This area has more Chinese character than the more modern, built-up parts of Hong Kong, particularly Tsim Sha Tsui and Central. Top hotels here include the Eaton as well as budget choices like the Booth Lodge. Also in the neighborhood is Sham Shui Po, where the world flocks for bargain-priced computers, games, and software.

Kowloon Tong. The railway crossroads to mainland China—where Hong Kong's MTR system meets the Kowloon–Canton Railway—is also home to the prestigious Festival Walk shopping mall and has an additional reputation for discreet "love hotels" that are familiar to every taxi driver.

Farther afield in Kowloon. Diamond Hill's only attraction is a replica Buddhist monastery and the Hollywood shopping mall. **Wong Tai Sin**'s temple hosts several spectacular festivals every year. If you find yourself in industrial **Kwun Tong** or **Hung Hom** you are probably lost.

The New Territories

Because of its distance (which in fact is not great) from the commercial hubs of Hong Kong Island and Kowloon, travelers often overlook the attractions of the New Territories. Parts of the area retain their isolated rural character, even if to find them you must make your way past massive housing developments called "new towns," which were built to house the burgeoning population of the territory.

Sha Tin. One of the "new towns," its main attraction is the ultramodern racecourse belonging to the Hong Kong Jockey Club, but the very old Temple of Ten Thousand Buddhas is also well worth the trip.

Sai Kung. East of Sha Tin, the village of Sai Kung has wonderful restaurants, and its Country Park is one of the most spectacular in the SAR.

Outer Islands

As popular getaways for locals and tourists alike, the islands around Hong Kong in the South China Sea have unique charms of their own, from beaches and old fishing villages to hiking trails and remote, ancient Buddhist monasteries. There are three main islands.

Lantau. The largest of Hong Kong's outer islands is actually larger than Hong Kong Island itself. It's main attraction is the Po Lin Monastery, with the largest seated, outdoor, bronze Buddha in the world.

Lamma. Though lacking in actual "sights," Lamma is famous for its seafood restaurants, which are worth the trip, and for village charm.

Cheung Chau. The most densely populated of the outer island, car-less Cheung Chau is known as an artist colony.

Macau

A tiny geographical remnant of the 16th-century Portuguese spice trade, Macau provides a pleasant respite from the nonstop bustle of Hong Kong, 65 km (40 mi) to the east. Construction has taken away some of the island's quieter charms, but Portuguese influence—especially in the food—is yet another fascinating Eurasian variation played out in the South China Sea. Macau is a peninsula, connected by bridge to Taipa Island, which is in turn connected to Coloane Island by a causeway. Both islands are easy to reach and have many attractions of their own.

If You Have 3 Days

Hong Kong is a complex city. On the surface it seems that every building is a high-rise sculpture of glass and steel and that every pedestrian is hurrying to a business meeting. But if you look past the shiny surface, you'll see the culture, heritage, and people that give this city its exotic flavor and unique outlook.

Day 1: To get a perspective on all the bustle, start your first day with a trip to the top of Victoria Peak by taking the Peak Tram, the steepest funicular railway in the world. From here you'll be able to get a bird's-eye view of Central's sparkling high-rises, the densely packed streets of Hong Kong Island, the harbor, and all the way to the outer edges of Kowloon. Descend back into Central and spend the rest of your first day checking out the centers of activity on Hong Kong Island: the upscale shopping and landmark skyscrapers of Central; the "old-fashioned" Western District, with its restored Western Market; the restaurants, lanes, and antiques shops alongside the Midlevels Escalator; and the megamalls and department stores of Causeway Bay and Admiralty. At night, look no further than trendy Lan Kwai Fong and SoHo in Central, or the more down-to-earth nightspots of Wanchai—which are best visited without carrying a credit card!

Day 2: If you're staying on Hong Kong Island, start your second day with a ride on the Star Ferry to arrive in the Tsim Sha Tsui neighborhood at the tip of Kowloon (if you're staying in Kowloon, you should use the ferry to arrive on Hong Kong Island on your first day). The view of the towering city from the water is always impressive. Not far from the Star Ferry Terminal are the Hong Kong Space and Art museums. Don't miss the new History Museum to learn about the amazing evolution of Hong Kong, from ancient times to the present day; you will learn more in two hours than from studying dozens of history books. On the street opposite the dome of the Space Museum is the grand Peninsula hotel, one of the historic landmarks of Hong Kong. Take a peek at the palatial lobby and stop for the justifiably popular afternoon high tea. Continue up Nathan Road, which is crammed with stores big and small, on your way to the temples of Tin Hau, the oldest in Hong Kong, and Wong Tai Sin, an explosively colorful and noisy spot with a full concourse of fortune-tellers. Also take this opportunity to visit some of the diverse markets that are unique to Hong Kong. The Bird Garden, with birdcages lining the walkways and busy vendors selling cricket treats for their beloved songbird pets, particularly stands out. Other markets in the area include the enclosed Jade Market, the Flower Market (most interesting in the time leading up to the New Year), and the Ladies' and Temple Street night markets (the latter starts around 6 PM). Wrap up your day in Kowloon with a drink or dinner at Knutsford Terrace, the area's top nightlife area, or in style at the Peninsula's Felix restaurant for unparalleled views of neon-lit Central.

Day 3: On your third day, take a hair-raising bus ride from Central to the south side of Hong Kong Island. You'll have an unforgettable view of the island's coastline as the double-decker bus descends from the peaks of the busy shopping and business districts into the sandy coves of Stanley and Repulse Bay. Try to sit in the front of the upper deck for a ride more exciting than any amusement park. Start your day in Stanley, wandering through the market before it gets too crowded. If you haven't bought souvenirs yet, this is the best—and usually the cheapest—place to do it. When you're ready for a break from the frenetic market, wander along the waterfront and choose a spot for lunch. Then hop the bus to Aberdeen, for an afternoon at Ocean Park, followed by dinner at the amazing Jumbo Floating Restaurant.

If You Have 5 Days

If you have a few more days, spend your first three days as laid out above, then it's time to go a bit farther afield.

Day 4: On your fourth day venture out to the New Territories. Your best bet is to head for little-visited Sai Kung, one of the most popular rural areas for expatriates. The port is delightful; enjoy lunch alfresco at one of the waterfront restaurants, and in the afternoon catch a bus into Sai Kung Country Park for a stroll in the countryside. If you'd like to see a lot of the New Territories in a short time, perhaps the easiest way is through an organized tour sponsored by the Hong Kong Tourism Bureau (HKTB). From Kowloon Tong MTR station, the KCR train will take you to Sha Tin, home of both a very modern horse-racing track and the time-honored Temple of Ten Thousand Buddhas. Continue on the train to the Chinese border and a shopping expedition to remember, directly across from the border post in Shenzhen.

Day 5: On your fifth day take a ride out to Lantau Island. Once again, you could spend several days exploring the outer islands, but if your time is limited, take the ferry from Central to the western side of Lantau. From here take a bus (or hike) to Po Lin Monastery where Tin Tan Buddha, the world's tallest outdoor bronze Buddha, is located. From here take the bus to Tai O, a quaint fishing village where you can have a seafood lunch. In the afternoon, take the bus back to the harbor and Silvermine Bay, where you can rent bikes to explore the small village of Mui Wo before taking the ferry back to Central.

If You Have 7 Days

If you have an entire week for your visit to Hong Kong, spend your first five days in Hong Kong as suggested above, but then pack a small bag and head out to Macau for an overnight stay. While Macau can be seen in one day—and can be reached in a little over an hour on the super-fast ferry—to really get a feel for its unique amalgam of Portuguese and Chinese charm you should spend the night.

Catch an early ferry to give yourself time to explore the Old Citadel section of the city, where you'll find the fascinating Museum of Macau and the landmark structure of the church of São Paulo. This Portuguese-influenced neighborhood also has reasonably priced shops that sell everything from furniture to polo shirts. You'll also want to set aside time to explore peninsular Macau, where you can visit the picturesque A-Ma Temple and the informative Maritime Museum. While you're in this neighborhood, stop by the Pousada de São Tiago, a tranquil inn built into the ruins of a 17th-century fort, for a meal or a drink. For dinner, make sure to sample the unique and tasty Macanese cuisine. After dinner, you can entertain yourself in a casino. On your last day, you might want to lay out on the white sands of a Macau beach to end your stay in this part of the world before boarding the ferry back to Hong Kong and home.

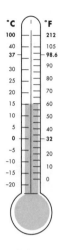

°C		°F
100		212
40		105
37		98.6
30		90
25		80
20		70
15		60
10		50
5		40
0		32
−5		20
−10		10
−15		0
−20		

October through December are among the most popular and expensive months in Hong Kong, not to mention the most pleasant. Because they coincide with typhoon season and summer's hot, sticky weather, June through September are usually the cheapest months. There's always a surge of visitors around Chinese New Year in late January or early February.

Climate

Hong Kong's high season, October through late December, is popular for a reason: the weather is pleasant, with sunny days and cool, comfortable nights. January, February, and sometimes early March are cooler and dank, with long periods of overcast skies and rain. March and April can be either chilly and miserable or sunny and beautiful. By May the temperature is consistently warm and comfortable.

June through September is typhoon season, when the weather is hot, sticky, and very rainy. Typhoons (called hurricanes in the Atlantic) must be treated with respect, and Hong Kong is prepared for these blustery assaults; if a storm is approaching, the airwaves will crackle with information, and your hotel and various public institutions will post the appropriate signals. When a No. 8 signal is posted, Hong Kong and Macau close down completely. Head immediately for your hotel and stay put. This is serious business—bamboo scaffolding can come hurtling through the streets like spears, ships can be sunk in the harbor, and large areas of the territory are often flooded.

Macau's summers are slightly cooler and wetter than Hong Kong's.

▣ Forecasts **Weather Channel Connection** ☎ 900/932-8437, 95¢ per minute from a Touch-Tone phone. **Hong Kong Observatory** ☎ 187-8066 ⊕ www.hko.gov.hk. **Hong Kong Time & Weather** ☎ 18501.

HONG KONG TEMPERATURES

Jan.	67F	19C	May	85F	29C	Sept.	86F	30C
	58	14		75	24		78	26
Feb.	67F	19C	June	86F	30C	Oct.	82F	28C
	58	14		78	26		73	23
Mar.	69F	21C	July	89F	32C	Nov.	75F	24C
	63	17		81	27		67	19
Apr.	77F	25C	Aug.	87F	31C	Dec.	69F	21C
	69	21		78	26		59	15

Top seasonal events in Hong Kong include the Chinese New Year, the Hong Kong Arts Festival, the Hong Kong Food Festival, and the Dragon Boat Festival. The most colorful shindigs of all are the many lunar festivals celebrated throughout the year. Contact the HKTB for exact dates and more information.

ONGOING

Late February–early March	The Hong Kong Arts Festival showcases four weeks of world-class music, dance, and drama from around the globe.
Late November–Early December	The Omega Hong Kong Open Golf Championship is co-sanctioned by the Asian PGA Tour and the European tour, and attracts top names in golf. It is held at the Hong Kong Golf Club in Fanling.

WINTER

Mid-December	The Hong Kong Judo Championship takes place at Queen Elizabeth Stadium.
January	The Fringe Club's City Festival showcases an assortment of international and local drama, dance, music, and light entertainment.
Early February	The Standard Chartered Hong Kong Marathon consists of three hot races—a full marathon, a half marathon, and a 10K race. The event attracts over 18,000 athletes every year, including many well-known foreign distance runners.
February	The Chinese New Year has the city at a virtual standstill as shops shut down for three days and people don their best attire to visit friends and relatives. A street parade is held on the first day of the new year, with large floats sponsored by local and international companies. There's a large fireworks display on the second night.
	For the Spring Lantern Festival, streets and homes are decorated with brightly colored lanterns for the last day of Chinese New Year celebrations.

SPRING

March	The Hong Kong International Literary Festival celebrates writing in English with Asian roots and attracts internationally acclaimed writers whose work is informed by Asia. Invited writers range from up-and-comings to Mann Booker Prize winners.
	The annual Hong Kong Food Festival is a two-week smorgasbord of events, including cooking classes with world-renowned chefs, tours of famous restaurants and teahouses, and an amusing waiters' race.

Late March–early April	The Rugby Sevens is the world's premier seven-a-side tournament usually held over Easter weekend in a sold-out 40,000-seat stadium.
Early April	The Ching Ming Festival, literally "bright and clear" is when families visit the burial plots of ancestors and departed relatives.
April	The Hong Kong International Film Festival focuses on hot spots in global cinema as well as special sections on restored Mandarin classics, commendable locally made films, and many other Asian productions.
	The Hong Kong Open tennis tournament attracts some of the biggest names in the sport.
Late April–early May	For the Birthday of Tin Hau, goddess of the sea, fishermen decorate their boats and converge on seaside temples to honor her, especially around the Tin Hau Temple in Junk Bay.
May 1	Labour Day is a public holiday in Hong Kong, as well as in China where the holiday often lasts a few days.
May	The Birthday of Buddha is celebrated on the eighth day of the fourth moon. The devout flock to major Buddhist shrines like the Temple of Ten Thousand Buddhas at Sha Tin or Po Lin Monastery on Lantau.
	The Bun Festival on Cheung Chau Island attracts thousands for a three-day rite dedicated to placating the spirits of the dead. It culminates in a grand procession.
	Le French May Festival of Arts attracts some of the best Gallic dance, music, and theater groups to the territory. There's also a mix of French films, plus art exhibitions at venues across Hong Kong.
SUMMER	
June	The Dragon Boat Festival pits long, multi-oared dragon-head boats against one another in races to commemorate the hero Chu Yuen, a 4th-century poet and scholar who drowned himself to protest the corruption of government officials. Afterwards, his friends and fishermen took to the water in boats in order to pound drums to scare away the fish who would have eaten his body.
	In the Fina Marathon Swimming World Cup, top-ranked swimmers compete in one of the legs of the international short courses series. World records have been set in previous years at the Kowloon Park indoor swimming pool.
July 1	Hong Kong SAR Establishment Day marks the day that Hong Kong reverted to Chinese sovereignty after 99 years of British rule.
August	The Hungry Ghosts Festival is a time when food is set out and elaborate ceremonies are performed to placate the angry roaming spirits of those buried without proper funeral rites, forgotten by their families, or deceased with no descendents to care for their grave sites.

Mid-August	The Seven Sisters (Maiden) Festival is a celebration for lovers, and a time when young girls pray for a good husband.
	The Women's Beach Volleyball Tour is part of the FIVB's (Federation of International Volleyball) world tour that has top-ranked players from around the globe competing on a man-made beach at Victoria Park. Dubbed "Sportainment," the five-day event has a carnival-like atmosphere alongside the action.
FALL	
September	The Chinese Opera Fortnight presents traditional Cantonese, Peking, Soochow, Chekiang, and Chiu Chow operas in the City Hall theater and concert hall, and the Ko Shan Theatre.
	The Mid-Autumn Festival, also known as the Lantern or Moon Festival, sees crowds with candle lanterns gather in parks and other open spaces sharing *yue bing* or "moon cakes," which are stuffed with red-bean or lotus-seed paste. Such hearty foods are said to symbolize happiness and completion.
Late September or early October	The Birthday of Confucius honors the revered philosopher.
October 1	National Day is a public holiday marking the anniversary of the 1949 founding of the People's Republic of China.
Mid-October	The Chung Yeung Festival commemorates a Han Dynasty tale about a man taking his family to high ground to avoid disaster. Like the Ching Ming Festival, this is a time to clean family graves and make offerings.
Late October or early November	The Chinese Arts Festival showcases more than 150 artistic events (dance, music, and theater) from as far afield as Australia, Bhutan, Hawaii, and Mongolia. It is held biennially, in even-numbered years.
Late November	The Macau Grand Prix takes over the city streets for a weekend.

PLEASURES & PASTIMES

Beaches Surprising as it may seem, splendid beaches are all over Hong Kong. Repulse Bay is a sort of Chinese Coney Island. Around the corner is the smaller and less crowded Deep Water Bay; Turtle Cove is isolated and beautiful; Shek O's Big Wave Bay has a Mediterranean feel; and in the New Territories you can catch a sampan from the Sai Kung waterfront to several idyllic island beaches, including Hap Mun (Half Moon) Bay.

Dining Aside from New York, no other city in the world can match the distinct variety and integrity of cuisines in Hong Kong. One of the most exciting aspects is obviously eating authentic Chinese food—which you will find far different from Chinatowns in the West. Expect a puzzled response if you request something like chop suey, chow mein, or fortune cookies, all of which were created in the United States. They just don't exist in Hong Kong. Subtlety and freshness of flavor are what count in Cantonese dishes, regarded as the prince of Chinese cuisine, although visitors frequently find themselves more familiar with the menus in the numerous Szechuan, Shanghainese, Peking, and Chiu Chow restaurants. At the same time, at a cultural crossroads like Hong Kong, the aromatic flavors of pan-Asian cuisine are another unique culinary opportunity, along with every style of international cuisine from Cajun to Cambodian, Lebanese to Moroccan, and Korean to Mexican. There's even an authentic New York deli.

Chinese Culture There are so many ways of absorbing Chinese culture. Even on public transport or in the street, you will be amazed by how polite and courteous people are obliged to behave as they move around a crowded city. This necessity to "get along" and respect an individual's personal space keeps Hong Kong one of the safest cities in the world to walk around, either by day or night. But there's probably no better way of pondering the culture than in the early morning, at any park, at the tai chi ritual. The calmness amid frenetic life beyond reflects the philosophy of yin and yang balance that essentially underlies what it means to be Chinese. This philosophy extends beyond exercising to eating, conversation, and meeting people for the first time, where such a simple matter as exchanging name cards assumes its own polite ritual. Appreciate this side of Hong Kong and you will go a long way to understanding why so many people, both Chinese and foreigners, fall in love with the city.

Shopping Hong Kong has some of the best shopping in the world, if you work at it. Although the thought of crowded streets and mind-boggling choices can be daunting, no place makes big spending easier than this center of international commerce. Every major designer label is here, including their bargain-priced factory overruns. Computers and software are famously good value in Sham Shui Po's many computer stores. Novelties and T-shirts galore are best sought at Stanley Market or Temple Street Night Market. Chinese antiques and paintings, handicrafts from all over Asia, electronic goods, and luxury accessories—you name it, Hong Kong sells it. Just as remarkable is the physical array of places to shop, from sophisticated boutique-lined malls to open-air markets and shadowy alleyways.

FODOR'S CHOICE

The sights, restaurants, hotels, and other travel experiences on these pages are our editors' top picks—our Fodor's Choices. They're the best of their type in the area covered by the book—not to be missed and always worth your time. In the chapters that follow, you will find all the details.

HOTELS

$$$$	**Mandarin Oriental Hong Kong,** Central. The Mandarin matches convenience with luxury, making it one of the world's great hotels. Celebrities and VIPs agree.
$$$$	**The Peninsula Hong Kong,** Tsim Sha Tsui. The Pen is the ultimate in colonial elegance, with its mix of European ambience and Chinese details.
$$$$	**Ritz-Carlton Hong Kong,** Central. Refined elegance is the name of the game at this luxury hotel with European details.
$$$$	**Westin Resort Macau,** Macau. When you want to get away from it all—but not too far from Hong Kong—this resort takes the cake, with a good beach, great facilities, and nearby golf courses.
$$$	**Harbour Plaza Hong Kong,** Hung Hom. This opulent hotel has a lovely rooftop pool and great harbor views, though it's a bit farther removed from the action in Kowloon—not a bad thing at all.
$$$	**Renaissance Harbour View,** Wanchai. This large hotel shares a beautiful pool area and a choice location with the much more expensive Grand Hyatt.
$$$	**Island Shangri-La,** Central. This hotel, which towers above the Pacific Place complex, has spacious rooms and spectacular views of the Peak and Victoria Harbour.
$$	**Bishop Lei International House,** Midlevels. The simple guesthouse has moderate prices and hotel-style amenities.
$	**Garden View International House,** Midlevels. This small, attractive hotel overlooks the Botanical Gardens and the harbor.
$	**Salisbury YMCA,** Tsim Sha Tsui. With excellent fitness facilities and a location next to the famed Peninsula, this "Y" is hardly a spartan affair, and it's worth paying a bit extra for the harbor view, which is four times more expensive across the street.

RESTAURANTS

$$$–$$$$	**Robuchon a Galera,** Macau. A slice of opulent Parisian fare has reached Macau through French celebrity chef Joël Robuchon.
$$–$$$$	**Yung Kee,** Central. What you expect from Cantonese dining—lightning-fast preparation, high-energy service, and reasonable prices—

is what you get at Yung Kee, which is why so many people keep coming back.

$$–$$$ **café TOO,** Admiralty. This Island Shangri-La takes the international food court to a whole new level of distinction, with made-to-order food from seven different cooking theaters.

$–$$$ **Café Deco Bar & Grill,** The Peak. Combining Hong Kong chic and pan-Asian cuisine with panoramic views from atop Victoria Peak, this has become an island favorite.

$–$$$ **M at the Fringe,** Central. It's hard to categorize the cuisine at what is, for many, Hong Kong's finest restaurant—unless the category is delicious and dazzling.

$–$$ **Dim Sum,** Happy Valley. Breaking with tradition, this small jewel serves the best dim sum in Hong Kong day and night.

EXCURSIONS

Largo do Senado, Macau. If you make the trek to Macau, be sure to stop by this quintessential town square, which is the heart of the city.

Ocean Park, Aberdeen. The view of the coastline from the cable car will make you think you're riding over the Mediterranean as you gaze down at a panorama of mountains, pastel villas, and the vast blue sea. It's also a great place to take the kids.

Po Lin Buddhist Monastery, Lantau. Built on a grander scale than most temple complexes in Hong Kong, Po Lin Monastery is home to Southeast Asia's largest seated, outdoor, bronze Buddha, more than 100 feet high.

Stanley Market, Stanley. You can't beat this market for cheerful Chinese souvenirs, sports goods, and designer outlet apparel, all situated by a seaside town.

Temple of Ten Thousand Buddhas, Sha Tin. You have to climb nearly 500 steps to reach this wonder, but with its 13,000 statues and gilded holy man, in addition to views of Amah Rock and a restaurant serving traditional Buddhist meals, it's worth the effort.

OUTDOOR ACTIVITIES

Dragon's Back in Shek O Country Park, Shek O. Bring your hiking boots and canteen and escape the urban madness on a moderately hilly trail where banana leaves grow to lengths of 3 feet and the view of the sea is nothing short of spectacular.

Hong Kong Jockey Club Golf Course, Kau Sai Chau. Hong Kong's only public golf course is well worth the trip, particularly on a weekday, when it's not quite so busy.

MacLehose Trail, New Territories. You don't have to hike the entire 97-km (60-mi) trail, but tackling the section in Sai Kung Country Park will give you an ideal excuse to see one of Hong Kong's best wilderness area.

Zhuhai Golden Gulf Golf Club, Jiwan District, Guangdong. If you aren't into shopping, Guangdong's newest golf course is reason enough to visit South China, and the attached country club offers activities for nongolfers in the family.

ONLY IN HONG KONG

Bird Garden, Prince Edward. The bird garden consists of various courtyards filled with trees and 70 stalls selling birds, cages, and such accoutrements as tiny porcelain feeders and fresh grasshoppers.

City Contemporary Dance Company. During the season, Hong Kong's best dance troupe presents modern performance pieces choreographed by predominantly local talent.

Happy Valley Racetrack, Happy Valley. Wednesday evenings come alive at one of the favorite destinations for Hong Kong locals.

International Rugby Sevens. Only Chinese New Year is a bigger celebration than Hong Kong's own version of March Madness.

Peak Tram, Central. Once you're seated on this historic tram, be prepared for a steep journey and a fantastic backwards view of Hong Kong Island and Kowloon.

Star Ferry, Central and Tsim Sha Tsui. Crossing the harbor is one of the quintessential Hong Kong experiences, particularly on the top deck, where the views are better. Feeling the wind of the South China Sea is vital to any experience of Hong Kong, whose very existence owes itself to the crossing of seas—not to mention today's stunning views.

Victoria Peak, The Peak. The city's best view is also its toniest residential neighborhood and a great destination if you want to get out and explore the surrounding parkland. Definitely visit both day and night to get the whole experience.

MUSEUMS

Hong Kong Museum of Art. This is the place in town to see ancient Chinese scrolls and sculpture along with the work of the territory's own contemporary masters.

Hong Kong Museum of History. See what Hong Kong looked like more than 6,000 years ago, when tigers and other animals ranged over the islands. Scenes of neolithic life, life-size dioramas, military displays, and artifacts trace the territory's development up to the present.

NIGHTLIFE

Club BBoss, Tsim Sha Tsui East. If you want to get a hint of what the big-business types are up to on their hours off, check out Hong Kong's grandest and most boisterous hostess club.

Felix, Tsim Sha Tsui. The Peninsula's penthouse bar is your best bet for a drink with a view Kowloon-side. The Philippe Starck–designed room is also beautiful.

Lan Kwai Fong. The tiny streets of Central's best nightlife area hide more than 100 restaurants and bars of every description and ethnic orientation, with celebrants often spilling out onto the streets with their drinks. It's a superb way to start, spend, or end an evening.

SHOPPING

The Admiralty, Central. Four gigantic malls converge here with several large hotels, creating a vast, interconnected shopping extravaganza.

Festival Walk, Kowloon Tong. Hong Kong's fanciest shopping mall is a bit off the beaten path, but it's worth the trip.

Harbour City, Tsim Sha Tsui. The city's largest mall, a collection of indoor and outdoor interconnected shopping plazas, has something for everyone.

Shanghai Tang, Central. The Peddar Street store is a throwback to a more elegant era, and the silk and cashmere designs are elegant. If it's just a cool souvenir you're looking for, those are available, too, as are classy—and pricey—kids clothes.

SMART TRAVEL TIPS

Finding out about your destination before you leave home means you won't squander time organizing everyday minutiae once you've arrived. You'll be more streetwise when you hit the ground as well, better prepared to explore the aspects of Hong Kong that drew you here in the first place. The organizations in this section can provide information to supplement this guide; contact them for up-to-the-minute details, and consult the A to Z sections that end the Side Trip to Macau and Side Trip to South China chapters for facts on the various topics as they relate to the areas around Hong Kong. Happy landings!

ADDRESSES

Hong Kong addresses often include the floor number in the format "1/F," which means "1st floor." And in keeping with the European style, "1st floor" actually designates the second floor of a building; the actual first floor is called the "ground floor" and is abbreviated "G/F." The floor number always precedes the street address and/or building name.

AIR TRAVEL TO & FROM HONG KONG

BOOKING

Most people choose a flight based on price, but because of the time and distance involved in traveling to Hong Kong, there are other issues to consider. These include connections, departure times, and a carrier's frequent-flyer partners, which allow you to credit mileage earned on one airline to your account with another.

When you book, look for nonstop flights and remember that "direct" flights stop at least once. Try to avoid connecting flights, which require a change of plane. Two airlines may operate a connecting flight jointly, so ask whether your airline operates every segment of the trip; you may find that the carrier you prefer flies you only part of the way. To find more booking tips and to check prices and make online flight reservations, log on to www.fodors.com.

CARRIERS

Cathay Pacific is Hong Kong's flagship carrier. It maintains high standards, with friendly service, good in-flight food, and a safe track record, all of which drive the price up slightly higher than some of the other regional carriers; there are flights from both Los Angeles and San Francisco on the west coast and from New York–JFK on the east coast, including a new nonstop flight from New York. Singapore Airlines is usually slightly less expensive and offers direct flights to San Francisco on the west coast and Newark on the east coast. Continental also frequently offers good price deals, and has a nonstop flight to Hong Kong from Newark Airport. Several other airlines offer service from the United States to Hong Kong, sometimes with connections in Asia.

⊞ From North America **Air Canada** ☎ 888/247–2262, 2867-8111 in Hong Kong ⊕ www.aircanada.com. **Asiana** ☎ 800/227–4262, 2523-8585 in Hong Kong ⊕ www.flyasiana.com. **Cathay Pacific Airways** ☎ 800/233–2742 in the U.S., 800/268–6868 in Canada, 2747-1888 in Hong Kong ⊕ www.cathay-usa.com. **China Airlines** ☎ 800/227–5118, 2868-2299 in Hong Kong ⊕ www.chinaairlines.com.hk. **Continental** ☎ 800/231–0856, 3198-5777 in Hong Kong ⊕ www.continental.com. **Korean Air** ☎ 800/438–5000, 2366-2001 in Hong Kong ⊕ www.koreanair.com. **Northwest** ☎ 800/447–4747, 2810-4288 in Hong Kong ⊕ www.nwa.com. **Qantas** ☎ 800/227–4500, 2822-9000 in Hong Kong ⊕ www.qantas.com. **Singapore Airlines** ☎ 800/742-3333, 2520-2233 in Hong Kong ⊕ www.singaporeair.com. **United Airlines** ☎ 800/241–6522, 2810-4888 in Hong Kong ⊕ www.united.com. **⊞ From the U.K.** **British Airways** ☎ 0845/773–3377, 2822-9000 in Hong Kong ⊕ www.britishairways.com. **Cathay Pacific Airways** ☎ 020/7747-8888, 2747-1888 in Hong Kong ⊕ www.cathaypacific.com. **Virgin Atlantic** ☎ 01293/747–747, 2532-3030 in Hong Kong ⊕ www.virgin-atlantic.com. **⊞ To Macau** **Asiana** ☎ 800/227–4262, 2523-8585 in Hong Kong. **Korean Air** ☎ 800/438–5000, 2366-2001 in Hong Kong. **Northwest** ☎ 800/447–4747, 2810-4288 in Hong Kong.

CHECK-IN & BOARDING

Always **find out your carrier's check-in policy.** Plan to arrive at the airport about 2 hours before your scheduled departure time for domestic flights and 2½ to 3 hours before international flights. You may need to arrive earlier if you're flying from one of the busier airports or during peak air-traffic times. In Hong Kong, check in at least 2 hours before departing from Hong Kong International Airport at Chek Lap Kok. If you are flying to anyplace but the United States and plan on taking the train to the airport, check your luggage at the Airport Express Railway station on Hong Kong Island. You must check in at least 3 hours in advance for this wonderfully efficient, time-saving service. Since September 11, 2001, carriers flying to the United States have discontinued check-in at the Airport Express terminal indefinitely. Check with your carrier beforehand. Remember to **retain your Hong Kong entry slip** which the customs official gives you at passport control. You will need to hand back this paper when you present your passport for your return trip home. To avoid delays at airport-security checkpoints, try not to wear any metal. Jewelry, belt and other buckles, steel-toe shoes, barrettes, and underwire bras are among the items that can set off detectors.

Assuming that not everyone with a ticket will show up, airlines routinely overbook planes. When everyone does, airlines ask for volunteers to give up their seats. In return, these volunteers usually get a several-hundred-dollar flight voucher, which can be used toward the purchase of another ticket, and are rebooked on the next flight out. If there are not enough volunteers, the airline must choose who will be denied boarding. The first to get bumped are passengers who checked in late and those flying on discounted tickets, so get to the gate and check in as early as possible, especially during peak periods.

Always **bring a government-issued photo ID** to the airport; even when it's not required, a passport is best.

CUTTING COSTS

The least expensive airfares to Hong Kong are priced for round-trip travel and must usually be purchased in advance. Airlines generally allow you to change your return date for a fee; most low-fare tickets, however, are nonrefundable. It's smart to call a number of airlines and check the Internet; when you are quoted a good price, book it on the spot—the same fare may not be available the next day, or even the next hour. Always check different routings and look into using alternate airports. Also, price off-peak flights, which may be significantly less expensive than others. Travel agents, especially low-fare specialists (⇨ Discounts & Deals), are helpful.

Consolidators are another good source. They buy tickets for scheduled flights at reduced rates from the airlines, then sell them at prices that beat the best fare available directly from the airlines. (Many also offer reduced car-rental and hotel rates.) Sometimes you can even get your money back if you need to return the ticket. Carefully read the fine print detailing penalties for changes and cancellations, purchase the ticket with a credit card, and confirm your consolidator reservation with the airline.

When you fly as a courier, you trade your checked-luggage space for a ticket deeply subsidized by a courier service. There are restrictions on when you can book and how long you can stay. Some courier companies list with membership organizations, such as the Air Courier Association and the International Association of Air Travel Couriers; these require you to become a member before you can book a flight.

Many airlines, singly or in collaboration, offer discount air passes that allow foreigners to travel economically in a particular country or region. These visitor passes usually must be reserved and purchased before you leave home. Information about passes often can be found on most airlines' international Web pages, which tend to be aimed at travelers from outside the carrier's home country. Also, try typing the name of the pass into a search engine, or search for "pass" within the carrier's Web site. The Cathay Pacific All Asia Pass is particularly useful for those travelers wishing to make a stopover in Hong Kong as part of a larger Asian or Southeast Asian

itinerary. The pass includes the flight from the United States or Canada to Hong Kong and then flights within 21 days to 17 other Asian cities served by Cathay Pacific. However, your itinerary must be set before you leave, and the pass must be purchased through a travel agent. To get the best price, you must register online at Cathay Pacific's Web site as a "CyberTraveler." The pass is generally not offered from mid-May through mid-August or during December and January.

🛫 Consolidators **AirlineConsolidator.com** ☎ 888/468-5385 ⊕ www.airlineconsolidator.com; for international tickets. **Best Fares** ☎ 800/880-1234 or 800/576-8255 ⊕ www.bestfares.com; $59.90 annual membership. **Cheap Tickets** ☎ 800/377-1000 or 800/652-4327 ⊕ www.cheaptickets.com. **Expedia** ☎ 800/397-3342 or 404/728-8787 ⊕ www.expedia.com. **Hotwire** ☎ 866/468-9473 or 920/330-9418 ⊕ www.hotwire.com. **Now Voyager Travel** ✉ 45 W. 21st St., Suite 5A, New York, NY 10010 ☎ 212/459-1616 🖷 212/243-2711 ⊕ www.nowvoyagertravel.com. **Onetravel.com** ⊕ www.onetravel.com. **Orbitz** ☎ 888/656-4546 ⊕ www.orbitz.com. **Priceline.com** ⊕ www.priceline.com. **Travelocity** ☎ 888/709-5983, 877/282-2925 in Canada, 0870/876-3876 in the U.K. ⊕ www.travelocity.com.

🛫 Courier Resources **Air Courier Association/Cheaptrips.com** ☎ 800/280-5973 or 800/282-1202 ⊕ www.aircourier.org or www.cheaptrips.com; $34 annual membership. **International Association of Air Travel Couriers** ☎ 308/632-3273 ⊕ www.courier.org; $45 annual membership. **Now Voyager Travel** ✉ 45 W. 21st St., Suite 5A, New York, NY 10010 ☎ 212/459-1616 🖷 212/243-2711 ⊕ www.nowvoyagertravel.com.

🛫 Discount Passes **All Asia Pass**, Cathay Pacific, ☎ 800/233-2742, 800/268-6868 in Canada ⊕ www.cathay-usa.com or www.cathay.ca.

ENJOYING THE FLIGHT

State your seat preference when purchasing your ticket, and then repeat it when you confirm and when you check in. For more legroom, you can request one of the few emergency-aisle seats at check-in, if you're capable of moving obstacles comparable in weight to an airplane exit door (usually between 35 pounds and 60 pounds)—a Federal Aviation Administration requirement of passengers in these seats. Seats behind a bulkhead also offer more legroom, but they don't have under-seat storage. Don't sit in the row in front of the emergency aisle or in front of a bulkhead, where seats may not recline.

Ask the airline whether a snack or meal is served on the flight. If you have dietary concerns, request special meals when booking. These can be vegetarian, low-cholesterol, or kosher, for example. It's a good idea to pack some healthful snacks and a small (plastic) bottle of water in your carry-on bag. On long flights, try to maintain a normal routine, to help fight jet lag. At night, get some sleep. By day, eat light meals, drink water (not alcohol), and **move around the cabin** to stretch your legs. For additional jet-lag tips consult *Fodor's FYI: Travel Fit & Healthy* (available at bookstores everywhere).

Airlines flying into Hong Kong usually no longer permit in-flight smoking. Check with your carrier before booking the flight. Smoking is also not permitted within the airport (the fine is HK$1,000) or on trains.

FLYING TIMES

Flying time to Hong Kong is around 16½ hours direct from Newark/New York, 13 hours direct from Los Angeles, or 12¼ hours direct from San Francisco. Macau is a 20-minute flight from Hong Kong.

Book yourself on a nonstop flight if at all possible as it will save you several hours of layover time en route, and eliminate the possibility of a missed connection—unfortunately a more frequently occurring problem.

HOW TO COMPLAIN

If your baggage goes astray or your flight goes awry, complain right away. Most carriers require that you **file a claim immediately.** The Aviation Consumer Protection Division of the Department of Transportation publishes *Fly-Rights,* which discusses airlines and consumer issues and is available online. You can also find articles and information on mytravelrights.com, the Web site of the nonprofit Consumer Travel Rights Center.

▓ Airline Complaints Aviation Consumer Protection Division ✉ U.S. Department of Transportation,

Office of Aviation Enforcement and Proceedings, C-75, 400 7th St. SW, Room 4107, Washington, DC 20590 ☎ 202/366-2220 ⊕ airconsumer.ost.dot.gov. **Federal Aviation Administration Consumer Hotline** ✉ for inquiries: FAA, 800 Independence Ave. SW, Washington, DC 20591 ☎ 800/322-7873 ⊕ www.faa.gov.

RECONFIRMING

Check the status of your flight before you leave for the airport. You can do this on your carrier's Web site, by linking to a flight-status checker (many Web booking services offer these), or by calling your carrier or travel agent. Always confirm international flights at least 72 hours ahead of the scheduled departure time. If you are flying on a mainland Chinese airline, you must reconfirm your ticket at least 24 hours before leaving Hong Kong or risk losing your seat. You can also call your travel agent to do this for you. Other airlines might not be as strict as the Chinese airlines operating out of Hong Kong. Check with your travel agent or contact your carrier when booking your flight.

AIRPORTS & TRANSFERS

The gateway to Hong Kong is the sleek and sophisticated Hong Kong International Airport at Chek Lap Kok. However, HKIA is never called by its official name; it's universally referred to as Chek Lap Kok. The airport is mammoth: the passenger terminal is a mile long and could encompass those at Heathrow and JFK combined. It is also well marked and employs a helpful staff. Note that passengers might have trouble finding those who come to meet them because the Arrivals Hall is quite vast. However, there are only two exit points, A and B, which are listed with other details on arrival monitors so it should not prove too difficult. Airport tax is normally included in your ticket price, but check with your travel agent to make sure. If it's not, you should hold on to HK$120 for the airport tax, payable on departure from the country. It is only levied on those 12 years and older and is waived for all transit and transfer passengers who arrive and leave on the same day.

The nearby Macau International Airport gives you more flight options; from here you can simply connect with sea transport for the one-hour journey to Hong Kong. ⏏ Hong Kong International Airport ☎ 852/2181-0000 ⊕ www.hkairport.com. Macau International Airport ☎ 853/861-111 ⊕ www.macau-airport.gov.mo.

AIRPORT TRANSFERS

The spectacular, high-speed, high-frequency **Airport Express** service run by the MTR Corporation, which also operates Hong Kong's subway system, whisks you between the airport and Kowloon in 19 minutes via Tsing Ma Bridge, and to and from Hong Kong Island (Central) in 23 minutes between 5:50 AM and 1:15 AM. This is the most convenient and economical way to get to and from the airport. There is plenty of luggage space, legroom, and comfortable seating with television screens on the backs of the passenger seats showing tourist information and the latest news. A noteworthy feature of Airport Express is the convenient in-town check-in for most destinations (except for the United States), whereby you check your luggage, get your boarding pass, and pay departure tax while still on Hong Kong Island. To do this, you must purchase an Airport Express ticket and get to the train station anytime from one day to 90 minutes before your flight. The office is open from 6 AM to 1 AM. The Airport Express station is connected to the MTR's Central station (albeit via a long, underground walkway with no luggage carts). One-way or same-day return fare to or from Central is HK$100; from Kowloon, HK$90. Round-trip tickets valid for one month cost HK$180 for Central and HK$160 for Kowloon.

The Airport Express also runs a free shuttle bus between major hotels and its Hong Kong and Kowloon stations. To board, you must show your ticket, boarding pass, or Airport Express ticket.

Airbus has eight routes covering just about every hotel and hostel in Hong Kong, Kowloon, and the New Territories. Prices range from HK$14 to HK$45 for the one-hour trip.

A 24-hour **Airport Shuttle** bus departs major hotels every 30 minutes and costs HK$120.

A number of regular public buses—including service by **Citybus, Kowloon Motor Bus,** and **Long Wing Bus Company**—serve the airport; though cheaper (HK$23 and under), these take longer than express options.

Taxis from the airport cost up to HK$330 for Hong Kong Island destinations and up to HK$270 for Kowloon destinations, plus HK$5 per piece of luggage.

DCH Limo Service is located at counter B13 in the Arrival Hall. Depending on the zone and the type of car, limo rides from the airport range from HK$390 to HK$600. A pick-up service is available at the same rates, as is a car service at HK$320 per hour not including tolls and parking, with a minimum of three hours. ⏏ Airbus ☎ 2745-4466. Airport Express ☎ 2881-8888 for MTR hotline. Airport Shuttle ☎ 2377-0733. Citybus ☎ 2873-0818. DCH Limo Service ☎ 2262-1888 🖷 2753-6768. Kowloon Motor Bus ☎ 2745-4466. Long Wing Bus Company ☎ 2261-2791. Taxis ☎ 2574-7311.

DUTY-FREE SHOPPING

In Hong Kong, the only place you can buy duty-free liquor and tobacco is at Chek Lap Kok, where shopping opportunities are many. Cigarettes are considerably cheaper than they are in the city, alcohol offers only moderate savings. Ten duty-free liquor and tobacco shops are located at the restricted boarding level, with two preorder shops on the nonrestricted departures check-in level. The shops are open from 7 AM to 11:30 PM. Airport tax is not levied on transit and transfer passengers.

BOAT & FERRY TRAVEL

Since December 1888, the Star Ferry has been running across Victoria Harbour; in fact, it is a Hong Kong landmark. Double-bowed, green-and-white vessels connect Hong Kong Island with Kowloon in just eight minutes daily from 6:30 AM to 11:30 PM; the ride costs HK$2.20 on the upper deck, HK$1.70 on the lower deck.

New World Ferry Services Ltd., better known as First Ferry, runs nine different ferry routes from Central to the outlying islands of Lantau, Cheung Chau, Lamma, and Peng Chau. Printed schedules are obtainable at the HKTB Information and gift centers at two locations: the Star Ferry Concourse, Kowloon, and the Center, 99 Queen's Road Central, Central; as well as through the HKTB Visitor Hot Line. Or, you can simply pick one up at the ferry ticket counters. Round-trip fares vary from HK$15 to HK$62.

For information about ferry service to Macau and locations in China, *see* Macau A to Z *in* Chapter 7 *and* South China A to Z *in* Chapter 8.

FARES AND SCHEDULES
You can pay in Hong Kong dollars or by using an "Octopus" stored-value card (⇨ Train Travel).
🚩 HKTB Visitor Hot Line ☎ 2508-1234. **New World First Ferry** ☎ 2131-8181 ⊕ www.nwff.com.hk. **Star Ferry** ☎ 2367-7065.

BUSINESS & TRADE SERVICES
BUSINESS CENTERS
Hong Kong supports many business centers outside hotels, and some are considerably cheaper than hotel facilities. Others cost about the same but offer private desks (from HK$250 per hour for desk space to upward of HK$8,000 a month for a private office). Amenities include a private address and phone-answering and forwarding services. Many centers are affiliated with accountants and lawyers who can expedite company registration. Some will even process visas and wrap gifts for you.

Harbour International Business Centre provides typing, secretarial support, and office rentals. Reservations are not required.

The American Chamber of Commerce can arrange a Breakfast Briefing Program at your hotel for a fee based on group size. The chamber hosts luncheons and seminars, and its Young Professionals Committee holds cocktail parties at least once a month. Facilities include a library and China trade services. Other business organizations of note are AMS Management Service Ltd., Business Executive Centre,

Business Station, and Central Executive Business Centre.
🚩 American Chamber of Commerce ⊠ Bank of America Tower, 12 Harcourt Rd., Room 1904, Central ☎ 2526-0165 🖷 2810-1289. **AMS Management Service Ltd.** ⊠ 18/F, Wilson House, 19–27 Wyndham St., Central ☎ 2846-3100 🖷 2810-7002. **Business Executive Centre** ⊠ 23/F, Kinwick Centre, 32 Hollywood Rd., Central ☎ 2827-7322 🖷 2827-4227. **Business Station** ⊠ 6/F, Cosmos Bldg., 8–11 Lan Kwai Fong, Central ☎ 2523-6810 🖷 2530-5071. **Central Executive Business Centre** ⊠ 11/F, Central Bldg., 1 Pedder St., Central ☎ 2841-7888 🖷 2810-1868. **Harbour International Business Centre** ⊠ 2802 Admiralty Centre Tower I, 18 Harcourt Rd., Central ☎ 2529-0356 🖷 2861-3420.

CHAMBERS OF COMMERCE
🚩 American Chamber of Commerce in Hong Kong ⊠ Bank of America Tower, 12 Harcourt Rd., Room 1904, Central ☎ 2526-0165 🖷 2810-1289 ⊕ www.amcham.org.hk. **Australian Chamber of Commerce** ⊠ 4/F, Lucky Bldg., 39 Wellington St., Central ☎ 2522-5054 🖷 2877-0860 ⊕ www.austcham.com.hk. **British Chamber of Commerce** ⊠ Emperor Group Centre, 288 Hennessy Rd., Room 1201, Wanchai ☎ 2824-2211 🖷 2824-1333 ⊕ www.britcham.com. **Chinese Manufacturers' Association** ⊠ 5/F, CMA Bldg., 64–66 Connaught Rd., Central ☎ 2542-8600 🖷 2541-4541 ⊕ www.cma.org.hk. **Federation of Hong Kong Industries** ⊠ 407 Hankow Centre, 5–15 Hankow Rd., Kowloon ☎ 2732-3188 🖷 2721-3494 ⊕ www.fhki.org.hk. **Hong Kong General Chamber of Commerce** ⊠ 22/F, United Centre, 95 Queensway, Admiralty ☎ 2529-9229 🖷 2527-9843 ⊕ www.chamber.org.hk. **Hong Kong Japanese Chamber of Commerce and Industry** ⊠ 38/F, Hennessy Centre, 500 Hennessy Rd., Causeway Bay ☎ 2577-6129 🖷 2577-0525 ⊕ www.hkjcci.com.hk. **Hong Kong Productivity Council** ⊠ HKPC Bldg., 78 Tat Chee Ave., Kowloon Tong ☎ 2788-5678 🖷 2788-5900 ⊕ www.hkpc.org. **Indian Chamber of Commerce Hong Kong** ⊠ 2/F, Hoseinee House, 69 Wyndham St., Central ☎ 2523-3877 🖷 2845-0300 ⊕ www.icchk.org.hk. **Swedish Chamber of Commerce** ⊠ China Resources Bldg., 26 Harbour Rd., Room 4401, Wanchai ☎ 2525-0349 🖷 2537-1843 ⊕ www.swedcham.com.hk.

CONVENTION CENTER
The Hong Kong Convention & Exhibition Centre is a state-of-the-art, 693,000-

square-foot complex on the Wanchai waterfront, capable of handling 140,000 visitors a day. There are five exhibition halls and two main convention halls; the section jutting into the harbor hosted the 1997 handover ceremony. The largest complex in Asia, the center houses two hotels, the 570-room Grand Hyatt, and the 860-room Renaissance Harbour View; an apartment block; and a 54-story trade center/office building.

🔳 **Hong Kong Convention & Exhibition Centre** ✉ 1 Expo Dr., Wanchai ☎ 2582-8888 📠 2802-0000 ⊕ www.hkcec.com.hk.

FAX SERVICES

Many convenience stores, such as 7-Eleven and Circle K, offer a fax service. Ask your concierge for directions to the closest one or call the hotline.

🔳 **Circle K** ☎ 2991-6300. **7-Eleven** ☎ 2299-1711.

MESSENGERS

Most business centers offer delivery service, and you can sometimes arrange a delivery through your hotel concierge. Couriers, including City-Link International, will pick up from your hotel. Price is based on weight and distance.

🔳 **City-Link International Courier Co. Ltd.** ☎ 2382-8289 ⊕ www.citylinkexpress.com.

TRADE INFORMATION

🔳 **Hong Kong Trade Development Council** ✉ 38/F, Office Tower Convention Plaza, 1 Harbour Rd., Wanchai ☎ 2584-4333 📠 2824-0249 ⊕ www.tdctrade.com. **Innovation & Technology Commission** ✉ 14/F, Ocean Centre, 5 Canton Rd., Tsim Sha Tsui ☎ 2737-2573 📠 2730-4633. **Trade & Industry Department** ✉ Trade Department Tower, 700 Nathan Rd., Mong Kok ☎ 2392-2922 📠 2789-2435 ⊕ www.tid.gov.hk.

TRANSLATION SERVICES

🔳 **CIAP Hong Kong** ☎ 2697-5114 ⊕ www.ciap.net. **Polyglot Translations** ✉ 14B Time Centre, 53 Hollywood Rd., Central ☎ 2851-7232 ⊕ www.polyglot.com.hk. **Translation Business** ✉ 22B Winsan Tower, 98 Thomson Rd., Wanchai ☎ 2893-5000 ⊕ www.translationbusiness.com.hk.

BUSINESS HOURS

Nearly all businesses, even tourist-related ones, will shut down for major holidays such as Chinese New Year, Christmas, and New Year's.

BANKS & OFFICES

Banks are open weekdays from 9 to 4:30 and Saturday from 9 to 12:30. ATMs are plentiful. Office hours are more or less the same as in the West: 9 to 5 or 6. Some offices are open from 9 to noon on Saturday. Lunch hour is 1 PM to 2 PM; don't be surprised if offices close during lunch.

MUSEUMS & SIGHTS

Museums and sights are usually open six days a week from 9 to 5. Each site picks a different day, usually a Monday or Tuesday, for its day off. Call the destination before visiting.

PHARMACIES

Pharmacies are generally open from about 10 AM until about 9 PM. There are no 24-hour pharmacies.

SHOPS

Stores usually open daily around 10 AM and stay open until 8:30 PM, especially in tourist and residential areas. Here's an estimate of store hours by neighborhood: Central, 10 to 6; Causeway Bay and Wanchai, 10 to 8:30; Tsim Sha Tsui East, 10 to 7:30; Tsim Sha Tsui, Yau Ma Tei, and Mong Kok, 10 to 8:30.

BUS TRAVEL WITHIN HONG KONG

Double-decker buses run from 6 AM to midnight and cover most parts of Hong Kong. Bus drivers usually don't speak English, so you may have to ask other passengers for help or you must know exactly where you want to disembark.

When determining bus direction, buses ending with the letter L will eventually connect to the Kowloon–Canton Railway; buses ending with the letter M connect to an MTR station; and buses ending with the letter X are express buses.

As with other big cities, buses can be quite busy during rush hours, public holidays, and at weekends, so it's best to use them during nonpeak times.

Maxicabs and minicabs both seat 16 people. Maxicabs are cream color, with green roofs, and a route number and fixed price prominently displayed. They stop at designated spots, and you usually pay as you board. Minibuses are also cream color but have red roofs. Minibuses display both fares and destinations (albeit in very small English letters), though these can change based on demand. They stop almost anywhere, and you pay as you get off the bus. Maxicabs and minibuses are both quick, though they cost slightly more than buses.

For information, call the HKTB Visitor Hot Line or, for double-decker-bus route maps, stop in at the HKTB Information and Gift Centres at the Center, 99 Queen's Road Central in Central or at the Star Ferry Concourse in Kowloon.

PAYING

Double-decker bus fares range from HK$1.20 to HK$45; the fare is paid when you enter the bus. Maxicab fares range from HK$1.50 to HK$18. Similarly, you pay as you board. Minibus fares range from HK$2 to HK$20, but you pay as you exit. For all three types of transportation you must pay exact change.

Long-staying visitors should consider purchasing an "Octopus" stored-value card (⇨ Train Travel), which you can use on the city bus as well as the MTR, Kowloon–Canton Railway, Light Rail, Airport Express, and ferries.
🚩 HKTB Visitor Hot Line ☎ 2508-1234.

CAMERAS & PHOTOGRAPHY

You are neither permitted to photograph customs and immigration procedures at border crossings nor allowed to photograph the police or military. At sites where photography is barred there are usually clearly marked NO PHOTOGRAPHY signs.

Although Hong Kong is picturesque, it can be quite cloudy, smoggy, or foggy, so be prepared for poor lighting at times.

Victoria Peak and Repulse Bay both offer visually stunning backdrops for photographs, but don't miss the unforgettable urban scenery of neon-lit streets at night or crowded market scenes by day. The *Kodak Guide to Shooting Great Travel Pictures* (available at bookstores everywhere) is loaded with tips.
🚩 Photo Help **Kodak Information Center** ☎ 800/242-2424 ⊕ www.kodak.com.

EQUIPMENT PRECAUTIONS

Humidity in Hong Kong—particularly from June through September—is extremely high, so try to store your equipment in air-conditioned rooms as much as possible. **Don't pack film or equipment in checked luggage,** where it is much more susceptible to damage. X-ray machines used to view checked luggage are extremely powerful and therefore are likely to ruin your film. Try to ask for hand inspection of film, which becomes clouded after repeated exposure to airport X-ray machines, and keep videotapes and computer disks away from metal detectors. Always keep film, tape, and computer disks out of the sun. Carry an extra supply of batteries, and be prepared to turn on your camera, camcorder, or laptop to prove to airport security personnel that the device is real.

FILM & DEVELOPING

Kodak and Fuji color film are easy to find in hotel shops, corner grocery stores, and camera shops throughout Hong Kong. Expect to pay about HK$30 for a 36-exposure roll of 200-speed film. For instant-print cameras, you will pay about HK$105 for a 10-picture pack of Polaroid Spectra Instant Film. One-hour developing is available at Kodak express stalls in malls, hotels, and street corners in Hong Kong. Expect to pay HK$48 to HK$80 for the speedy service.

VIDEOS

Hong Kong uses the PAL system, which is driven by the camera rather than the tape itself, so any video tape you purchase in Hong Kong should work in your camera. Ask if you aren't sure. Blank VHS tapes are available for about HK$20 but are not very widely available. Smaller tapes used by digital camcorders are widely available in most camera and electronic shops.

CAR RENTAL

Avoid renting a car on Hong Kong Island or Kowloon. Driving conditions, traffic jams, and limited parking are bound to make your life difficult. Public transportation is excellent here, and taxis are inexpensive. If you do decide to rent a car, you may want to hire a driver as well; this can be arranged through your hotel. The fee is HK$800 to HK$1,200 for the first four hours (depending on car model) and HK$200 to HK$300 for each subsequent hour.

Rental rates begin at HK$702 per day and HK$2,900 per week for an economy car with air-conditioning, automatic transmission, and unlimited mileage.

Major Agencies Alamo ☎ 800/522-9696 ⊕ www.alamo.com. **Avis** ☎ 800/331-1084, 800/879-2847 in Canada, 0870/606-0100 in the U.K., 02/9353-9000 in Australia, 09/526-2847 in New Zealand ⊕ www.avis.com. **Budget** ☎ 800/527-0700, 0870/156-5656 in the U.K. ⊕ www.budget.com. **Dollar** ☎ 800/800-6000, 0800/085-4578 in the U.K. ⊕ www.dollar.com. **Hertz** ☎ 800/654-3001, 800/263-0600 in Canada, 0870/844-8844 in the U.K., 02/9669-2444 in Australia, 09/256-8690 in New Zealand ⊕ www.hertz.com. **National Car Rental** ☎ 800/227-7368, 0870/600-6666 in the U.K. ⊕ www.nationalcar.com.

CUTTING COSTS

For a good deal, book through a travel agent who will shop around. Fung Hing Hire Co. rents only chauffeured cars.

Local Agencies Ace Hire Car ⊠ 16 Min Fat St., Happy Valley, turn left at Hong Kong Bank ☎ 2893-0541. **Fung Hing Hire Co.** ⊠ G/F, 58 Village St., Happy Valley ☎ 2572-0333.

INSURANCE

When driving a rented car you are generally responsible for any damage to or loss of the vehicle. You also may be liable for any property damage or personal injury that you may cause while driving. Before you rent, see what coverage you already have under the terms of your personal auto-insurance policy and credit cards.

REQUIREMENTS & RESTRICTIONS

You may use your valid driver's license in Hong Kong if you are 18 years old or above. Drivers over 70 years old must pass a physical examination before driving. However, you'll need an International Driver's Permit for longer stays. They're available from the American and Canadian automobile associations and, in the United Kingdom, from the Automobile Association or Royal Automobile Club. These permits are universally recognized, so having one in your wallet may save you a problem with the local authorities.

SURCHARGES

Before you pick up a car in one city and leave it in another, ask about drop-off charges or one-way service fees, which can be substantial. Also inquire about early-return policies; some rental agencies charge extra if you return the car before the time specified in your contract while others give you a refund for the days not used. To avoid a hefty refueling fee, fill the tank just before you turn in the car, but be aware that gas stations near the rental outlet may overcharge. It's almost never a deal to buy the tank of gas that's in the car when you rent it; the understanding is that you'll return it empty, but some fuel usually remains.

CAR TRAVEL

The best advice we can give is don't drive in Hong Kong. In addition to the fact that gasoline and parking are so prohibitively expensive that the only cars you're likely to see on Hong Kong Island are chauffeured Rolls-Royces driven by former race-car-driving Triad members, the local bus and truck drivers seem to think slamming on their breaks (and sending their passengers flying forward) is the only way to stop—making it an exceptionally difficult city to drive in.

CHILDREN IN HONG KONG

If you are renting a car, don't forget to arrange for a car seat when you reserve. For general advice about traveling with children, consult *Fodor's FYI: Travel with Your Baby* (available in bookstores everywhere).

BABY-SITTING

Most hotels offer babysitting service. The price is about HK$50 an hour on average.

FLYING

If your children are two or older, ask about children's airfares. As a general rule, infants under two not occupying a seat fly at greatly reduced fares or even for free.

But if you want to guarantee a seat for an infant, you have to pay full fare. Consider flying during off-peak days and times; most airlines will grant an infant a seat without a ticket if there are available seats. When booking, confirm carry-on allowances if you're traveling with infants. In general, for babies charged 10% to 50% of the adult fare you are allowed one carry-on bag and a collapsible stroller; if the flight is full, the stroller may have to be checked or you may be limited to less.

Experts agree that it's a good idea to use safety seats aloft for children weighing less than 40 pounds. Airlines set their own policies: if you use a safety seat, U.S. carriers usually require that the child be ticketed, even if he or she is young enough to ride free, because the seats must be strapped into regular seats. And even if you pay the full adult fare for the seat, it may be worth it, especially on longer trips. Do **check your airline's policy about using safety seats during takeoff and landing.** Safety seats are not allowed everywhere in the plane, so get your seat assignments as early as possible.

When reserving, request children's meals or a freestanding bassinet (not available at all airlines) if you need them. But note that bulkhead seats, where you must sit to use the bassinet, may lack an overhead bin or storage space on the floor.

LODGING

🚩 Best Choices **Grand Hyatt** ✉1 Harbour Rd., Wanchai ☎ 2588-1234 🖷 2802-0677 ⊕ www. hongkong.grand.hyatt.com. **Holiday Inn Golden Mile** ✉ 50 Nathan Rd., Tsim Sha Tsui ☎ 2369-3111 🖷 2369-8016 ⊕ goldenmile-hk.holiday-inn.com. **Marco Polo Hongkong** ✉ Harbour City, Canton Rd., Tsim Sha Tsui ☎ 2113-0088 🖷 2113-0011 ⊕ www. marcopolohotels.com. **Peninsula Hong Kong** ✉ Salisbury Rd., Tsim Sha Tsui ☎ 2366-6251 🖷 2722-4170 ⊕ www.peninsula.com. **Renaissance Harbour View** ✉1 Harbour Rd., Wanchai ☎ 2802-8888 🖷 2802-8833 ⊕ www.renaissancehotels.com/hkghv. **Ritz-Carlton, Hong Kong** ✉3 Connaught Rd., Central ☎ 800/241-3333 in the U.S., 2877-6666 🖷 2877-6778 ⊕ www.ritzcarlton.com.

PRECAUTIONS

The traffic flows by quickly, so be especially careful to warn children to look

both ways. Otherwise Hong Kong is as safe as any major city in the world. Simply use common sense.

SIGHTS & ATTRACTIONS

Places that are especially appealing to children are indicated by a rubber-duckie icon (🐥) in the margin. Hong Kong's Ocean Park is perhaps one of the top destinations for children. For a free option, consider Hong Kong Park; the koi fish and turtles in the ponds nearly always captivate children's imaginations.

SUPPLIES & EQUIPMENT

Baby supplies such as diapers range in price from HK$64 for a box of 30 medium-size Huggies to HK$76 for a box of 28 extra-large Pampers, and are widely available throughout the city. Similarly, a variety of brands of powdered baby formula, sold in 1 kilogram–size tin containers, are available for about HK$150. Heinz baby foods, Johnson & Johnson lotions and powders, and Gerber plastic nursers and silicone nipples are all readily found. You can shop in supermarkets, or at pharmaceutical/cosmetics chain stores such as Watson's, which are scattered throughout Hong Kong, or specialist stores like Mothercare. Call for the nearest location.

🚩 **Mothercare** ☎ 2523-5704. **Watson's** ☎ 2868-4388.

COMPUTERS ON THE ROAD

Hong Kong is computer friendly. If your spare battery or adapter fails you, don't worry; you can buy a new one in Hong Kong. In general, for computer purchases make sure the product's voltage compatibility is that of your home country and verify that all parts, pieces, and an international warranty are packed with your purchase. Shop around, as prices may vary widely. Consider purchasing your product with a credit card, which might increase the price by 3% to 5%, but will make it easier if you need to return or claim a refund for your purchase from the manufacturer or store once you return home.

While using surge protection is a good computer habit, you'll have no problems plugging your computer directly into the socket at a Hong Kong hotel or business building. The electricity is stable. Also, many hotels now offer wireless Internet (Wi-Fi) or some other form of broadband Internet connection in rooms.

CONCIERGES

Concierges, found in many hotels, can help you with theater tickets and dinner reservations: a good one with connections may be able to get you seats for a hot show or prime-time dinner reservations at the restaurant of the moment. You can also turn to your hotel's concierge for help with travel arrangements, sightseeing plans, services ranging from aromatherapy to zipper repair, and emergencies. **Always tip** a concierge who has been of assistance (⇨ Tipping).

CONSUMER PROTECTION

Be wary of anything too cheap; it probably *is* worth what you're paying for it. If you are buying electronic equipment, inspect it carefully. And in all instances, make sure that the product you initially look at is the one that you take home with you.

Whether you're shopping for gifts or purchasing travel services, **pay with a major credit card** whenever possible, so you can cancel payment or get reimbursed if there's a problem (and you can provide documentation). If you're doing business with a particular company for the first time, contact your local Better Business Bureau and the attorney general's offices in your state and (for U.S. businesses) the company's home state as well. Have any complaints been filed? Finally, if you're buying a package or tour, always consider travel insurance that includes default coverage (⇨ Insurance).

🚩 Consumer Resources In Hong Kong **Consumer Council** ✉ G/F, Harbour Bldg., 38 Pier Rd., Central ☎ 2929-2222 ⊕ www.consumer.org.hk
🚩 BBBs **Council of Better Business Bureaus** ✉ 4200 Wilson Blvd., Suite 800, Arlington, VA 22203 ☎ 703/276-0100 🖷 703/525-8277 ⊕ www. bbb.org.

CUSTOMS & DUTIES

When shopping abroad, keep receipts for all purchases. Upon reentering the country, **be ready to show customs officials what you've bought.** Pack purchases together in an easily accessible place. If you think a duty is incorrect, appeal the assessment. If you object to the way your clearance was handled, note the inspector's badge number. In either case, first ask to see a supervisor. If the problem isn't resolved, write to the appropriate authorities, beginning with the port director at your point of entry.

IN AUSTRALIA

Australian residents who are 18 or older may bring home A$400 worth of souvenirs and gifts (including jewelry), 250 cigarettes or 250 grams of cigars or other tobacco products, and 1,125 ml of alcohol (including wine, beer, and spirits). Residents under 18 may bring back A$200 worth of goods. Members of the same family traveling together may pool their allowances. Prohibited items include meat products. Seeds, plants, and fruits need to be declared upon arrival.

🚩 **Australian Customs Service** ⊘ Regional Director, Box 8, Sydney, NSW 2001 ☎ 02/9213-2000 or 1300/363-263, 02/9364-7222 or 1800/020-504 quarantine-inquiry line 🖷 02/9213-4043 ⊕ www. customs.gov.au.

IN CANADA

Canadian residents who have been out of Canada for at least seven days may bring in C$750 worth of goods duty-free. If you've been away fewer than seven days but more than 48 hours, the duty-free allowance drops to C$200. If your trip lasts 24 to 48 hours, the allowance is C$50. You may not pool allowances with family members. Goods claimed under the C$750 exemption may follow you by mail; those claimed under the lesser exemptions must accompany you. Alcohol and tobacco products may be included in the seven-day and 48-hour exemptions but not in the 24-hour exemption. If you meet the age requirements of the province or territory through which you reenter Canada, you may bring in, duty-free, 1.5 liters of wine *or* 1.14 liters (40 imperial ounces) of liquor *or* 24 12-ounce cans or bottles of beer or ale. Also, if you meet the local age requirement for tobacco products, you may bring in, duty-free, 200 cigarettes and

50 cigars. Check ahead of time with the Canada Customs and Revenue Agency or the Department of Agriculture for policies regarding meat products, seeds, plants, and fruits.

You may send an unlimited number of gifts (only one gift per recipient, however) worth up to C$60 each duty-free to Canada. Label the package UNSOLICITED GIFT—VALUE UNDER $60. Alcohol and tobacco are excluded.

🛂 **Canada Customs and Revenue Agency** ✉ 2265 St. Laurent Blvd., Ottawa, Ontario K1G 4K3 ☎ 800/461-9999 in Canada, 204/983-3500, 506/636-5064 ⊕ www.ccra.gc.ca.

IN HONG KONG

Except for the usual prohibitions against narcotics, explosives, firearms, and ammunition (all but narcotics must be declared upon arrival and handed over for safekeeping until departure), and modest limits on alcohol, tobacco products, and perfume, you can bring anything you want into Hong Kong, including an unlimited amount of money.

Nonresident visitors may bring in, duty-free, 200 cigarettes or 50 cigars or 250 grams of tobacco, and 1 liter of alcohol.

🛂 **Hong Kong Customs & Excise Department** ✉ Canton Road Government Offices, 10/F, 393 Canton Rd., Kowloon ☎ 2815-7711 ⊟ 2542-3334 ⊕ www.info.gov.hk/customs.

IN NEW ZEALAND

All homeward-bound residents may bring back NZ$700 worth of souvenirs and gifts; passengers may not pool their allowances, and children can claim only the concession on goods intended for their own use. For those 17 or older, the duty-free allowance also includes 4.5 liters of wine or beer; one 1,125-ml bottle of spirits; and either 200 cigarettes, 250 grams of tobacco, 50 cigars, *or* a combination of the three up to 250 grams. Meat products, seeds, plants, and fruits must be declared upon arrival to the Agricultural Services Department.

🛂 **New Zealand Customs** ✉ Head office: The Customhouse, 17–21 Whitmore St., Box 2218, Wellington ☎ 09/300-5399 or 0800/428-786 ⊕ www.customs.govt.nz.

IN THE U.K.

From countries outside the European Union, including Hong Kong, you may bring home, duty-free, 200 cigarettes, 50 cigars, 100 cigarillos, or 250 grams of tobacco 1 liter of spirits or 2 liters of fortified or sparkling wine or liqueurs; 2 liters of still table wine; 60 ml of perfume; 250 ml of toilet water; plus £145 worth of other goods, including gifts and souvenirs. Prohibited items include meat and dairy products, seeds, plants, and fruits.

🛂 **HM Customs and Excise** ✉ Portcullis House, 21 Cowbridge Rd. E, Cardiff CF11 9SS ☎ 0845/010-9000 or 0208/929-0152 advice service, 0208/929-6731 or 0208/910-3602 complaints ⊕ www.hmce.gov.uk.

IN THE U.S.

U.S. residents who have been out of the country for at least 48 hours may bring home, for personal use, $800 worth of foreign goods duty-free, as long as they haven't used the $800 allowance or any part of it in the past 30 days. This exemption may include 1 liter of alcohol (for travelers 21 and older), 200 cigarettes, and 100 non-Cuban cigars. Family members from the same household who are traveling together may pool their $800 personal exemptions. For fewer than 48 hours, the duty-free allowance drops to $200, which may include 50 cigarettes, 10 non-Cuban cigars, and 150 ml of alcohol (or 150 ml of perfume containing alcohol). The $200 allowance cannot be combined with other individuals' exemptions, and if you exceed it, the full value of all the goods will be taxed. Antiques, which U.S. Customs and Border Protection defines as objects more than 100 years old, enter duty-free, as do original works of art done entirely by hand, including paintings, drawings, and sculptures. This doesn't apply to folk art or handicrafts, which are in general dutiable.

You may also send packages home duty-free, with a limit of one parcel per addressee per day (except alcohol or tobacco products or perfume worth more than $5). You can mail up to $200 worth of goods for personal use; label the package PERSONAL USE and attach a list of its contents and their retail value. If the package contains your used personal belongings, mark it AMERICAN GOODS RETURNED to avoid paying duties. You may send up to $100 worth of goods as a gift; mark the package UNSOLICITED GIFT. Mailed items do not affect your duty-free allowance on your return.

To avoid paying duty on foreign-made high-ticket items you already own and will take on your trip, register them with Customs before you leave the country. Consider filing a Certificate of Registration for laptops, cameras, watches, and other digital devices identified with serial numbers or other permanent markings; you can keep the certificate for other trips. Otherwise, bring a sales receipt or insurance form to show that you owned the item before you left the United States.

For more about duties, restricted items, and other information about international travel, check out U.S. Customs & Border Protection's online brochure, *Know Before You Go.*

🚩 **U.S. Customs & Border Protection** ✉ for inquiries and equipment registration: 1300 Pennsylvania Ave. NW, Washington, DC 20229 ☎ 877/287-8667 or 202/354-1000 ⊕ www.cbp.gov ✉ for complaints: Customer Satisfaction Unit, 1300 Pennsylvania Ave. NW, Room 5.2C, Washington, DC 20229.

DISABILITIES & ACCESSIBILITY

Hong Kong is not the easiest of cities for people in wheelchairs since few ramps or other provisions for access are provided. Progress is being made, however; the airport, City Hall, the Academy for Performing Arts and the Hong Kong Arts Centre have made efforts to assist people in wheelchairs. For more information, consult the *Hong Kong Access Guide for Disabled Visitors,* available from the Hong Kong Tourist Board (HKTB). The guide lists those rare places that have special facilities for people with disabilities, in addition to the best access to hotels, shopping centers, government offices, consulates, restaurants, and churches.

LODGING

All hotels are supposed to be in compliance with basic standards for travelers with disabilities, but in reality that may not be the case, particularly in older hotels. Newer hotels—particularly upscale ones—usually have a number of rooms suitable for persons with various disabilities. Be sure to ask before making your reservations.

RESERVATIONS

When discussing accessibility with an operator or reservations agent, ask hard questions. Are there any stairs, inside *or* out? Are there grab bars next to the toilet *and* in the shower/tub? How wide is the doorway to the room? To the bathroom? For the most extensive facilities meeting the latest legal specifications, opt for newer accommodations. If you reserve through a toll-free number, consider also calling the hotel's local number to confirm the information from the central reservations office. Get confirmation in writing when you can.

TRANSPORTATION

The vast airport has moving walkways that transport arriving or departing passengers from the most remote gates in about 70 seconds. Ramps, elevators, and escalators are provided for unavoidable changes of level.

While taxis in Hong Kong do not adapt to special needs of passengers with physical disabilities, walking aids such as wheelchairs and crutches are carried free of charge.

The Kowloon–Canton Railway (KCR), which operates along North East New Territories, has elevators at all stations except the Racecourse Station. The KCR Light Rail, which operates in the North West New Territories, has ramps from the street to the platform at all stations. The Mass Transit Railway (MTR), which services Hong Kong and Kowloon and also connects to Tung Chung and the Chek Lap Kok airport, has ramps or elevators at 19 stations. Ancillary facilities such as tactile guide paths, escalator audible devices, and light-emitting diode (LED) display boards are available at most stations.

The lower deck on the ferries is more accessible than the upper deck for passengers using wheelchairs.

⫶ Complaints Aviation Consumer Protection Division (⇨ Air Travel to & from Hong Kong) for airline-related problems. **Departmental Office of Civil Rights** ⊠ for general inquiries, U.S. Department of Transportation, S-30, 400 7th St. SW, Room 10215, Washington, DC 20590 ☎ 202/366-4648 ⊟ 202/366-9371 ⊕ www.dot.gov/ost/docr/index.htm. **Disability Rights Section** ⊠ NYAV, U.S. Department of Justice, Civil Rights Division, 950 Pennsylvania Ave. NW, Washington, DC 20530 ☎ 800/514-0301, 800/514-0383 or 202/514-0383 TTY, 202/514-0301 ADA information line ⊕ www.ada.gov. **U.S. Department of Transportation Hotline** ☎ for disability-related air-travel problems: 800/778-4838 or 800/455-9880 TTY.

TRAVEL AGENCIES

In the United States, the Americans with Disabilities Act requires that travel firms serve the needs of all travelers. Some agencies specialize in working with people with disabilities.

⫶ Travelers with Mobility Problems Access Adventures/B. Roberts Travel ⊠ 206 Chestnut Ridge Rd., Scottsville, NY 14624 ☎ 585/889-9096 ⊕ www.brobertstravel.com ✍ dltravel@prodigy.net, run by a former physical-rehabilitation counselor. **CareVacations** ⊠ No. 5, 5110-50 Ave., Leduc, Alberta, T9E 6V4 Canada ☎ 780/986-6404 or 877/478-7827 ⊟ 780/986-8332 ⊕ www.carevacations.com, for group tours and cruise vacations. **Flying Wheels Travel** ⊠ 143 W. Bridge St., Box 382, Owatonna, MN 55060 ☎ 507/451-5005 ⊟ 507/451-1685 ⊕ www.flyingwheelstravel.com.

DISCOUNTS & DEALS

Be a smart shopper and compare all your options before making decisions. A plane ticket bought with a promotional coupon from travel clubs, coupon books, and direct-mail offers or purchased on the Internet may not be cheaper than the least expensive fare from a discount ticket agency. And always keep in mind that what you get is just as important as what you save.

For the avid museumgoer, the Hong Kong Tourist Board (HKTB) offers a Museum Tour pass for HK$30 that includes visits to the Museum of Art, and the Space, Science, History, and Heritage museums. The pass also includes a shuttle bus to each location. Buses depart throughout the day so you can spend as much time in each place as you wish. For tickets and bus timetable, visit any HKTB Visitor Information Centre.

DISCOUNT RESERVATIONS

To save money, look into discount reservations services with Web sites and toll-free numbers, which use their buying power to get a better price on hotels, airline tickets (⇨ Air Travel to & from Hong Kong), even car rentals. When booking a room, always **call the hotel's local toll-free number** (if one is available) rather than the central reservations number—you'll often get a better price. Always ask about special packages or corporate rates.

When shopping for the best deal on hotels and car rentals, look for guaranteed exchange rates, which protect you against a falling dollar. With your rate locked in, you won't pay more, even if the price goes up in the local currency.

⫶ Airline Tickets Air 4 Less ☎ 800/AIR4LESS; low-fare specialist.

⫶ Hotel Rooms Accommodations Express ☎ 800/444-7666 or 800/277-1064 ⊕ www.acex.net. **Asia-Hotels.com** ⊕ www.asia-hotels.com. **Hotel Club** ⊕ www.hotelclub.net. **Hotels.com** ☎ 800/246-8357 ⊕ www.hotels.com. **Steigenberger Reservation Service** ☎ 800/223-5652 ⊕ www.srs-worldhotels.com. **Turbotrip.com** ☎ 800/473-7829 ⊕ www.turbotrip.com. **VacationLand** ☎ 800/245-0050 ⊕ www.vacation-land.com.

PACKAGE DEALS

Don't confuse packages and guided tours. When you buy a package, you travel on your own, just as though you had planned the trip yourself. Fly/drive packages, which combine airfare and car rental, are often a good deal. In cities, ask the local visitor's bureau about hotel and local transportation packages that include tickets to major museum exhibits or other special events.

ELECTRICITY

To use electric-powered equipment purchased in the United States or Canada, **bring a converter and adapter.** The electrical current in Hong Kong and Macau is

220 volts, 50 cycles alternating current (AC). Some outlets in Hong Kong take plugs with three round prongs, while others use plugs with two square prongs. There is no standard plug size in Macau; check with your hotel regarding its setup.

If your appliances are dual-voltage, you'll need only an adapter. Don't use 110-volt outlets marked FOR SHAVERS ONLY for high-wattage appliances such as blow-dryers. Most laptops operate equally well on either 110 and 220 volts and so require only an adapter.

EMBASSIES & CONSULATES

There are no embassies in Hong Kong; all embassies in China are in Beijing. However, many countries have consulates in Hong Kong to deal with the needs of their nationals. Most consulates are on Hong Kong Island.

🔖 Australia **Australian Consulate** ✉ 23/F, Harbour Centre, 25 Harbour Rd., Wanchai ☎ 2827-8881 🖨 2585-4457 ⊕ www.australia.org.hk.

🔖 Canada **Canadian Consulate** ✉ 11/F-14/F, Tower 1, Exchange Sq., 8 Connaught Pl., Central ☎ 2810-4321 🖨 2810-8736 ⊕ www.dfait-maeci.gc.ca.

🔖 New Zealand **Consulate General** ✉ 18 Harbour Rd., 6508 Central Plaza, Wanchai ☎ 2525-5044 🖨 2845-2915 ⊕ www.nzembassy.com.

🔖 United Kingdom **British Consulate General** ✉ Visa Section, 3/F, 1 Supreme Court Rd., Central ☎ 2901-3000 🖨 2901-3066 ⊕ www. britishconsulate.org.hk.

🔖 United States **U.S. Consulate General** ✉ 26 Garden Rd., Central ☎ 2523-9011 🖨 2845-1598 ⊕ www.usconsulate.org.hk.

EMERGENCIES

Locals and police are usually quite helpful in an emergency situation. Most police officers speak some English or will contact someone who does. There are no 24-hour pharmacies; however, Fanda Perfume Co., Ltd., and Watson's both have pharmacy departments and numerous shops throughout the city; they are usually open until 9 PM.

🔖 **Police, fire & ambulance** ☎ 999. **Hong Kong Police & Taxi Complaint Hotline** ☎ 2527-7177.

🔖 Hospitals **Prince of Wales Hospital** ✉ 30-32 Ngan Shing St., Sha Tin, New Territories

☎ 2632-2211. **Princess Margaret Hospital** ✉ 2-10 Princess Margaret Hospital Rd., Lai Chi Kok ☎ 2990-1111. **Queen Elizabeth Hospital** ✉ 30 Gascoigne Rd., Yau Ma Tei ☎ 2958-8888. **Queen Mary Hospital** ✉ 102 Pok Fu Lam Rd., Pok Fu Lam ☎ 2855-3838. **Ruttonjee Hospital** ✉ 266 Queen's Rd. East, Wanchai ☎ 2291-2000.

🔖 Pharmacies **Fanda Perfume Co., Ltd.** ☎ 2526-6623. **Watson's** ☎ 2868-4388.

ENGLISH-LANGUAGE MEDIA

English-language newspapers are available in Hong Kong. Two English television channels broadcast local English programs weekday mornings and evenings and all day on weekends and holidays. Satellite and cable TV are also widely available.

BOOKS

Most bookstores throughout the city have English-language selections. Dymocks has a number of shops around Hong Kong and offers a wide selection of books and magazines in English.

🔖 Bookstore **Dymocks** ✉ Unit EP1, Star Ferry Concourse, Central ☎ 2801-4423.

NEWSPAPERS & MAGAZINES

English-language newspapers printed in Hong Kong include the *South China Morning Post*, the *Standard*, the *Asian Wall Street Journal*, the *International Herald Tribune*, and *USA Today International*.

HK Magazine and the *BC Magazine* are free. The former is an alternative weekly tabloid, the latter a twice-a-month magazine; both provide comprehensive weekly listings.

The *Far Eastern Economic Review* is a Dow Jones publication, and is a serious, locally produced business and regional politics publication. *Time* also prints an edition in Hong Kong.

RADIO & TELEVISION

There are 13 radio channels, with everything from Cantonese pop music to English news. Stations with English-speaking disc jockeys include: RTHK Radio 3 (AM 567 or 1584, FM 97.9 or 106.8), which airs news, finance, and current affairs; RTHK Radio 4 (FM 97.6 to 98.9), which plays Western and Chinese classical music; and RTHK Radio 6 (AM 675), which airs the BBC World Service relay. Metro Plus (AM 1044) has regional news, finance programs, and international music.

English-language television channels include ATV World and TVB Pearl. Satellite selections include Star TV; on cable you can get BBC, CNN, ESPN, and HBO.

ETIQUETTE & BEHAVIOR

It won't hurt to brush up on your use of chopsticks. Silverware is common in Hong Kong, but it might be seen as a respectful gesture if you try your hand at chopsticks. Dining is a communal event. Everyone orders at least one dish, which are then placed in the center of the table and shared. Your meal will usually include rice or soup. It is considered proper to hold the bowl close to your lips and shovel the rice or soup into your mouth. At the end of the meal, most Chinese will use a toothpick at the table while covering their mouth with the non-toothpick-holding hand. This is common at all gatherings at all types of restaurants.

Smoking is common in Hong Kong, yet it is officially banned in all indoor public areas, including malls, banks, department stores, and supermarkets. It's also banned on all public transportation. There is a movement afoot to ban it in restaurants and bars, as well, but a strong opposition so far has prevented this effort from becoming law.

Hong Kong is extremely crowded; pushing, shoving, and gentle nudges are commonplace. As difficult as this may be to accept, it's not considered rude, it's unavoidable. Becoming angry or taking offense to an inadvertent push is considered rude.

However, while a gentle shove on the streets may be common, it is not typical of strangers to be excessively touchy-feely with one another. A gregarious hug and boisterous hello will be off-putting to Hong Kongers who don't know you. When you are first meeting local people, try to be low-key and subdued, even if it's not in your nature.

BUSINESS ETIQUETTE

Hong Kongers have a keen sense of hierarchy in the office. Egalitarianism may be admired in the United States, but it's often insulting in Hong Kong. Let the tea lady get the tea and coffee—that's what she's there for. Your assistant or Chinese colleague is thought to have better things to do than make copies or deliver messages. Hong Kongers are very attached to business cards, presumably because they're tangible evidence of one's place in the hierarchy. Have plenty of business cards available (printed, if possible, in English on one side and Chinese on the other). Exchange cards by proffering yours with both hands and a slight bow, and receiving one in the same way. Once your receive the card, you should stop, read the card, and then try to make an admiring comment about the card, the person's title, or the company.

GAY & LESBIAN TRAVEL

Criminal sanctions on homosexual relations between consenting adults in Hong Kong were lifted in the 1980s. Today, gay men and women have a higher profile than ever before in professional and social circles. As in many large cities, Hong Kong's gay nightlife and clubs are some of the best in town, and the envy of heterosexuals.

Contacts, a magazine covering the local gay scene, is available for HK$35 at the **Fetish Fashion** boutique. Among popular nightspots is **Propaganda,** the largest gay and lesbian bar in Hong Kong.

🛄 Local Resources **Fetish Fashion** ✉ 32 Cochrane St., mezzanine, Central ☎ 2544-1155. **Propaganda** ✉ 1 Hollywood Rd., Central ☎ 2868-1316. **Rice Bar** ✉ 33 Jervois St., Sheung Wan ☎ 2851-4800.

🛄 Gay- & Lesbian-Friendly Travel Agencies **Different Roads Travel** ✉ 8383 Wilshire Blvd., Suite 520, Beverly Hills, CA 90211 ☎ 800/429-8747 or 323/651-5557 [Ext. 14 for both] 🖷 323/651-5454 ✉ lgernert@tzell.com. **Kennedy Travel** ✉ 130 W. 42nd St., Suite 401, New York, NY 10036 ☎ 800/237-7433 or 212/840-8659 🖷 212/730-2269 ⊕ www.kennedytravel.com. **Now, Voyager** ✉ 4406 18th St., San Francisco, CA 94114 ☎ 800/255-6951 or 415/626-1169 🖷 415/626-8626 ⊕ www.nowvoyager.com. **Skylink Travel and Tour/Flying Dutchmen Travel** ✉ 1455 N. Dutton Ave., Suite A, Santa Rosa,

CA 95401 ☎ 800/225-5759 or 707/546-9888
🖷 707/636-0951; serving lesbian travelers.

HEALTH
FOOD & DRINK
The major health risk for travelers overseas is traveler's diarrhea, caused by eating
contaminated fruit or vegetables or drinking contaminated water. So watch what
you eat. Stay away from ice, uncooked
food, and unpasteurized milk and milk
products. Water from government mains
satisfies World Health Organization
(WHO) standards, but it's wise to **drink
only bottled water,** particularly if you have
never traveled to Hong Kong. Expect to
pay HK$7 to HK$20 for a liter bottle of
purified water.

Severe Acute Respiratory Syndrome
(SARS), also known as atypical pneumo-
nia, is a respiratory illness caused by a new
strain of coronavirus that was first reported in parts of Asia in early 2003.
Symptoms include a fever greater than
100.4°F (38°C), shortness of breath, and
other flulike symptoms. The disease is
thought to spread by close person-to-per-
son contact, particularly respiratory
droplets and secretions transmitted
through the eyes, nose, or mouth. To prevent SARS, the Hong Kong Health Department recommends maintaining good
personal hygiene, washing hands frequently, and wearing a face mask in
crowded public places. SARS did not return in 2004, but many experts believe
that it or other contagious, upper-respira-
tory viruses will continue to be a seasonal
health concern. At this writing, all travelers are still asked to submit a health ques-
tionnaire as they disembark in Hong
Kong, and those with fever will probably
be asked to comply with further health
checks.

OVER-THE-COUNTER REMEDIES
Familiar over-the-counter medications
such as aspirin, Tylenol, and so on, are
available in supermarkets such as Wellcome or 7-Eleven shops, which are scattered throughout the city. The drugstore
chains Fanda Perfume Co., Ltd. and Watson's (⇨ Pharmacies *in* Emergencies) both

have pharmacy departments and numerous shops throughout the city.

🛈 Local Health Information **Department of
Health Hotline** ☎ 2961-8968 ⊕ www.info.gov.hk/
dh. **Traveller's Health Service** ☎ 2150-7235.

🛈 Health Warnings **National Centers for Disease
Control and Prevention** (CDC) ✉ Office of Health
Communication, National Center for Infectious Dis-
eases, Division of Quarantine, Travelers' Health,
1600 Clifton Rd. NE, Atlanta, GA 30333 ☎ 877/394-
8747 international travelers' health line, 800/311-
3435 other inquiries, 404/498-1600 Division of
Quarantine 🖷 888/232-3299 ⊕ www.cdc.gov/
travel. **World Health Organization** (WHO)
⊕ www.who.int.

HOLIDAYS
Major holidays in Hong Kong include
New Year's (the first weekday in January),
Chinese New Year (end of January/early
February), Easter, Labour Day (May 1),
National Day (October 1), and Christmas
and Boxing Day (December 25 and 26).
There are also numerous Chinese holidays
throughout the year.

INSURANCE
The most useful travel-insurance plan is a
comprehensive policy that includes coverage for trip cancellation and interruption,
default, trip delay, and medical expenses
(with a waiver for preexisting conditions).

Without insurance you'll lose all or most
of your money if you cancel your trip, regardless of the reason. Default insurance
covers you if your tour operator, airline, or
cruise line goes out of business—the
chances of which have been increasing.
Trip-delay covers expenses that arise because of bad weather or mechanical delays. Study the fine print when comparing
policies.

If you're traveling internationally, a key
component of travel insurance is coverage
for medical bills incurred if you get sick on
the road. Such expenses aren't generally
covered by Medicare or private policies.
U.K. residents can buy a travel-insurance
policy valid for most vacations taken during the year in which it's purchased (but
check preexisting-condition coverage).
British and Australian citizens need extra
medical coverage when traveling overseas.

Always **buy travel policies directly from the insurance company**; if you buy them from a cruise line, airline, or tour operator that goes out of business you probably won't be covered for the agency or operator's default, a major risk. Before making any purchase, review your existing health and home-owner's policies to find what they cover away from home.

🔳 Travel Insurers In the United States: **Access America** ✉ 2805 N. Parham Rd., Richmond, VA 23294 ☎ 800/284-8300 🖨 800/346-9265 or 804/673-1491 ⊕ www.accessamerica.com. **Travel Guard International** ✉ 1145 Clark St., Stevens Point, WI 54481 ☎ 800/826-1300 or 715/345-0505 🖨 800/955-8785 ⊕ www.travelguard.com.

🔳 In Australia: **Insurance Council of Australia** ✉ Insurance Enquiries and Complaints, Level 12, Box 561, Collins St. W, Melbourne, VIC 8007 ☎ 1300/780-808 or 03/9629-4109 🖨 03/9621-2060 ⊕ www.iecltd.com.au. In New Zealand: **Insurance Council of New Zealand** ✉ 111-115 Customhouse Quay, Level 7, Box 474, Wellington ☎ 04/472-5230 🖨 04/473-3011 ⊕ www.icnz.org.nz. In the United Kingdom: **Association of British Insurers** ✉ 51 Gresham St., London EC2V 7HQ ☎ 020/7600-3333 🖨 020/7696-8999 ⊕ www.abi.org.uk. In Canada: **RBC Insurance** ✉ 6880 Financial Dr., Mississauga, Ontario L5N 7Y5 ☎ 800/668-4342 or 905/816-2400 🖨 905/813-4704 ⊕ www.rbcinsurance.com.

LANGUAGE

Hong Kong's official languages are English and Cantonese. Mandarin—the official language of China, known in Hong Kong as Putonghua—is gaining in popularity. Macau's official languages are Portuguese and Cantonese, but many people speak English. There, too, Mandarin is growing in popularity.

In hotels, major restaurants, stores, and tourist centers, almost everyone speaks English. This is not the case, however, with taxi drivers, bus drivers, and workers in small shops, cafés, and market stalls.

Local language study courses are available, but most last at least one month. Peruse the Web site of the New Asia Yale in China Chinese Language Centre at the Chinese University of Hong Kong for more information.

🔳 **New Asia Yale in China Chinese Language Centre** ⊕ www.cuhk.edu.hk/clc.

MAIL & SHIPPING

Hong Kong has an excellent reputation for its postal system. Airmail letters to any place in the world should take three to eight days. The Kowloon Central Post Office and the General Post Office in Central are open 8 AM to 6 PM Monday through Saturday.

🔳 Post Offices **General Post Office** ✉ 2 Connaught Rd., Central ☎ 2921-2222 ⊕ www.hongkongpost.com. **Kowloon Central Post Office** ✉ 10 Middle Rd., Tsim Tsa Shui.

OVERNIGHT SHIPPING

The post office has an overnight express service called Speedpost. Large international couriers in Hong Kong include DHL, Federal Express, and UPS.

🔳 **DHL** ☎ 2765-8111 🖨 2334-1228 ⊕ www.dhl.com.hk. **Federal Express** ☎ 2730-3333 🖨 2730-6588 ⊕ www.fedex.com.hk. **General Post Office** ✉ 2 Connaught Rd., next to Star Ferry Terminal, Central ☎ 2921-2222 ⊕ www.hongkongpost.com. **UPS** ☎ 2735-3535 🖨 2738-5070 ⊕ www.ups.com.

POSTAL RATES

Letters sent from Hong Kong are thought of as going to one of two zones. Zone 1 includes China, Japan, Taiwan, South Korea, Southeast Asia, Indonesia, and Asia. Zone 2 is everywhere else. International airmail costs HK$3 for a letter or postcard weighing under 10 grams mailed to a Zone 1 or 2 address. To send a letter within Hong Kong, the cost is HK1.40.

RECEIVING MAIL

The General Post Office has a *poste restante* (general delivery) counter. Have mail addressed as following: Your Name, Poste Restante, GPO, Hong Kong. To pick up mail you'll need to present yourself at the counter with a valid picture ID—a passport is preferred. Travelers with American Express cards or traveler's checks can receive mail at the American Express office. Have mail addressed c/o Client Mail Service at the main Amex office.

🔳 Addresses for Receiving Mail **American Express** ✉ 5 Queen's Rd., Central ☎ 2811-6888. **General Post Office** ✉ 2 Connaught Rd., next to Star Ferry, Central ☎ 2921-2222.

SHIPPING PARCELS

Packages sent airmail to the United States often take two weeks. Airmail shipments to the United Kingdom—both packages and letters—arrive within three or five days, while mail to Australia often arrives in as little as three days.

You are probably best off shipping your own parcels instead of letting shop owners do this for you, both to save money and to ensure that you are actually shipping yourself what you purchased and not a quick substitute—though most shop owners are honest and won't try to cheat you in this way. The workers at Hong Kong Post are extremely friendly and they will sell you all the packaging equipment you need, at unbelievably reasonable prices.

MONEY MATTERS

The Hong Kong dollar is closely pegged to the U.S. dollar, and exchange rates don't usually vary too widely.

Prices throughout this guide are given for adults. Substantially reduced fees are almost always available for children, students, and senior citizens. For information on taxes, *see* Taxes.

ATMS

Reliable and safe, ATMs are widely available throughout Hong Kong. If your card was issued from a bank in an English-speaking country, the instructions on the ATM machine will appear in English.

CREDIT CARDS

Major credit cards are widely accepted in Hong Kong, though they may not be accepted at small shops. However, prices are often 3% to 5% higher if you pay by credit card to compensate for the processing fees charged by the card companies.

Throughout this guide, the following abbreviations are used: **AE,** American Express; **DC,** Diners Club; **MC,** MasterCard; and **V,** Visa.

🛈 Reporting Lost Cards **American Express** ☎ 2811-6122. **Diners Club** ☎ 2860-1888. **Master-Card** ☎ 800/966-677. **Visa** ☎ 2810-8033.

CURRENCY

Units of currency are the Hong Kong dollar ($) and the cent. Bills come in denomi-nations of 1,000, 500, 100, 50, 20, and 10 dollars. Coins are 10, 5, 2, and 1 dollar and 50, 20, and 10 cents. At this writing, the Hong Kong dollar was pegged to the U.S. dollar at approximately 7.8 Hong Kong dollars to 1 U.S. dollar, approxi-mately 5.8 Hong Kong dollars to 1 Cana-dian dollar, and 14.05 Hong Kong dollars to 1 British pound. Although the image of Queen Elizabeth II does not appear on new coins, old ones bearing her image are still valid.

The official currency unit in Macau is the pataca, which is divided into 100 avos. Bank notes come in five denominations: 500, 100, 50, 10, and 5 patacas. Coins are 5 and 1 patacas and 50, 20, and 10 avos. The pataca is pegged to the Hong Kong dollar (within a few cents); at this writing there were 8 patacas to the U.S. dollar. Hong Kong currency circulates freely in Macau but not vice versa, so remember to change your patacas before you return to Hong Kong.

CURRENCY EXCHANGE

There are no currency restrictions in Hong Kong. You can exchange currency at the airport, in hotels, in banks, and through private money changers scattered through the tourist areas.

For the most favorable rates, **change money through banks.** Although ATM transaction fees may be higher abroad than at home, ATM rates are excellent be-cause they're based on wholesale rates of-fered only by major banks. You won't do as well at exchange booths in airports or rail and bus stations, in hotels, in restau-rants, or in stores. To avoid lines at airport exchange booths, get a bit of local cur-rency before you leave home.

🛈 Exchange Services **International Currency Ex-press** ✉ 427 N. Camden Dr., Suite F, Beverly Hills, CA 90210 ☎ 888/278-6628 orders 🖷 310/278-6410 ⊕ www.foreignmoney.com. **Travel Ex Currency Services** ☎ 800/287-7362 orders and retail loca-tions ⊕ www.travelex.com.

TRAVELER'S CHECKS

Do you need traveler's checks? It depends on where you're headed. If you're going to rural areas and small towns, go with cash;

traveler's checks are best used in cities. Lost or stolen checks can usually be re-placed within 24 hours. To ensure a speedy refund, buy your own traveler's checks—don't let someone else pay for them: irregularities like this can cause delays. The person who bought the checks should make the call to request a refund. In Hong Kong, banks and hotels will accept traveler's checks, but you may find local restaurateurs and shop assistants confused by them. It's best to change them into small amounts of local currency at banks in Hong Kong.

PACKING

Appearances in Hong Kong are impor-tant. This is a city where suits are still *de rigueur* for meetings and business func-tions. From May through September, Hong Kong's high humidity warrants light clothing; but air-conditioning in ho-tels and restaurants can be arctic, so bring a sweater or shawl for evening use indoors. Don't forget your swimsuit and sunscreen; most of the large hotels have pools, and you may want to spend some time on one of Hong Kong's many beaches. In October, November, March, and April, a jacket or sweater should suf-fice, but from December through Febru-ary bring a raincoat or a light overcoat. At any time of year it's wise to pack a folding umbrella.

In your carry-on luggage, pack an extra pair of eyeglasses or contact lenses and enough of any medication you take to last a few days longer than the entire trip. You may also ask your doctor to write a spare prescription using the drug's generic name, as brand names may vary from country to country. In luggage to be checked, **never pack prescription drugs, valuables, or un-developed film.** And don't forget to carry with you the addresses of offices that han-dle refunds of lost traveler's checks. Check *Fodor's How to Pack* (available at online retailers and bookstores everywhere) for more tips.

To avoid customs and security delays, carry medications in their original packag-ing. Don't pack any sharp objects in your carry-on luggage, including knives of any size or material, scissors, nail clippers, and corkscrews, or anything else that might arouse suspicion.

To avoid having your checked luggage chosen for hand inspection, don't cram bags full. The U.S. Transportation Security Administration suggests packing shoes on top and placing personal items you don't want touched in clear plastic bags.

CHECKING LUGGAGE

You're allowed to carry aboard one bag and one personal article, such as a purse or a laptop computer. Make sure what you carry on fits under your seat or in the overhead bin. Get to the gate early, so you can board as soon as possible, before the overhead bins fill up.

Baggage allowances vary by carrier, desti-nation, and ticket class. On international flights, you're usually allowed to check two bags weighing up to 70 pounds (32 kilograms) each, although a few airlines allow checked bags of up to 88 pounds (40 kilograms) in first class. Some inter-national carriers don't allow more than 66 pounds (30 kilograms) per bag in business class and 44 pounds (20 kilo-grams) in economy. On domestic flights, the limit is usually 50 to 70 pounds (23 to 32 kilograms) per bag. In general, carry-on bags shouldn't exceed 40 pounds (18 kilograms). Most airlines won't accept bags that weigh more than 100 pounds (45 kilograms) on domestic or international flights. Expect to pay a fee for baggage that exceeds weight lim-its. Check baggage restrictions with your carrier before you pack.

Airline liability for baggage is limited to $2,500 per person on flights within the United States. On international flights it amounts to $9.07 per pound or $20 per kilogram for checked baggage (roughly $640 per 70-pound bag), with a maximum of $634.90 per piece, and $400 per pas-senger for unchecked baggage. You can buy additional coverage at check-in for about $10 per $1,000 of coverage, but it often excludes a rather extensive list of items, shown on your airline ticket.

Before departure, itemize your bags' contents and their worth, and label the bags with your name, address, and phone number. (If you use your home address, cover it so potential thieves can't see it readily.) Include a label inside each bag and **pack a copy of your itinerary.** At check-in, make sure each bag is correctly tagged with the destination airport's three-letter code. Because some checked bags will be opened for hand inspection, the U.S. Transportation Security Administration recommends that you leave luggage unlocked or use the plastic locks offered at check-in. TSA screeners place an inspection notice inside searched bags, which are resealed with a special lock.

If your bag has been searched and contents are missing or damaged, file a claim with the TSA Consumer Response Center as soon as possible. If your bags arrive damaged or fail to arrive at all, file a written report with the airline before leaving the airport.

🔳 Complaints **U.S. Transportation Security Administration Contact Center** ☎ 866/289–9673 ⊕ www.tsa.gov.

PASSPORTS & VISAS

When traveling internationally, carry your passport even if you don't need one (it's always the best form of ID) and **make two photocopies of the data page** (one for someone at home and another for you, carried separately from your passport). If you lose your passport, promptly call the nearest embassy or consulate and the local police.

U.S. passport applications for children under age 14 require consent from both parents or legal guardians; both parents must appear together to sign the application. If only one parent appears, he or she must submit a written statement from the other parent authorizing passport issuance for the child. A parent with sole authority must present evidence of it when applying; acceptable documentation includes the child's certified birth certificate listing only the applying parent, a court order specifically permitting this parent's travel with the child, or a death certificate for the nonapplying par-

ent. Application forms and instructions are available on the Web site of the U.S. State Department's Bureau of Consular Affairs (⊕ travel.state.gov).

ENTERING HONG KONG

Citizens of the United Kingdom need only a valid passport to enter Hong Kong for stays of up to six months. Australian, Canadian, New Zealand, and U.S. citizens need only a valid passport to enter Hong Kong for stays up to three months. It is best to have at least six months' validity on your passport before traveling to Asia.

PASSPORT OFFICES

The best time to apply for a passport or to renew is in fall and winter. Before any trip, check your passport's expiration date, and, if necessary, renew it as soon as possible.

🔳 Australian Citizens **Passports Australia** Australian Department of Foreign Affairs and Trade ☎ 131–232 ⊕ www.passports.gov.au.

🔳 Canadian Citizens **Passport Office** ✉ to mail in applications: 200 Promenade du Portage, Hull, Québec J8X 4B7 ☎ 800/567–6868 or 819/994–3500 ⊕ www.ppt.gc.ca.

🔳 New Zealand Citizens **New Zealand Passports Office** ☎ 0800/225–050 or 04/474–8100 ⊕ www.passports.govt.nz.

🔳 U.K. Citizens **U.K. Passport Service** ☎ 0870/521–0410 ⊕ www.passport.gov.uk.

🔳 U.S. Citizens **National Passport Information Center** ☎ 877/487–2778, 888/874–7793 TDD/TTY ⊕ travel.state.gov.

RESTROOMS

Public restrooms are difficult to find in Hong Kong. Clean, Western-style restrooms (as opposed to squatters, which are merely holes in the ground) are even more difficult to find. Although the situation is gradually improving, bring tissues or a toilet-paper roll. Using hotel and restaurant bathrooms is the best bet for a clean environment.

SAFETY

Don't wear a money belt or a waist pack, both of which peg you as a tourist. Distribute your cash and any valuables (including your credit cards and passport) between a deep front pocket, an inside jacket or vest pocket, and a hidden money pouch. Do not reach for the money pouch once you're in public.

Safety is not usually a problem in Hong Kong, which remains relatively safe day or night. The Hong Kong Police do a good job maintaining law and order, but pickpockets are an increasing problem. So exercise the same caution you would in any large city and avoid carrying large amounts of cash or valuables with you, and you should have no problems.

WOMEN IN HONG KONG

If you carry a purse, choose one with a zipper and a thick strap that you can drape across your body; adjust the length so that the purse sits in front of you at or above hip level. (Don't wear a money belt or a waist pack.) Store only enough money in the purse to cover casual spending. Distribute the rest of your cash and any valuables between deep front pockets, inside jacket or vest pockets, and a concealed money pouch.

SENIOR-CITIZEN TRAVEL

To qualify for age-related discounts, mention your senior-citizen status up front when booking hotel reservations (not when checking out) and before you're seated in restaurants (not when paying the bill). Be sure to have identification on hand. When renting a car, ask about promotional car-rental discounts, which can be cheaper than senior-citizen rates.

🖬 Educational Programs **Elderhostel** ⊠ 11 Ave. de Lafayette, Boston, MA 02111-1746 ☎ 877/426-8056, 978/323-4141 international callers, 877/426-2167 TTY 🖶 877/426-2166 ⊕ www.elderhostel.org.

SHOPPING

If you buy and ship home Chinese lacquer or other breakable keepsakes, buy an all-risk insurance policy. Ivory has long been a prized souvenir of trips to Asia, but the Hong Kong government has imposed a stringent policy on the import and export of this bone derivative. As a result, you must get an import license from your country of residence, as well as an export license to take ivory out of Hong Kong. Failure to comply may result in a fine and forfeiture of the purchase. If you're considering buying ivory, check with your home

consulate or trade commission for the latest regulations. Remember that all goods—with the exceptions of alcohol, tobacco, petroleum, perfume, cosmetics, and soft drinks—are duty-free everywhere in Hong Kong, not just in "duty-free" stores. Bargaining, even at street markets, has become increasingly rare.

Beware of merchants who claim to be giving you a "special" price; you may not get what you actually pay for.

SMART SOUVENIRS

Refrigerator magnets of a dim sum dish or rickshaw, inexpensive silk pajamas, fans and chopsticks—and of course postcards—are the typical tourist souvenirs you can find in shops along Nathan Road in Kowloon, on Li Yuen East and Li Yuen West alleys in Central in Hong Kong, and by the Star Ferry in both Hong Kong and Kowloon. Expect to pay about HK$10 to $40 for magnets, HK$50 to HK$150 for silk robes or pajamas, HK$20 for fans and chopsticks. Postcards cost about HK$2 each.

SIGHTSEEING TOURS

The HKTB offers walking and exploring tours in Hong Kong, many of which can be personalized, including a very informative feng shui tour of Central. In addition to standard tours of Hong Kong, Splendid Tours & Travel offers tailor-made trips that can take you hiking through the jungle—or through a jungle of shops.

The HKTB also offers several tours of the outlying New Territories; these tours are an easy way to get out into the countryside without having to rent a car to drive yourself. The Heritage tour focuses on the territory's fast-disappearing traditional walled villages and ancestral halls. The six-hour Land Between tour takes you through the rural countryside, including Chuk Lam Shim Yuen (Bamboo Forest Monastery) and Hong Kong's tallest mountain, Tai Mo Shan. Your hotel's tour desk will be able to help you, or you can book a tour directly with the HKTB Visitor Hot Line, which is open from 8 to 6 daily.

🖬 Sightseeing Tours **HKTB Visitor Hot Line** ☎ 2508-1234. **Splendid Tours & Travel** ⊠ 26/F,

Lockville Commercial Bldg., 25–27 Lock Rd., Tsim Sha Tsui ☎ 2316–2151 🖷 2312–2031 ⊕ www. splendidtours.com.

STUDENTS IN HONG KONG

To save money, look into deals available through student-oriented travel agencies. You need only a valid student ID card to qualify. Members of international student groups are also eligible.

🖪 **IDs & Services STA Travel** ✉ 10 Downing St., New York, NY 10014 ☎ 800/777–0112 24-hr service center, 212/627–3111 🖷 212/627–3387 ⊕ www.sta. com. **Travel Cuts** ✉ 187 College St., Toronto, Ontario M5T 1P7 Canada ☎ 800/592–2887 in the U.S., 416/979–2406 or 866/246–9762 in Canada 🖷 416/ 979–8167 ⊕ www.travelcuts.com.

SUBWAY TRAVEL

The four-line Mass Transit Railway (MTR) links Hong Kong Island to Kowloon (including the shopping area Tsim Sha Tsui) and parts of the New Territories. Trains run frequently and are safe and easy to use. Station entrances are marked with a simple line symbol resembling a man with arms and legs outstretched. You buy tickets from ticket machines or from English-speaking workers at the counters by the turnstile entrances. For the machines, change is available at the stations' Hang Seng Bank counters and from the machines themselves. Fares range from HK$4 to HK$26.

DISCOUNT PASSES

The special Tourist MTR 1-Day Pass (HK$50) allows you unlimited rides in one day. The Airport Express Tourist Octopus (HK$220/HK$300) includes single journeys from/to the airport.

🖪 **HKTB Visitor Hot Line** ☎ 2508–1234. **Mass Transit Railway (MTR)** ☎ 2881–8888.

TAXES

Hong Kong levies a 10% service charge and a 3% government tax on hotel rooms.

TAXIS

Taxis in Hong Kong and Kowloon are usually red. A taxi's roof sign lights up when the car is available. Fares in urban areas are HK$15 for the first 2 km (1 mi) and HK$1.20 for each additional ⅓ km

(⅒ mi). There is luggage surcharge of HK$5 per large piece, and surcharges of HK$20 for the Cross-Harbour Tunnel, HK$30 for the Eastern Harbour Tunnel, and HK$45 for the Western Harbour Tunnel. The Tsing Ma Bridge surcharge is HK$30. The Aberdeen, Lion Rock, and Junk Bay tunnels also carry small surcharges (HK$3 to HK$8). Taxis cannot pick up passengers where there are double yellow lines. Note that it's hard to find a taxi around 4 PM when the drivers switch shifts.

Many taxi drivers do not speak English, so you may want to ask someone at your hotel to write out your destination in Chinese.

Backseat passengers must wear a seat belt or face a HK$5,000 fine. Most locals do not tip; however, if you do—HK$5 to HK$10—you're sure to earn yourself a winning smile from your underpaid and overworked taxi driver.

Outside the urban areas, taxis are green (blue on Lantau Island). Cabs in the New Territories cost less than urban taxis: HK$11.80 for the first 2 km (1 mi) and HK$1.10 for each additional ⅓ km (⅒ mi). Urban taxis may travel into rural zones, but rural taxis must not cross into urban zones. There are no interchange facilities for the two, so do not try to reach an urban area using a green taxi.

COMPLAINTS

Taxis are usually reliable, but if you have a problem, note the taxi's license number, which is usually on the dashboard, and call the Transport Complaints Unit.

🖪 **Transport Complaints Unit** ☎ 2889–9999.

TELEPHONES

Hong Kong phone numbers are comprised of eight digits. The local telephone system is efficient and telephone owners pay a flat monthly fee, not a per-call tariff; international calls are inexpensive relative to those in the United States. You can expect a clear-sounding connection. Directory assistance is helpful. Don't hang up if you hear Cantonese when calling automated and prerecorded hotlines; English is usually the second or third language option.

AREA & COUNTRY CODES

The country code for Hong Kong is 852. When dialing a Hong Kong number from abroad, drop the initial 0 from the local area code. The country code is 1 for the United States and Canada, 61 for Australia, 64 for New Zealand, and 44 for the United Kingdom.

The country code for Macau is 853; for China, 086.

CELLULAR PHONES

CSL rents out cellular phones for HK$250 per week with the purchase of a phone card of HK$300 or more.

⚑ CSL ✉ 2/F, 168 Sai Yeung Choi St., Mong Kok ☎ 2393-5597 ✉ Shop 5, 1/F, Ying Kong Mansion, 2-6 Yee Woo St., Causeway Bay ☎ 2512-3123 ⊕ www.one2free.com.

DIRECTORY & OPERATOR ASSISTANCE

Dial 1081 for directory assistance from English-speaking operators. If a number is constantly busy and you think it might be out of order, call 109 and the operator will check the line. The operators are very helpful, if you talk slowly and clearly. However, do not be surprised if you call a local business and they simply hang up on you; often when local, nonnative English speakers don't understand you, they simply hang up rather than stammer through a conversation and lose face.

LOCAL CALLS

Given that your hotel will likely charge you for a local call, you might consider simply walking out of your hotel, stopping at the nearest shop, and asking the shopkeeper if you can use the phone. Most locals will not charge you to you use their phone for a local call since the phone company does not charge for individual local calls.

LONG-DISTANCE CALLS

You can dial direct from many hotel and business centers, but always with a hefty surcharge. Dial 10013 for international inquiries and for assistance with direct dialing. Dial 10010 for collect and operator-assisted calls to most countries, including the United States, Canada, and the United Kingdom. Dial 10011 for credit-card, collect, and international conference calls.

LONG-DISTANCE SERVICES

AT&T, Sprint, and MCI services are all available in Hong Kong.

AT&T, MCI, and Sprint access codes make calling long-distance relatively convenient, but you may find the local access number blocked in many hotel rooms. First ask the hotel operator to connect you. If the hotel operator balks, ask for an international operator, or dial the international operator yourself. One way to improve your odds of getting connected to your long-distance carrier is to travel with more than one company's calling card (a hotel may block Sprint, for example, but not MCI). If all else fails, call from a pay phone.

⚑ Access Codes **AT&T Direct** ☎ 800/96-1111. **MCI WorldPhone** ☎ 800/96-1121. **Sprint International Access** ☎ 800/96-1877.

PHONE CARDS

Phone cards are available throughout Hong Kong in 7-Eleven shops. Directions are written in English on the back of the cards, and they can be used on nearly all public phones.

PUBLIC PHONES

To make a local call from a pay phone, use a HK$1 coin or, at some phones, a credit card. Pay phones are not hard to find, but locals generally pop into a store and ask to use the phone there, as local calls are free on residence and business lines. Many small stores keep their telephone on the counter facing the street.

To make international calls from a pay phone, stop by a 7-Eleven or other convenience store and purchase a prepaid phone card.

Watch for multimedia Powerphones, whose touch screens allow you to check e-mail and send faxes as well as phone home.

TIME

Hong Kong is 12 hours ahead of Eastern Standard Time and 7 hours ahead of Greenwich Mean Time. Remember during daylight savings time to add an hour to the time difference (so it's 13 hours ahead of EST and 8 hours ahead of GMT).

TIPPING

Hotels and major restaurants usually add a 10% service charge; however, in almost all cases, this money does not go to the waiters and waitresses. Proprietors will tell you it goes to the cost of replacing broken crockery, napkins, and so on. If you want to tip a waiter or waitress, be sure to give it directly to that person and no one else. It is generally not the custom to leave an additional tip in taxis and beauty salons; but, if you do choose to tip, you'll receive more attentive service and make the usually not-very-well-paid employees immensely happy. If you buy your newspaper from a corner vendor, consider searching for one of the numerous octogenarians who are sadly still working for a living—leaving your extra change with these people is also another much-appreciated tip.

TOURS & PACKAGES

Because everything is prearranged on a prepackaged tour or independent vacation, you spend less time planning—and often get it all at a good price.

BOOKING WITH AN AGENT

Travel agents are excellent resources. But it's a good idea to collect brochures from several agencies, as some agents' suggestions may be influenced by relationships with tour and package firms that reward them for volume sales. If you have a special interest, find an agent with expertise in that area; the American Society of Travel Agents (ASTA; ⇨ Travel Agencies) has a database of specialists worldwide. You can log on to the group's Web site to find an ASTA travel agent in your neighborhood.

Make sure your travel agent knows the accommodations and other services of the place being recommended. Ask about the hotel's location, room size, beds, and whether it has a pool, room service, or programs for children, if you care about these. Has your agent been there in person or sent others whom you can contact?

Do some homework on your own, too: local tourist offices can provide information about lesser-known and small-niche operators, some of which may sell only direct.

BUYER BEWARE

Each year consumers are stranded or lose their money when tour operators—even large ones with excellent reputations—go out of business. So check out the operator. Ask several travel agents about its reputation, and try to **book with a company that has a consumer-protection program.** (Look for information in the company's brochure.) In the United States, members of the United States Tour Operators Association are required to set aside funds ($1 million) to help eligible customers cover payments and travel arrangements in the event that the company defaults. It's also a good idea to choose a company that participates in the American Society of Travel Agents' Tour Operator Program; ASTA will act as mediator in any disputes between you and your tour operator.

Remember that the more your package or tour includes, the better you can predict the ultimate cost of your vacation. Make sure you know exactly what is covered, and beware of hidden costs. Are taxes, tips, and transfers included? Entertainment and excursions? These can add up.

⧉ Tour-Operator Recommendations American Society of Travel Agents (⇨ Travel Agencies). **National Tour Association (NTA)** ✉ 546 E. Main St., Lexington, KY 40508 ☎ 800/682-8886 or 859/226-4444 🖷 859/226-4404 ⊕ www.ntaonline.com. **United States Tour Operators Association** (USTOA) ✉ 275 Madison Ave., Suite 2014, New York, NY 10016 ☎ 212/599-6599 🖷 212/599-6744 ⊕ www.ustoa.com.

TRAIN TRAVEL

The **Kowloon–Canton Railway** (KCR) has 13 commuter stops on its 34-km (22-mi) journey through urban Kowloon (from Kowloon to Lo Wu) and Sha Tin and Taipo on its way to the Chinese border. The main station is at Hung Hom, Kowloon, where you can catch express trains to China. Fares range from HK$7.50 to HK$40, and no reservations are required. The KCR meets the MTR at the **Kowloon Tong** station. In the New Territories, the **Light Rail Transit** connects Tuen Mun and Yuen Long.

TRAVEL CARD

The electronic Octopus Card (HK$100) is accepted on Airport Express, the MTR,

Kowloon–Canton Railway (KCR), Kowloon Motor Bus (KMB), Citybus, and ferries. Plus you can use it at 7-Eleven shops, Starbucks, and select stores. You can buy the card at ticket offices and HKTB outlets; you place a refundable deposit of HK$50 on it, then reload it with HK$50 or HK$100 increments at Add Value machines or at one of the service counters inside the station.

f **HKTB Visitor Hotline** ☎ 2508-1234. **Octopus Hotline** ☎ 2266-2266.

TRAMS

STREET TRAMS

Trams run along the north shore of Hong Kong Island from Kennedy Town (in the west) all the way through Central, Wanchai, Causeway Bay, North Point, and Quarry Bay, ending in the former fishing village of Shaukeiwan. A branch line turns off in Wanchai toward Happy Valley, where horse races are held in season. Destinations are marked on the front of each tram; the fare is HK$2. Avoid trams at rush hours, which are generally weekdays from 7:30 to 9 AM and 5 to 7 PM. Trams are generally quite slow, and a great way to inhale a lung full of car fumes, but they also give you an opportunity to see the city from a slow-moving vehicle.

PEAK TRAM

Dating from 1888, this railway rises from ground level to Victoria Peak (1,805 feet), offering a panoramic view of Hong Kong. Both residents and tourists use it; most passengers board at the lower terminus between Garden Road and Cotton Tree Drive. (The tram has five stations.) The fare is HK$20 one-way, HK$30 round-trip, and the tram runs every 10 to 15 minutes daily from 7 AM to midnight. A shuttle bus runs between the lower terminus and the Star Ferry.

TRAVEL AGENCIES

A good travel agent puts your needs first. Look for an agency that has been in business at least five years, emphasizes customer service, and has someone on staff who specializes in your destination. In addition, **make sure the agency belongs to a professional trade organization.** The

American Society of Travel Agents (ASTA)—the largest and most influential in the field with more than 20,000 members in some 140 countries—maintains and enforces a strict code of ethics and will step in to help mediate any agent-client disputes involving ASTA members if necessary. ASTA (whose motto is "Without a travel agent, you're on your own") also maintains a Web site that includes a directory of agents. (If a travel agency is also acting as your tour operator, *see* Buyer Beware *in* Tours & Packages.)

f Local Agent Referrals **American Society of Travel Agents (ASTA)** ✉ 1101 King St., Suite 200, Alexandria, VA 22314 ☎ 800/965-2782 or 703/739-2782 24-hr hotline 📠 703/684-8319 ⊕ www. astanet.com. **Association of British Travel Agents** ✉ 68-71 Newman St., London W1T 3AH ☎ 020/7637-2444 📠 020/7637-0713 ⊕ www.abta.com. **Association of Canadian Travel Agencies** ✉ 130 Albert St., Suite 1705, Ottawa, Ontario K1P 5G4 ☎ 613/237-3657 📠 613/237-7052 ⊕ www.acta.ca. **Australian Federation of Travel Agents** ✉ 309 Pitt St., Level 3, Sydney, NSW 2000 ☎ 02/9264-3299 or 1300/363-416 📠 02/9264-1085 ⊕ www.afta.com. au. **Travel Agents' Association of New Zealand** ✉ Tourism and Travel House, 79 Boulcott St., Level 5, Box 1888, Wellington 6001 ☎ 04/499-0104 📠 04/499-0786 ⊕ www.taanz.org.nz.

VISITOR INFORMATION

Learn more about foreign destinations by checking government-issued travel advisories and country information. For a broader picture, consider information from more than one country.

When you arrive, stop by an HKTB information center in Hong Kong. For phone assistance, call the multilingual hotline, which operates from 8 AM to 6 PM; for a printout of specific details, contact the 24-hour fax information service.

f Web sites **Hong Kong Tourist Board** (HKTB) ⊕ www.discoverhongkong.com. **Macau Government Tourist Office** ⊕ www.macautourism.gov.mo. **f** Government Advisories **U.S. Department of State** ✉ Overseas Citizens Services Office, 2100 Pennsylvania Ave. NW, 4th fl., Washington, DC 20520 ☎ 888/407-4747, 202/647-5225 interactive hotline ⊕ travel.state.gov. **Consular Affairs Bureau of Canada** ☎ 800/267-6788 or 613/944-6788 ⊕ www.voyage.gc.ca. **U.K. Foreign and Common-**

wealth Office ✉ Travel Advice Unit, Consular Division, Old Admiralty Bldg., London SW1A 2PA ☎ 0870/606-0290 or 020/7008-1500 ⊕ www.fco.gov.uk/travel. **Australian Department of Foreign Affairs and Trade** ☎ 300/139-281 travel advice, 02/6261-1299 Consular Travel Advice Faxback Service ⊕ www.dfat.gov.au. **New Zealand Ministry of Foreign Affairs and Trade** ☎ 04/439-8000 ⊕ www.mft.govt.nz.

WEB SITES

Do check out the World Wide Web when planning your trip. You'll find everything from weather forecasts to virtual tours of famous cities. Be sure to visit Fodors.com (⊕ www.fodors.com), a complete travel-planning site. You can research prices and book plane tickets, hotel rooms, rental cars, vacation packages, and more. In addition, you can post your pressing questions in the Travel Talk section. Other planning tools include a currency converter and weather reports, and there are loads of links to travel resources.

For a comprehensive guide to what's happening in Hong Kong, check out the HKTB's excellent site. For weather info, check out the Hong Kong Observatory. For the latest political information plus news and interesting business links try the official Hong Kong government site. For an overview of tourism information and sites in Macau, visit the site of the Macau Government Tourist Office.

🚩 **Hong Kong Government** ⊕ www.info.gov.hk. **Hong Kong Observatory** ⊕ www.weather.gov.hk **Hong Kong Tourist Board** (HKTB) ⊕ www.discoverhongkong.com. **Macau Government Tourist Office** ⊕ www.macautourism.gov.mo.

EXPLORING HONG KONG

1

Updated by
Eva Chui
Loiterton

TO STAND ON THE TIP OF KOWLOON PENINSULA and look out across the harbor to the full expanse of the Hong Kong island skyline—as awesome in height as Manhattan's, but only a few blocks deep and strung along the entire north coast—is to see the triumph of ambition over fate. Whereas it took Paris and London 10 to 20 generations to build the spectacular cities seen today, and New York 6, Hong Kong built almost everything you see before you in the time since today's young investment bankers were born. It is easy to perceive this tremendous creation of wealth as an inevitable result of Hong Kong's strategic position, but at any point in the territory's history things might have happened slightly differently, and the island would have found itself on the margins of world trade rather than at the center.

When the 78-square-km (30-square-mi) island of Hong Kong was ceded to the British after the Opium War of 1841, it consisted, in the infamous words of the British minister at the time, of "barren rock" whose only redeeming feature was the adjacent deep-water harbor. For the British, though, it served another purpose: Hong Kong guarded the eastern edge of the Pearl River delta, and with it access to Guangzhou (Canton), which in the mid-19th century was China's main trading port. By controlling Hong Kong, Britain came to control the export of Chinese products such as silk and tea, and to corner the Chinese market for Western manufactured goods and opium. The scheme proved highly profitable.

If British trade were all Hong Kong had going for it, however, its prosperity would have faded with the rest of the empire. No, the real story of Hong Kong began in the 1920s, when the first wave of Chinese refugees settled here to avoid civil unrest at home. They were followed in the '30s and '40s by refugees fleeing the advance of the invading Japanese army. But the biggest throngs of all came after the 1949 Communist revolution in China—mostly from the neighboring province of Guangdong, but also from Fujian, Shanghai, and elsewhere. Many of these mainland arrivals came from humble farming backgrounds, but many others had been rich and had seen their wealth and businesses stripped away by the revolutionaries. They came to Hong Kong poorer than their families had been in generations, yet by virtue of their labor, their descendants are the wealthiest generation yet.

Hong Kong has always lived and breathed commerce, and it is the territory's shrines to Mammon that will make the strongest impression when you first arrive. The Central district has long been thick with skyscrapers bearing the names of banks and conglomerates, and yet more continue to be built, squeezed into irregular plots of land that would seem insufficient for buildings half the size. When that doesn't work, the city simply reclaims more land from the harbor and builds on it almost before it dries. For a few years it will be obvious which land is reclaimed and which is old as the ground is turned and foundations laid, but soon enough the two will meld into one, just as they have before: you now have to walk four blocks from the Star Ferry Terminal, through streets shaded by office towers, to reach Queen's Road Central, the former waterfront. You may well ask what one can know for sure in this world if

MEGA MILLIONS

PLAY CASH WINFALL!
MONDAY'S EST JKPT-$525,000!

A. 10 32 41 46 48 - (37) QP

----

1 DRAW   TUE NOV15 05
018585   PRICE ✳   1.00
97905300   970-044512770-132510

above will be paid by the Lottery Commission after ticket is validated as a winner, Claim Form is filed, and proof of positive identification is provided. All prizes must be claimed within one (1) year following the drawing date.

RULES AND REGULATIONS

This ticket is a bearer instrument and unless signed by owner, prize may be claimed by anyone in possession of the winning ticket. SIGN YOUR TICKET IMMEDIATELY. BETTORS AGREE TO ABIDE BY MASSACHUSETTS STATE LOTTERY COMMISSION RULES AND REGULATIONS. Applicable Rules are available for inspection by Bettors by contacting the Lottery at the address below.

NAME (Please Print)
_____

ADDRESS
_____

CITY, STATE, ZIP
_____

PHONE   OWNER'S SIGNATURE

RN

Joseph C. Sullivan
JOSEPH C. SULLIVAN
Executive Director

Timothy P. Cahill
TIMOTHY P. CAHILL
State Treasurer

MASSACHUSETTS STATE LOTTERY, 60 COLUMBIAN ST., BRAINTREE, MA 02184

660312232

IMPORTANT NOTICE

CHECK THIS TICKET TO BE SURE IT REPRESENTS DESIRED BET(S) AS IT IS YOUR ONLY PROOF OF BET(S) PLACED.

HOW TO CLAIM PRIZE

Present winning ticket to any ON-LINE Lottery Sales Agent for payment up to $600.00. Claims for $600.00 and above will be paid by the Lottery Commission after ticket is validated as a winner, Claim Form is filed, and proof of positive identification is provided. All prizes must be claimed within one (1) year following the drawing date.

RULES AND REGULATIONS

This ticket is a bearer instrument and unless signed by owner, prize may be claimed by anyone in possession of the winning ticket. SIGN YOUR TICKET IMMEDIATELY. BETTORS AGREE TO ABIDE BY MASSACHUSETTS STATE LOTTERY COMMISSION RULES AND REGULATIONS. Applicable Rules are available for inspection by Bettors by contacting the Lottery at the address below.

NAME (Please Print)
_____

ADDRESS
_____

CITY, STATE, ZIP
_____

PHONE   OWNER'S SIGNATURE

not where the earth ends and the oceans begin, but Hong Kongers have gotten used to such vagaries.

Watching young investment bankers out on a Friday night in Hong Kong's nightspot haven of Lan Kwai Fong, reveling in their outrageous good fortune at being in this place at this time in history, you can't help but wonder whether this can possibly last. There's a heady, end-of-an-era exuberance to it all—a decadence that portends doom ahead. Yet visitors to Hong Kong have felt this same sentiment for almost a century and a half and, save for the rare economic downturn, the day of reckoning has not come. One of those rare exceptions came within a month after Hong Kong's handover back to China. But the change of sovereignty was not the issue which many expected to be the source of problems. Rather, it was the Asian crisis which took almost everyone by surprise. For a moment during these uncertain times, it seemed Hong Kongers would have to permanently scale back their ambitions. But then the moment passed and the usual breakneck growth returned.

Rapid change has not been limited to Hong Kong Island or the crowded Kowloon Peninsula, but extends up through the "new towns" of the New Territories. Some of these, like Sha Tin, were rice paddies 20 years ago and now form thriving cities of a half million people. The most ambitious project of all is the one you see on arrival: the leveling of Chek Lap Kok, an uninhabited island of rock and scrub, that made way for Hong Kong's stylish, ultraefficient international airport, the final legacy of British-ruled Hong Kong. Arriving in Hong Kong may now lack the rooftop-grazing shock of flying into the old Kai Tak, but you're whisked through the airport in no time and can then zip into Central in just 23 minutes on the Airport Express train. In a fairly short time, Lantau Island will be the location of the new Disneyland Hong Kong, which is scheduled at this writing to open by late 2005 or 2006; this will no doubt make the island an important destination for tourists from Hong Kong, the rest of China, and the rest of the world.

Amid all the change it can be easy (even for residents) to forget that most of Hong Kong has nothing to do with business or skyscrapers: three-quarters of it is actually rural land and wilderness. A bird's-eye view reveals the 236 islands that make up the lesser-known parts of Hong Kong; most are nothing but jagged peaks and tropical scrub, just as Hong Kong Island itself once was. Others are time capsules of ancestral China, with tiny temples, fishing villages, and small vegetable farms. Even Hong Kong Island, so relentlessly urban on its north coast, consists mostly of rolling green hills and sheltered bays on its south side. So whether you're looking for the hectic Hong Kong or the relaxed one, both are easy enough to find—indeed, sometimes only a few minutes apart.

Getting Your Bearings

Hong Kong Island and Kowloon are divided both physically and psychologically by Victoria Harbour. On Hong Kong Island, the central city stretches only a few kilometers south into the island before mountains rise up, but the city goes several more kilometers north into Kowloon. In the main districts and neighborhoods, luxury boutiques are a stone's

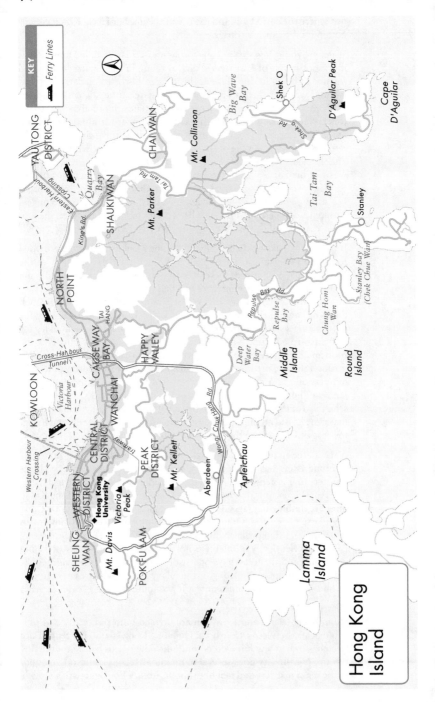

KEY

Ferry Lines

Hong Kong
Island

YAU TONG
DISTRICT

Quarry Bay

Eastern Harbour Crossing

King's Rd.

SHAUKIWAN

NORTH
POINT

Mt. Parker ▲

Tai Tam Rd.

CHAI WAN

Mt. Collinson ▲

Big Wave
Bay

Shek O

Shek O Rd.

D'Aguilar Peak ▲

Cape
D'Aguilar

Tai Tam
Bay

Stanley

Stanley Bay
(Chek Chue Wan)

Chung Hom
Wan

Round
Island

Cross-Harbour
Tunnel

KOWLOON

Victoria Harbour

Western Harbour
Crossing

CAUSEWAY
BAY

TAI
HANG

WANCHAI

HAPPY
VALLEY

Repulse Bay Rd.

Repulse
Bay

Deep
Water
Bay

Middle
Island

SHEUNG
WAN

WESTERN
DISTRICT

CENTRAL
DISTRICT

(tramway)

PEAK
DISTRICT

Mt. Kellett ▲

Wong Chuk Hang Rd.

Apleichau

Aberdeen

Hong Kong
University ▲

Victoria
Peak ▲

Mt. Davis ▲

POKFULAM

Lamma
Island

throw away from old hawker stalls, and a modern, high-tech horse-racing track is just around the corner from a temple housing over 10,000 buddhas. If you're on Hong Kong Island and feeling a little disorientated, remember that the water is always north; in Kowloon it's always south. If you want to escape the bustling city and walk in wide open spaces, there are always options.

HONG KONG ISLAND—NORTH SIDE

Just 78 square km (30 square mi), Hong Kong Island is where the action is, from high finance to nightlife to luxury shopping. As a result—even though Kowloon is just a short ride away—many residents feel little reason to ever leave the island. One of Hong Kong's unexpected pleasures is that, despite what sometimes feels like unrelenting urbanity, property development has actually been restricted to a few small areas. As a result, a 20-minute taxi ride from downtown Central can have you breathing fresh air and seeing only lush green vegetation.

Hong Kong has few historical landmarks (largely because soaring property values have long since caused most older buildings to be torn down and replaced) and no more than a handful of cultural sights, but it pulses with an extraordinarily dynamic contemporary life. In general, the commercial and shopping districts are on the island's north coast, interspersed with the ubiquitous apartment blocks, while the towns on the rest of the island tend to be more residential. Each district has a name (and the name of its MTR stop usually corresponds) and a slightly distinct character, but the borders tend to blur together (⇨ What's Where at the beginning of this book for descriptions of major neighborhoods).

Central & Western Districts

The office towers and opulent shopping centers of Hong Kong's core business district occupy one of the most expensive stretches of land on earth. It may be fitting, then, that Central also houses nearly every major investment and commercial bank, fashion designer, and luxury-goods boutique the world has yet produced. The streets are often so crowded with bankers and shoppers that a pedestrian can feel like a salmon trying to swim upstream to spawn. Fortunately, most of the buildings are connected by elevated covered walkways that can also be handy in the rain. Bear in mind that on Sunday, many Central shops close and the district teems with thousands of maids, mostly Filipinas, who, with nowhere else to spend their day off, congregate en masse in the public gardens, sidewalks, and plazas of the area.

The Western district is gradually becoming more like Central, but it still retains a traditional feel that many other areas have lost. Most of the buildings are high-rises (and older and more run-down than those in Central), but it's in some of the small alleys off Western's main streets that the old China Coast comes alive. Traditional shops sell dried sea horses, curled snakes, salted fish, aromatic mushrooms, herbal medicines, steaming noodles, and, of course, tea, by the glass or by the bushel.

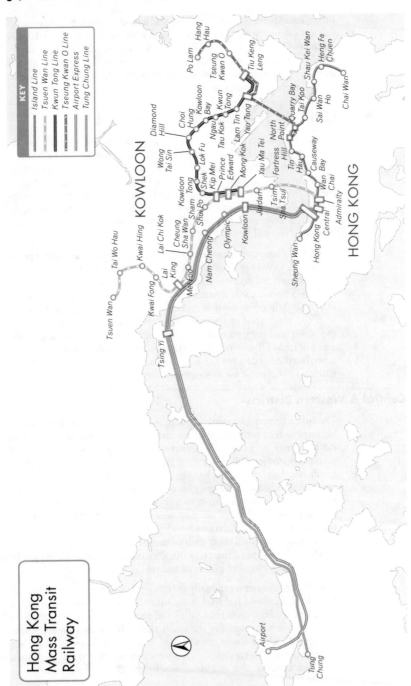

Hong Kong
Mass Transit
Railway

KEY
Island Line
Tsuen Wan Line
Kwun Tong Line
Tseung Kwan O Line
Airport Express
Tung Chung Line

KOWLOON

HONG KONG

Tsuen Wan
Tai Wo Hau
Kwai Hing
Kwai Fong
Lai King
Mei Foo
Lai Chi Kok
Cheung Sha Wan
Sham Shui Po
Kowloon Tong
Wong Tai Sin
Diamond Hill
Choi Hung
Kowloon Bay
Ngau Tau Kok
Kwun Tong
Lam Tin
Yau Tong
Tiu Keng Leng
Po Lam
Hang Hau
Tseung Kwan O
Lok Fu
Shek Kip Mei
Prince Edward
Mong Kok
Yau Ma Tei
Jordan
Tsim Sha Tsui
Olympic
Nam Cheong
Kowloon
Tsing Yi
Airport
Tung Chung
Sheung Wan
Hong Kong
Central
Admiralty
Tin Hau
Fortress Hill
North Point
Quarry Bay
Tai Koo
Sai Wan Ho
Shau Kei Wan
Heng Fa Chuen
Chai Wan
Causeway Bay
Wan Chai

The two major MTR stops for the Central and Western districts are Central and Sheung Wan. Most of the sights are easily accessible from the Central MTR. Once you arrive at the station, head for the Star Ferry exit. From here, you can spend the day exploring Central, winding down to Upper Lascar Row, Wing Lok Street, and Western Market, where the closest MTR stop is Sheung Wan. Once you have explored the districts, you have essentially walked the distance between two stations.

Numbers in the text correspond to numbers in the margin and on the Exploring the Central & Western Districts map.

a good walk

Walking is by far the best way to get around Central and Western, and orientation is easy since the harbor is always north. Start at the **Star Ferry Pier ❶** ▶, where sturdy green-and-white boats deposit passengers arriving from Kowloon. With your back to the harbor (and stepping out from the awning to get a better view), you can see many of Hong Kong's most significant buildings, as well as a number of practical landmarks. Just in front of you is a parking garage, to the east (left) of which is the double-decker, open-air shuttle to the Peak Tram and the unattractive City Hall complex, which has a good—and vast—dim sum restaurant. To your right is the General Post Office, a squat white building, and behind it is the towering **Jardine House ❷** with its many round windows, and on its right the marble-and-mirrored-glass stripes of Exchange Square, which houses the stock exchange and the American Club and has a bus terminal underneath. Just north of Exchange Square are the Hong Kong station Airport Express Terminal and, along the water, the piers for ferries to the outlying islands.

Follow the awnings to the right and go through the underground walkway to **Statue Square ❸**. The intriguing Victorian/Chinese hybrid building on the east side of the square is the **Legislative Council Building ❹**. Along the southern end of the square are the three buildings of Hong Kong's note-issuing banks: the art deco former headquarters of the **Bank of China ❺**, the spectacular strut-and-ladder facade of the **Hongkong & Shanghai Bank (HSBC) ❻**, and, pressing up against it, the rose-color wedge of Standard Chartered Bank. The HSBC building is one of the most important buildings in 20th-century architecture; walk under it and look up into the atrium through the curved glass floor, or go inside for a view of its details. Exiting HSBC on the south side, cross the street (Queen's Road Central) and turn left past the giant yet unimaginative Cheung Kong building (on your right) and Chater Garden (on your left) until you come to the triangle-shape Bank of China Tower, with its adjacent Chinese waterfall garden. This is the headquarters of the largest mainland China bank and was built a few years before the handover in an effort to architecturally one-up its local rival, HSBC.

Head back on Queen's Road Central toward HSBC and walk until you get to the intersection with Pedder Street, where you'll find the **Landmark ❼**, the mother of all luxury shopping centers. Having paid your respects, exit and turn left (south) on Pedder Street and walk straight up the steep hill until you pass the colonial red-and-white-striped building on the left that hosts the Fringe Club, an avant-garde arts center. At

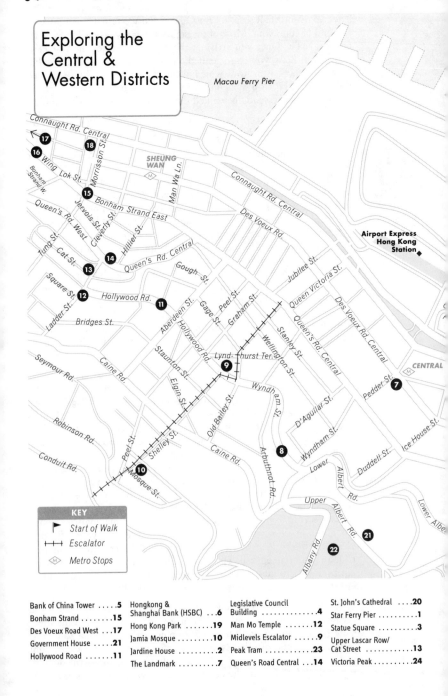

Exploring the Central & Western Districts

Macau Ferry Pier

Connaught Rd. Central

SHEUNG WAN

Connaught Rd. Central

Des Voeux Rd.

Wing Lok St.

Bonham Strand W.

Bonham Strand East

Queen's Rd. West

Jervois St.

Cleverly St.

Hillier St.

Morrison St.

Man Wa Ln.

Tung St.

Cat St.

Queen's Rd. Central

Gough St.

Square St.

Hollywood Rd.

Ladder St.

Bridges St.

Peel St.

Gage St.

Graham St.

Aberdeen St.

Hollywood Rd.

Jubilee St.

Queen Victoria St.

Des Voeux Rd. Central

Stanley St.

Wellington St.

Queen's Rd. Central

Seymour Rd.

Caine Rd.

Staunton St.

Elgin St.

Lynd-hurst Ter.

Wyndham St.

D'Aguilar St.

CENTRAL

Pedder St.

Robinson Rd.

Old Bailey St.

Caine Rd.

Wyndham St.

Ice House St.

Conduit Rd.

Peel St.

Shelley St.

Arbuthnot Rd.

Lower

Albert

Rd.

Duddell St.

Lower Albe

Mosque St.

Upper

Albert Rd.

Airport Express Hong Kong Station

Albany Rd.

KEY
⚑ Start of Walk
┼┼┼ Escalator
◇ Metro Stops

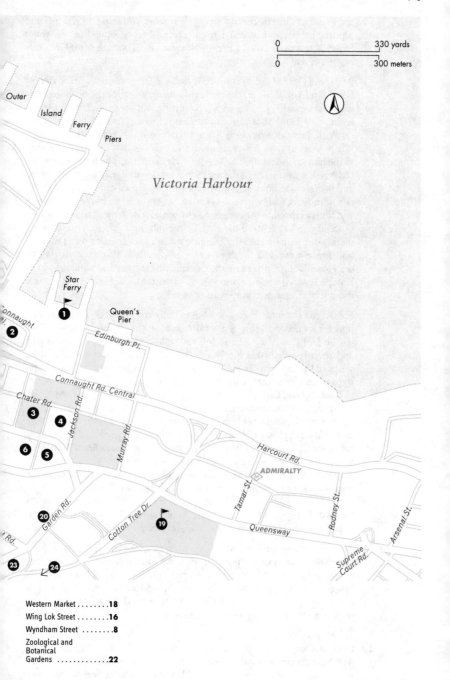

330 yards
0
0
300 meters

Outer
Island
Ferry
Piers

Victoria Harbour

Star
Ferry
1

Queen's
Pier

Edinburgh Pl.

onnaught
l.
2

Connaught Rd. Central

Chater Rd.
3   **4**

Jackson Rd.

Murray Rd.

Harcourt Rd.

ADMIRALTY

6   **5**

20

Garden Rd.

Cotton Tree Dr.

19

Tamar St.

Queensway

Rodney St.

Arsenal St.

Rd.

23   **24**

Supreme
Court Rd.

the five-street intersection, a sharp right takes you into Lan Kwai Fong, a prime entertainment district, but veering right gets you to **Wyndham Street** ⑧ and the start of a breathtaking series of antiques and Oriental-rug galleries.

At the old Central Police Station, Wyndham Street turns into Hollywood Road, and you'll see an overpass that forms a link in the open-air **Mid-levels Escalator** ⑨. Join up with it by turning left up an incline. Midlevels is the wide band of land south of Central that runs halfway up Victoria Peak. Long one of Hong Kong's most desirable residential districts, it is now lined with towering apartment blocks that cling precariously to the hillside. Bisecting it is the Midlevels Escalator, which connects Central Market with some of the area's main residential roads. Free of charge and protected from the elements, the multilevel escalator—actually a series of moving walkways—has proved a great way to move commuters and tourists through the congested city without destroying the landscape. Once aboard, take it all the way up the hill until you see an elaborate metalwork gate on the left. The gate hides a small garden and the tranquil **Jamia Mosque** ⑩, built in 1915. Midlevels is also worth a visit to see Hong Kong University, the Botanical Gardens, and some of Hong Kong's few remaining examples of Victorian apartment architecture, though the latter are disappearing rapidly.

Follow the escalator back downhill to **Hollywood Road** ⑪, perhaps stopping for a meal in the hip Elgin and Staunton streets area en route. Turn left on Hollywood Road and follow the antiques shops to the colorful and incense-filled **Man Mo Temple** ⑫. To reach the curio and trinket shops of **Upper Lascar Row** ⑬ (also known as Cat Street), walk down the steps of Ladder Street, just across from Man Mo Temple. Continue down to **Queen's Road Central** ⑭ and turn left (west) to see a bit of the old Hong Kong that may otherwise seem to have disappeared. Turn right on Cleverly Street, then left. Both the eastern and western branches of **Bonham Strand** ⑮ have plenty of little shops to explore, as does the adjacent **Wing Lok Street** ⑯. Follow Bonham Strand West to **Des Voeux Road West** ⑰ to see the dried-food and medicine shops. When you're just about ready to turn back, head toward the harbor and follow Connaught Road east until you come to the cream-and-brown **Western Market** ⑱, built in 1906 and lovingly restored. From here it's an easy tram ride back to Central. The quaint trams are known commonly as "ding ding," for the sound the bell makes when starting and stopping.

TIMING   Allow a full day, perhaps two if you want to spend any appreciable time shopping. It's physically possible to do the tour from the Star Ferry Terminal to Cat Street in three hours, but you won't be able to see anything in depth. The Man Mo Temple will add 20 minutes. The second half of the walk, from Cat Street to Western Market, will take an hour or two, and you'll want to factor in time for a lunch break and rest stops.

What to See

❺ **Bank of China Tower.** In the politics of Hong Kong architecture, the stylish art deco building that served as the old **Bank of China headquarters** was the first trump: built after World War II, it was 20 feet higher than the adjacent Hongkong & Shanghai Bank (HSBC). It is now one of the smallest buildings in Central, utterly dwarfed by the imposing steel-and-glass structure HSBC finished in 1985. The Bank of China refused to take this challenge lying down, however, and commissioned the Chinese-American architect I. M. Pei to build a bigger, better headquarters nearby to supersede HSBC. The result: the Bank of China Tower, completed in the early 1990s, a masterful twisting spire of replicating triangles and the first building to break the ridgeline of Victoria Peak. It may not be as innovative as the HSBC building, but it dominates Hong Kong's urban landscape and embodies the post-handover balance of power. For a panoramic, and uncrowded, viewing spot of Central, head to the 43rd floor. The observation deck is open weekdays from 9 to 5 and Saturday 9 to 1; and best of all, it's free. The old building now houses Sin Hua Bank and, on the top floors, David Tang's exclusive China Club, which manages to be both postmodern and nostalgic for pre-Communist Shanghai. ⌗ *Bank St., Central.*

★ ⓯ **Bonham Strand.** A major thoroughfare in one of Hong Kong's most charmingly traditional areas, Bonham Strand is lined with shops selling goods that evoke the old China Coast trade merchants. A few shops sell live snakes, whose meat is used in winter soups to ward off colds and whose gallbladders reputedly improve vigor and virility. Bonham Strand West, in particular, is known for its Chinese medicines and herbal remedies. Many of its old shops have their original facades, and inside, the walls are lined with drawers and shelves of jars filled with hundreds of pungent ingredients such as wood barks and insects. These are consumed dried and ground up, infused in hot water or tea, or taken as powders or pills.

⓱ **Des Voeux Road West.** You'll recognize the tram tracks when you get to the west end of Bonham Strand West. On the left (south) side of the street is a cluster of shops selling preserved foods—everything from dried and salted fish to black mushrooms to vegetables—and herbal medicines. This is a good area for lunchtime dim sum.

⓫ **Hollywood Road.** Many of Hong Kong's best antiques, furniture, and classical-art galleries are concentrated on Wyndham Street, at the road's eastern end. As the road heads west, the shops gradually move down-market, selling mostly porcelain, curios, and not-very-old trinkets masquerading as ancient artifacts. Look to the left for a sign saying POSSESSION STREET, where Captain Charles Elliott of the British Royal Navy stepped ashore in 1841 and claimed Hong Kong for the British empire. It's interesting to note how far today's harbor is from this earlier shoreline—the result of a century of aggressive land reclamation.

off the beaten path

HONG KONG MUSEUM OF MEDICAL SCIENCES – Tucked away in an Edwardian-style building behind a small park in Midlevels, this museum is worth the climb through tiny backstreets for anyone interested in the history of Chinese medicine in Hong Kong. Exhibits compare the uses of Chinese and Western medicines and show Chinese medicines of both animal and herbal origin as well as a traditional Chinese medical practitioner's equipment. Several other rooms are devoted to Western medical subjects. To get here from Hollywood Road, follow Ladder Street behind Man Mo Temple, going south and uphill to Square Street, which veers right, then left to Caine Lane. Follow a circular path up about 300 feet around Caine Lane Garden, a park with colorful stucco structures, until you reach Number 2. ⊠ *2 Caine La., Midlevels* ☎ *2549–5123* ⊕ *www. hkmms.org.hk* 🎫 *HK$10* ⊘ *Tues.–Sat. 10–5, Sun. 1–5.*

★ ❻ **Hongkong & Shanghai Bank (HSBC).** With its distinctive ladder facade, this striking building is a landmark of modern architecture. Designed by Sir Norman Foster as the headquarters of Hong Kong's premier bank (you'll see it depicted on most of the territory's paper money) and completed in 1985, the building sits on four props, which allow you to walk under it and look up through its glass belly into the soaring atrium within. Imposing as that may be, the building is most interesting for its sensitive use of high-tech details: the mechanics of everything from the elevators' gears and pulleys to the electric signs' circuit boards are visible through smoked glass. In addition to its architectural triumph, the building served a symbolic function as well: built at a time of insecurity vis-à-vis China at a cost of almost US$1 billion, it was a powerful statement that the bank had no intention of taking its money out of the territory. ⊠ *1 Queen's Rd., across from Statue Sq., Central.*

❿ **Jamia Mosque.** This attractive gray-and-white mosque was built by Essack Elias of Bombay in 1915, and it shows its Indian heritage in the perforated arches and decorative work on the facade. The mosque itself is not open to non-Muslims, but it occupies a small verdant enclosure that offers a welcome retreat from the city. It once had a nice view down toward the water, but that was disrupted by an apartment tower— one of many now ringing this site. ⊠ *30 Shelley St., just off Midlevels Escalator, Midlevels.*

❷ **Jardine House.** To the west of the Star Ferry Terminal, recognizable by its signature round windows, this 1973 building was once the tallest in Central. It houses Jardine, Matheson & Co., the greatest of the old British *hongs* (trading companies) that dominated trade with imperial China. Jardines has come a long way from the days when it trafficked opium; today, its investment-banking arm, Jardine Fleming, is one of the most respected in Asia. ⊠ *Connaught Pl. across from the Central Post Office, Central.*

❼ **The Landmark.** Few fashion designers, watch craftsmen, or other makers of luxury goods do not have—or do not crave—a boutique in the Landmark. The building is no longer the city's poshest, but its Pedder Street location is still priceless, and it has its own MTR entrance. Classical music performances, art exhibitions, and the odd fashion show are occasionally staged near the fountain in the high-ceiling atrium. ⊠ *Des Voeux Rd. between Ice House and Pedder Sts., Central* ⊘ *Building, daily 9 AM–midnight; most shops, daily 10–6.*

❹ **Legislative Council Building.** Built for the Supreme Court in 1912 and now home to the Legislative Council (known as LegCo), this building is one of the few grand Victorian structures left in this area. Note the eaves of the Chinese-style roof, a modest British concession to local culture. The council had no real power in the British days, but in the last decade of British law, it did have a majority of elected members who challenged the administration every Wednesday. Since the handover in 1997, mainland attempts to muzzle LegCo's pro-democracy members have been only moderately successful, so it continues to serve as a forum for debate, if not as an organ of political power. In front of the Council Building is the **Cenotaph,** a monument to all who lost their lives in the two world wars. ⊠ *Statue Sq. at Jackson Rd., Central.*

⑫ **Man Mo Temple.** Built in 1847 and dedicated to the gods of literature and of war—Man and Mo, respectively—this is Hong Kong Island's oldest temple. It now serves primarily as a smoke-filled haven for elderly women paying respects; ashes flutter down onto your clothes from the enormous spirals of incense hanging from the beams. The statue of Man is dressed in green and holds a writing brush, while Mo is dressed in red and holds a sword. To their left is a shrine to Pao Kung, god of justice, whose face is painted black; to the right is Shing Wong, god of the city. The temple bell, cast in Canton in 1847, and the drum next to it are sounded to attract the gods' attention when a prayer is being offered. To check your fortune, stand in front of the altar, take one of the small bamboo cylinders available there, and shake it until one of the sticks falls out. The number on the stick corresponds to a written fortune. The English translation of said fortune is in a book that the temple will happily sell you. ⊠ *Hollywood Rd. at Ladder St., Central* ◷ *Daily 8–6.*

⑨ **Midlevels Escalator.** A practical human mover, this is actually a 1-km-long (½-mi-long) combination of escalators and walkways that provide free, glass-covered transport up or down the steep incline between Central and Midlevels. The painless uphill trip provides a view of small Chinese shops and gleaming residential high-rises, as well as the Jamia Mosque, at Shelley Street. **Staunton Street,** one level above Hollywood Road, is now known as Hong Kong's SoHo (South of Hollywood), with an eclectic collection of cafés and bars, including the Sherpa Himalayan Coffee Shop and the hole-in-the-wall Le Rendezvous French crêperie.

Plan to ride the escalators up between 10:20 AM and 11:30 PM. From 6 to 10 AM the escalators move downhill, so commuters living in Midlevels can get to work, or to the public transportation, down in Central; and after 11:30 they shut down. You can get off at any point and explore the side streets where vendors sell porcelain, clothes, and antiques (not necessarily authenticated). Almost every building has a tiny makeshift altar to the ancestors, usually made of red paper with gold Chinese characters, with offerings of fruit and incense. ⊠ *Enter across from Central Market, at Queen's Rd. Central and Jubilee St., Central* ◷ *Daily 6 AM–11:30 PM.*

⑭ **Queen's Road Central.** This street once ran along the waterfront. It is, at various points, one of Hong Kong's most prestigious shopping addresses and among its quaintest and most traditional streets. Of the countless shops and market stalls selling dried herbs, live snakes, and everything else imaginable to treat the body's vital energies, the **Eu Yan Sang Medical Hall** (✉ 152 Queen's Rd., Central) is the one to visit for an education in traditional Chinese medicines. Glass cases display reindeer antlers, dried fungi, ginseng, and other standard medicinal items; English-language cards explain some of the items' uses, and men behind the counters will happily sell you purported cures for anything from the common cold to impotence (the cure for the latter is usually slices of reindeer antler boiled into tea). A note of caution: look all you want, but remember that Chinese medicines are not regulated by the Hong Kong government, and anything that sounds dubious or dangerous might be just that.

▶ ☾ ❶ **Star Ferry Pier.** Since 1898 the ferry pier has been the gateway to the is-

Fodor$Choice land for commuters and travelers coming from Kowloon. First-time vis-

★ itors are all but required to cross the harbor on the Star Ferry at least once and ride around Hong Kong Island on a double-deck tram. In front of the pier you will usually see a few red rickshaws; once numbering in the thousands, these two-wheel man-powered taxis are all but gone. You'll have a choice between buying a first-class or second-class ticket for the ferry ride: first class is the upper deck of the ferry and has air-conditioned compartments, while second class is the lower deck and tends to be noisy due to the proximity to the engine room. ✉ *Enter pier through tunnel next to Mandarin Hotel, Connaught Rd. and Connaught Pl., Central* ⌚ *1st class HK$2.20, 2nd class HK$1.70* ☉ *Daily 6 AM–midnight.*

off the beaten path

HONG KONG DOLPHIN WATCH – The Chinese white dolphin (actually from pink to dark gray, and found in waters from South Africa to Australia) is on its way to extinction in the South China Sea, mainly because of the dredging to create the Chek Lap Kok airport. Hong Kong Dolphin Watch sponsors a Dolphin Discovery Cruise three times a week (Wednesday, Friday, and Sunday), weather permitting—there's no guarantee, but on most trips you'll catch one or two dolphins playing in the water. They claim a 96% success rate in spotting dolphins, and if you don't see a dolphin, you get to go again for free. Tours leave from Tung Chung New Pier on North Lantau, but you get there by coach, departing from central points on Hong Kong Island or Kowloon: at 8:30 AM from the east lobby entrance of the Mandarin Oriental Hotel in Central, or at 9 AM from the Kowloon Hotel in Tsim Sha Tsui (⇨ *Where to Stay for exact addresses*). The trip makes for an enjoyable half day at sea, and tickets help raise money to build a sanctuary that will ensure the dolphins' survival. Try to reserve at least two weeks in advance, but also be aware that you must pay in advance—either in cash or by credit card—in person at the Dolphin Watch office; no payments are accepted on the day of the tour. ✉ *1528A Star House, 3 Salisbury Rd., Tsim Sha Tsui* ☎ *2984–1414* 🖷 *2984–7799* ⊕ *www.hkdolphinwatch.com* ⌚ *HK$280* ☉ *Wed., Fri., Sun.*

❸ **Statue Square.** This piece of land was gifted to the public by the Hongkong & Shanghai Bank (whose headquarters dominate the southern end), with the proviso that nothing built on it could block the bank's view of the water. The square is named for the statue of Sir Thomas Jackson (1841–1915), who was the bank's chief manager for more than 30 years in the late 19th century. The square is surrounded by some of the most important buildings in Hong Kong, including those housing the Hong Kong Club, the Legislative Council, and the Bank of China, and has an entrance to the Central MTR station. On Sunday it becomes the hub for thousands of Filipina maids enjoying their day off.

> **need a break?** On the west side of Statue Square is the **Mandarin Oriental Hotel** (⊠ 5 Connaught Rd., Central ☎ 2522–0111), one of the finest hotels in the world. The mezzanine coffee lounge is a pleasant place to have a drink (they also have an excellent high tea), or you can people-watch at the **Captain's Bar,** where billion-dollar deals are consummated over cognac.

🔟 **Upper Lascar Row.** Cat Street, as Upper Lascar Row is often called, is a vast flea market. You won't find Ming vases here—or anything else of significant value—but you may come across an old Mao badge or an antique pot or tea kettle.

More worthwhile for the art or antiques collector is the section of shops and stalls known as **Cat Street Galleries** (⊠ 38 Lok Ku Rd., Sheung Wan), adjacent to the flea market, open from 10 to 6 every day but Sunday. This is a bustling and growing complex, with galleries selling every kind of craft, sometimes old but more often new. You can rest your feet and have coffee in the convenient little European café Somethin' Brewin'. The nearest MTR station is Sheung Wan.

🔞 **Western Market.** Erected in 1906, this is the only surviving segment of a larger market building built in 1858. It functioned as a produce market for 83 years and included living quarters for coolies and inspectors in the four corner towers. Threatened with demolition, it was exquisitely restored and turned into a unique shopping outlet. Alas, they've never gotten the retail mix quite right, filling the place with souvenir and trinket shops on the ground floor, fabrics on the middle floor, and a Chinese restaurant on the top floor. The building, however, gorgeously decorated with Chinese bunting, is worth a trip. ⊠ 323 Connaught Rd. W, Sheung Wan ☉ Daily 10 AM–11:45 PM.

🔟 **Wing Lok Street.** You can find fascinating traditional items on this street (off Queen's Road Central) lined with Chinese shops selling dried fish and seafood, rattan goods, medicines, and the engraved seals called chops. You can have your initials engraved in Roman letters or Chinese characters on a chop made of plastic, bone, or jade. (Ivory is also available all over Hong Kong, but it's illegal to bring it into the United States.) It takes about an hour to engrave a chop, which you can pick up later or the following day.

★ 🔟 **Wyndham Street.** The galleries that pack the curving block of Wyndham Street from the Fringe Club to where Wyndham becomes Hollywood Road can be approached more as a collection of miniature museums than as mere shops. Their showrooms hold some spectacular antique furniture, art, and artifacts (albeit perhaps smuggled out of their countries of origin) at prices that, while not cheap by any means, are a fraction of what they would be outside the region. Most stores are open daily from 10 to 7, though some have shorter hours or close altogether on Sunday. Here is a rough guide, starting from the western end: the **Oriental Rug Gallery** and **Oriental Carpets Gallery** specialize in rugs from the Middle East and Central Asia. **Artemis** has gorgeous but expensive furniture, along with statuary and stonework. **MinGei Antiques** has Chinese furniture and an interesting collection of birdcages. **Zitan** has chests and old doors, many in a more authentic state than the restored pieces sold elsewhere. **Zee Stone Gallery** specializes in Tibetan arts, including silver work, silk hangings, and robes. **Ad Lib** has kiln work, statues, and the ubiquitous Ming and Qing Dynasty reproduction furniture. **Teresa Coleman Fine Arts,** opposite the police station at the corner of Pottinger Street, is among the premier galleries in Asia, with an ability to find little treasures others miss, like embroidered dragon robes and collars or vibrant-blue "kingfisher" jewelry. **Chu's** focuses on artifacts from Tibet, including carpets and chests. **Schoeni** is actually on Hollywood Road, near the police station, and is better known as a promoter of contemporary mainland Chinese art, but has an antiques gallery on nearby Old Baily Street. For more on shopping, *see* the Shopping chapter.

From Central to the Peak

Victoria Peak, high above Midlevels, is known simply as the Peak, and soars 1,805 feet above sea level. Residents here take special pride in the positions to which they have, quite literally, risen; theirs is the most exclusive residential area on the island—perhaps in all of Asia.

To get to Hong Kong Park, take the Chater Garden exit at the Central MTR stop, and you'll be a hop, skip, and jump away.

Numbers in the text correspond to numbers in the margin and on the Central and Western Districts map.

a good tour

Start your walk at 2 Queen's Road Central, diagonally across the street from Chater Garden. Head uphill on Garden Road and cross the street at the pedestrian overpass to Cotton Tree Drive. You should be facing **Hong Kong Park** ⑲ ⌐, where you'll find the **Museum of Tea Ware** and a large aviary and conservatory.

Leave the garden and return to Garden Road. On the right heading up Garden Road is **St. John's Cathedral** ⑳. Continue up the road and turn right on Upper Albert Road, passing **Government House** ㉑, which was the official residence of the British colonial governor of Hong Kong. Farther up Garden Road are the United States Consulate General and the **Zoological and Botanical Gardens** ㉒.

Stroll through the gardens, zoo, and aviary. Swing back down Garden Road, cross it, and go to the **Peak Tram** ㉓, just behind St. John's Building (not to be confused with the cathedral). Take the tram to **Victoria Peak** ㉔.

For a scenic alternative to the Peak Tram, you can catch Bus 15 or a cab from Central. Both go through the steep roads of the residential areas

FENG SHUI AT WORK

THERE'S A BATTLE going on in Central, a battle between good and evil forces. Feng shui (pronounced fung shoy in Cantonese, foong shway in Mandarin, and literally translated as "wind" and "water") is the traditional Chinese art that determines the placement of objects to enhance the natural yin/yang balance. The principles governing positioning are highly complex. The most popular school of thought in Hong Kong emphasizes general geographic orientation, such as the relationship to nearby mountains or bodies of water. Another school of thought focuses on the symbolic importance of shapes in the surrounding environment, with triangles (such as those on the headquarters of the Bank of China) giving off particularly bad feng shui. In general, the principles of both schools relate to the flow of energies in nature. Some are considered beneficial (thus an entrance will be positioned to allow them to enter) and others are considered to be negative (in which case objects such as metal bars can be introduced to deflect them). The ideal orientation of a building, for example, is facing out to sea with a mountain behind—which also happens to afford the best view and a cooling breeze. Even in modern Central, where feng shui is regarded as something akin to superstition, most developers figure it's better to be safe than sorry, so it's the rare skyscraper that's built without consulting a feng shui expert. Indeed, rumor has it that when the HSBC headquarters were built in the mid-1980s (at a cost of nearly US$1 billion) the escalators were reset from their original straight position so that they would be at an angle to the entrance of the building. Because evil spirits can only travel in a straight line, this realignment was thought to prevent waterborne spirits from flowing in off Victoria Harbor. The escalators are also believed to resemble two whiskers of a powerful dragon, sucking money into the bank.

The Bank of China Tower—designed by Chinese-American I. M. Pei—with its many triangular angles, however, does not have such good feng shui. A popular notion is that the building, which thins at the top, resembles a screwdriver that is drilling the wealth out of Hong Kong. Another is that buildings facing the sharp edges of the building will encounter negative feng shui and resulting problems. The Lippo Centre, which faces one of the triangles, was formerly the Bond Centre, owned by disgraced Australian businessman Allen Bond who was forced to sell the building after experiencing financial troubles. Government House, originally considered to be one of the best feng shui locations in Hong Kong, with clear, uninterrupted views of the mountains and sea. However, one of the angles of the Bank of China Tower bisects the Government House and caused, among other things, a nasty fall by Margaret Thatcher. The building is considered so unlucky that it now sits empty most of the year.

If you look up at the HSBC building, you'll notice two metal rods on top that look like a window-washing apparatus. Look more closely and you'll see that the rods are pointed at the Bank of China, a classic feng shui technique to protect the building from the negative energy of the dreaded triangles by deflecting the energy back to its source.

The HKTB leads interesting weekly tours. Contact any HKTB bureau for more details.

of Midlevels, a route just as beautiful as the tram's. You can also get to the Peak on Minibus 1 from the terminal behind the former HMS *Tamar* site (now occupied by the People's Liberation Army), next to the City Hall complex.

TIMING This walk is largely uphill and is complicated somewhat by the elaborate road system that crisscrosses the area. A tour of this entire area takes about three hours. This time period includes about 40 minutes for the Museum of Tea Ware and at least 45 minutes to stroll through Hong Kong Park's greenhouses and aviary, both of which can get crowded. Add another half hour or more for the zoo at the Zoological and Botanical Gardens. The tram ride up the mountain will take about 20 minutes. Allow about an hour for the Peak.

What to See

㉑ Government House. Constructed in 1855, this handsome white Victorian building was the official residence of the British governor. During the Japanese occupation it was significantly rebuilt, so it now exhibits a subtle Japanese influence, particularly in the roof eaves. The SAR's chief executive, Tung Chee Hwa, had no wish to reside here—some say because of perceived negative feng shui—so Government House is used periodically for state occasions. It is not open to the public. ⊠ *Upper Albert Rd. just west of Garden Rd., Central.*

▶ ★ ☾ **⑲ Hong Kong Park.** Hoarding 25 acres of prime real estate, this park has to be one of the world's most valuable. Built by the Hong Kong Jockey Club with the abundant revenues from its racetracks, it comprises lakes, gardens, sports areas, a café, a rain-forest aviary with 500 species of birds, and a greenhouse with 200 species of tropical and arid-region plants. Although some of the artificial rocks and waterfalls in the lower gardens can feel a little unnatural, the park is a blessedly quiet and lush oasis within the urban melee.

Flagstaff House, the former official residence of the commander of the British forces and the city's oldest colonial building (built in 1846), is now the **Museum of Tea Ware.** The museum's fascinating exhibit chronicles the history of tea and its various accessories (including the famous Yixing tea ware) from the 7th century on. Who knew, for example, that Tibetan cream tea could be made with cheese by-products, or that the method of steeping leaves in water came relatively late, following a preference for whipped tea? ⊠ *Cotton Tree Dr. at park entrance, Central* ☎ *2869–0690* ⊕ *www.lcsd.gov.hk* ⊠ *Free* ☉ *Park, daily 6 AM–11 PM; museum, Wed.–Mon. 10–5.*

☾ **㉓ Peak Tram.** Housed in the Lower Peak Tram Terminus is the world's steepest funicular railway. It passes five intermediate stations on its way to the upper terminal, 1,805 feet above sea level. The tram was opened in 1880 to transport people to the top of Victoria Peak, the highest hill overlooking Hong Kong Harbour. Before the tram, the only way to get to the top was to walk or take a bumpy ride up the steep steps in a sedan chair. The tram has two 72-seat cars, which are hauled up the hill by cables attached to electric motors. Bus 15C, an antique double-decker, shuttles you to the Peak Tram Terminal from Edinburgh Place, next to

FodorśChoice
★

City Hall. ⊠ *Between Garden Rd. and Cotton Tree Dr., Central* ☎ *2522–0922* ⊕ *www.thepeak.com.hk* ✍ *HK$20 one way, HK$30 round-trip* ⊙ *Daily every 15 mins 7 AM–midnight.*

㉒ St. John's Cathedral. Completed in 1849, this Anglican cathedral was built with Canton bricks in the shape of a cross. It serves as a good example of both Victorian-Gothic and Norman architecture. ⊠ *4–8 Garden Rd., up from Queen's Rd. Central, on west side of the street just past the large parking lot, Central* ⊙ *Daily 9–5, Sun. services.*

Fodor'sChoice
★

㉔ Victoria Peak. Known in Chinese as Tai Ping Shan, or Mountain of Great Peace, the Peak is Hong Kong's one truly essential sight. On a clear day, nothing rivals the view of the dense, glittering string of skyscrapers that line Hong Kong's north coast and the carpet of buildings that extend to the eight mountains of Kowloon. It's well worth timing your visit to see the view both by day and at night, perhaps by taking in a meal at one of the restaurants near the upper terminus. The Peak is more than just a view, however; it also contains extensive parkland, perfect for a picnic or a long walk.

With the opening of the **Peak Tower** (⊠Peak Rd., The Peak ☎2849–7654) the commercial complex of shops, restaurants, and diversions up top, the site's developers have tried to re-brand a visit to the Peak, spectacular enough in the old days, as "the Peak Experience," complete with shopping, amusements, and restaurants. This has been a mixed success, but children might enjoy some of the activities: the Peak Explorer is a virtual-reality ride through outer space, while the Rise of the Dragon takes you on a railcar through a series of animated scenes from Hong Kong's history, including a frighteningly accurate rendition of the 1907 typhoon that devastated the territory. There's also a branch of Ripley's Believe It or Not! Odditorium. The tower is open daily from 7 AM to midnight.

At the top of Victoria Peak, in the Peak Tower complex is a **Madame Tussaud's** wax museum with lifelike wax figures of famous Asian celebrities including Jackie Chan and Michelle Yeoh; and, not to be upstaged, a replica of Chinese President Jiang Zemin. ⊠ *128 Peak Tower, Peak Rd., level 2 The Peak* ☎ *2849–6966* ✍ *HK$95* ⊙ *Daily 10–10.*

off the
beaten
path

YAN YUEN SHEK – Also known as Lovers' Rock, Yan Yuen Shek is a shrine that some Chinese women visit daily, burning joss sticks and making offerings in hopes of finding a husband. The 6th, 16th, and 26th days of each lunar month are the most popular times, and during the Maidens' Festival, in August, fortune-tellers set up shop for the lovelorn. A visit here is best combined with a visit to the Zoological & Botanical Gardens. Leave the gardens by the upper exit, east of the aviaries; cross Garden Road and take the left fork (Magazine Gap Road) at the traffic circle. Take a sharp left onto Bowen Road, a pleasant, tree-lined street that becomes a traffic-free path all the way to Happy Valley. From there Lovers' Rock is a 20- to 30-minute stroll. To get back to town, walk to the Wong Nai Chung Gap Road traffic circle at the end of Bowen Road, where you can catch Bus 15 or 15B to the Peak or Bus 6 or 61 back to Exchange Square, or you can take a taxi.

Zoological & Botanical Gardens. A visit here is a delightful way to escape the city's traffic and crowds. In the early morning the spectacle of mainly elderly people practicing *Tai Chi Chuan* (the ancient art of meditative shadow boxing, more popularly known as Tai Chi) is an inspiring sight. The quiet pathways are lined with semitropical trees, shrubs, and flowers. The zoo has a black jaguar and orangutans, which for years were a source of friction between the government and animal-rights groups, but the cages have been expanded to better simulate the animals' natural habitats; as a result, you can usually see the jaguar swimming in its pool or sunbathing. There is also an aviary with more than 300 species of birds, including a spectacular flock of pink flamingos. ⊠ *Upper Albert Rd. opposite Government House; enter on Garden Rd., Central* ☎ *2530–0155* ⊕ *www.lcsd.gov.hk* ⊠ *Free* ☉ *Zoological Garden daily 6 AM–7 PM; Botanical Garden daily 6 AM–10 PM.*

Wanchai

Wanchai was once one of the five *wan*—areas the British set aside for Chinese residences—but it developed a reputation for vice and became a magnet for sailors on shore leave, as during the Vietnam War. How times have changed: Wanchai is still as risqué an area as Hong Kong has to offer, but that says more about the city's overall respectability than it does about its available indulgences. For all its bars and massage parlors, Wanchai is now so safe that it seems a pale version of the "Wanch" of Richard Mason's novel *The World of Suzie Wong*.

The city's high real-estate prices have inevitably turned parts of Wanchai into an area of office towers, but it comes as a pleasant surprise to see how many crowded little alleys remain. A chance wrong turn can lead you into an outdoor wet market for vegetables and meat (so called because the sellers constantly hose down their produce), a tiny furniture maker's shop, or an age-old temple. At night, the area comes alive with bars, restaurants, and discos, as well as establishments offering some of Wanchai's more traditional services.

While Wanchai has its own MTR stop, a pleasant way to arrive from Central is a 10-minute ride by tram or Bus 10. This area is also just a few blocks from the Admiralty MTR stop.

Numbers in the text correspond to numbers in the margin and on the Exploring Wanchai, Causeway Bay, Happy Valley & North Point map.

a good walk

Walking is the best way to get around Wanchai, as the district's charms are more in its aura than in specific sights. Take a circular walking tour starting from the junction of Queensway and **Queen's Road East** ❶ ▷. Continue on Queen's Road East and turn left onto Wanchai Road, a busy market area selling food, clothing, and household goods. This is a good place for browsing, especially in the narrow side alleys. To the left, several small lanes lead to Johnston Road and more tram lines; this area contains many shops that make rattan furniture, picture frames, and curtains to order. Turn left on Johnston Road and follow the edge of Southorn Playground, a popular meeting place, especially for those looking for a game of cards or Chinese chess.

Luard Road—along with cross streets Hennessy, Lockhart, and Jaffe roads—is the heart of old Wanchai. At night the area is alive with multicolor neon signs and a lively trade in bars, pubs, massage parlors, and restaurants. Hennessy Road, which roughly follows the line of the original harbor front, is another good place to browse. Walk east on Hennessy Road to Fleming Road and turn north. Continue to Harbour Road, then head west to the **Academy for Performing Arts & Hong Kong Arts Centre ②**, in two adjacent buildings that function as the core of Hong Kong Island's cultural activity.

Continue on Harbour Road to Seafront Road and the **Hong Kong Convention & Exhibition Centre ③**. Circle back to Harbour Road and head east for a look at the **Central Plaza ④**, one of the world's tallest buildings. From here you can taxi back to your hotel, catch the MTR at the Wanchai station, or continue walking along the harbor front to the Wanchai Ferry Pier for a ferry to Kowloon.

TIMING If you stop to take in views and exhibits, this walk takes about two hours.

What to See

② Academy for Performing Arts & Hong Kong Arts Centre. Hong Kong is often maligned, not least by its foreign residents, as a cultural desert, but these two adjacent buildings help defuse this charge, with excellent facilities for both exhibits and the performing arts. Find out about the busy schedule of activities—dance, classical music, and theater by local and visiting artists—in local newspapers or at the ticket reservations office. While you're at the Arts Centre, visit the **Pao Gallery** (fourth and fifth floors), which hosts both local and international exhibits. The Academy for Performing Arts was financed with horse-racing profits donated by the Hong Kong Jockey Club. ✉ *2 Harbour Rd., Wanchai* ☎ *2582–0200* ⊕ *www.hkac.org.hk* 🖃 *Free* ☉ *Daily 10–8.*

> **need a break?**
>
> **Open Kitchen** (✉ 2 Harbour Rd., Wanchai ☎ 2827–2923), on the sixth floor of the Hong Kong Arts Centre, serves delicious international cuisine in a self-serve-style environment. It's open daily from 11 to 9.

④ Central Plaza. In Asia's ongoing race to build ever-taller skyscrapers, this modern triangular office complex (completed in 1992) briefly held the title as the region's tallest. It has long since been surpassed, but at 78 stories it's still quite striking. ✉ *Harbour Rd. and Fleming Rd., Wanchai.*

③ Hong Kong Convention & Exhibition Centre. The original center opened in 1988 as one of the largest and best-equipped meeting facilities in the world, but—in typical Hong Kong fashion—it was quickly deemed insufficient. Needing a suitable venue for the 1997 handover ceremonies, the city decided to build—in a mad, furious dash—the extension that now sits prominently on a spit of reclaimed land jutting into the harbor. With its glass walls and swooping curved roof the whole structure resembles from afar a tortoise entering the sea. It's an outstanding venue for the international trade fairs, regional conferences, and hundreds of local events held here annually. An exceptionally long walk through the center yields

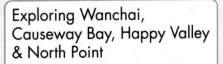

Exploring Wanchai, Causeway Bay, Happy Valley & North Point

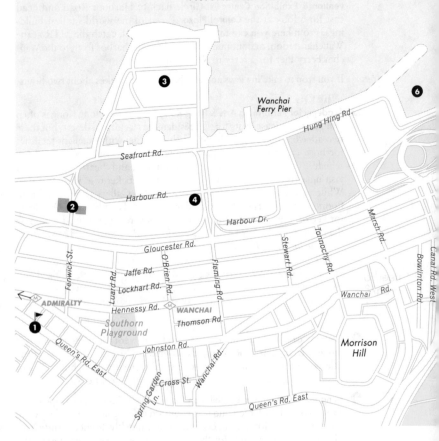

Victoria Harbour

Wanchai Ferry Pier

Hung Hing Rd.

Seafront Rd.

Harbour Rd.

Harbour Dr.

Gloucester Rd.

Stewart Rd.

Tonnochy Rd.

Marsh Rd.

Bowrinton Rd.

Canal Rd. West

Jaffe Rd.

Fenwick St.

Luard Rd.

O'Brien Rd.

Fleming Rd.

Lockhart Rd.

Wanchai Rd.

ADMIRALTY

Hennessy Rd.

WANCHAI

Southorn Playground

Thomson Rd.

Morrison Hill

Queen's Rd. East

Johnston Rd.

Spring Garden Ln.

Cross St.

Wanchai Rd.

Queen's Rd. East

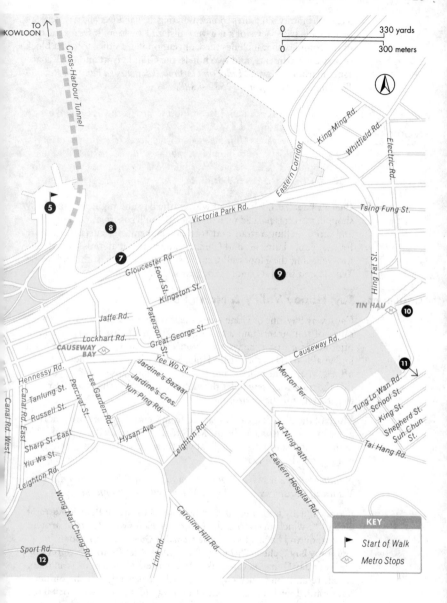

TO ↑
KOWLOON

Cross-Harbour Tunnel

0 _____ 330 yards
0 _____ 300 meters

King Ming Rd.
Whitfield Rd.
Electric Rd.

Eastern Corridor

Tsing Fung St.

Victoria Park Rd.

5

8

7
Gloucester Rd.

Food St.

Kingston St.

Hing Fat St.

9

TIN HAU
10

Jaffe Rd.

Paterson St.

Great George St.

Lockhart Rd.

CAUSEWAY BAY

Yee Wo St.

Causeway Rd.

11

Hennessy Rd.

Jardine's Bazaar

Jardine's Cres.

Morton Ter.

Tung Lo Wan Rd.

School St.

King St.

Shepherd St.

Sun Chun St.

Tanlung St.

Percival St.

Lee Garden Rd.

Yun Ping Rd.

Russell St.

Ka Ning Path

Sharp St. East

Hysan Ave.

Leighton Rd.

Tai Hang Rd.

Yiu Wa St.

Canal Rd. West

Canal Rd. East

Leighton Rd.

Caroline Hill Rd.

Eastern Hospital Rd.

Wong Nai Chung Rd.

Link Rd.

Sport Rd.
12

KEY	
▶	*Start of Walk*
◈	*Metro Stops*

a few celebratory sculptures commemorating the handover and a waterfront promenade with views of a not-very-distant Kowloon. It forms the core of the complex that includes the Convention Plaza office tower, a block of service apartments, and two hotels, the Grand Hyatt and the Renaissance Harbour View. ⊠ *Enter on Harbour Rd. between Fenwick Rd. and Fleming Rd., Wanchai* ☎ *2582–8888.*

> **need a break?**
>
> Next to the Convention and Exhibition Centre is the **Grand Hyatt Hotel** (⊠ 1 Harbour Rd., Wanchai ☎ 2588–1234). From its polished marble and enormous Chinese vases to the jungle-size flower displays and grand staircases, this hotel just manages to stay on the tasteful side of opulence. The second-floor lounge is an exceptionally relaxing place to sit and chat over a drink or two.

▶ ❶ **Queen's Road East.** It's choked with traffic day and night, but this busy shopping street is packed with diversions. You'll pass rice and food shops and stores selling rattan and traditional furniture, curtains, picture frames, paper lanterns, and Chinese calligraphic materials. Shortly before reaching the Hopewell Centre, stop at the altar of the **Tai Wong Temple** and smell its smoldering joss sticks.

Causeway Bay, Happy Valley & North Point

Causeway Bay, one of Hong Kong's best shopping areas, also has a wide range of restaurants and a few sights. The areas east of Victoria Park offer little for first-time visitors. North Point and Quarry Bay are both undeniable parts of the "real" Hong Kong, which means they're full of offices, apartment blocks, and factories. From Causeway Bay you can ride the tram for a few miles through these areas, perhaps the best way to get a feel for the environment.

Much of the district is easily reached from Central by the tram that runs along Hennessy Road, or by the MTR to the Causeway Bay station. This underground station is a small labyrinth, so read the signs carefully to head to the desired exit.

Numbers in the text correspond to numbers in the margin and on the Wanchai, Causeway Bay, Happy Valley & North Point map.

> **a good tour**

If you come by taxi, a good starting point is the **Royal Hong Kong Yacht Club** ❺ ▶, which overlooks the **Cargo Handling Basin** ❻. Stroll around the harbor and have a look at the **Noonday Gun** ❼ and the boats in the **Causeway Bay Typhoon Shelter** ❽. From Gloucester Road, which runs by the Noonday Gun, you can walk to **Victoria Park** ❾, where you can roam at leisure and, on a nice day, have lunch or beverages in the outdoor restaurant. Exit from there onto Causeway Road, and walk or take a taxi to **Tin Hau Temple** ❿. Take another taxi to **Kwun Yum Temple** ⓫. Hop aboard Bus 19 or grab another taxi and continue to the **Happy Valley Racetrack** ⓬ in Happy Valley which is an interesting area with pockets of large middle-class housing, a legacy of life in less hectic, more spacious times. While the racetrack is the center point of the valley, there are several quaint *dai pai dong* or tea cafés and restaurants and shops to wander through.

TIMING Allow three to four hours so you'll have plenty of time to stroll around the park, catch taxis, and find the museum. Try to set out late in the morning, just after rush hour, as the traffic in Causeway Bay—both pedestrian and vehicular—can be extremely daunting. The busiest intersection is right in front of the Sogo department store, which, with its skyscraper-size advertisements, looks a bit like an Asian Times Square.

What to See

❻ Cargo Handling Basin. West of the Yacht Club and east of the Wanchai Ferry Pier (which sends ferries to Kowloon), you can watch the unloading of boats bringing cargo ashore from ships anchored in the harbor. ⊠ *Hung Hing Rd., Causeway Bay.*

❽ Causeway Bay Typhoon Shelter. This boat basin was originally built as a bad-weather haven for sampan dwellers. In the 1960s and '70s, tourists could have dinner on a sampan, but this is no longer possible, as the number of fishing families who live in those small open-air boats has dwindled and the basin has filled with pleasure craft. A few traditional sampans, crewed primarily by elderly toothless women, still putter around ferrying owners to their sailboats.

⓬ Happy Valley Racetrack. Hong Kong punters are the world's most avid horse-racing fans, and the track in Happy Valley—opened soon after the British first arrived in the territory—is one of their headquarters (the other being the newer, larger track in Sha Tin, in the New Territories). Races alternate between the tracks but are generally held in Happy Valley on Wednesday night or weekends from September through June. The joy of the Happy Valley track, even for those who aren't into horses, is that it's smack in the middle of the city and surrounded by towering apartment blocks—indeed, people whose balconies hang over the backstretch often have parties on racing days. There are members-only stands, for HK$50 (to purchase one you'll need to bring your passport to one of the off-track betting locations in the city), but the Hong Kong Tourist Board (HKTB) organizes special day-tours that allow you to experience the exclusive high-roller lounges. However, if you're game, it's just HK$10 to join in at the public stands where feverish gamblers wave their newspapers madly during races. ⊠ *Hong Kong Jockey Club, 2 Sports Rd., Happy Valley* ☎ *2966–8111* ⊕ *www.hongkongjockeyclub. com* 🎟 *HK$10* ☉ *Most Wed. nights and a few weekend days from Sept.–Jun.; call to verify schedule.*

⓫ Kwun Yum Temple. A shrine to the goddess of mercy has stood on this site for 200 years, but the current structure is mostly new, dating from 1986. Constructed on top of a huge boulder, it has a high ceiling and gallery and is very popular with local worshippers. ⊠ *Lin Fa Kung St. W, Causeway Bay* ☉ *Daily 9 AM–nightfall.*

off the beaten path

LAW UK FOLK MUSEUM – It's worth a trip to the end of the MTR line to see this 200-year-old house, which belonged to a family of Hakkas, the farmers who originally inhabited Hong Kong Island and the peninsula all the way into what is now southern Guangdong. Decorated in period style, the museum displays rural furniture and farm implements. Photos show you what bustling industrial Chai Wan looked like in the 1930s, when it was a peaceful bay inhabited only by fishermen and squatters. The museum is a block from Chai Wan station; outside the station, turn left and follow Kut Shing Street as it turns to the right. ⊠ *14 Kut Shing St., Chai Wan* ☎ *2896–7006* ⊕ *www.lcsd.gov.hk* ⌑ *Free* ☯ *Mon.–Wed., Fri., and Sat. 10–1 and 2–6, Sun. 1–6* Ⓜ *Chai Wan.*

❼ Noonday Gun. "In Hong Kong they strike a gong and fire off a noon-day gun," wrote Noël Coward in his song "Mad Dogs and English-men." They still fire that gun at noon each day from a small enclosure overlooking the Royal Yacht Club Basin & Typhoon Shelter, which is reached via a long walk (follow the signs) through the parking garage next to the Excelsior Hotel. The tradition was started by Jardine Math-eson & Co., the great hong that inspired James Clavell's novels *Taipan* and *Noble House*: Jardine would fire a salute each time their *taipan*, who ruled over the company like a lord, would enter or leave the har-bor. This angered the local governor, who ordered the company to use a gun instead of a cannon, and to fire it only as a noontime signal. The gun itself, with brass work polished bright, is a 3-pound Hotchkiss that dates back to 1901. ⊠ *Across from Excelsior Hotel, 281 Gloucester Rd., Causeway Bay.*

need a break? Have coffee or lunch in the first-floor coffee shop of the **Excelsior Hotel** (⊠ 281 Gloucester Rd., Causeway Bay ☎ 2894–8888), overlooking the Yacht Club, and gaze at the yachts docked in the harbor.

▶ ❺ Royal Hong Kong Yacht Club. The yacht club is worth a visit, but it's not open to the public, so try to find a local who is a member (or knows one) to give you guest privileges. If you belong to a yacht club at home, you may have reciprocal guest privileges. Once inside, you're surrounded by display cabinets full of silver prize trophies and welcomed by a de-lightfully old-fashioned bar with magnificent views of the harbor. On weekends the place hums with activity, especially when there are races, common from spring through fall. The **China Sea Race** (☎ 2239–0362 ⊕ www.chinasearace.com) to Manila is held every two years (in even-numbered years) at Easter time; call the race office for details. ⊠ *Kel-let Island, off Hung Hing Rd., Causeway Bay* ☎ *2832–2817* ⊕ *www.rhkyc.org.hk.*

❿ Tin Hau Temple. Located on a street of the same name off Causeway Road (behind Park Cinema on the southeast side of Victoria Park), this tem-ple is one of several in Hong Kong similarly named and dedicated to the goddess of the sea. Its decorative roof and old stone walls are worth a peek; the date of construction is unknown, but the temple bell was made in 1747. ⊠ *Tin Hau St. off Causeway Rd., Tin Hau.*

❾ Victoria Park. Beautifully landscaped with trees, shrubs, flowers, and lawns, the park has an aviary and recreational facilities for swimming, lawn bowling, tennis, roller-skating, and even go-cart racing. At dawn every morning the park fills with hundreds of tai chi chuan practitioners. The Lantern Carnival is held here in mid-autumn, with the trees a mass of colored lights. Just before Chinese New Year (late January to early February), the park hosts a huge flower market. On the eve of Chinese New Year, after a traditional family dinner at home, much of Hong Kong happily gathers here to shop and wander until the early hours of the new year. ⊠ *Bounded by Victoria Park, Hing Fat, Gloucester, and Causeway Rds., Causeway Bay.*

HONG KONG ISLAND—SOUTH SIDE

One of Hong Kong's unexpected pleasures is that, for all the unrelenting urbanity of the north coast of the island, the south side consists largely of rolling green hills and a few residential areas that have sprung up around picturesque bays. A few points of interest nestle within the rolling hills.

Since you won't be able to go from spot to spot by foot, it's best to choose two or three places to walk around in one day, but you'll still need to take a taxi or bus from one place to the next as no mass transit links all the points on the south side.

If your time in Hong Kong is short, you might want to limit yourself to Stanley and Shek O. If you want to squeeze more in, set out early in the morning and plan to make Shek O your dinner stop. Alternatively, you could easily spend an entire day shopping in Stanley and another day on the beach at Shek O or hiking through Shek O Country Park. The wonderful museum on the University of Hong Kong campus is closer to the city center. The most popular beaches are in Deep Water Bay and Repulse Bay, and along the same main road you'll find Ocean Park.

The beaches are worth visiting only in good weather. You can hike there year-round, although the beach is best from June through November.

Numbers in the text correspond to numbers in the margin and on the Exploring Hong Kong Island–South Side map.

Hong Kong University

❶ *20 mins from Central via Bus 3A or 40M.*

Established in 1911, the university has almost 10,000 undergraduate and graduate students. Most of its buildings are spread along Bonham Road, the most interesting of which is the 19th-century University Hall, designed in a hybrid Tudor-Gothic style.

The **University Museum & Art Gallery** has an excellent collection of Chinese antiquities including ceramics and bronzes, some dating from 3000 BC; fine paintings; lacquerware; and carvings in jade, stone, and wood. It also has the world's largest collection of Nestorian crosses from the Yuan Dynasty (1280–1368), and some superb ancient pieces: ritual vessels, decorative mirrors, and painted pottery. The museum is a bit out of the way, but it's a must for the true Chinese-art lover. ⊠ *94 Bonham Rd., Midlevels* ☎ *2241–5500* ⊕ *www.hku.hk/hkumag* ⊠ *Free* ☉ *Mon.–Sat. 9:30–6, Sun. 1:30–5:30.*

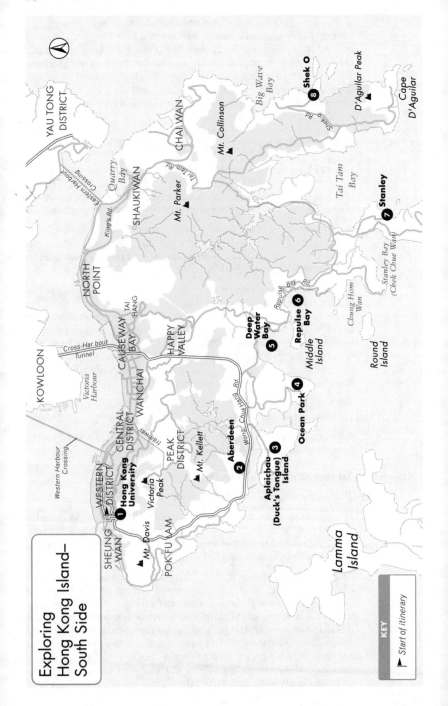

Exploring
Hong Kong Island–
South Side

YAU TONG
DISTRICT

Eastern Harbour
Crossing

Quarry
Bay

Tai Tam Rd

Big Wave
Bay

Shek O **8**

D'Aguilar Peak ▲

Cape
D'Aguilar

CHAI WAN

Mt. Collinson ▲

SHAUKIWAN

King's Rd.

Mt. Parker ▲

Tai Tam Bay

Stanley **7**

NORTH
POINT

Stanley Bay
(Chek Chue Wan)

KOWLOON

Cross-Harbour
Tunnel

CAUSEWAY
BAY

TAI
HANG

HAPPY
VALLEY

Repulse Bay Rd.

**Deep
Water
Bay**

5

Repulse Bay **6**

Chung Hom
Wan

Victoria
Harbour

WANCHAI

Middle
Island

Round
Island

Western Harbour
Crossing

CENTRAL
DISTRICT

WESTERN
DISTRICT

**Hong Kong
University** **1**

SHEUNG
WAN

PEAK
DISTRICT

Mt. Kellett ▲

Victoria
Peak ▲

Wong Chuk Hang Rd.

Aberdeen

2

**Apleichau
(Duck's Tongue)
Island**

3

Ocean Park **4**

▲ Mt. Davis

POKFULAM

Lamma
Island

KEY

▶ Start of itinerary

Aberdeen

② *30 mins from Central via Bus 70 or 91.*

Named after an English lord, not the Scottish city, Aberdeen got its start as a refuge for pirates some 200 years ago. After World War II Aberdeen became fairly commercial as the *tanka* (boat people) attracted tourists to their floating restaurants. In the harbor are some 3,000 junks and sampans, still interspersed with floating restaurants. You'll notice the famous Jumbo restaurant just offshore, its faux-Chinese decorations shrouded in lights. The tanka continue to live on houseboats, and although they may appear picturesque to passersby, their economic conditions are depressing.

You will undoubtedly be "invited" on board one of the sampans for a ride through the harbor by elderly women with sea- and sun-weathered skin, enticing you with loud croaking voices. It's best if you use one of the licensed operators, which depart on 20-minute tours daily from 8 to 6 from the main Aberdeen seawall opposite Aberdeen Centre. Groups can bargain: a trip for four to six people should cost from HK$100 to HK$150. Individual tickets are HK$40. A tour enables you to see how a portion of the fishing community live and work from their sampans and how the simple boats are also homes for families, sometimes with three generations on one small vessel. Ironically, only about 110 yards away, at the two marina clubs, some of the territory's most exclusive yachts and boats are moored.

On the town's side streets you'll find outdoor barbers at work and any number of dim sum restaurants. You can still see much of traditional Aberdeen, such as the **Aberdeen Cemetery,** with its enormous gravestones.

Aberdeen has its own famous **Tin Hau Temple,** whose ancient original bell and drum are still used at its opening and closing each day. Currently in a state of decline, this is one of several shrines to the goddess of the sea celebrated in the Tin Hau Festival in April and May, when hundreds of boats converge along the shore.

Apleichau (Duck's Tongue) Island

③ *15 mins from Aberdeen on Bus 90B or 91.*

To get here, take a bus across the bridge or arrive by sampan from Aberdeen. Apleichau Island has a boatbuilding yard where junks, yachts, and sampans are constructed, almost all without formal plans. Look to your right when crossing the bridge for a superb view of the harbor and its countless junks. Vehicles are not allowed to stop on the bridge, so you'll have to walk back if you want to take a picture.

On your left are boats belonging to members of the Marina Club and the slightly less exclusive Aberdeen Boat Club, as well as the famous Jumbo Floating Restaurant. Quiet and unspoiled just a decade ago, Apleichau is now bursting at the seams with development—both public housing and a number of gleaming private residential estates and shopping malls.

Ocean Park

☺ ❹ *30 mins from Central via Bus 29R or M590.*

Fodor'sChoice
★

The Hong Kong Jockey Club built this large amusement park, which occupies 170 hilly acres overlooking the sea just east of Aberdeen and has one of the world's largest oceanariums, Marine Land, where a variety of fish, sharks, and other sea life swim in the aquarium. On the lowland side are gardens, parks, and a children's zoo, where the highlight is undoubtedly the giant pandas, An An and Jia Jia. A cable car with spectacular views of the entire south coast can take you to the headland side and Ocean Theatre, the world's largest marine-mammal theater, where dolphins, seals, and a killer whale perform for crowds of up to 4,000. There are also various thrill rides, including a mammoth roller coaster and the gravity-defying Abyss Turbo Drop. ⊠ *Tai Shue Wan Rd., Aberdeen* ☎ *2873–8888* ⊕ *www.oceanpark.com.hk* ☒ *HK$180* ⊙ *Tues.–Sun. 10–6.*

Deep Water Bay

❺ *20 mins from Central via Bus 6, 64, or 260.*

On Island Road, just to the east of Ocean Park, this bay was the setting for the William Holden film *Love Is a Many Splendored Thing* (1955), and its deep coves are still lovely. This is the first beach you will reach on the south side after you leave Central, and though it is much smaller than the popular Repulse Bay beach, it is undoubtedly a scenic spot. Near Deep Water Bay are the manicured greens of the Deep Water Bay Golf Course, which is owned by the **Hong Kong Golf Club** (⊠ Deep Water Bay ☎ 2812–7070 ⊕ www.hkgolfclub.org), which welcomes visitors but recommends they call first. Not surprisingly, the area has become a multimillionaires' enclave and is home to Hong Kong's richest man, Li Ka-shing, a very private real-estate tycoon.

Repulse Bay

❻ *30 mins from Central via Bus 6, 6X, 64, or 260.*

Named after the British warship HMS *Repulse* (not, as some local wags say, after the pollution of its waters), the beach is a wonderful place to while away an afternoon. This was the site of the famed Repulse Bay Hotel, which gained notoriety in December 1941 when invading Japanese clambered over the hills behind it and entered its gardens, which were being used as headquarters by the British. After a brief battle, the British surrendered. The hotel was demolished in 1982 and eventually replaced with a luxury residential building, but replicas of its Repulse Bay Verandah Restaurant & Bamboo Bar were opened in 1986, run by the same people who operated the hotel.

> **need a break?**
>
> To taste the experience of colonial pampering, treat yourself to British high tea at the **Repulse Bay Verandah Restaurant & Bamboo Bar** (⊠ 109 Repulse Bay Rd., Repulse Bay ☎ 2812–2722). Tea is served weekdays from 3 to 5:30, weekends from 3:30, and costs HK$128.

Stanley

❼ *40 mins from Central via Bus 6, 6X, 64, or 260.*

Notorious during World War II as the home of Japan's largest POW camps in Hong Kong, Stanley is now known for its picturesque beaches and its market. The old police station, built in 1859, is open to the public and now houses a restaurant. Past the market, on Stanley Main Street, a strip of restaurants and pubs faces the bay. On the other side of the bay is a Tin Hau Temple, wedged between giant modern housing estates.

Fodor'sChoice **Stanley Market** is the place to buy casual clothing and tourist knick-
★ knacks at wholesale prices. Hong Kong has dozens of shops offering similar bargains, but it's more fun to shop for them in Stanley's coun-trified atmosphere. You can also buy ceramics, paintings and, ironically, snow-skiing gear at rock-bottom prices.

Shek O

❽ *45 mins from Central via Bus 309.*

The easternmost village on the south side of Hong Kong Island is a pop-ular weekend retreat. It's filled with old houses, great mansions, a su-perb golf course and club, a few simple restaurants, a pretty beach, and fine views, albeit marred by some ugly modern housing developments. Leave the town square, full of small shops selling inflatable toys and other beach gear, and take the curving path across a footbridge to the "island" of **Tai Tau Chau,** really a large rock with a lookout for scan-ning the South China Sea. Little more than a century ago, this open water was ruled by pirates.

You can hike through **Shek O Country Park** in less than two hours. Look here for birds that are hard to find in Hong Kong, such as Kentish plovers, reef egrets, and black-headed gulls, as well as the colorful rufus-backed shrike and the ubiquitous chatty bulbul.

| need a break? | A favorite place for lunch, drinks, or just alfresco lounging is Shek O's **Black Sheep Restaurant** (⊠ G/F, 452 Shek O Village ☎ 2809–2021), a small place with an eclectic menu and the kind of relaxed vibe that makes you wonder if you're still in Hong Kong. Clusters of palm fronds give it the feel of a tropical island hideaway. From Shek O Village, turn left at the Thai restaurant by the small traffic circle; continue down the road and around the corner on the right. Major credit cards are accepted. |

KOWLOON

Kowloon Peninsula is on the Chinese mainland just across the harbor from Central, bounded in the north by the string of mountains that give Kowloon its poetic name: *gau lung,* "nine dragons" (there are actually eight mountains, the ninth represented the emperor who named them). Kowloon is closer to China than Hong Kong in more ways than just geography: although the island's glittering skyscrapers are suffused with international commerce, Kowloon's urban fabric is even denser but has an older look to it. The proximity of the old Kai Tak airport kept building heights down (though landings still made you feel like you were scraping Kowloon's rooftops), but with the opening of Chek Lap Kok airport on Lamma Island, Kowloon will no doubt rival the physical heights of Hong Kong at some point. The peninsula has many of the territory's best hotels as well as a mind-boggling selection of shopping options; and no visit to Hong Kong is complete without taking in the commercial chaos of Nathan Road.

The southernmost part of Kowloon is called Tsim Sha Tsui, where such landmarks as the Star Ferry Pier and the elegant Peninsula Hotel stand proudly. A series of cultural buildings lines the waterfront, including the bold parabolic curves of the Cultural Centre and the golf ball–shape Space Museum. North of Tsim Sha Tsui are the market districts of Jordan and Mong Kok, where you can buy everything from pirated videos to electronics to name-brand clothes at fire-sale prices. A 75-meter Observation Wheel, which is being built atop the Ocean Terminal Mall, is expected to open in 2006; the wheel will be much like the London Eye, with self-rotating capsules that carry about a dozen people for magnificent views of the harbor.

Tsim Sha Tsui is best reached by the Star Ferry from Central or Wanchai, while the rest of Kowloon is easily accessible by MTR or taxi.

Numbers in the text correspond to numbers in the margin and on the Kowloon Peninsula map.

a good tour

From the Kowloon tip, wend your way into the urban jungle of Tsim Sha Tsui from the **Star Ferry Pier** ❶ ▶, which is a 10-minute ferry ride from the pier on the Hong Kong Island side—and, incidentally, the most romantic way to see the harbor, day or night.

Stroll east along the pedestrian waterfront to the Victoria Clock Tower, then visit the **Hong Kong Cultural Centre** ❷. Note the luxurious **Peninsula Hotel** ❸, across from which you'll find the **Hong Kong Space Museum** ❹. The **Hong Kong Museum of Art** ❺ is behind the Space Museum.

Continue east on Salisbury Road and turn left on Chatham Road South and continue north to the corner of Cheong Wan Road, where you'll find the **Hong Kong Science Museum** ❻ and the **Hong Kong Museum of History** ❼. Backtrack a bit on Chatham Road to Granville Road or Cameron Road and turn right. The next main boulevard will be **Nathan Road** ❽. Head south a short way on Nathan Road, then turn right onto Haiphong Road to get to **Kowloon Park** ❾.

Return to Nathan Road and continue north to Jordan Road, then make a left and then a right onto **Temple Street** ❿. Follow Temple Street north to the **Kansu Street Jade Market** ⓫, to the west. Continue one block north of Kansu Street to the **Tin Hau Temple** ⓬.

From here you can either walk or take the MTR to Prince Edward to see the more modern **Bird Garden** ⓭, which replaced the old Bird Market.

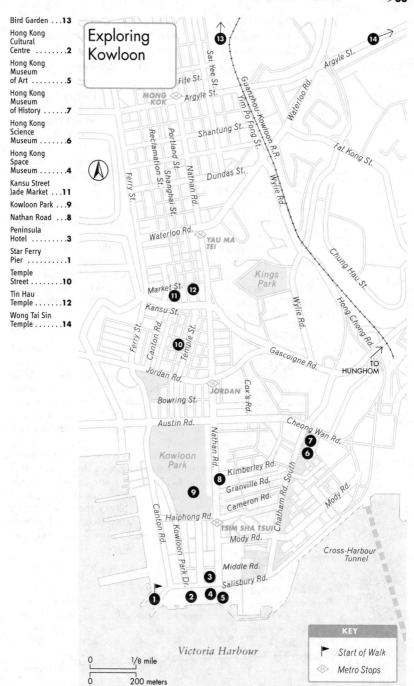

Exploring
Kowloon

MONG
KOK

Fife St.

Argyle St.

Sai Yee St.

Guanzhou-Kowloon R.R.

Yim Po Fong St.

Argyle St.

Waterloo Rd.

Fat Kong St.

Shantung St.

Reclamation St.

Portland St.

Shanghai St.

Nathan Rd.

Ferry St.

Dundas St.

Wylie Rd.

Chung Hau St.

Waterloo Rd.

YAU MA
TEI

Kings
Park

Wylie Rd.

Hong Chong Rd.

Market St.

12

11

Kansu St.

Ferry St.

Canton Rd.

Temple St.

10

Gascoigne Rd.

TO
HUNGHOM

Jordan Rd.

JORDAN

Cox's Rd.

Bowring St.

Austin Rd.

Cheong Wan Rd.

7

6

Kowloon
Park

Nathan Rd.

Kimberley Rd.

8

Granville Rd.

Chatham Rd. South

Cameron Rd.

Mody Rd.

9

Haiphong Rd.

Canton Rd.

Kowloon Park Dr.

TSIM SHA TSUI

Mody Rd.

Cross-Harbour
Tunnel

Middle Rd.

3

Salisbury Rd.

1

2

4 **5**

Victoria Harbour

0   1/8 mile

0   200 meters

KEY	
▶	*Start of Walk*
◈	*Metro Stops*

The **Wong Tai Sin Temple** ⑭ is best reached by MTR. The Wong Tai Sin station is four stops from Prince Edward on the green Kwun Tong line; the temple is directly opposite the station.

TIMING You can take this tour in one day, but it will be a tiring day, as Kowloon is crowded, noisy, and often frustrating to walk or drive through. Plan a half day to stroll from the Star Ferry Pier to the Tin Hau Temple, stopping to see sights and shops along the way. Allow at least an hour for the Space Museum and the Museum of Art, another 45 minutes for the Science Museum, and an hour for the Museum of History. Be flexible with your shopping time; you'll want to compare prices before you make decisions. If you have two days in Kowloon, take the walk from Star Ferry to Kowloon Park the first day, then start at Temple Street and continue to Wong Tai Sin Temple the next day.

Start around 10 AM to avoid rush-hour traffic. Note that all museums offer free admission on Wednesday, though they're quite inexpensive normally. For the avid museumgoer, the Hong Kong Tourist Board (HKTB) offers a Museum Tour pass for HK$30 that includes visits to the Museums of Art and History, and the Space, Science, and Heritage museums. The pass also includes a shuttle bus to each location. Buses depart throughout the day so you can spend as much time in each place as you wish. For tickets and bus timetable, visit any HKTB Visitor Information Centre.

What to See

☺ ⑬ **Bird Garden.** On Yuen Po Street, 10 minutes from the Prince Edward
Fodor'sChoice MTR station, this garden replaced the old Bird Market, whose narrow
★ streets of bird shops have been redeveloped. What the garden lacks in spontaneous tumult it makes up for with an attractive outdoor setting in the shadow of the Kowloon–Canton Railway (KCR) railroad tracks—and the rumble of each passing train sends the birds into a frenzy. The garden is composed of various courtyards filled with trees and surrounded by 70 stalls selling birds, cages, and such accoutrements as tiny porcelain feeders and fresh grasshoppers. Plenty of free birds also swoop in to gorge on spilled food and commiserate with their imprisoned brethren. If you walk from the MTR, you'll enjoy an aromatic approach through the flower market. Take the Police Station exit, walk east along Prince Edward Road for three short blocks, then turn left onto Sai Yee Street, and then right onto Flower Market Road. The bird garden is at the end of this flower market street. ⊠ *Yuen Po St., Prince Edward* ☎ *Free* ☉ *Daily 7 AM–8 PM.*

off the
beaten
path

CHI LIN NUNNERY – Originally built in 1934 and considered a gem of Chinese monastic architecture, the nunnery was reopened in 2000 after a multimillion-dollar renovation completed in traditional Tang-era style—no nails were used in the construction, only wooden dowels and brackets, a truly marvelous architectural achievement. The 8-acre site includes 16 Buddhist halls, a Zen-style lotus-pond rock garden, and a Ten Thousand Buddhas pagoda. ⊠ *5 Chi Lin Dr., Diamond Hill, 15-min walk from Diamond Hill MTR* ☎ *2354–1770* ☎ *Free* ☉ *Monastery, Thurs.–Tues. 9–4:30; lotus-pond garden, daily 7–7.*

SYMPHONY OF LIGHTS

One of Hong Kong's newer nightly attractions may make you think you're in Las Vegas rather than China. Each night, starting at 8 pm, multicolored lights on 18 of the Central district's big skyscrapers are synchronized to a musical accompaniment for a light show that uses the city's own skyline as its canvas. The best place to see and hear the show is the so-called "Avenue of Stars," an enhanced section of the Tsim Sha Tsui waterfront promenade near the Star Ferry (follow exit E from the Tsim Sha Tsui MTR station and then follow the signs). Stars honor important figures from Hong Kong cinema. If you stand or stroll around here, you'll be able to hear the music to which Central's light show is synchronized. During special events, fireworks are shot from the tops of each of the 18 skyscrapers, adding pyrotechnics to the show.

② Hong Kong Cultural Centre. This stark, architecturally controversial building (which looks better by its flattering nighttime lighting than by day) has tile walls inside and out, sloped roofs, and no windows—an irony, since the view of the harbor would be superb. Its concert hall and two theaters host almost every major artist who performs in the territory. Exhibits are occasionally mounted in the atrium, which has its own three-story metallic mural by Van Lau called *The Meeting of Yin and Yang*. In front of the center is a long, two-level promenade with plenty of seating and a view of the entire north coast of Hong Kong. The center is a few minutes' walk from either the Star Ferry or Tsim Sha Tsui MTR stop. ⊠ *10 Salisbury Rd., Tsim Sha Tsui* ☎ *2734–2010* ⊕ *www.hkculturalcentre.gov.hk.*

⑤ Hong Kong Museum of Art. The exterior is unimaginative, but inside are
FodorśChoice five floors of innovatively designed galleries. One is devoted to historic
★ photographs, prints, and artifacts of Hong Kong, Macau, and other parts of the Pearl River delta; other galleries highlight Chinese antiquities, fine art, and visiting exhibits. The museum is a few minutes' walk from either the Star Ferry or Tsim Sha Tsui MTR stop. ⊠ *10 Salisbury Rd., Tsim Sha Tsui* ☎ *2721–0116* ⊕ *www.lcsd.gov.hk* ☒ *HK$10, or included in Museum Tour pass; free Wed.* ☉ *Fri.–Wed. 10–6.*

⑦ Hong Kong Museum of History. The museum, in an ungainly building
FodorśChoice adjacent to the Science Museum, covers a broad expanse of Hong Kong's
★ past with life-size dioramas. Exhibits outline 6,000 years of the territory's cultural heritage and history. Special themed exhibits are often on display as well. The museum is a few minutes' walk from either the Star Ferry or Tsim Sha Tsui MTR stop. ⊠ *100 Chatham Rd. S, Tsim Sha Tsui* ☎ *2724–9042* ⊕ *www.lcsd.gov.hk* ☒ *HK$10, or included in Museum Tour pass; free Wed.* ☉ *Mon. and Wed.–Sat. 10–6, Sun. 10–7.*

★ ⏰ ❻ **Hong Kong Science Museum.** More than 500 scientific and technological exhibits—including an energy machine and a miniature submarine—emphasize interactive participation. The highlight is a series of experiments that test memory and cognitive ability. The museum is less than a 10-minute walk from the Tsim Sha Tsui MTR stop. ⊠ *2 Science Museum Rd., corner of Cheong Wan Rd. and Chatham Rd., Tsim Sha Tsui East* ☎ *2732–3232* ⊕ *www.lcsd.gov.hk* ⊠ *HK$25, or included in Museum Tour pass; free Wed.* ⏰ *Mon.–Wed. and Fri. 1–9, weekends 10–9.*

⏰ ❹ **Hong Kong Space Museum.** Across from the Peninsula Hotel, this dome-shape museum houses one of the most advanced planetariums in Asia. Interactive models help to explain basic aspects of space exploration (though some of these are less than lucid); fly wires let you experience weightlessness and such. It also contains the **Hall of Solar Science,** whose solar telescope permits you to take a close look at the sun, and the **Space Theatre** (seven shows daily from 11:10 to 9:25), with Omnimax movies on space travel, sports, and natural wonders. Children under three are not admitted. It's a few minutes' walk from either the Star Ferry or Tsim Sha Tsui MTR stop. ⊠ *10 Salisbury Rd., Tsim Sha Tsui* ☎ *2734–2722* ⊕ *www.lcsd.gov.hk* ⊠ *HK$10, or included in Museum Tour pass; free Wed.; Omnimax and Sky shows HK$24–HK$32* ⏰ *Mon. and Wed.–Fri. 1–9, weekends 10–9.*

⓫ **Kansu Street Jade Market.** The old jade market was a sea of pavement trading, but this more orderly market has 450 stalls, selling everything from priceless ornaments to fake pendants. If you don't know much about jade, take along someone who does or you might pay a lot more than you should. Try to come between 10 and noon, as many traders close shop early. The market is a 10-minute walk from the Yau Ma Tei MTR stop. ⊠ *Kansu and Battery Sts., Yau Ma Tei* ⏰ *Daily 10–3:30.*

⏰ ❾ **Kowloon Park.** The former site of the Whitfield Military Barracks is now a restful, green oasis. Signs point the way to gardens with different landscaping themes—the sculpture garden is particularly interesting, and the Chinese Garden has a lotus pond, streams, a lake, and a nearby aviary with a colorful collection of rare birds. Take the Mosque exit of the Tsim Sha Tsui MTR stop. The **Jamia Masjid & Islamic Centre** is in the south end of the park, near the Haiphong Road entrance. This is Hong Kong's principal mosque, albeit not its most graceful; built in 1984, it has four minarets, decorative arches, and a marble dome. It is not open to visitors. At the northern end of the park sits an extraordinary **public swimming complex** built, like so much else in the city, by the Hong Kong Jockey Club with revenues from the races. Admission is HK$19, and it's open year-round. ⊠ *Just off Nathan Rd., Tsim Sha Tsui* ☎ *2724–3344 park, 2724–3846 swimming complex* ⊕ *www.lcsd.gov.hk* ⊠ *Free* ⏰ *Park daily 6 AM–midnight; pool Apr.–Oct., daily 6:30 AM–noon, 1 to 5 PM, and 6–10 PM; call to determine winter opening schedule.*

off the beaten path

LEI CHENG UK HAN TOMB MUSEUM – This small museum in Sham Shui Po houses a 1,600-year-old vault and is worth a trip for its age alone. The four barrel-vaulted brick chambers form a cross around a domed vault, and the funerary objects are typical of the tombs of the Han Dynasty (AD 25–AD 220). The vault was discovered in 1955 during excavations for the huge housing estate that now surrounds it. To get here, take Bus 2 from Kowloon's Star Ferry Terminal to Tonkin Street (drops you closer), or catch the MTR to the Cheung Sha Wan station (faster trip). ⊠ *41 Tonkin St., Lei Cheng UK Resettlement Estate, Sham Shui Po* ☎ *2386–2863* ⊕ *www.lcsd.gov.hk* ⊠ *Free* ⊙ *Mon.–Wed., Fri., and Sat. 10–1 and 2–6, Sun. 1–6.*

❽ Nathan Road. The densest shopping street in town, the so-called Golden Mile runs for several miles north from Salisbury Road in Tsim Sha Tsui and is filled with hotels, restaurants, and shops of every description. To the left and right are mazes of narrow streets lined with even more shops crammed with every possible type of merchandise—jewelry, electronics, clothes, souvenirs, cosmetics, and so on. Expect to be besieged with street hawkers trying to sell you cheap "Rolexes."

❸ Peninsula Hotel. The grande dame of Hong Kong hotels, the Peninsula is a local institution. The exterior of this sumptuous hotel is lined with a fleet of Rolls-Royce taxis and doormen in white uniforms, while the huge colonnaded lobby has charm, grandeur, string quartets, and the sedate air of excessive wealth tastefully enjoyed. Even if you're not staying here, stop inside to browse the upscale shopping arcade, partake of high tea, or just marvel at the architecture. ⊠ *Salisbury Rd., Tsim Sha Tsui* ☎ *2920–2888* ⊟ *2722–4170* ⊕ *www.peninsula.com.*

need a break?

Tsim Sha Tsui is short on quiet cafés, but the **Peninsula Hotel** serves high tea—the perfect way to rest your shopping feet in style. Nibble on a majestic selection of scones and pastries in the grand lobby (for HK$180 per person, a bargain considering all you get) daily from 2 to 7. Or settle down for à la carte tea in the Verandah restaurant Friday through Sunday 3 to 5. You can't make reservations for tea, so arrive early if you don't want to stand in line.

▶ ❶ Star Ferry Pier. The pier makes a convenient starting point for any tour of Kowloon. (It also has a bus terminal, which sends buses to all parts of Kowloon and to the New Territories.) As you face the bus station, Ocean Terminal, where luxury cruise ships berth, is on your left; inside this terminal, and in adjacent Harbour City, are miles of air-conditioned shopping arcades. To the right of the ferry pier is **Victoria Clock Tower**, which dates from 1915 and is all that remains of the old Kowloon–Canton Railway Station. (The train station, for travel within China, is 2 km [1 mi] to the east in Hung Hom.)

★ ❿ Temple Street. The heart of a busy shopping area, Temple Street is ideal for wandering and people-watching. By day you'll find market stalls with plenty of kitsch and plenty of bargains in clothing, handbags, accessories, tapes, and CDs, so it's worth it to stroll through if you visit the nearby Kansu Street Jade Market, but the best time to come is after 8 PM, when the streets become an open-air bazaar of fortune-tellers, prostitutes, street doctors offering cures for almost any complaint, and occasionally Chinese opera.

Such nearby lanes as **Shanghai Street** and **Canton Road** are also worth a peek for their shops and stalls selling everything from herbal remedies to jade and ivory. **Ning Po Street** is known for its paper kites and for the colorful paper and bamboo models of worldly possessions (boats, cars, houses) that are burned at Chinese funerals.

⑫ Tin Hau Temple. One of Kowloon's oldest temples, this sensual site is filled with incense and crowds of worshippers. You'll probably be encouraged to have a try with the fortune sticks, known as *chim* sticks. Each stick is numbered, and you shake them in a cardboard tube until one falls out. A fortune-teller asks you your date of birth and makes predictions from the stick based on numerology. ⊠ *Market St., 1 block north of Kansu St., Yau Ma Tei* ☉ *Daily 7–5:30.*

★ ⑭ Wong Tai Sin Temple. Have your fortune told at this large vivid compound, whose Buddhist shrine is dedicated to a shepherd boy who was said to have magic healing powers. In addition to the main altar, the pavilions, and the arcade—where soothsayers and palm readers are happy to interpret Wong Tai Sin's predictions for a small fee—there are two lovely Chinese gardens and a Confucian Hall. The temple is in front of the Wong Tai Sin MTR stop. ⊠ *2 Chuk Yuen Village, Wong Tai Sin* ☎ *2327–8141* 🕮 *Small donation expected* ☉ *Daily 7–5:30.*

THE NEW TERRITORIES

Until a generation ago, the expansive New Territories consisted almost exclusively of farmland and traditional walled villages. Today, following a government housing program that created "new towns" such as Sha Tin and Tuen Mun with up to 500,000 residents, parts of the New Territories are beginning to feel more like the rest of Hong Kong. Within its expansive 518 square km (200 square mi), however, you'll still feel far removed from the congestion and urban rigors of Hong Kong Island and Kowloon. It's here you'll find many of the area's lushest parks and therapeutic nature walks. In addition, you'll be able to sneak glimpses of traditional rural life in the restored walled villages and ancestral clan halls scattered throughout the area.

The New Territories got their name when the British acquired this area. Whereas Hong Kong Island and Kowloon were taken outright following the Opium War of 1841, the land that now constitutes the New Territories was handed over much later on a 99-year lease. It was this lease that expired in 1997 and was the catalyst for the return of the entire colony to China. Because of its size, the New Territories can be difficult to explore without a car, but between the bus, MTR, and the Kowloon–Canton Railway, you can at least get close to many sights.

Perhaps the best way to see some of the smaller villages is to go on one of the HKTB's organized tours (even if you don't think of yourself as a tour type), which loop through the region. In addition to the tours' convenience, the guides are knowledgeable and helpful (⇨ Sightseeing Tours *in* Smart Travel Tips).

Numbers in the text correspond to numbers in the margin and on the New Territories and the Outer Islands map.

Western New Territories

a good tour

It's possible to do a tour of the Western New Territories by taxi, but you'll save money by hiring a new taxi at each stop; the other option, which is sometimes cost-effective if you are a group of three or more, is to hire a car and driver for the day from your hotel, but depending on your hotel this can also be an expensive option. Start at **Sam Tung Uk Museum ❶** ☞, an 18th-century walled village in Tsuen Wan. From here take a taxi to the **Yuen Yuen Institute ❷**, which brings together Buddhism, Taoism, and Confucianism. From there take another taxi to **Ching Chung Koon Taoist Temple ❸**, near the town of Tuen Mun, and then a little farther north to the **Miu Fat Buddhist Monastery ❹** on Castle Peak Road, which is a popular place for a vegetarian lunch. From here, Bus 51 will take you to the **Kam Tin Walled Village ❺**, a 17th-century enclave.

After wandering the old village, you can take a taxi east to go up to the peak of **Tai Mo Shan ❻** or north to visit the scenic town of **Lok Ma Chau ❼**. End your tour at **Tai Fu Tai ❽**, a 19th-century mansion that illustrates the conflicted political times during which it was built.

If you prefer to tour at your own pace and want to see this large area without hopping from public transport to taxi and back again, you have two options. The first is to hire a car for a few hours or even a full day. **Ace Hire Car** (☎ 2893–0541) offers a driver and sedan car for HK$160 per hour with a minimum of three hours. **DCH Transport** (☎ 2768–2977) is HK$280 an hour, also with a minimum charge of three hours. A full-day hire is a little less, and bargaining is recommended. Some taxis can also be hired on an hourly rate from around HK$100 per hour, but be sure to hire a green **New Territories taxi** (☎ 2527–6324 or 2574–7311), whose driver will be familiar with the area, rather than a red Hong Kong and Kowloon taxi. If you choose to hire a taxi, ask the taxi to meet you at a convenient train station in the Western New Territories.

TIMING Allow at least a full day for this tour, or more, depending on your pace. Plan to start in the morning and have lunch at the Miu Fat Buddhist Monastery.

What to See

❸ **Ching Chung Koon Taoist Temple.** This huge temple near the town of Tuen Mun has room after room of altars, all filled with the heady scent of incense burning in bronze holders. On one side of the main entrance is a cast-iron bell with a circumference of about 5 feet—all large monasteries in ancient China rang such bells at daybreak to wake the monks

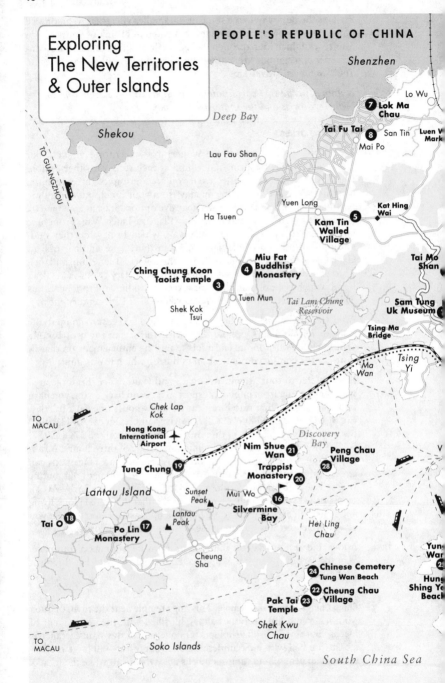

Exploring The New Territories & Outer Islands

PEOPLE'S REPUBLIC OF CHINA

Shenzhen

Deep Bay

Shekou

Shekou

TO GUANGZHOU

Lo Wu

7 Lok Ma Chau

Tai Fu Tai

8 San Tin

Mai Po

Luen W Mark

Lau Fau Shan

Yuen Long

Kat Hing Wai

5

Ha Tsuen

Kam Tin Walled Village

Tai Mo Shan

Miu Fat Buddhist Monastery **4**

Ching Chung Koon Taoist Temple **3**

Tuen Mun

Tai Lam Chung Reservoir

Shek Kok Tsui

Sam Tung Uk Museum

Tsing Ma Bridge

Ma Wan

Tsing Yi

TO MACAU

Chek Lap Kok

Hong Kong International Airport

Discovery Bay

Nim Shue Wan **21**

Peng Chau Village

28

Tung Chung **19**

Trappist Monastery **20**

Lantau Island

Sunset Peak

Mui Wo

16

Tai O **18**

Lantau Peak

Silvermine Bay

Hei Ling Chau

Yun War

Po Lin Monastery **17**

Cheung Sha

Chinese Cemetery **24** Tung Wan Beach

Hun Shing Ye Beach

22 **Cheung Chau Village**

Pak Tai Temple **23**

Shek Kwu Chau

TO MACAU

Soko Islands

South China Sea

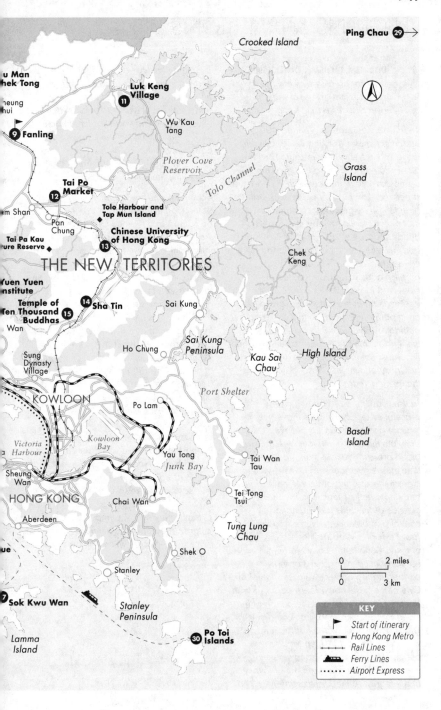

Ping Chau **29** →

Crooked Island

u Man
hek Tong

heung
hui

9 Fanling

**11 Luk Keng
Village**

Wu Kau
Tang

*Plover Cove
Reservoir*

Tolo Channel

*Grass
Island*

**12 Tai Po
Market**

m Shan

Pan
Chung

**Tolo Harbour and
Tap Mun Island**

**13 Chinese University
of Hong Kong**

Tai Pa Kau
ure Reserve ◆

Chek
Keng

THE NEW TERRITORIES

Yuen Yuen
nstitute

**Temple of
Ten Thousand
Buddhas 15**

14 Sha Tin

Sai Kung

Wan

*Sai Kung
Peninsula*

Ho Chung

*Kau Sai
Chau*

High Island

Sung
Dynasty
Village

KOWLOON

Po Lam

Port Shelter

*Basalt
Island*

Victoria
a Harbour

*Kowloon
Bay*

Yau Tong

Junk Bay

Tai Wan
Tau

Sheung
Wan

HONG KONG

Chai Wan

Tei Tong
Tsui

Aberdeen

*Tung Lung
Chau*

ue

Shek O

Stanley

0 ——— 2 miles

0 ——— 3 km

7 Sok Kwu Wan

*Stanley
Peninsula*

*Lamma
Island*

**30 Po Toi
Islands**

KEY
▶ *Start of itinerary*
▬▬ *Hong Kong Metro*
┼─┼ *Rail Lines*
⛴ *Ferry Lines*
...... *Airport Express*

RELIGIONS & TRADITIONS

B UDDHISM, TAOISM, CONFUCIANISM—the three great strands of Chinese religious thought are at work everywhere in Hong Kong.

Buddhism. There are more than 400 Buddhist temples in Hong Kong, from the large Po Lin Monastery in Lantau, with its giant seated Buddha, to the small smoky shrine covered with incense in a dead-end street near Lan Kwai Fong. Lord Buddha's birthday, the eighth day of the fourth moon, is a public holiday in Hong Kong. Buddhist devotees give offerings to the gods in return for luck, health, and of course, prosperity. One of the most popular gods is Tin Hau, Queen of Heaven and Protector of all Seafarers. The territory's maritime history has given her an important place in Hong Kong, and her birthday is celebrated on the 23rd day of the third month of the lunar calendar when fishermen colorfully decorate their boats and pray at temples for good catches in the coming year.

Taoism. Tai chi, or "shadow boxing" is a graceful series of exercises that combines thought and action and is believed to stimulate the central nervous system, lower blood pressure, relieve stress, and gently tone muscles without strain. The rhythmic movements also massage internal organs and improve their functionality. The essence of tai chi is a combination of control and balance, which embodies Taoist thought. Walking through any part of Hong Kong in the early morning, you'll no doubt encounter groups or individuals performing this ancient Chinese martial art. One of the best known Taoist gods is Kwan Tai, the God of War and the patron of the Hong Kong police, and, ironically, of the Triads as well. Tai was a historical figure who lived during the Three Kingdoms period (AD 220–AD 265) and who was later deified as a Taoist symbol of loyalty and integrity. At the 19th-century Man Mo

Temple on Hollywood Road, an ever-burning lamp stands before his statue. Sung Dynasty general Che Kung is another god who was elevated to a Taoist deity. Legend has it that he saved the inhabitants of Sha Tin Valley from the plague centuries ago. Now, believers gather at his major temple in Sha Tin on his birthday, the third day of the lunar New Year.

Confucianism. The fundamental concerns of the Confucian tradition are learning to be human and filial devotion. Respecting elders is considered one of the most important values in families, and this is reflected in the Ching Ming Festival or "Remembrance of Ancestors Day," when families visit cemeteries to sweep their ancestors' graves and clean headstones in a sign of respect. The importance of the family gathering on Chinese New Year's Eve is equivalent to Christmas in the West. It is a time for celebrations and a huge feast. Traditionally, lai see, or red pockets, with tokens of cash, are handed out from the elders to the young, and are considered lucky money. The period leading up to New Year's Day is very busy, too, with superstitious families taking steps to avoid any chance of bad luck in the coming year. It's believed that you must not wash your hair in the first few days of the new year, otherwise your life span will be shortened. Also, sweeping the floors during this same time is considered unlucky, because all the money and good fortune will be swept out the door.

— Eva Chui Loiterton

and nuns for a day of work in the rice fields. On the other side of the entrance is a huge drum that was used to call the workers back in the evenings. Inside, some of the rooms are papered with small pictures; their relatives pay the temple to have these photos displayed so they can see their dearly departed as they pray. The temple also includes a retirement home, built from donations, which provides a quiet and serene spot for the elderly. Colorful plants and flowers, hundreds of dwarf shrubs, ornamental fishponds, and pagodas bedeck the grounds. Take the MTR to Tsuen Wan station and then Bus 66M or 66P to Tuen Mun. Alternatively, you can take the MTR to Kwai Fong Station, then board Bus 58M, alighting at the Tuen Mun Catholic Secondary School. The temple is nearby, but the entrance is not obvious, so ask for directions. ⊠ *Adjacent to Ching Chung LRT station, Tuen Mun.*

⑤ Kam Tin Walled Village. This village was built in the 1600s as a fortified town belonging to the Tang clan. Six walled villages surround Kam Tin, but **Kat Hing Wai** is the most popular. The original walls are intact, with guardhouses on the four corners and arrow slits for fighting off attackers; but the image of antiquity is somewhat marred by the modern homes and TV antennas looming over the ancient fortifications. Just inside the main gate is a narrow street lined with shops selling souvenirs and mass-produced oil paintings. Take the MTR to the Tsuen Wan stop, then catch a taxi to the village. Alternatively, take the MTR to Tsuen Wan station, then board Bus 51 from the Tsuen Wan Ferry Pier, which is a short taxi ride from the MTR station. The bus will take you over the hills along scenic Route Twisk. Alight at the last stop and then continue walking in the same direction the bus was going, past the open-fronted shops. Kam Tin is less than five minutes away, on your left. The bus takes approximately 50 minutes.

⑦ Lok Ma Chau. Once, the hillside view from Lok Ma Chau was of bucolic rice paddies and duck ponds. Now it's the best vantage point in Hong Kong of mainland China and the high-rise urban developments of the Shenzhen Special Economic Zone. This sleepy border town is facing development of its own with the construction of the Lok Ma Chau rail terminus, a US$250 million (HK$2 billion) project, that will become the second cross-border facility in the territory. The project is expected to be completed at the end of 2007. To reach Lok Ma Chau, take the KCR to Lo Wu station and then a taxi.

④ Miu Fat Buddhist Monastery. On Castle Peak Road near Tuen Mun, Miu Fat is a popular place for a vegetarian lunch. Like many large monasteries, this one also has a restaurant that serves meals; dishes include lots of greens, mushrooms, and "meat" that is actually made from rice flour. Lunch is served between noon and 3:30 PM. The monastery itself is ornate, with large carved-stone animals guarding the front. Farther on is the former clan village of **Yuen Long,** now almost completely redeveloped as an industrial and residential complex. Take the MTR to Tsuen Wan, then a taxi to the monastery. Alternatively, take the Airport Railway train to Tsing Yi station and then take Bus 53, 63M, 63X, or 68A. ⊠ *Castle Peak Rd., Tuen Mun* ☜ *Free* ☉ *Daily 9–5.*

▶ ❶ **Sam Tung Uk Museum.** This walled village, built in 1786, looks more like a single large house with numerous interlocking chambers and white-washed interior courtyards. Set in a forested area incongruously amid the residential towers and chaotic commercial life of Tsuen Wan, its construction obeys a rigid symmetry, with the ancestral hall and two common chambers forming the central axis and the more private areas flanking it. The front door is angled to face west–southwest, in keeping with feng shui principles of alignment between mountain and water. The village is easily reached by MTR; it's a five-minute walk from the Tsuen Wan stop to the museum. ⊠ *2 Kwu Uk La., Tsuen Wan* ☎ *2411–2001* ☜ *Free* ☉ *Mon. and Wed.–Sun. 9–5.*

★ ❽ **Tai Fu Tai.** Built in 1865 by a scholar of the gentry class, this exquisitely preserved home reflects the European architectural influence on China, which was a result of the Western victory over China in the Opium War of 1841 and the gradual encroachment of colonialism. With loyalties divided, the scholar-gentry class decided to incorporate a few European design elements to indicate their open-mindedness. French rococo moldings and stained glass above the doorways belie the home's tra-ditional Qing Dynasty style. Other charming idiosyncrasies include an upper floor that allowed women to watch guests unobserved and an enclosed courtyard called a "moon playing" chamber for examining the night sky. To reach the house take Bus 76K from Sheung Shui KCR and alight on Castle Road at the gas station. Follow the signs to the mansion (it's a five-minute walk). ⊠ *San Tin, Yuen Long* ☜ *Free* ☉ *Wed.–Mon. 9–1 and 2–5.*

❻ **Tai Mo Shan.** Rising 3,230 feet above sea level, Tai Mo Shan—which trans-lates as Big Hat Mountain—is Hong Kong's highest peak, which has been cordoned off as a country park. Access is via a former military road (you can see the old British barracks, now occupied by the People's Lib-eration Army, en route), and a lookout about two-thirds of the way up gives you a chance to see both sides of the territory: rolling green hills in the foreground and dense urban development in the distance. On a clear day you can even see the spire of the Bank of China building in Central. Take the MTR to Tsuen Wan and exit the station at Shiu Wo Street, then catch Minibus 82.

❷ **Yuen Yuen Institute.** This complex of pavilions and prayer halls was built in the 1950s to bring together the three streams of Chinese thought: Bud-dhism (which emphasizes nirvana and physical purity), Taoism (nature and inner peace), and Confucianism (which follows the practical and philosophical beliefs of Confucius). The main three-tier red pagoda is a copy of the Temple of Heaven in Beijing, and houses 60 statues rep-resenting the full cycle of the Chinese calendar—you can look for the one that corresponds to your birth year and make an offering of incense. To reach the institute, take the MTR to Tsuen Wan and exit the station at Shiu Wo Street, then catch Minibus 81. ⊠ *Lo Wai Village, Tsuen Wan* ☎ *2492–2220* ☜ *Free* ☉ *Daily 8:30–5.*

Central & Eastern New Territories

a good tour

Although parts of this tour are accessible by KCR train, you should consider hiring a taxi and driver for the day for visiting some of the more remote sights. Otherwise, if you take a taxi to a sight you may not be able to find one to take you back.

You can begin by taking the train to **Fanling** ○ ►, then take a taxi from the KCR stop to the Luen Wo Market. From there, drive to the nearby village of Sheung Shui to see the ancestral hall of **Liu Man Shek Tong** ⑩, then head northeast to **Luk Keng village** ⑪, which is close to the Chinese border. It is a scenic drive past Plover Cove Reservoir to **Tai Po market** ⑫, which runs along the streets near the Tai Po KCR stop. Wander around the market, then take the KCR south one more stop to the University station to find the **Chinese University of Hong Kong** ⑬. Take a campus bus or taxi to the Art Museum, in the university's Institute of Chinese Studies Building.

Go back to the University station and take the train another stop south to the Sha Tin Racecourse, which adjoins the Racecourse station. Take a look around, then take the train one more stop south if you want to see the hub of the "new town" **Sha Tin** ⑭. From here you can take a taxi or go to Sha Tin KCR station and walk to the **Temple of Ten Thousand Buddhas** ⑮, which provides a view of Amah Rock and Tai Mo Shan, Hong Kong's highest peak.

If you want to spend some time enjoying the outdoors, the Eastern New Territories has several attractive undeveloped areas that are off the beaten path: you can explore the beaches and fishing villages of Tap Mun Island or wander the forest and seaside trails of the Sai Kung Peninsula.

TIMING   This entire tour takes a couple of days. If you don't have that much time to devote to this area, you may want to select sights that are geographically close together. If you want to visit Tap Mun Island or the Sai Kung Peninsula, set aside a separate day for each.

What to See

⑬ **Chinese University of Hong Kong Art Museum.** The Art Museum in the Institute of Chinese Studies Building is well worth a visit for its large exhibits of paintings and calligraphy from the Ming period to modern times. There are also important collections of bronze seals, carved jade flowers, and ceramics from South China. Take the KCR to University station, then a campus bus or taxi. ⊠ *Tai Po Rd., Sha Tin* ☎ *2609–7416* ⊕ *www.cuhk.edu.hk/ics/amm* ☜ *Free* ☉ *Mon.–Sat. 10–4:45, Sun. 12:30–5:30.*

need a break?

Across from the Chinese University campus is the popular restaurant **Yucca de Lac** (⊠ Tai Po Rd., Ma Liu Shui Village, Sha Tin ☎ 2691–1630), which serves Chinese meals outdoors in the green hills along Tolo Harbour, affording a pleasant view of the university.

off the
beaten
path

TAP MUN ISLAND – About a 15-minute walk from the Chinese University along Tai Po Road is the Ma Liu Shui Ferry Pier, the starting point for a ferry tour of the harbor and Tap Mun Island. The ferry makes many stops, and if you take the 8:30 AM trip you'll have time to hike around Tap Mun Island and still turn back by late afternoon. The last ferry returning from the island is at 5:30 PM. Tap Mun has a small village with a few Chinese restaurants, but you can also bring a picnic lunch. This trip is better by far in sunny weather. The New Fisherman's Village, on the southern tip of the island, is populated mainly by Hakka fisherwomen. About 1 km (½ mi) north, near the western shore, is the ancient village of Tap Mun, where you'll see old women playing mah-jongg. The huge Tin Hau Temple, dedicated to the goddess of the sea, is one of the oldest temples in Hong Kong and is less than ½ km (¼ mi) north of the village. It sits at the top of a flight of steps that leads down into the water of the harbor; inside are old model junks and, of course, a veiled figure of the goddess herself. Go to the east side of the island to see the Tap Mun Cave and some of the best-kept beaches in the territory. ☎ 2527–2513 for Tsui Wah Ferry schedule ☒ Round-trip ferry: HK$32 weekdays, HK$50 weekends.

▶ **❾ Fanling.** Although this town has the rather spare functional feel of many of the "new towns" and may be of little interest to you, the nearby **Luen Wo Market** is one of the territory's most impressive and well worth a look. A grid of small stalls selling everything from T-shirts to pigs' lungs and the bustle and pungent aromas prove that local merchants can quickly make even a relatively new marketplace feel traditional.

❿ Liu Man Shek Tong. Approached down a small unmarked path in the village of Sheung Shui, this ancestral hall was built in 1751 and was one of few such halls that survived the antihistorical Cultural Revolution of the mid-1960s–mid-1970s. A restoration preserved the spectacular original roofs and ornamentation but substituted concrete walls to take the weight off the rickety pillars—at some cost to the site's aesthetic unity, unfortunately. It is interesting to note that the Liu clan, for whom this hall was built, was obsessed with education: the wood panels hung in the rear hall indicate the education levels achieved by various clan members under the old imperial civil-service-exam system of the Qing Dynasty. Take the KCR to Sheung Shui, then Bus 73K and alight at Sheung Shui Wai on Jockey Club Road. ☒ Sheung Shui ☎ Free ☉ Wed., Thurs., weekends, and public holidays 9–1 and 2–5.

⓫ Luk Keng village. This tiny Hakka village is home to fewer than 200 residents, most of them widows. While most of the existing buildings were constructed in the 1960s (the dates are marked above the entryways), the village abuts the Luk Keng Country Park, which is an egret sanctuary, lending the place a superbly tranquil air. From the KCR stop, take Minibus 56K.

⓮ Sha Tin. Whether you enter Sha Tin by road or rail, you'll be amazed to find this metropolis smack dab in the middle of the New Territories. One of the so-called "new towns," Sha Tin underwent a population explosion starting in the mid-1980s that transformed it from a town of 30,000 to a city of more than a half million in less than 15 years. The town of Sha Tin is where you'll find the popular **Sha Tin Racecourse** (⊠ Sha Tin ☎ 2966–8111 💷 HK$10), Hong Kong's largest and a spectacular place to watch a race. Racing season is from September through June. The racecourse has its own stop on the KCR (stop name is "Racecourse").

The **Hong Kong Heritage Museum** is devoted to Chinese history, art, and culture. Exhibitions are housed in a five-story building surrounded by a traditional Chinese courtyard. Take the KCR to Tai Wai, and then cross the river and walk along it heading northeast. Turn left at Sha Tin Government Secondary School. ⊠ *1 Man Lam Rd., Sha Tin* ☎*2180–8188* ⊕*www.heritagemuseum.gov.hk/eng_main.htm* 💷*HK$10, or included in Museum Tour pass; free Wed.* ☉ *Mon. and Wed.–Sat. 10–6, Sun. 10–7.*

off the
beaten
path

SAI KUNG PENINSULA – To the east of Sha Tin, Sai Kung Peninsula has a few small towns and Hong Kong's most beloved nature preserve. The hikes through the hills surrounding High Island Reservoir are spectacular, and the beaches are among the territory's cleanest, largely because they are sheltered from the effluent that flows out of the Pearl River delta. A number of open-air seafood restaurants dot the area as well. (If you choose to eat in a seafood restaurant, note that physicians caution against eating raw shellfish here because of hepatitis outbreaks.) Take the MTR to Choi Hung and then Bus 92 or 96R, or Minibus 1 to Sai Kung Town. Instead of taking the bus, you can also catch a taxi along **Clearwater Bay Road,** which will take you into forested areas and land that is only partially developed, with Spanish-style villas overlooking the sea. To cruise around the harbor, rent a *kaido* (pronounced "guy-doe"; one of the small boats run by private operators for about HK$130 round-trip), and stop at tiny **Yim Tin Tsai Island,** which has a rustic Catholic mission church built in 1890. **Sai Kung Country Park** has several hiking trails that wind through majestic hills overlooking the water. This excursion will take a full day, and you should go only in sunny weather.

⓬ **Tai Po.** *Tai po* means "shopping place," and the town more than lives up to its name. In the heart of the region's breadbasket, Tai Po is fast becoming a utilitarian "new town," but its main open-air market is a feast for the eyes, with baskets of lush green vegetables, freshly cut meat hanging from great racks overhead, fish swimming in tanks awaiting selection, and all types of baked and steamed treats. Adjacent to the Tai Po market is the 100-year-old **Man Mo Temple;** you'll smell the incense offered by worshippers. The temple is open daily from 9 to 6. To reach the village, take the KCR to the Tai Po Market stop.

⓯ **Temple of Ten Thousand Buddhas.** You have to climb some 500 steps to reach this temple, nestled in the foothills of Sha Tin, but it's worth every step: inside the main temple are nearly 13,000 (a few thousand more

Fodor'sChoice
★

than the name implies) gilded ceramic statues of Buddha, all virtually identical. They were made by Shanghai craftsmen and donated by worshippers. You can also take in a vegetarian meal at a small, no-frills restaurant. From here you can also see the nearby Amah Rock. Amah means "nurse" in Cantonese, and the rock resembles a woman with a child on her back; it's popular with Chinese women. Take the KCR to Sha Tin, and at the exit turn left and walk until you reach Pai Tau Street. At the end of Tai Pau Street are signs that lead to the temple. ⊠ *Sha Tin* 🖾 *Free* ☉ *Daily 9–5.*

THE OUTER ISLANDS

It's easy to forget that Hong Kong is not the only island in these parts. But for residents, the Outer Islands are a popular and important chance to escape the city and enjoy the waterfront, good seafood, and a little peace and quiet. The islands' villages are very much up to speed (and, to the regret of many, cellular phones still work here), but they run at a more humane pace. For maximum relaxation, try to come on a weekday, as the Hong Kong weekenders often come in large numbers and bring their stresses with them.

In addition to Hong Kong Island and the mainland sections of Kowloon and the New Territories, 235 islands were under the control of the British until the handover back to China. The largest, Lantau, is bigger than Hong Kong Island; the smallest is just a few square feet of rock. Most are uninhabited. Others are gradually being developed, but at nowhere near the pace of the main urban areas. A few of the outlying islands are off-limits, occupied by prisons or military bases. The four that are most easily accessible by ferry—Lantau, Lamma, Cheung Chau, and Peng Chau—have become popular residential areas and welcome visitors.

You can reach the islands by scheduled ferry services operated by the **New World First Ferry.** The ferries are easy to recognize by the large letters HKF on their funnels. For most destinations you'll leave from the Outlying Districts Services Pier, in Central, on the land reclamation area just west of the Star Ferry Terminal. Boats to Discovery Bay on Lantau leave from the Star Ferry Terminal itself. For more information, *see* Boat & Ferry Travel *in* Smart Travel Tips.

Numbers in the text correspond to numbers in the margin and on the New Territories and the Outer Islands map.

Lantau

The island of Lantau lies due west of Hong Kong. At 143 square km (55 square mi), it is almost twice the size of Hong Kong Island. Hong Kong's impressive airport Chek Lap Kok is on Lantau, and the island will someday have Disneyland Hong Kong, which is currently under construction at Penny's Bay and due for completion in late 2005 or 2006. In early 2006, another development will likely increase tourism to Lantau. A 5.7-km cable car is being constructed at this writing between the town of Tung Ching and Po Lin Monastery; travelers will be shisked along to the monastery in about 15 minutes. The latter may eventually change the face of Lantau, but for the time being the island is sparsely populated and makes a nice getaway from the city.

a good tour

Because of Lantau's size, you should limit yourself to either the western half (Silvermine Bay, Po Lin Monastery, and Tung Chung) or the eastern half (Discovery Bay, the Trappist monastery, and perhaps Peng Chau) instead of combining both on a single visit. To do the western tour, take the ferry to the town of Mui Wo on **Silvermine Bay** ⑯ ▶, an area being developed as a commuter suburb of Hong Kong Island. Lantau is very mountainous, so for a tour of the outlying villages, plan to hike or take a bus. From Mui Wo, the island's buses head out to the **Po Lin Monastery** ⑰, home of a giant Buddha; **Tai O** ⑱, an ancient fishing village; and **Tung Chung** ⑲, which has a Sung Dynasty fort.

Although the **Trappist Monastery** ⑳ near **Nim Shue Wan** ㉑ can be reached by bus from Silvermine Bay, one alternative is to combine the monastery with other sights on the eastern end of the island by taking the ferry from Central to Discovery Bay. From there it is half-hour walk to the monastery. Ferries for Discovery Bay leave from the Star Ferry Terminal; from the pier in Discovery Bay turn left and walk to Nim Shue Wan, then follow the signs to the monastery. You can also take a small passenger ferry, or kaido, between Peng Chau Island and Nim Shue Wan.

TIMING   The ferry ride from Central to Silvermine Bay takes about an hour, while the trip to Discovery Bay (via faster boats) takes about 25 minutes; after that, you can spend as long on Lantau as you like. The island is worth at least a full day's visit, even two; and you could easily spend a day on just one or two of the attractions listed below, so choose the ones that interest you most. The best overnight accommodations are at the Silvermine Beach Hotel; there's also a hostel next to Po Lin Monastery (the S. G. Davis Hostel), or you can also stay at the Trappist monastery if you write or call for permission far in advance. The HKTB has information on these and other Lantau lodgings.

What to See

㉑ **Nim Shue Wan.** For quiet and solitude, take the 90-minute hike through this old fishing village—where you might see fishermen's grandchildren talking on their cellular phones—and the unspoiled woods and hills beyond. The beaches here would be beautiful except for the astounding amount of trash thrown on them or washed ashore.

⑰ **Po Lin Monastery.** Within the Po Lin, or "Precious Lotus," Monastery in Lantau's mountainous interior, is the world's tallest outdoor bronze statue of Buddha, the **Tin Tan Buddha**—measuring more than 100 feet high and weighing 275½ tons. The statue is all the more impressive for its situation at the peak of a hill, which essentially forces pilgrims to stare up at it as they ascend. The adjacent monastery, gaudy and exuberantly commercial, is known for the vegetarian meals served in the temple refectory. Take the bus marked PO LIN MONASTERY from Mui Wo and ask the driver to let you off at the monastery stop, from which you follow signs. A new cable-car connection to the monastery is expected, at this

FodorśChoice
★

writing, to open in early 2006. ⊠ *Po Lin, Lantau Island* 🎫 *Free* ⊙ *Daily dawn–dusk.*

▶ **⑯ Silvermine Bay.** This area is being developed as a commuters' suburb of Hong Kong Island, but right now the area is still surrounded by terraced fields. You can rent bicycles in front of the **Silvermine Beach Hotel** (⊠ Silvermine Bay, Mui Wo, Lantau Island ☎ 2984–8295) to ride around the village of Mui Wo.

⑱ Tai O. Divided into two parts connected by a modern drawbridge, the village still has many waterfront stilt houses and fishing shanties. However, a fire that devastated part of the old village subsequently raised concerns about the safety of the traditional stilt houses. The fires reportedly spread quickly throughout the homes because of inadequate safety measures when they were built. Today there are plans to rebuild homes under modern safety guidelines, while the dwellings that were spared from the fire are a reminder of earlier village life. Visit the local temple dedicated to Kuanti, the god of war, and taste the local catch at one of Tai O's seafood restaurants. To reach the town, take the bus marked TAI O from the village of Mui Wo.

⑳ Trappist Monastery. Despite its unexpectedly futuristic 1950s architecture, the monastery and its adjacent chapel exude a wonderfully placid air. Founded in 1951, the monastery is reached by a steep wooded path that ends at a footbridge suspended over a small stream. Like many Trappist monasteries, this one served as a working dairy for many years. The walk from Discovery Bay takes about 30 minutes, and you'll know you're on the right path if you find yourself walking through the backyards of the ramshackle huts en route. Follow the poorly marked concrete path from the southwest end of Discovery Bay to the forest, where the signs become more useful. The monastery has simple accommodations, where you can spend the night, but you must make reservations well in advance by writing to or calling the Grand Master. ⊠ *Discovery Bay, Lantau Island* ✑ *Grand Master, Trappist Haven, Lantau Island, Box 5, Peng Chau* ☎ 2987–6292 🎫 *Free* ⊙ *Daily dawn–dusk.*

⑲ Tung Chung. Here an ancient Sung Dynasty fort was evacuated by the Qing Dynasty army in 1898, when the New Territories were leased to Britain. The fort is now an elementary school. Tung Chung's other attraction is its view of Chek Lap Kok Airport. The government plans to build a "new town" here, similar to Sha Tin, which aims to move people from the crowded cities and into the New Territories.

Cheung Chau

Cheung Chau, southwest of Lantau and about one hour from Central by ferry, is Hong Kong's most crowded outlying island (all things being relative), with about 22,000 people. It is most well known as the home of Hong Kong's only Olympic gold medalist, Lee Lai Shan, who won for women's mistral sailing and is affectionately known to the locals as San San. At the tip of the beach is a lovely outdoor restaurant owned by relatives of San San, who have proudly hung a large framed picture of the athlete in her golden moment. The island community mostly live on the sandbar that connects the two hilly tips of this dumbbell-shape entity. Its Mediterranean flavor has attracted artists and writers from around the world, some of whom have formed an expatriate artists' colony here. Cheung Chau also draws Hong Kongers for another reason: its hotels rent by the hour (you'll see their booths in front of the ferry terminal), offering young lovers a brief escape from the congested living quarters and parental oversight of home.

There are no vehicles here—with the exception of a miniature red fire truck—so be prepared to walk around the island. As an alternative, you can take one of the small sampans that ferry year-round from Hong Kong Island to Cheung Chau's beaches, which are virtually deserted and have clear water.

TIMING The ferry from Central takes an hour each way. You can make Cheung Chau a day trip, or you can stay in reasonable comfort at the Cheung Chau Warwick hotel, on East Bay at Tung Wan Beach, just north of Cheung Chau Village.

What to See

②② Cheung Chau Village. The entry into Cheung Chau's harbor, through lines of gaily bannered fishing boats, is an exhilarating experience. Cheung Chau is highly historical, with pirate caves and ancient rock carvings along the waterfront just below the Warwick hotel. Dining out here is also a joy, as there are dozens of open-air cafés on either side of the crowded sandbar township—both on the waterfront **Praya Promenade** and overlooking the main public beach at **Tung Wan.**

②④ Chinese Cemetery. These graves are generally modest and are set very close together, but each one bears a photo, etched onto a porcelain plate, of the person buried below. The ground is littered with fake money (belonging to the Bank of Hell, and denominated in the millions of dollars) that relatives burn to bring the deceased prosperity in the afterlife. The cemetery is 1 km (½ mi) from the ferry pier; turn right from pier and walk along the waterfront until you leave town, then follow paths veering left up the hill. ⊠ *Sin Yan Tseng Village* 🎟 *Free* ⊙ *Daily dawn–dusk.*

②③ Pak Tai Temple. Dedicated to the protector of fishermen, this 200-year-old temple hosts the colorful, springtime Bun Festival, one of Hong Kong's most popular community galas. The festival originated in the 18th century as an appeasement for the spirits of people killed by pirates—spirits thought to wreak plagues upon the village. Beside the main altar are four whalebones from the nearby sea. The temple is ½ km (¼ mi) from the ferry pier; turn left from the pier and walk along the waterfront until you see the temple, a slight uphill walk, next to Fortuna Village. ⊠ *Fortuna Village* 🎟 *Free* ⊙ *Daily dawn–dusk.*

Lamma Island

What Lamma lacks in sights, it makes up for with an abundance of quaint, lackadaisically bustling port-side village charm. The waterfront is lined with restaurants offering alfresco dining and the pleasure of exquisitely fresh seafood plucked live from tanks and cooked on the spot. Once you've feasted, you can work off the meal by taking the hour-long walk through rolling green hills that connects the two main villages.

In addition to its other attractions, Lamma is as close to a 1960s bohemian scene as Hong Kong gets, full of laid-back expatriates driven out of Central by high rents. They have spawned a subculture of vegetarian restaurants, Western health-food shops, and Tibetan crafts stores.

TIMING The ferry from Central to either Sok Kwu Wan or Yung Shue Wan takes about 25 minutes and leaves from the outlying islands ferry piers in front of Exchange Square. It doesn't matter which village you go to first, since the one-hour walk between them is a Lamma highlight. Plan to visit both in a leisurely afternoon.

What to See

26 **Hung Shing Ye Beach.** "Beach" overstates the scale of this small, sandy ocean-side strip next to the Hong Kong Electric power plant. Roughly midway between Sok Kwu Wan and Yung Shue Wan, Hung Shing Ye Beach is a pleasant place to enjoy the sun and is sometimes swimmable, but don't go in if you see plastic bags or other refuse on the water. You can spend the night at the modest 12-room **Concerto Inn** (☎ 2982–1668 🖷 2982–0022 ⊕ www.concertoinn.com.hk); some rooms have nice views, and the inn has a garden café.

27 **Sok Kwu Wan.** The smaller and grittier of Lamma's two villages, Sok Kwu Wan is notable mainly for the string of cavernous seafood restaurants that line the path leading from the pier. If you arrive on foot from Yung Shue Wan, however, your first glimpse of the bay from the hills will be quite stunning.

25 **Yung Shue Wan.** By comparison with Sok Kwu Wan, Yung Shue Wan whirrs with activity. Formerly a farming and fishing village, it has since the early 1980s become an enclave for expats, especially artists and journalists. Main Street is lined with small shops selling handicrafts and the occasional bohemian outpost, although the lingering smell of the fish markets is a reminder of Lamma's humbler, less cosmopolitan origins. **Craft Inn** (✉ 56 Main St., Yung Shue Wan ☎ 2982–2120) sells handmade crafts and jewelry from across the region.

need a break? The hub of expat community life (and a great place for vegetarian food) is the **Bookworm Café** (✉ 79 Main St., Yung Shue Wan ☎ 2982–4838), which bills itself as a "health café with net surfing and community happenings."

Peng Chau

The tiniest of Hong Kong's four major Outer Islands, Peng Chau was once home to a few farmers, fishermen, and a fireworks factory. Although the factory has long since closed and the island has been discovered as a weekend retreat for Hong Kong's city folk, the port-side community feeling remains.

Stand on the Peng Chau ferry quay and watch the kaido for Lantau's Trappist monastery sputter toward dark-green hills. Breathe in that stirring aroma of Hong Kong's islands—a mix of salt air, shrimp paste, and dried fish combined with a strong dose of local pride and a sense of independence, both of which have been lost in urban Hong Kong.

The ferry from Central takes an hour each way; alternatively, you can make a short hop from Nim Shue Wan on Lantau in about 15 minutes. Go on a sunny afternoon, if possible, and plan to spend about two hours.

28 **Peng Chau Village.** The village is small and charming, and its shopping district is known for its unpretentious little stores selling locally made porcelain at remarkably low prices.

> **need a break?** Peng Chau doesn't have Lamma's lively café scene, but the **Forest** (⊠ 38C Wing Hing St., Peng Chau ☎ 2983–8837), a stone's throw away from the ferry pier, is a popular watering hole that also serves Thai food.

Other Islands

If you have extra time or a venturesome spirit, try one of Hong Kong's more out-of-the-way islands, not so easy to reach but all the more rewarding for their isolation.

Ping Chau

29 This minuscule island, not to be confused with Peng Chau, is 2½ square km (1 square mi) of land in the far northeast of the New Territories, near the mainland coast. Now almost deserted, it has a checkered history. Guns and opium were once smuggled out of China through Ping Chau, and during the Cultural Revolution many mainlanders swam through shark-infested waters in hope of reaching Ping Chau and the freedom of Hong Kong. The island's largest village, **Sha Tau,** is something of a ghost town, with many cottages boarded up, but here and there you'll find old farming families eager to take you in, maybe even for the night.

A large part of the island is country parkland, with footpaths overgrown with orchids, wild mint, and morning glories. Look for the strange rock formations at either end of the island. At the south end are two huge rocks known as the **Drum Rocks,** or Watchman's Tower Rocks. At the north end is a chunk of land that has broken away from the island; the Chinese say it represents the head of a dragon.

Plan your visit for a weekend and be prepared to stay the night, as the ferry to Ping Chau departs only on Saturday at 11:15 AM and returns only on Sunday at 11:15 AM. Bring camping gear, or accept lodging from villagers if they offer. You board the ferry at Ma Liu Shui, near the University KCR stop. Since there is only one daily ferry, be sure to verify the timing with the HKTB before you leave.

Po Toi Island

30 A chain of three barren little fishing islands, virtually unchanged since medieval times, sits in the extreme southeast of Hong Kong's waters. Only Po Toi Island itself is inhabited (sort of), with a population of fewer than 100. It offers spectacular walks and a fine seafood restaurant, which is the only restaurant on the island.

Walk uphill past primitive dwellings, many deserted, to the Tin Hau Temple, or walk east through the hamlet of Wan Tsai, past banana and papaya groves, to Po Toi's famous **rock carvings.** The geometric patterns on these rocks are believed to have been carved during the local Bronze Age, about 2,500 years ago.

A trip to the Po Toi Islands is an all-day affair. There's only one restaurant on the island, which is very popular with day-trippers. **Ferries to Po Toi** leave Aberdeen on Sunday and public holidays at 8 AM and from St. Stephen's Beach in Stanley at 10 or 11:30 AM. Ferries return at 3 and 4:30 PM directly to St. Stephen's Beach, or at 6 PM to Aberdeen via St. Stephen's Beach. You can call to make reservations, but you'll need the help of a Cantonese speaker. A round-trip costs HK$40.

WHERE TO EAT

2

Updated by
Tim Metcalfe

WHEREVER YOU GO IN HONG KONG, you're bound to see a restaurant sign. Establishments that sell prepared food are as old as Chinese culture itself, and because most people live in small apartments and have little space to entertain at home, restaurants are usually the chosen venues for special occasions and family gatherings. Cooking may be more varied in Hong Kong than anywhere else in the world. Cantonese cuisine, for which Hong Kong is famous since most residents trace their roots to Guangdong (Canton) Province, has been long regarded by Chinese gourmands as the most intricate and sophisticated in Asia. However, the Cantonese are noted for cooking foods you might not think edible; as one saying goes, if it has four legs and isn't a table, the Cantonese will steam, stir-fry, or boil it. Specialties include pigeon, bird's nest soup, shark's-fin soup, and abalone.

You shouldn't leave Hong Kong without trying Cantonese dim sum. These light snacks, served for lunch or breakfast in local teahouses as well as fine restaurants, are usually served in steaming bamboo baskets. Dim sum includes a variety of dumplings, buns, and pastries containing meat and vegetables.

Seafood is another year-round favorite in Hong Kong. Plentiful and delicious, live fish and shellfish are kept in tanks at many restaurants, so you can handpick your dinner and be assured of freshness. Steamed *garoupa* (grouper) and poached shrimp with chili and soy sauce are two specialties.

Of course, you can also find restaurants serving specialties from throughout China. Beijing-style cuisine is based on noodles and dumplings and is often strongly spiced with coriander, peppers, and garlic. Shanghainese cuisine is typically seasoned with sugar, soy sauce, and wine. Late autumn is the best time to try a Shanghainese specialty, freshwater hairy crabs. Szechuan food includes some of the spiciest dishes in China (check the chili codes on the menus) but not all dishes are spicy.

The deeply rooted Chinese love of good food also extends here to French, Italian, Portuguese, British, Spanish, Australian, Japanese, Indian, Thai, Vietnamese, Korean, Mexican, and specialty American fare. It's likely you will be able to find something from almost every culinary region on earth.

Be advised, however, that Hong Kong's extraordinary culinary vitality is offset by some of Asia's worst restaurants. It's possible to find a hole-in-the-wall with unexpectedly exciting food, but don't expect any old neighborhood restaurant to turn out dreamy dishes. In fact, you might expect more exciting food in places that are often shunned in other cities. Hong Kongers regularly patronize hotel restaurants, bars, and coffee shops. Service is usually better, and the quality of the food more consistent, than in many independent restaurants.

Restaurants in Hong Kong tend to change menus as often as people change their clothes, following the season and the clientele's tastes. Don't be surprised if your favorite dish is no longer on the list the second time you visit.

2

Dress "Smart-casual" is the norm for dress in most restaurants in Hong Kong. Even top-class venues like Gaddi's at the Peninsula have abandoned their old-fashioned jacket-and-tie policy—a change that is long overdue given the stifling heat during much of the year. Shorts and sneakers are the telltale signs of a tourist and are generally tolerated, but they should not normally be worn at pricier restaurants. If you're off the beaten track—on Lamma Island or in Sai Kung, for example—you can turn up barefoot in a wet swimsuit and nobody will bat an eye. We mention dress only when men are required to wear a jacket or a jacket and tie.

Hours Dim sum restaurants normally open about 7:30 AM and close about 2:30 PM. Some are shut between 10 and 11:30 AM. Dim sum restaurants often teem with people on weekends, so expect to wait at the more popular places. Western-style restaurants, such as Irish pubs and steak houses, are open from about 11 AM to 10:30 PM; dinner is busiest, around 7 PM. Unless otherwise noted, the restaurants listed in this guide are open daily for lunch and dinner.

Ordering For many kinds of Asian cuisines, in particular Chinese cuisine, food is meant to be shared. Instead of having an entrée for yourself, a table—whether it's 2 or 12 people—will order several dishes to share. For example, a table of 4 might order a whole or half chicken, a vegetable, a fish dish, a meat dish, and fried noodles, all of which are placed on a lazy Susan and made available to everyone at the table. The sizes and prices of the dishes can also be altered according to the number of diners.

Prices In this chapter, the price ranges reflect the range of actual prices of main courses on the dinner menu (unless dinner isn't served), but keep in mind that an average main dish is normally shared among two to four diners and several are ordered for the table, and this will affect the final cost of your dinner. Please note that market prices of seafood, and prices of outrageously expensive dishes and specialties—abalone, bird's nest, shark's fin—are not included in the price range to avoid misleading conclusions. In many sophisticated restaurants, fresh seafood prices vary daily and are determined by the weight (ask the waiter for the market price). Some restaurants are marked with a price range ($$–$$$$), for example, which indicates that the main course prices straddle two or more categories.

WHAT IT COSTS In HK$				
$$$$	$$$	$$	$	¢
AT DINNER over $300	$200–$300	$100–$200	$60–$100	under $60

Prices are per person for a main course at dinner and do not include the customary 10% service charge.

Paying

Try not to be shocked when you get your bill. You'll be charged for everything, including tea, rice, and even those side dishes placed automatically on every table, which are often mistaken for complimentary snacks.

Reservations

Reservations are always a good idea, but they are often essential at lunchtime (between 1 and 2) and at dinnertime (between 7 and 10) on weekends; additionally, reservations are often necessary in the big hotel restaurants, and in the trendy SoHo and Lan Kwai Fong restaurants during Chinese holidays. Large parties should always call ahead to check the reservations policy. Hong Kongers have a nasty habit of reserving tables at several restaurants for the same night then deciding which one to honor at the last moment without calling the other restaurants to cancel; so don't be surprised if the restaurant calls you to double-check to make sure you indeed intend on dining at their establishment.

Tipping

Tips are expected (10% average gratuity) at most restaurants, even if the bill includes a service charge—the service charge on your check does not go to the waiters, the restaurants actually keep that money.

Wine, Beer & Spirits

The drinking age in bars is 18, although it doesn't appear to be enforced. You can find most brands of imported alcohol and an excellent array of imported beers as well as the locally brewed San Miguel. Most nightlife spots offer happy-hour specials, sometimes starting as early as 3 PM and continuing until 10 PM. It's worth shopping around for happy-hour prices since a small bottle of Heineken, one of the most available bottled beers, costs about HK$62 outside happy hour at many nightspots.

HONG KONG ISLAND

Central & SoHo

One of the busiest sections of Hong Kong, Central is a madhouse at lunchtime, when hungry office workers crowd the streets and eateries. Most restaurants have set lunches with speedy service, making it possible for most customers to get in and out within an hour; these are generally good values. Evening dining is either formal or a quick bite followed by many drinks, especially in Central's nightlife center, a warren of cobbled backstreets called Lan Kwai Fong. Another social area is just a few minutes' walk uphill in SoHo (the area south of Hollywood Road), spreading mainly along Elgin Street, Staunton Street, and Old Bailey Street, accessible by the long, outdoor Midlevels Escalator. Almost every kind of cuisine can be found here, including Spanish, Italian, Indian, Argentinian, Cuban, Cajun, French, Portuguese, and Russian. Quality and authenticity of the food varies—but it's worth a visit to experience the SoHo atmosphere. Restaurants in both Lan Kwai Fong and SoHo have a somewhat contrived quality, with highly stylized themes and menus, along with relatively steep prices. All these places are near the Central MTR stop.

Asian

CANTONESE   ✕ **China Lan Kwai Fong.** In the heart of trendy Lan Kwai Fong and styled
$$–$$$$ after "old Shanghai," this elegant restaurant serves up a culinary jour-
ney through China, with regional delicacies from Guangdong, Chiu Chow,
Szechuan, Beijing, and Shanghai. Traditional touches include ceiling fans,
terra-cotta warriors, and chirping birds in antique cages. Specialties in-
clude panfried Szechuan-style king prawns, Shanghainese crystal river
shrimp, and diced beef tenderloin with chili and black pepper served in
a potato basket. Check out the all-you-can-eat dim sum brunch on
weekends (HK$128). Reservations are recommended for weekend
brunch. ✉ *17–22 Lan Kwai Fong, Lan Kwai Fong* ☎ 2536–0968
▭ *AE, DC, MC, V.*

$$–$$$$ ✕ **Luk Yu Tea House.** Food takes a backseat to atmosphere in this institution. Luk Yu is a living museum with extraordinary character—it's
been in business since the 1940s, offering a rare glimpse of old colonial
Hong Kong from the Chinese perspective. Don't expect top-notch service and attentive waiters. It's a traditional and typically noisy Chinese
teahouse with carved wooden doors, hardwood panels, marble facings,
and spittoons—and waiters dressed in traditional Chinese garb. Morning dim sum is especially popular and seats can be hard to come by at
peak afternoon hours (1–2 PM) unless you're a regular. ✉ *24–26 Stanley St., Central* ☎ 2523–1970 ▭ *MC, V.*

★ $$–$$$$ ✕ **Man Wah.** Unlike most bustling Cantonese restaurants, this is a re-
fined haven, with panoramic views over Victoria Harbor. Hand-carved
gold-and-ebony chopsticks polish off each place setting, the service is
impeccable, and the rosewood decor is elegant. The cuisine is exquisite,
though pricey: this is definitely a place to impress a guest. Lychee prawns
are a seasonal specialty in summer. Steamed chicken in ginger and rice
wine is a year-round signature dish, along with sautéed fillet of sole with
chilies in black-bean sauce. For dessert try the poached pear in tanger-
ine tea. ✉ *Mandarin Oriental Hotel, 5 Connaught Rd., Central*
☎ *2522–0111 Ext. 4025* ▭ *AE, DC, MC, V.*

$$–$$$$ ✕ **Yung Kee.** Since 1950 this massive eatery has served Cantonese food
Fodor'sChoice   amid riotous decor and writhing gold dragons. Convenient to both ho-
★   tels and businesses, Yung Kee specializes in roast goose with beautifully
crisp skin. More adventurous palates may wish to check out the famous
thousand-year-old eggs with ginger, which melt in your mouth. Among
the good seafood offerings are sautéed fillet of pomfret with chili and
black-bean sauce or braised garoupa. ✉ *32–40 Wellington St., Central*
☎ *2522–1624* ▭ *AE, DC, MC, V.*

¢–$ ✕ **Tsui Wah Restaurant.** Looking for a hearty meal in Central doesn't mean
you have to spend a fortune, as is the case here. Join the locals and order
a mixture of milk, tea, and coffee. From toasted sandwiches to noodles,
fried rice to steak, this joint has almost anything you could possibly want.
Although it's not quite what typical Hong Kongers would make at
home, it's as close as you can come to Chinese comfort food. Noodles
and fried rice are some of the safest bets for timid palates. There's also
a wide range of set meals with very reasonable prices. ✉ *15 Wellington St., Central* ☎ *2525–6338* ▭ *No credit cards.*

¢   ✕ **Mak's Noodles Limited.** Mak's looks like any other Hong Kong noodle shop, but it's one of the best known in town, with a reputation far exceeding its humble decor. The restaurant takes such pride in its fame that copies of its reviews—including a write-up in *Time* magazine—are displayed at every table. The premises are clean, the attentive staff wear smart-looking uniforms, and the menu includes some particularly inventive dishes, such as tasty pork-chutney noodles. The real test of a good noodle shop, however, is its wontons, and here they're fresh, delicate, and filled with whole shrimp. ⊠ *77 Wellington St., Central* ☎ *2854–3810* ▭ *No credit cards.*

HUNAN   ✕ **Hunan Garden.** This serene restaurant serves spicy-hot Hunan cuisine.
$–$$ Crispy fried-fish "butterflies" (thinly sliced carp pieces deep-fried and dipped in a very sweet coating) are a recommended appetizer. The spicy fried chicken with chili may well set your lips and throat on fire; if you like things milder, stick with the codfish fillet with fried minced beans— the chewy and nutty bean paste goes perfectly with the fillet's soft texture. For an authentic experience try the warm Shaoxing wine; request lemon slices with the wine for a zestier aroma. Chinese musicians provide an instrumental accompaniment for your meal. ⊠ *3/F, The Forum, Exchange Sq., Central* ☎ *2868–2880* ▭ *AE, DC, MC, V.*

INDIAN   ✕ **VEDA.** Hong Kong's only "new wave" Indian restaurant is a culinary
$$–$$$ journey to the best of India's regional cuisines, presented in a refreshingly modern style. Main courses like venison with Himalayan berry chutney, tandoori lobster, and roast duck with coconut, or desserts like coconut crème brûlée, underline how VEDA is revolutionizing Indian cuisine in Hong Kong. Chef Rajiv Singh Gulshan is simply a master of his craft. The South India lunch thali, with lassi, is a remarkable value at HK$88, as is the two-course set lunch at HK$128 (three courses, HK$148). Reservations are necessary on weekends. ⊠ *8 Arbuthnot Rd., Central* ☎ *2868–5885* ▭ *AE, DC, MC, V.*

$–$$$ ✕ **Tandoor.** One of Hong Kong's oldest Indian restaurants closed for several years but is back in a new location with a renewed sense of adventure for those seeing more than standard fare. This classy curry house has long been a favorite among the business community, and despite a new design with touches resembling a maharajah's palace, the alcoves and wooden floors remain. Chef Anil Khurana's exceptional dishes include spicy prawns and lamb with fresh fenugreek leaves. The lunch buffet gives you the most value for your money. At night a traditional live Indian band performs. ⊠ *1/F, Lyndhurst Tower, 1 Lyndhurst Terr., Central* ☎ *2845–2262* ▭ *AE, DC, MC, V.*

ITALIAN   ✕ **DiVino.** This ultracool wine bar feels like something straight out of
$$–$$$ Milan, bringing with it small plates for casual snacking and mixed platters ideal for sharing. Tempting morsels are scallop risotto and an aubergine tartlet. Tailor-made cold-cut platters are superb; the cheese board is served with crusty, oven-warm bread. Unusual main courses like gnocchi with lamb and mushroom sauce, or salmon with lentils, make a nice change. Desserts embrace all the Italian classics. You get complimentary savory treats with your wine from 6 to 8 PM, and at 7:30 a special surprise dish of the day is shared with all the restau-

For those times when all you want is a quick bite, consider these local chains, which have locations all over Hong Kong.

Cafe de Coral: Hong Kong's biggest fast-food chain caters to the lunch-box crowd with hearty, wholesome, value-for-money Chinese dishes of mostly pork or chicken served with a large helping of rice and vegetables. It's not the fanciest Chinese food around, but if you're not too fussy, it inexpensively fills empty stomachs.

2

Delifrance: French-style baguette rolls, quiche, "combo" breakfasts, and pastries are the specialty of Delifrance, which has over 20 branches. The cheese-puff is highly recommended, and so are the Danish pastries. Inexpensive and tasty fare plus a decent cup of coffee keeps most branches full all day.

KFC: Of all the international fast-food chains, KFC is the one that is most like those at home. If you enjoy your seasoned fried chicken with mashed potato and coleslaw in New York or London, you won't be disappointed at any of the dozens of branches here, which is more than can be said for some of the other fast-food icons.

Oliver's: Made-to-order sandwiches and fresh coffee are the favorites at Oliver's, with a dozen branches around Hong Kong, including one at the airport. The fillings are fresh, full, and tasty. You can get such standbys as egg salad, turkey, ham, beef, and cheese, all with lettuce and tomato.

Pacific Coffee: Starbucks has a rival in Pacific Coffee, where Hong Kong yuppies take café latte or cappuccino while immersed in their laptops. There's not much solid food served here, except for muffins, but this is for the same crowd who hit the gyms regularly, so perhaps they don't eat. A big plus is the free Internet service in most stores, though you're limited to 15 minutes at a time if other people are waiting.

Prêt à Manger: The upmarket British chain has exported its brand of fresh, wholesome sandwiches, coffees, cakes, sushi, and salads that have proved so popular with London's office workers to several outlets in Hong Kong, including one at the Central MTR station, a location above the check-in desk for the Airport Express in Central, and in the Lippo Centre in Admiralty.

---

rant's patrons. ⊠ *G/F, 73 Wyndham St., Central* ☎ *2167–8883* ▭ *AE, DC, MC, V.*

$$ ✕ **Nove.** Seductively draped in burgundy, Nove is Central's most elegant and romantic newcomer, matched by an authentic northern Italian menu from the repertoire of a Tuscan farmhouse kitchen. Good choices from a tradition-minded menu include monkfish wrapped in salted pork fat, panfried pigeon with cabbage, porcini mushroom flan, and black-

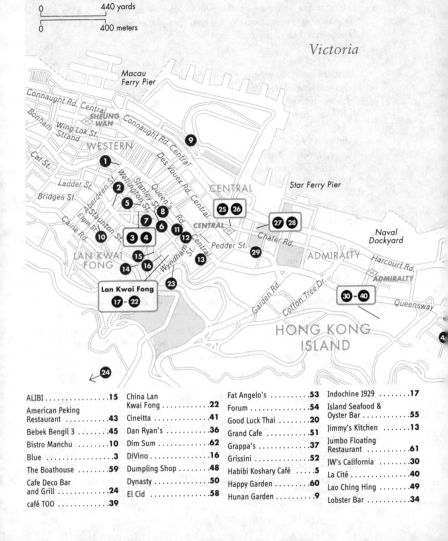

Where to Eat on Hong Kong Island

0 _____ 440 yards
0 _____ 400 meters

Victoria

Macau
Ferry Pier

Connaught Rd. Central

SHEUNG WAN

Connaught Rd. Central

Bonham Strand

Wing Lok St.

WESTERN

Cat St.

Des Voeux Rd. Central

Ladder St.

Bridges St.

Aberdeen St.

Staunton St.

Wellington St.

Stanley St.

Queen's Rd.

CENTRAL

Star Ferry Pier

Elgin St.

Caine Rd.

Queen's Rd. Central

CENTRAL

Chater Rd.

Naval Dockyard

LAN KWAI FONG

Wyndham St.

D'Aguilar St.

Pedder St.

ADMIRALTY

Harcourt Rd.

Lan Kwai Fong

Garden Rd.

Cotton Tree Dr.

ADMIRALTY

Queensway

HONG KONG ISLAND

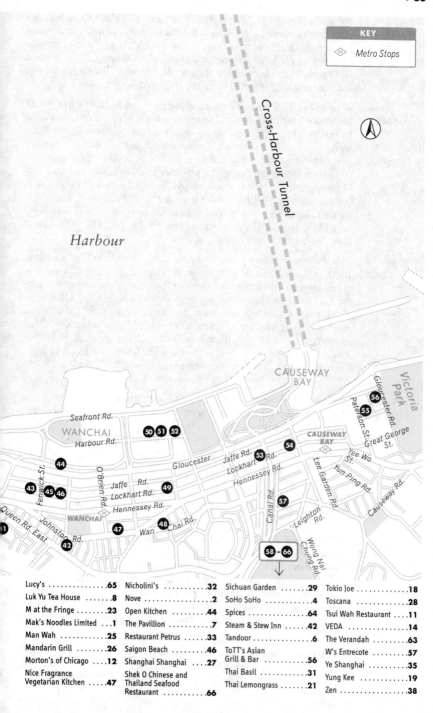

KEY

◈ Metro Stops

Cross-Harbour Tunnel

Harbour

CAUSEWAY BAY

Victoria Park

Seafront Rd.

WANCHAI

Harbour Rd.

Gloucester St.

Paterson St.

Great George St.

50 **51** **52**

56

55

CAUSEWAY BAY Ⓜ

Yee Wo St.

Gloucester

Jaffe Rd.

53

Lockhart Rd.

54

Yun Ping Rd.

44

O'Brien Rd.

Jaffe Rd.

Hennessey Rd.

Lee Garden Rd.

Causeway Rd.

43 **45** **46**

Lockhart Rd.

49

Fenwick St.

Hennessey Rd.

57

Canal Rd.

Leighton Rd.

Queen Rd. East

WANCHAI Ⓜ

47

48

Wan Chai Rd.

58 – 66

Johnston Rd.

42

↓

Wong Nai Chung Rd.

eye cod with polenta. Half-baked chocolate cake with Grand Marnier, passion-fruit essence, and pistachio ice cream—though hardly traditional—is the popular signature dessert. "Lite Lunch" is invitingly priced at HK$108 or HK$128 for two or three courses. Boutique Italian wines and exotic cocktails complete the decadent formula. ⊠ *49 Hollywood Rd., Central* ☎ *2545–9889* ⊟ *AE, DC, MC, V* ☉ *Closed Sun.*

JAPANESE ✕ **Tokio Joe.** This funky casual Japanese joint serves "user-friendly Jap-
$$–$$$$ anese food" with attentive and courteous finesse, yet without intimidating formality. The atmosphere is fun—beautiful ceramic pots line faux-fur walls. Chefs work in a central bar area, lending a wonderfully contemporary twist to some classic dishes: the house sushi roll, for example, contains a mixture of deep-fried soft-shell crab, avocado, and crab roe. Other options include seafood ramen, battered tempura shrimp, and broiled sea bass. Ask for a recommended sake. For dessert, try homemade sesame ice cream. ⊠ *16 Lan Kwai Fong, Lan Kwai Fong* ☎ *2525–1889* ⌘ *Reservations essential* ⊟ *AE, DC, MC, V* ☉ *Closed Sun. No lunch.*

MANCHURIAN ✕ **Bistro Manchu.** This smart and cozy little bistro serves up warming,
$–$$$ soothing, stomach-filling Manchurian cuisine. Noodles, dumplings, vegetables, and meat are mainstays of these rarely encountered northern Chinese specialties. The vegetable stew is a large bowl full of eggplant, potato, cabbage, and green beans in a clear broth. Other menu staples include smoked chicken, cumin lamb, refreshing *lapi* salad (potato noodles and thinly sliced bean curd in sesame dressing), and handmade sorghum noodles. To complement the hearty dishes savor from the vast array of Chinese teas or sweet Harbin beer. ⊠ *33 Elgin St., SoHo* ☎ *2536–9218 or 2536–9996* ⊟ *AE, DC, MC, V.*

SHANGHAINESE ✕ **Shanghai Shanghai.** This retro-Chinese restaurant with art deco
★ ¢–$$ touches, stained glass, discreet private rooms, and wooden booths captures the atmosphere of 1930s Shanghai. The menu ranges from simple Shanghainese midnight snacks and cold appetizers, such as mock goose and smoked fish, to pricey delicacies such as abalone. After 9 PM the lights dim and a chanteuse croons favorites requested by diners. This intimate restaurant has become a hot spot for affluent Chinese reminiscing about the good old days. ⊠ *Ritz-Carlton Hotel, 3 Connaught Rd., basement, Central* ☎ *2869–0328* ⌘ *Reservations essential* ⊟ *AE, DC, MC, V* ☉ *Closed Sun.*

SZECHUAN ✕ **Sichuan Garden.** This spacious restaurant is renowned for its exotic
¢–$$ Szechuan delicacies such as the delectable deep-fried bean curd stuffed with mashed shrimp. Fried sliced mutton with spring onion and sesame pockets is another menu highlight; to eat this delicacy you stuff the warm sesame pocket with the tender fried meat and make your own Szechuan-style mutton sandwich. Friendly and attentive service adds to the overall score. ⊠ *The Landmark, 3/F, Gloucester Tower, Central* ☎ *2521–4433* ⊟ *AE, DC, MC, V.*

THAI ✕ **Thai Lemongrass.** Regional Thai cuisine is served with a modern twist
$–$$$ in this relaxed and comfortable restaurant with large windows providing some natural light. The menu highlights dishes from three different

A CHINESE SAMPLER

CHINESE CUISINE is as varied as the country is large. However, you'll find that five major styles are prominent in Hong Kong cooking, and not all of these will be familiar to the Western palate.

Beijingese. This hearty fare is designed for the chilly climate of northern China—noodles, dumplings, and breads are more evident than rice. Peking duck is a perennial favorite. Firm flavors—such as garlic, ginger, and leek—are popular.

Cantonese. The most popular cuisine in Hong Kong favors meats and fresh vegetables. The Cantonese ideal is to bring out the natural taste of each ingredient by cooking them all quickly at very high temperatures. The result must be served and eaten immediately.

Chiu Chow. The Chiu Chow have a gutsy, hearty cuisine that has never caught on in the West. Specialties include Iron Buddha

tea (a very strong, dark tea), thick shark's-fin soup, soya goose, whelk (snails), bird's nest soup, and dumplings; irresistible cold crabs are served with vinegar.

Shanghainese. Shanghai has a cosmopolitan cuisine that especially favors seafood. Rich-flavored Shanghainese hairy crabs are winter favorites; sautéed freshwater shrimp are also a staple. Many dishes are fried and can be a bit greasy. Shanghai is also famous for its great varieties of buns and dumplings.

Szechuan. Szechuan (more often rendered as Sichuan now) is renowned for its spicy flavors. Szechuan rice, bamboo, wheat, river fish, shellfish, chicken, and pork dishes are all prepared with plenty of salt, anise, fennel seed, chili, and coriander. The ingredients are cooked slowly for an integrated flavor—the opposite of Cantonese food. The cooking style features an eye-watering array of chilis.

regions of Thailand. Your gourmet tour could include grilled, whole, freshwater fish and herbs cooked in banana leaves with coriander-chili sauce (north and northeast); sizzling seafood mousse with light red curry and coconut milk, or roast duck in red curry (Central Plains); or Thai barbecued lamb cutlets (south). ☒ *30–32 D'Aguilar St., California Tower, Lan Kwai Fong* ☎ *2905–1688* ▤ *AE, DC, MC, V* ☉ *No lunch Sun.*

¢–$$ ✕ **Good Luck Thai.** If you're around Lan Kwai Fong at meal time but don't feel like spending a fortune, this Thai spot is one of your best options. Tucked in a dead-end street, the hole-in-the-wall offers hearty and unpretentious Thai food with very friendly prices and service. Pad thai, grilled chicken, and diced beef wrapped in lettuce are just some of the favorites here. Enjoy the alfresco seating as you watch the world go by. The nearby bars and pubs are great choices for a pre-meal aperitif and after-dinner drinks. ☒ *13 Wing Wah La., Lan Kwai Fong* ☎ *2877–2971* ▤ *No credit cards* ☉ *Closed Sun.*

VIETNAMESE   ✕ **Indochine 1929.** This stunningly successful restaurant resembles a
★ $–$$$ French plantation veranda in colonial Indochina. The food is as tasty as it is authentic; in fact, most of the ingredients are imported from Viet-

nam. Highlights include soft-shell crab, fried beef and tomato, stir-fried fillet of pork, and fried fish Hanoi style (using northern spices). This is not the cheapest Vietnamese food in town, but it's arguably the best. The staff's traditional costumes—*ao dais,* straight, elegant silk gowns worn over flowing pants—and the surrounding old maps and antique fans and lamps add to the authentic atmosphere. ⊠ *2/F, California Tower, 30–32 D'Aguilar St., Lan Kwai Fong* ☏ *2869–7399* ▤ *AE, DC, MC, V* ⊘ *No lunch Sun.*

European

MODERN BRITISH

★ **$$**

✕ **SoHo SoHo.** Modern British cuisine is creating culinary waves, and this smart little restaurant is a prime representative in Hong Kong. SoHo SoHo takes traditional dishes, combines them with eclectic ingredients, and transforms them into modern classics. The roast cod with white beans, chorizo, and garlic aioli is Mediterranean-influenced, while the lamb shank shepherd's pie with parsnip carrot topping is a more traditionally British culinary highlight. Don't miss the sticky toffee and the bread-and-butter puddings. The crowds testify to a winning formula of high-quality and delicious food, helpful service, and value for money. ⊠ *43 Lyndhurst Terr., Central* ☏ *2147–2618* ▤ *AE, DC, MC, V* ⊘ *Closed Sun.*

CONTINENTAL

★ **$$$–$$$$**

✕ **Mandarin Grill.** The colonial atmosphere, impeccable service, and deliciously comfortable seats make this a particular treat. You can start your day with kippers and kedgeree for breakfast and end with a dinner of duck pressed table-side, or top-quality meat such as Angus or Kobe beef, Dutch veal, or Australian lamb, prepared on the open grill. Live lobsters and bouillabaisse are highlights for those who favor *fruits de mer.* Sunday champagne brunch (HK$350) is popular for its vast selection and is a good choice for families. ⊠ *1/F, Mandarin Oriental Hotel, 5 Connaught Rd., Central* ☏ *2522–0111 Ext. 4020* ⌕ *Reservations essential* ▤ *AE, DC, MC, V.*

$$–$$$

✕ **ALIBI Bar & Brasserie.** Sleek and chic, ALIBI attracts the so-called beautiful people, including visiting celebrities, for brasserie cuisine using organically farmed meats, wild seafood, and organic whole grains. Specialties of British chef David Maclean include beef carpaccio with caramelized pork, ravioli stuffed with Persian feta, and double-roasted duck with jasmine tea and fresh peach sauce (which takes three days to make). For dessert, his mascarpone *crème vanille* with champagne fruit is exceptional. An all-day prix-fixe menu from brunch through the afternoon is in the HK$90–HK$175 range. Last orders aren't until 1 AM in case you get peckish in the cosmopolitan bar downstairs. ⊠ *73 Wyndham St., Central* ☏ *2167–1676* ▤ *AE, DC, MC, V.*

$$–$$$

✕ **Jimmy's Kitchen.** One of the oldest restaurants in Hong Kong, Jimmy's opened in 1928 and has been catering to a loyal clientele of mostly "old China" hands ever since. The setting is shamelessly colonial, with dark-wood booths and brass fittings. The menu features comfort food as charmingly old fashioned as the place itself: everything from corned beef and cabbage to a traditional mixed grill. Other specialties include borscht, goulash, and bangers and mash, plus Asian selections ranging from curry to fried rice. Homey desserts include rhubarb tart and bread-and-butter pudding. ⊠ *South China Bldg., 1 Wyndham St., basement, Central* ☎ *2526–5293* ▤ *AE, DC, MC, V.*

$–$$$
Fodor'sChoice
★

✕ **M at the Fringe.** M is consistently hailed as Hong Kong's best restaurant by magazine food critics and polls alike, and deservedly so. Michelle Garnaut, the founder, sets herself above the rest with a menu and style that defies categorization, embracing French, European, Turkish, Lebanese, and Italian cuisines. The common denominator is, she says, "simple, good, down-to-earth food that I like to eat and cook," from rabbit, homemade sausages, and her trademark slow-cooked lamb to antipasto or meze platters, suckling pig, and creamy fish pie. Her pavlova is legendary, but try it amid her grand dessert platter of eight bite-size desserts (HK$198 for two). ⊠ *1/F, South Block, 2 Lower Albert Rd., Central* ☎ *2877–4000* ⌂ *Reservations essential* ▤ *AE, MC, V* ⊙ *No lunch Sun.*

$$
✕ **The Pavilion.** Located in one of the best-hidden alleys in the hub of the city, the Pavilion is a secret gem. The 17th-century French decor is quite different from anywhere else in Hong Kong. The well-prepared food complements the refined setting—appetizers of seared scallops and beef tenderloin carpaccio share the menu with roast cod fillets and rack of lamb on rosemary polenta. The restaurant's sister, El Pomposo, which is next door, offers a mellow ambience for a glass of wine and Spanish tapas. ⊠ *3 Tun Wo La., Central* ☎ *2869–7768* ▤ *AE, DC, MC, V.*

ITALIAN
★ **$$$–$$$$**

✕ **Toscana.** One of the best Italian restaurants in Asia, Toscana is classical dining at its finest; sumptuous, elegant, and relaxed—equally ideal for an impressive business lunch or a romantic dinner. The opulent atmosphere is matched by chef Umberto Bombana's cuisine, hand-picked wines, and friendly service. Signature dishes include braised veal shank, pigeon served with foie gras, rack of lamb, and sea bass—all prepared with outstanding originality. A roasted mango, banana, and wild berry tart is a perfect finale. The three-course executive lunch is a bargain treat at HK$338. ⊠ *Ritz-Carlton, 3 Connaught Rd., Central* ☎ *2532–2062* ▤ *AE, DC, MC, V* ⊙ *Closed Sun.*

International

AMERICAN/
STEAK
$$$$

✕ **Morton's of Chicago.** Unashamedly carnivorous, the American steak house has finally extended its global chain to Hong Kong. If you crave the best-quality steak money can buy, this is it. All the classics are here: double filet mignon, porterhouse, New York strip sirloin, and Cajun rib eye, together with such Morton's trademarks as Sicilian veal chop, jumbo lump crab cakes, shrimp Alexander, and Maine lobster. You're charged extra for any potato or vegetables (even fried onions) so the bill mounts up. But you can't beat it for an expense-account lunch. Don't miss the calorie-packed Godiva hot chocolate cake. ⊠ *3/F and 4/F, Entertainment Bldg., 30 Queen's Rd., Central* ☎ *2804–6996* ▤ *AE, DC, MC, V.*

AUSTRALIAN
$$–$$$

✕ **Blue.** Renowned for its fusion cuisine and savvy decor, Australian-owned Blue is one of the most stylish restaurants in Hong Kong and *the* place to see and be seen around SoHo. High ceilings, soft lighting, and glass-and-chrome furnishings set the scene for imaginative dishes like sliced beef stacked with layers of crisp Parmesan wafers and Stilton mayonnaise. Blue also serves an imaginative range of pastas and fresh seafood. ✉ *43–45 Lyndhurst Terr., SoHo* ☎ *2815–4005* ▭ *AE, MC, V* ☯ *No lunch weekends.*

MIDDLE EASTERN   ✕ **Habibi Koshary Cafe.** Egyptian café-style cuisine at affordable prices
☪ ¢–$ has made this one of Central's most popular fast-food outlets. Simple Middle Eastern fare includes vegetarian mezes, hummus, tabbouleh, lamb kofta (ground lamb kebabs), dawud beef balls (beef mixed with ground chickpeas), and elegant doner kebabs (reminiscent of gyros). Leave room for authentic sweet pastry baklava, halvah, or a Moorish rice pudding with nuts and raisins for dessert, and, of course, powerful Egyptian coffee. More formal, but equally good value, is owner Hosni Emam's restaurant Habibi next door to the café, which is like walking into a casbah. ✉ *112–114 Wellington St., Central* ☎ *2544–6190* ▭ *AE, DC, MC, V.*

Admiralty

Since this is essentially an office area wedged between Central and Wanchai made up of a series of large shopping malls, much of the food is aimed at meeting the lunch needs of workers and shoppers. However, with a major cinema and several good restaurants in the Pacific Place mall, it's a convenient destination for dinner as well. All the places here can be reached from the Admiralty MTR stop.

Asian

CANTONESE   ✕ **Zen.** The dim sum is a highlight at this upscale nouveau Cantonese
$–$$$ eatery that belongs to a group of ultrachic London restaurants of the same name. Recommended small dishes include deep-fried boneless chicken wings stuffed with glutinous rice and deep-fried shrimp with chili and garlic. More familiar Cantonese dishes are delicately prepared and presented. Service is flawless, and the decor is contemporary, with dramatic hanging lights and a central waterfall. ✉ *The Mall, Pacific Place 1, 88 Queensway, Admiralty* ☎ *2845–4555* ▭ *AE, DC, MC, V.*

SHANGHAINESE   ✕ **Ye Shanghai.** This nostalgic replica of old Shanghai is part of a chain
$$–$$$$ expanding across Asia. The old-fashioned setting includes 1950s furnishings and ceiling fans. Authentic Shanghainese appetizers such as chicken in spicy sauce and tea-leaf–smoked egg complement entrées of delicate stir-fried river shrimp in dark vinegar and minced chicken with pine nuts in steaming sesame pockets. For dessert, try the Shanghai staple, deep-fried egg white stuffed with banana and mashed red-bean paste. Reserve early for comfortable booth seats or window tables. A band plays Chinese oldies on Thursday, Friday, and Saturday nights. ✉ *Level 3, Pacific Place, 88 Queensway, Admiralty* ☎ *2918–9833* ▭ *AE, DC, MC, V.*

THAI   ✕ **Thai Basil.** At this smart mall restaurant at the entrance to Pacific Place
¢–$$ an Australian chef artfully presents Asian creations with a contemporary twist. Innovative dishes include scampi and banana bud with lime and mint leaves, stingray salad with green mango, and green papaya and crispy fish. Also highly recommended in winter is the braised lamb

shank. The homemade ice cream selection is eclectic: from ginger to honeycomb. For a price, you can watch the cuisine being created as you dine at an exclusive table called the Kitchen. ⊠ *Lower G/F, Shop 005, Pacific Place, Admiralty* ☎ *2537–4682* ▤ *AE, DC, MC, V.*

European

FRENCH

★ $$$$

✕ **Restaurant Petrus.** Commanding breathtaking views atop the Island Shangri-La Hotel, Restaurant Petrus is as prestigious as it gets. Considered by many to be one of the best French restaurants in the world, it attracts the finest chefs and features a premium collection of Petrus wine and 900 celebrated vintages. Signature dishes include foie gras and roast-braised suckling pig. À la carte dining is pricey, but lunch menus are an affordable HK$290–HK$340, while the five-course Menu Gourmand dinner is HK$750. ⊠ *56/F, Island Shangri-La, Pacific Place, Supreme Court Rd., Admiralty* ☎ *2820–8590* ⌕ *Reservations essential* ⌂ *Jacket required* ▤ *AE, DC, MC, V.*

☾ $$

✕ **La Cité.** A Parisian sidewalk café without sky—the "outdoor" café has umbrellas and is circled by a wrought-iron fence—this is the spot for bistro-style dining in Pacific Place shopping mall. It serves simple tasty French food, from escargots, pâté, and French onion soup to pastas, roast chicken, and steak. Panfried sea bass with artichokes, potatoes, and mussel-tarragon sauce bewitches the most jaded palate. Save room for a stunning dessert: brioche-and-rhubarb crumble topped with white chocolate mousse and raspberry sauce. ⊠ *007 Pacific Place, 88 Queensway, Admiralty* ☎ *2522–8830* ▤ *AE, DC, MC, V.*

ITALIAN

$$$–$$$$

✕ **Nicholini's.** This elegant restaurant regularly picks up local dining awards. Highlighting northern Italian dishes, the menu includes a wide range of pastas, fish, fowl, and meat. Homemade black fettuccine with shrimp, clams, and asparagus tips is delicious, while linguine with clams is a delight. The roast rack of lamb with green tomato compote is young enough to be sweet without overpowering the palate. For dessert, try a soufflé. The wine list is handpicked. ⊠ *8/F, Conrad Hotel Hong Kong, Pacific Place, 88 Queensway, Admiralty* ☎ *2521–3838 Ext. 8210* ▤ *AE, DC, MC, V.*

$$–$$$

✕ **Grappa's.** Don't let the mall location mislead you. Once inside, you can turn your back on the mall and let the kindly staff serve you superb Italian food. The endless selection of pastas can prolong your decision, but nothing will disappoint. Panfried foie gras makes an excellent kickoff, and osso buco, smothered in a rich flavorful sauce, is a dish you shouldn't miss. Game hen stuffed with sun-dried tomatoes, garlic, and fresh rosemary tastes as good as it sounds. With excellent coffee and a range of bottled beers, Grappa's is equally useful for a quick pick-me-up or a post-shopping rendezvous. ⊠ *132 Pacific Place, 88 Queensway, Admiralty* ☎ *2868–0086* ▤ *AE, DC, MC, V.*

International

★ $$–$$$$

✕ **JW's California.** Lobster is the star of this sleek, light, trendy flagship of the JW Marriott Hotel which is a popular choice for business lunches. Australian chef Todd Farr defies mainstream conventions to create his own unique cosmopolitan cuisine. The JW's Taster Plate, which adequately serves two, perfectly introduces his appetizers. Alternatives to

WITH CHILDREN

SOME WESTERN-STYLE RESTAURANTS—like Dan Ryan's—offer children's meals, but Cantonese restaurants do not. However, the individual dishes are "child size" anyway. A selection is placed on the table, and everyone helps themselves. You'll see children at all but the most upscale restaurants, and indulgent parents often allow them to run around. But some places are more geared toward family dining than others. Jaspa's in Sai Kung even provides toys and crayons if you ask and encourages children to draw on paper tablecloths.

On Sunday, whether for Western-style brunch or Chinese-style dim sum, children are not only welcome but expected. Since Sunday is traditionally "family day" in Hong Kong, even the fanciest restaurant wouldn't dare turn them away. Indeed, the Mandarin Grill, which during the week targets high-flying executives, becomes practically a glorified crèche on Sunday,

as the rich and famous acquaint their broods with the finer things in life. Cafe Deco on the Peak has special games and attractions to keep the little ones occupied.

There is one final point to remember about taking children out to eat in Hong Kong. In either Chinese or other Asian-style restaurants, don't be too certain what your child might or might not enjoy. Parents are constantly surprised when their offspring cheerfully chew on dishes that adults are programmed by age and ethnic snobbery to reject with horror—like chicken feet, duck web, dried squid, and barbecued intestine. For some reason, youngsters take great delight in the rare opportunity for one-upmanship and sometimes find it highly amusing that their parents are so unadventurous.

---

lobster are char-grilled steaks and favorite creations including salmon with artichokes and chorizo, corn-fed chicken breast, and spring lamb done "three ways" (cutlet, confit, and liver). The Napa Valley dessert sampler of chocolate napoleon, peanut butter mousse, and a raspberry tart is mouthwatering. ⊠ 5/F, JW Marriott Hotel, Pacific Place, Supreme Court Rd., Admiralty ☎ 2841–3889 ⊟ AE, DC, MC, V.

$$–$$$
Fodor's Choice
★
✕ **café TOO.** The innovative café TOO introduces all-day dining and drama with seven separate cooking "theaters" and a brigade of 30 chefs. Take your pick from seafood, sushi, and sashimi; Peking duck and dim sum; a carving station for roasts, poultry, and game; noodles and pastas; and pizzas, curries, tandooris, antipasto, cured meats, salads, or sandwiches—all made to order and all exceptionally good. Finish with a choice of hot and cold desserts. Try lunch (HK$235), dinner (HK$308), or even a late-night snack from 10:30 AM to midnight, priced at just HK$128 with two-for-one drinks. ⊠ 7/F, Island Shangri-La, Pacific Place, Supreme Court Rd., Admiralty ☎ 2820–8571 ⊟ AE, DC, MC, V.

North American

★ **$–$$$** ✕ **Dan Ryan's.** This popular bar and grill is often standing room only, so call ahead for a table. Apart from beer, the menu offers a smattering of international dishes—pasta and the like—but Dan Ryan's is known for its great burgers—the kind ex-pats dream about when they think of the States. It's simple, rib-sticking fare, served up without fuss or formality. ⊠ *114 Pacific Place, 88 Queensway, Admiralty* ☎ *2845–4600* ⌲ *Reservations essential* ▤ *AE, DC, MC, V.*

Seafood

$$–$$$$ ✕ **Lobster Bar.** The giant tropical-fish tank at the entrance sets the scene here. As the name suggests, lobster is the feature presentation, whipped into soups, appetizers, and various entrées. Lobster bisque is creamy yet light, with great chunks of meat at the bottom. The seafood platter—half a lobster thermidor, whole grilled langoustine, prawns, baked oysters, creamy scallops, crab cakes, black cod—doesn't disappoint. Decorated in blue and gold, with mahogany timbers, leather upholstery, and the sparkle of stained glass, the restaurant has a vibe that is at once formal and cozy. Besides seafood, a selection of pasta is also available. ⊠ *Island Shangri-La, Pacific Place, Supreme Court Rd., lobby level, Admiralty* ☎ *2877–3838 Ext. 8560* ⌲ *Reservations essential* ▤ *AE, DC, MC, V.*

The Peak

On a clear day, even the views en route via the Peak Tram, which is on every tourist's itinerary, will justify a trip to the highest dining point in Hong Kong. (Note that if there are low clouds, you won't be able to see a thing; you'll just hear the city beneath you.)

Eclectic

☕ **$–$$$** ✕ **Cafe Deco Bar & Grill.** If you're in Hong Kong on a clear day, take the
Fodor's Choice   Peak Tram to the top and dine at this 1930s-inspired art deco restau-
★   rant overlooking the city. The views are stunning. The menu—which includes Chinese, Thai, Indian, Italian, Mexican, and Japanese cuisine as well as Angus beef steaks from the grill and gourmet pizzas—is prepared by chefs in open kitchens; a culinary theater to rival the magnificent panorama. Food festivals are regularly staged here, and nightly live jazz transforms the venue into a swinging supper club. ⊠ *1st level, Peak Galleria, 118 Peak Rd., The Peak* ☎ *2849–5111* ▤ *AE, DC, MC, V.*

Wanchai

At lunchtime Wanchai is just another jumble of people, not a particularly invigorating shopping area; but after dark it comes into its own. This is Hong Kong's prime nightlife area, its long roads lined with fluorescent lights and jam-packed with taxis and wide-awake crowds. The range of dining options is extreme—from fail-safe five-star luxury to authentic and welcoming street-level spots with fine food. All the restaurants in this neighborhood are easily reached from the Wanchai MTR stop.

Asian

BEIJINGESE   ✕ **American Peking Restaurant.** Blazoned in red and gold, this Beijing-
$–$$$ style Chinese restaurant has been a Hong Kong institution for more than 40 years, so it must be doing something right. Favorites include hot-and-sour soup, fried and steamed dumplings, and, in winter, delicious hot

pots; you might also try the excellent beggar's chicken cooked in clay (order one day in advance), minced pigeon and, of course, Peking duck. The name was designed to attract American GIs during the Vietnam War, and the Chinese cuisine may be more familiar to international visitors than locals, since Cantonese cuisine is the norm in Hong Kong while Beijing-style is much less common. ⊠ *20 Lockhart Rd., Wanchai* 🕾 *2527–7770* ⌕ *Reservations essential* ▤ *AE, DC, MC, V.*

¢   ✕ **Dumpling Shop.** Beijing street-stall specialties are the attraction at this clean and smart outlet with a friendly staff. Thick northern Chinese noodles are accompanied by a rich minced-pork sauce—China's version of spaghetti Bolognese. Even a small portion is enough for two, so be careful not to over-order. Buns and dumplings are also in abundance and the panfried spring-onion cakes are typical starters. Leave room for the luscious bean-ball dessert—sweet red-bean paste encased in a light dough made of fluffy egg whites. You can only use your credit card if you spend over HK$200. ⊠ *138 Wanchai Rd., Wanchai* 🕾 *2771–2399* ▤ *DC, MC, V.*

CANTONESE   ✕ **Dynasty.** The haute Cantonese cuisine with panoramic views over Victoria Harbor from the highest Chinese restaurant in Hong Kong makes

★ **$$–$$$$**   this a memorable experience. Award-winning Tam Sek Lun comes from a long line of chefs and is famed for adapting family-style recipes into works of art. Lunchtime dim sum is recommended. The menu changes, as it should, with the seasons and heavily leans towards fresh seafood, plus top-end temptations like bird's nest soup, abalone, and shark's fin. Try the signature dessert of chilled sago cream with mango and grapefruit to finish. ⊠ *3/F, Renaissance Harbour View, 1 Harbour Rd., Wanchai* 🕾 *2802–8888* ▤ *AE, DC, MC, V.*

¢–$$ ✕ **Steam & Stew Inn.** Red lanterns mark the entrance to this hole-in-a-wall at the end of a short alley. It serves healthful, home-style Cantonese food—with red rice and no MSG, both rare occurrences in Hong Kong. Steamed fish and eggplant casserole are the most popular dishes; the double-boiled chicken with ginseng is said to help lower body heat. There's also a seasonal menu and dim sum at lunchtime. This gem was opened by a group of young professionals who craved inexpensive, healthful Chinese food, and it draws a young crowd. ⊠ *21–23 Tai Wong St. E, Wanchai* 🕾 *2529–3913* ▤ *MC, V* ☾ *No lunch Sun.*

SHANGHAINESE   ✕ **Lao Ching Hing.** One of the oldest Shanghainese restaurants in Hong

$$–$$$$ Kong (open since 1955), Lao Ching Hing has earned its good name over the years. From simple stuff such as the Shanghainese noodles to deluxe abalone, you're bound to find something intriguing on the menu. Chicken in wine sauce and sautéed river shrimp are popular choices. Also check out the Shanghainese dumplings and buns. For a real adventure, investigate the braised sea cucumber in brown sauce for its distinct texture and strong sauce. Try the freshwater crab if you're here in September or October. ⊠ *Novotel Century Hong Kong Hotel, 238 Jaffe Rd., basement, Wanchai* 🕾 *2598–6080* ▤ *AE, MC, V.*

VEGETARIAN   ✕ **Nice Fragrance Vegetarian Kitchen.** Simple bean curd, mushrooms, and

¢–$$ taro are whipped into unexpected and delicious forms here. Don't be surprised to see a whole fish on the next table: taro paste, molded into a fish shape and deep-fried, is one of the most popular dishes in Chinese vegetarian cooking. Crispy on the outside and succulent inside, the "fish" is served with a tangy sweet-and-sour sauce. Vegetarian dim sum and a snack counter at the door round out the offerings. You must spend a minimum of HK$200 to use your credit card. ✉ *105–107 Thomson Rd., Wanchai* ☎ *2838–3608 or 2838–3067* ▭ *AE, DC, MC, V.*

VIETNAMESE ✕ **Saigon Beach.** This tiny place can seat only about 20, so avoid the
¢–$ lunch rush unless you don't mind standing in line. The interior, an amalgam of nautical paraphernalia—cheap plastic fish hung from nets, folding chairs, and Formica tables—isn't likely to impress. Rather, the authentic Vietnamese fare and the opportunity to rub convivial elbows with people who know the place well more than make up for the unprepossessing environs. Soft-shell crab and lemon chicken, washed down with French 33 beer, are always a pleasure. Set meals are a good value. ✉ *66 Lockhart Rd., Wanchai* ☎ *2529–7823* ▭ *No credit cards.*

INDONESIAN ✕ **Bebek Bengil 3** (Dirty Duck Diner). Inspired by a tiny but legendary
$–$$ institution in Bali, this re-creation in the heart of Wanchai similarly specializes in crispy duck, marinated for 36 hours in an age-old recipe of spices. Decor is Balinese, and the seating is sala-style (at a low table, sitting on pillows on the floor), on a terrace outside overlooking bustling Lockhart Road. Familiar Indonesian dishes like *nasi goreng* (fried rice with satay) and beef *rendang* are on the menu. Breaching tradition is the black Russian pie dessert, laced with chocolate, vodka, and Kahlua. Finish with drinks at BB's lively sister establishment on the ground floor, the Bangkok-styled Klong Bar & Grill. ✉ *5/F, The Broadway, 34-62 Lockhart Rd., Wanchai* ☎ *2217–8000* ▭ *AE, DC, MC, V.*

European

ITALIAN ✕ **Grissini.** Taking its name from an Italian bread stick, this is one of
$$$–$$$$ Hong Kong's top Italian restaurants. To start, try the hot tomato soup topped with a surprising chilled tomato emulsion. Porcini-mushroom-and-pumpkin risotto is moist and subtly sweet, and roasted quail wrapped in pancetta and stuffed with foie gras is rich and flavorful. The wine gallery houses 1,000 bottles of mainly Italian wines. The dessert sampler comprises perfect miniportions of five delectable sweets including sabayon and sherbet, panna cotta with red-wine cherry compote, ricotta mousse and hot chocolate, and gianduja pudding. ✉ *2/F, Grand Hyatt Hotel, 1 Harbour Rd., Wanchai* ☎ *2588–1234 Ext. 7313* ⚲ *Reservations essential* ▭ *AE, DC, MC, V.*

$$–$$$ ✕ **Cinecitta.** Named after the fabled Italian film studio, Cinecitta serves Roman classics according to chef Michele Rodelli's distinctive style. A wine cellar immediately inside the entrance sets the tone for the modern sophisticated design. The set-price lunches and the fresh interior attract ladies who lunch as well as business types. Freshly made pasta is a trademark. Spoil yourself with an appetizer of panfried foie gras and baked pear, then move on to sea bass, swordfish, or tuna if you're a seafood lover. Beef tournedos in Parma ham with melted Gorgonzola is inspired. After-dinner/theater desserts are served after 10 PM. ✉ *Starcrest Bldg., 9 Star St., Wanchai* ☎ *2529–0199* ▭ *AE, DC, MC, V.*

International

ECLECTIC
$$–$$$

✕ **Grand Cafe.** It's grander than you'd expect for a coffee shop. Choose from eclectic "sandwiches" including lamb fillet on naan, or quesadillas, pastas, Asian-style noodles and rice, in addition to free-range chicken, panfried veal chops, and oven-glazed king prawns. Start with a salad or creative appetizer such as steamed asparagus with cold-pressed olive oil, poached egg, and shaved Parmesan. Also served is a creditable version of the famous Chinese dish, Hainanese chicken rice with soup. Desserts—sorbets, tarts, and cakes—are heavenly. ⊠ *Grand Hyatt Hotel, 1 Harbour Rd., Wanchai* ☎ *2588–1234 Ext. 7273* ▭ *AE, DC, MC, V.*

¢–$

✕ **Open Kitchen.** This sit-down cafeteria in the Hong Kong Arts Centre has a large selection of well-prepared, eclectic dishes and a nice view of the harbor. It's ideal for a pre- or post-performance meal or coffee. Dishes include Malaysian *laksa* (a rich and flavorsome noodle with bean curd, shrimp, fish ball, and spices), Indian curries, fresh Italian pasta, Chinese casseroles, and fish-and-chips, not to mention a selection of pastries for dessert. You must spend at least HK$150 to use your credit card. ⊠ *6/F, Hong Kong Arts Centre, 2 Harbour Rd., Wanchai* ☎ *2827–2923* ▭ *AE, MC, V.*

Causeway Bay

Home to a series of large Japanese department stores and a number of shopping malls, Causeway Bay is one of Hong Kong's busiest shopping districts and becomes a real cultural phenomenon on Saturday afternoon. Adjoining Causeway Bay on its southern edge is Happy Valley. The density of the population can be overwhelming. Several pubs are in the vicinity, but they're not concentrated on one strip; likewise, there are several good restaurants, but they can be hard for the uninitiated to find. Times Square, a huge, modern shopping mall, has four floors of restaurants in one of its towers, serving international cuisines including Korean, French, steak, and regional Chinese. All the restaurants in this area are easily accessible from the Causeway Bay MTR stop.

Asian

CANTONESE
$$–$$$

✕ **Forum.** The name of this prestigious restaurant connotes two things: chef Yeung Koon Yat and his special abalone. Yeung has earned an international reputation with his Ah Yat abalone. The price is steep, but if you want to experience this luxurious Asian ingredient, you really must come here. Your beautiful abalone is boiled and braised to perfection and served with a rich brown sauce—one of the most extravagant dishes in Cantonese cooking. If you want to leave with some cash in hand, you can choose from several more affordable choices, including boiled chicken and a noodle broth that lures regulars back time and again. ⊠ *485 Lockhart Rd., Causeway Bay* ☎ *2891–2516* ▭ *AE, DC, MC, V.*

$–$$
Fodor'sChoice
★

✕ **Dim Sum.** This elegant jewel breaks with tradition and serves dim sum all day and night. The original menu goes beyond common Cantonese morsels like *har gau* (steamed shrimp dumplings), embracing dishes more popular in the north, including chili prawn dumplings, Beijing onion cakes, and steamed buns. Lobster bisque and abalone dumplings are also popular. Lunch reservations are not taken on weekends, so there's always a long line. Arrive early, or admire the antique telephones and old Chinese posters while you wait. It's worth it. ⊠ *63 Sing Woo Rd., Happy Valley* ☎ *2834–8893* ▤ *AE, DC, MC, V.*

European

CONTEMPORARY ✕ **ToTT's Asian Grill & Bar.** The funky decor, which includes zebra-
$$-$$$$ stripe chairs, a central oval bar, and designer tableware, is matched by the East-meets-West cuisine at this restaurant that sits atop the Excelsior hotel looking down on Causeway Bay and the marina. Caesar salad with tandoori chicken is a good example of the culinary collision as is the red-crab bisque served in a baby papaya. The grilled rare tuna steak is another long-standing favorite, and the sampler platter of desserts is a grand finale. Live music kicks in late during the evening, offering a chance to burn a few calories on the dance floor. ⊠ *Excelsior hotel, 281 Gloucester Rd., Causeway Bay* ☎ *2837–6786* ▤ *AE, DC, MC, V.*

ITALIAN ✕ **Fat Angelo's.** Diners cram into this place—partly for the lively atmo-
$$ sphere, but mostly for the huge portions. Fat Angelo's is an Italian-American–style diner, with green-checked tablecloths and wooden chairs. Portions come in "big" (serving five–eight) and "not so big" (serving two–four). Favorites are mounds of steamed green-lipped mussels in tomato sauce, massive meatballs, roast chicken with rosemary, and pastas of every kind. Linguine with pesto is hearty and filling. Meals come with a salad and a bread basket. Wine is served in water glasses. The branches in SoHo and Tsim Sha Tsui are equally as fun. ⊠ *414 Jaffe Rd., Causeway Bay* ☎ *2574–6263* ▤ *AE, DC, MC, V.*

Seafood

$$-$$$ ✕ **Island Seafood & Oyster Bar.** Tucked into a Causeway Bay shopping area that was once Hong Kong's Food Street, this laid-back spot is drawing foodies back. The deliciously fresh oysters come in several varieties from around the world; pick them as creamy or firm as you like from the oyster bar, where the staff will happily make suggestions and serve the sexy mollusk on ice or cooked hot to your liking. Read the chalkboard for daily specials, which are bound to include seafood and meat. ⊠ *Shop C, Towning Mansion, 50–56 Paterson St., Causeway Bay* ☎ *2915–7110* ▤ *AE, DC, MC, V.*

Steak

$$-$$$ ✕ **W's Entrecote.** W's is a dining dictatorship: you can order steak, steak, or steak. Your only choices have to do with size and cooking time. Some call this the best steak in town, and the price includes a salad and as many fries as you can eat. The wine list is French, as is the interior: red-and-white–checked tablecloths and French posters. Service is attentive and friendly, and it's a good place for a family meal. If you come with children and want to share a portion, just ask and the waiters will happily help you. Perched at the top of bustling Times Square, it's ideal for a bout of protein replenishment after battling the crowds. ⊠ *13/F, 1303 Times Square, Causeway Bay* ☎ *2506–0133* ▤ *AE, DC, MC, V.*

Aberdeen

Seafood

★ ☺
$$–$$$

✕ **Jumbo Floating Restaurant.** This is the floating restaurant you see on postcards: a huge, pagoda-shape vessel burning with a thousand lights at night, it floats replete with a throne for visiting emperors. It's as much a sightseeing outing as a meal—and is one of the most interesting dining experiences in Hong Kong. Jumbo comprises three floating outlets: Tai Pat, Sea Palace, and Jumbo Palace. Naturally enough, seafood is the draw (market price), but the set meals, including Peking duck, are a reasonably priced alternative. Shuttle ferries depart every two or three minutes; don't forget your camera. ✉ *Shum Wan Pier Path, Wong Chuk Hang, Aberdeen* ☎ *2553–9111* ▭ *AE, DC, MC, V.*

Repulse Bay

The south side of Hong Kong Island is a string of beaches, rocky coves, and luxury developments, and Repulse Bay, 20 minutes by bus from Central, comprises all three. Popular on weekends and in summer, its beach is one of the best on the island, and the Repulse Bay complex houses a number of quality restaurants and shops along with corporate apartments. A taxi is a faster option to reach this area, though the bus is much cheaper.

Asian

PAN-ASIAN
$$

✕ **Spices.** Alfresco dining is rare in Hong Kong, but at Spices you can dine on classic Asian food surrounded by lawns and patios. (If the weather fails, there's an elegant interior.) The menu flies from India to Japan and back again. Singaporean satay or Indonesian *kuwe udang goreng* (deep-fried prawn cakes) make good starters. Main courses include Indian tandoori plates, Vietnamese fried soft-shell crabs, Japanese beef *shogayaki* (panfried fillet with sake sauce), and Malaysian *char kwayt teow* (seafood fried noodles). Curry lovers can try different versions from India, Vietnam, Singapore, and Indonesia. ✉ *The Repulse Bay, 109 Repulse Bay Rd., Repulse Bay* ☎ *2812–2711* ▭ *AE, DC, MC, V.*

European

CONTEMPORARY
★ $$$

✕ **The Verandah.** Step into another era here with antique fans, champagne-cocktail trolleys, cool, granite-tile floors and palm trees waving through the arched teak windows. Tuxedoed waiters attend to your every whim at this unashamed celebration of the halcyon days of colonial rule, which also serves an excellent Sunday brunch and daily afternoon tea. It comes into its own at night, however, when the chef whips up an impressive array of Continental dishes, from lobster to rack of lamb. The soufflé is reputedly the finest "this side of Suez." ✉ *The Repulse Bay, 109 Repulse Bay Rd., Repulse Bay* ☎ *2812–2722* ▭ *AE, DC, MC, V.*

Stanley

A visit to Stanley Village reveals another side of Hong Kong: a much slower pace of life than in the city. After exploring the market, historical sights, and beaches, take a leisurely meal at one of the top-notch but laid-back restaurants scattered around, some of which have harbor views. Stanley is 30 minutes by bus or taxi from Central.

European

MEDITERRANEAN ✗ **The Boathouse.** With a lovely view of the seafront and a cozy decor,
$$–$$$ the Boathouse is a perfect spot to hang out with friends and family. A bucket of mussels, served with nicely toasted garlic bread, goes down well with a glass of chilled white wine. Sandwiches and pastas are good bets for casual dining. The cobbler, a crumble with wild berries, will send you home happy. ⊠ *86–88 Stanley Main St., Stanley* ☎ *2813–4467* ▤ *DC, MC, V.*

★ **$$** ✗ **Lucy's.** The lighting is low, the decor warm, and the waiters friendly and casual. Laid-back and intimate, Lucy's draws regulars back again and again. The food is fresh, lovingly presented, and unpretentious. Stilton, spinach, and walnuts in phyllo pastry is a perfect starter. Veal with polenta and crispy Parma ham is delicate but powerful in taste; sea bass with pumpkin mash is delightfully light. Leave room for Lucy's quintessential chocolate cake for dessert. ⊠ *64 Stanley Main St., Stanley* ☎ *2813–9055* ▤ *MC, V.*

SPANISH ✗ **El Cid.** It may sound a bit weird to eat Spanish food and have a fiesta
$$–$$$ at the former British Army Officers' quarters; however, this restaurant is definitely worth the visit. Enjoy a few tapas and a sangria or Rioja as you admire the beautiful sea view and ponder what it must have been like here in 1848 when the structure was built. Garlic prawns and stuffed mushrooms are some of the best choices here. Ask for a table with a view. ⊠ *1/F, Murray House, Stanley Plaza, Stanley* ☎ *2899–0858* ▤ *AE, DC, MC, V.*

Shek O

Shek O is a tiny seaside village, but it has a few decent open-air restaurants. And once you've made the trek—the longest overland trip possible from Central—you'll need some sustenance. You can reach the village by bus or minibus from the Chai Wan MTR stop.

Asian

PAN-ASIAN ✗ **Shek O Chinese & Thailand Seafood Restaurant.** Nothing particularly
☺ **¢–$$** stands out about the food at this legendary restaurant—it's just such *fun.* On summer weekends, people arrive en masse and sit for hours despite the relentless heat. The curious hybrid cuisine ensures plenty of rice, noodle, and fish dishes. The *tom yung kung* (spicy prawn and coconut soup) is guaranteed to bring color to your cheeks; the green curry is a safe chicken choice; and the honey-fried squid is quite good. The festive ambience is a real experience, and you'll eat heartily without breaking the bank, but you have to spend over HK$300 to use your credit cards. ⊠ *303 Shek O Village (main intersection, next to the bus stop), Shek O* ☎ *2809–4426* ⌕ *Reservations essential* ▤ *AE, DC, MC, V.*

THAI ✗ **Happy Garden.** This restaurant is definitely named properly—you
¢–$$ can tell from the diners' faces. There's nothing gimmicky or fancy here, just simple Thai treats with reasonable prices and huge portions. The appetizer sampler—prawn cakes, fish cakes, chicken in vine leaves, and

spring rolls—is the house specialty. Steamed fish in sour soup finds its way to almost every table. Thai fried rice and fried Chinese broccoli with salty fish are both down-to-earth goodies. Only one drawback: there's usually a line on weekends. ⊠ *786 Shek O Village, Shek O* ☎ *2809–4165 or 2809–2770* ⚏ *Reservations not accepted* ▤ *No credit cards.*

KOWLOON

Parts of Kowloon are among the most densely populated areas on the planet, and support a corresponding abundance of restaurants. Many hotels, planted here for the view of Hong Kong Island (spectacular at night), also have excellent restaurants, though they're uniformly expensive. You may have just as much luck walking into places on a whim, though of course you'll take your chances. Some of the best food in Kowloon is served in the backstreets, where immigrants from Vietnam, Thailand, and all over Asia keep their native cooking skills sharp.

Kowloon City

Locals flock to Kowloon City, a 10-minute taxi ride north from Tsim Sha Tsui, adjoining Hong Kong's former international airport at Kai Tak, for casual, authentic, tasty meals at affordable prices.

Asian

CANTONESE ✕ **Tso Choi Koon.** If you're of delicate constitution, or insist on fine food,
¢ pass on this home-style Cantonese restaurant. Tso Choi (which translates as rough dishes) is not everyone's cup of tea. Tripe lovers and haggis fans, however, might like to try the Chinese versions of some of their favorites: fried pig tripe, fried pig brain (served as an omelet), double-boiled pig brain . . . you get the idea. The older Hong Kong generation still likes this stuff; younger folks may demur. The wary can still opt for creamy congee, fried chicken, or a fish fillet. ⊠ *17–19A Nga Tsin Wai Rd., Mong Kok* ☎ *2383–7170* ▤ *No credit cards.*

THAI ✕ **Golden Orchid Thai Restaurant.** Golden Orchid serves some of Hong
¢–$$ Kong's best and most innovative Thai cuisine. The curried crab and the seafood curry in pumpkin are excellent. If you like to be involved with your food preparation don't miss *mein come,* a kind of Thai leaf served with little bowls of spices and fixings such as fried coconut, peanuts, garlic, chili, lime, and dried shrimp. Wrap your choices in the leaf and enjoy. The steamed seafood cakes, served in Thai stone pots, are also delicious. Try the roasted pork-neck slices, prawn cakes, and rice with olives. There's no service charge or tipping, making this cheap place a major bargain. ⊠ *12 Lung Kong Rd., Mong Kok* ☎ *2383–3076* ▤ *MC, V.*

Sai Kung

Renowned for its seafood restaurants and neighborhood hill-walking tracks, Sai Kung is off most tourist itineraries, but only a 20-minute taxi ride north of Tsim Sha Tsui (or Minibus 1 from Choi Hung MTR) and a town worth investigating. Many restaurants run adjoining seafood shops,

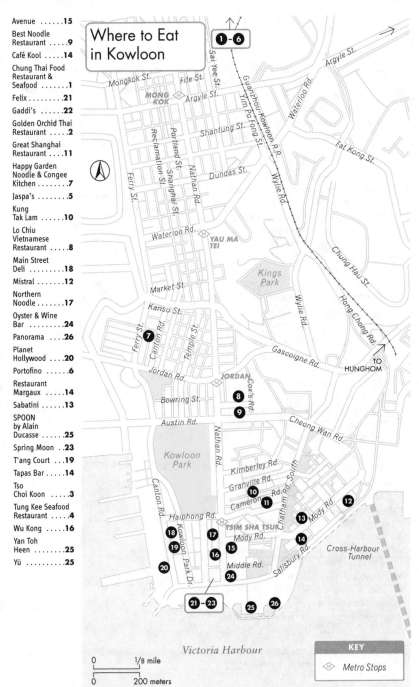

Where to Eat
in Kowloon

CloseUp

THE DIM SUM EXPERIENCE

A VISIT TO HONG KONG IS NOT COMPLETE without a visit to a dim sum restaurant. Dim sum is the staple food in Hong Kong and is always accompanied by Chinese tea. You'll be able to find dim sum from before dawn to around 5 or 6 PM, but these traditional Cantonese daytime tidbits—works of art, really—are most often served for breakfast (from about 7:30 to 10 AM) and lunch (from about 11:30 AM to 2:30 PM. More than 2,000 kinds of dim sum are in the Cantonese repertoire, and most dim sum restaurants prepare 100 varieties daily. Many are filled with such ingredients as pork, prawns, rice, and flour, and can efficiently fill up your stomach before you even notice it.

In the old days, dim sum restaurants were always associated with noise. Trolleys filled with steaming dishes were pushed around in restaurants while dim sum ladies shouted the names of the dishes. Today, in many of Hong Kong's hundreds of dim sum restaurants, a dim sum order form awaits you at the table and is subsequently stamped as your dishes arrive, creating a much quieter dining experience.

Generally steamed in bamboo steamers, panfried, baked, or deep-fried, the buns, crepes, and cakes are among the world's finest hors d'oeuvres. Many are minor culinary achievements—such as a soup with prawns served in a translucent rice-pastry shell, or a thousand-layer cake, or the ubiquitous spring roll. Most items come in a serving for three or four, allowing diners to share a good variety of delicacies around a table. Although every restaurant has its own dim sum menu, certain traditional items can be found in almost all dim sum outlets.

Popular dim sum items you need to know before a fun and fulfilling dim sum hunting meal include:

Cha siu bao: barbecued pork buns

Cha siu so: baked barbecued pork pastry

Cheong fun: steamed rice rolls (with various fillings such as prawns, beef, barbecued pork, and more)

Chun kuen: spring rolls

Dan tart: baked egg tarts

Har gau: steamed prawn dumplings with a light translucent wrap

Har kok: deep-fried prawn dumplings

Lou mei gai: glutinous rice wrapped in lotus leaf

Ngau yuk: steamed beef balls

Siu mai: steamed pork dumplings

Don't be surprised, however, if you discover some novelty items that you, or even your Hong Kong friends, have never heard of. Dim sum chefs in Hong Kong like to come up with innovative ideas and introduce creative elements to make a dim sum meal satisfying.

so you can select a fresh catch from tanks and have it cooked to order—steamed, fried, sautéed, or deep-fried with salt and pepper. You'll also find a good selection of Western restaurants serving delicious food with an easy, intimate, and laid-back feel.

International

$–$$ ✕ **Jaspa's.** What could be better than heading straight to a cozy restaurant after a day out in the countryside? Here the food is always delicious and filling, perfect after a day walking in the hills or enjoying the water and sun. Whether sitting out on the terrace or indoors, an enjoyable dining experience is guaranteed. The goat cheese parcel makes a delectable starter, and tasty chicken fajitas arrives on your table sizzling hot. Pasta with bay bugs (large crayfish) and lamb chops never disappoint. The hearty food and friendly service makes Jaspa's a key culinary attraction in Sai Kung. ⊠ *13 Sha Tsui Path, Sai Kung* ☎ *2792–6388* ⊟ *AE, MC, V.*

$–$$ ✕ **Portofino.** Home-style Mediterranean dining at pizzeria prices on the Sai Kung waterfront makes Portofino a firm favorite among locals. Authentic Italian pizzas and pastas are the specialty, but the menu extends to Spanish paella, French bouillabaisse and quiche, Greek salad and moussaka, and Middle Eastern meze platters. Grilled seafood, steaks, veal chops, and chicken are simply cooked in fresh herbs, drizzled with olive oil and lemon. An all-you-can-eat Sunday brunch is a good value at HK$195 with wine. Wines are reasonably priced with some interesting rarities. Tiramisu is a must-try dessert. ⊠ *Shop 3, G/F, Fiu Yat Bldg., Hoi Tong Sq., Sai Kung* ☎ *2791–5818* ⊟ *AE, DC, MC, V.*

Seafood

$$–$$$ ✕ **Tung Kee Seafood Restaurant.** Lobsters, slipper lobsters, clams, abalone, crabs, prawns, fish, and everything else from the deep blue sea are here for the tasting on Sai Kung's picturesque harborside. Crustaceans and fish are quickly cooked by steaming and wok-frying and are presented whole, leaving no illusions as to the freshness of your food. A quick look inside the tank is better than a marine biology lesson. Pick your favorites, and leave the rest for the chef. From lobster sashimi to steamed fish, this well-established eatery will impress you with a feast *de la mer.* ⊠ *96–102 Man Nin St., Sai Kung* ☎ *2792–7453* ⊟ *AE, DC, MC, V.*

¢–$$ ✕ **Chung Thai Food Restaurant & Sea Food.** As its name suggests, this seafood corner is best known for both Chinese and Thai cooking, prepared separately by chefs of both nationalities. Those with a taste for spice can try the Thai fried crabs with curry or fried prawns with chili; otherwise, pick any seafood you like from the store next door, and the chef will prepare it to order. Steaming is highly recommended for fresh fish, as the fish will retain its fresh taste and tender texture. Prices depend on the type and weight of the seafood you choose. ⊠ *93 Man Nin St., Sai Kung* ☎ *2792–1481* ⊠ *Seafood shop* ⊠ *5 Siu Yat Bldg., Hoi Pong Sq., Sai Kung* ☎ *2792–8172* ⊟ *MC, V.*

Tsim Sha Tsui

Tsim Sha Tsui, on the tip of Kowloon, is crammed with shops and dining options, from five-star hotels to holes-in-the-wall. Starting from the

Kowloon-side Star Ferry Terminal, the district embraces the most glittering end of the famous Nathan Road's "Golden Mile," snakes around the harbor front to Tsim Sha Tsui East, and extends to the end of Kowloon Park at Austin Road, marking the boundary of Jordan. The restaurants here are easily accessible from either the Tsim Sha Tsui MTR stop or Kowloon's Star Ferry Terminal.

Asian

CANTONESE ✕ **Spring Moon.** This prestigious restaurant is modeled on 1930s Shang-
★ **$$–$$$$** hai with antique-style teak floors, Oriental rugs, stained glass, and a traditional tea cabinet; but the cuisine is first-rate Cantonese fare. Start with typical Cantonese barbecued chicken and delicious barbecued pork. Or watch waiters prepare Shaoxing-wine-infused drunken prawns at your table—tasty to eat but slightly torturous to watch being prepared. Braised abalone in oyster sauce melts in your mouth as does the roast pigeon. A tea master is on hand to help you choose a perfect infusion and afternoon dim sum is as elegant as it is delicious. ⊠ *Peninsula Hong Kong, Salisbury Rd., Tsim Sha Tsui* ☎ *2315–3160* ▤ *AE, DC, MC, V.*

★ **$$–$$$$** ✕ **T'ang Court.** Bedecked with golden silk curtains, T'ang Court is one of Hong Kong's most elegant Cantonese restaurants—impressive for a lunch with either business associates or Chinese friends. The dining room covers two floors connected by a spiral staircase. The cuisine is faithfully traditional yet creatively original—from home-style Cantonese soups and baked oysters with port as appetizers, to baked salty chicken with crispy skin for a main course. Desserts are irresistible: try the steamed pumpkin dumplings with egg-yolk cream. ⊠ *Langham Hong Kong, 8 Peking Rd., Tsim Sha Tsui* ☎ *2375–1133 Ext. 2250* ▤ *AE, DC, MC, V.*

★ **$$–$$$$** ✕ **Yan Toh Heen.** This internationally acclaimed Cantonese restaurant is the showpiece of the Hotel InterContinental Hong Kong and the top of its class in town. The *International Herald Tribune* once named it the third-best restaurant in the world. Exquisite is hardly the word for place settings: handcrafted with green jade, each one is conservatively valued at US$1,000. Over 30 types of exemplary dim sum are served at lunchtime, including signature creations with steamed shark's fin and Yunnan ham. A vast selection of seafood—the largest range in Hong Kong—is the star of the main menu. ⊠ *Hotel InterContinental Hong Kong, 18 Salisbury Rd., Tsim Sha Tsui* ☎ *2721–1211* ⌔ *Reservations essential* ▤ *AE, DC, MC, V.*

¢–$ ✕ **Happy Garden Noodle & Congee Kitchen.** For a taste of down-to-earth Hong Kong fare without the fear of feeling like an interloper in Chinese-only local joints, this is the place to go. Bright and clean, with helpful waitresses and an English menu, this small place works for a typical local breakfast, an easy lunch, and even a big dinner. A popular morning combination is Cantonese congee and a glutinous rice dumpling wrapped in a lotus leaf. A bowl of wonton soup or a plate of fried rice or noodles makes a simple but satisfying lunch. For dinner, the diced chicken with cashews and sweet-and-sour pork are delicious Cantonese staples. ⊠ *76 Canton Rd., Tsim Sha Tsui* ☎ *2377–2603 or 2377–2604* ▤ *No credit cards.*

SEAFOOD

$$$–$$$$

✕ **Yü.** You're welcomed by denizens of the deep, who peer out from a huge curving aquarium at this seafood-lover's dream. Oysters come in all shapes, sizes, and preparations. Lobster bisque and sautéed jumping shrimp are perfect hot appetizers. Fresh seafood of all sorts are cooked to either Asian or Western tastes. This is not a cheap place, but it is extremely popular and has a spectacular view of Hong Kong Island by day or night. The lunchtime starter buffet with a main course is an exceptional value at HK$220, or HK$250 with dessert. A "suchi" master prepares ocean-fresh sushi and sashimi at the new Yü Sushi Bar. ⊠ *Hotel InterContinental Hong Kong, 18 Salisbury Rd., Tsim Sha Tsui* ☎ *2721–1211* ⌖ *Reservations essential* ▭ *AE, DC, MC, V.*

$$–$$$$

✕ **Oyster & Wine Bar.** Atop the Sheraton Hong Kong Hotel & Towers, against the romantic backdrop of Hong Kong's twinkling harbor, this is the top spot in town for oyster-lovers. More than 30 varieties are flown in fresh daily and kept alive on ice around the horseshoe oyster bar, ready for shucking. Staff cheerfully explain the characteristics of the available oysters and guide you to ones to suit your taste. Also on the aphrodisiac menu is San Francisco fisherman's stew, clams, mussels, crab, and black cod. An extensive wine cellar lines the walls. ⊠ *Sheraton Hong Kong Hotel & Towers, 20 Nathan Rd., Tsim Sha Tsui* ☎ *2369–1111* ▭ *AE, DC, MC, V* ☾ *No lunch.*

SHANGHAINESE

$–$$$

✕ **Great Shanghai Restaurant.** Great Shanghai is not esteemed for its decor (which is old and dingy), but it's perfect if you prefer the bold flavors of Shanghainese food to the more delicate tastes of local Cantonese fare. You may not be ready for the sea blubber or braised turtle with sugar candy, but do consider one of the boneless eel dishes, the Shanghai-style yellow fish soup, the beggar's chicken (order before noon for dinner), or the excellent spiced soy duck. For less adventurous palates there are more fundamental Shanghainese goodies such as sautéed river shrimp, Chinese cabbage with Yunnan ham, tasty fried noodles, or juicy dumplings. ⊠ *26–36 Prat Ave., Tsim Sha Tsui* ☎ *2366–8158* ▭ *AE, DC, MC, V.*

¢–$$

✕ **Wu Kong.** At the intersection of Nathan Road and Peking Road, this big basement dining room serves first-rate Shanghainese fare at reasonable prices. Pigeon in wine sauce is an excellent appetizer. Goose wrapped in crispy bean curd skin is delicious and authentic, as is the fish smothered in a sweet-and-sour sauce. The Shanghai-style doughnut on the dessert menu is a deep-fried sweet ball whipped up with fluffy egg whites and stuffed with red bean and banana. ⊠ *Alpha House, 23–33 Nathan Rd., basement (entrance on Peking Rd.), Tsim Sha Tsui* ☎ *2366–7244* ▭ *AE, DC, MC, V.*

¢–$

✕ **Best Noodle Restaurant.** Tucked on a side street off Nathan Road, near the Jordan MTR station, just beyond the northern boundary of Tsim Sha Tsui, this humble place is popular among locals seeking a quick bowl of noodles or a simple, tasty Shanghainese dish. Shanghainese rice with vegetables, topped with your choice of meats and vegetables, is a favorite, as are fried noodles, soup noodles, and sweet spareribs. ⊠ *105 Austin Rd., Jordan* ☎ *2369–0086 or 2736–2786* ▭ *No credit cards.*

¢

✕ **Northern Noodle.** Conveniently located near the Tsim Sha Tsui MTR and shopping area, this smart little joint has a great variety of northern

Chinese dishes (think hot and spicy) and makes a nice spot for a quick lunch or snack. Chow down on a bowl of noodles or dumplings accompanied with a chilled soya drink, or sample the typical northern specialties such as braised bean curd or spicy diced chicken. It's cramped and crowded, but the staff are friendly and cheerful. ⊠ *44 Hankow Rd., Tsim Sha Tsui* ☎ *2367–9011* ▭ *No credit cards.*

VEGETARIAN ✕ **Kung Tak Lam.** Health-conscious diners will appreciate this simple Shang-
¢–$ hainese vegetarian food. Don't turn your back when you see the no-frills interior; it's the food that makes this place so popular. Try the cold noodle plates, which come with an array of sauces to mix and match for as sweet or sour a flavor as you want. The bean curd ravioli also gets a big thumbs up. Set-price meals are incredibly cheap. ⊠ *1/F, 45–47 Carnarvon Rd., Tsim Sha Tsui* ☎ *2367–7881* ▭ *AE, DC, V.*

VIETNAMESE ✕ **Lo Chiu Vietnamese Restaurant.** The spartan interior may not impress
¢–$$ you at first glance, but pay no heed since what you're here for is the hearty authentic food. Take your time and try not to burn your tongue on the sizzling hot and wonderfully flavorsome lemongrass chicken wings. Deep-fried sugarcane with minced shrimp is sweet and juicy. There are also a good variety of noodles and vermicelli served in soup or with fish sauce. A bottle of imported French beer is just the thing to wash it all down. ⊠ *17–19 Hillwood Rd., Tsim Sha Tsui* ☎ *2314–7983 or 2314–9211* ▭ *MC, V.*

European

FRENCH ✕ **Gaddi's.** With exemplary service, world-class French cuisine, and a
$$$$ magnificent wine list, the Peninsula's flagship restaurant is a world of neoclassical elegance unto itself. With British chef Philip Sedgwick at the helm, the dress code has been relaxed and prices have been brought down: set lunches start at HK$340, set dinner menus at HK$650. Braised veal shank is an eternally popular signature dish, and twice-cooked suckling pig is remarkable. For dessert, the lightly caramelized lemon tart will melt in your mouth. For a gourmet treat, dine at the Gaddi's Chefs' Table in the kitchen (HK$688 for lunch, HK$1,188 for dinner). ⊠ *Peninsula Hong Kong, Salisbury Rd., Tsim Sha Tsui* ☎ *2315–3171 or 2366–6251 Ext. 3989* ⌑ *Reservations essential* ⌂ *Jacket and tie* ▭ *AE, DC, MC, V.*

International

CONTEMPORARY ✕ **SPOON by Alain Ducasse.** This "bistro" is Hong Kong's highest-pro-
$$$–$$$$ file arrival in 2004. High prices are balanced against a prestigious venue, stunning harbor views, and the very best ingredients. A novel mix-and-match concept offers several choices of sauces and condiments for each dish. Despite the odd Asian influence (seaweed pesto and shiitake mushrooms), the menu is contemporary French at heart, with signature dishes such as lobster "glamour" salad, veal and pasta with black truffles, and succulent lamb chops. Pumpkin soup is an unlikely highlight. A multi-course tasting menu introduces the Ducasse experience to the uninitiated for HK$750. ⊠ *Hotel InterContinental Hong Kong, 18 Salisbury Rd., lobby level, Tsim Sha Tsui* ☎ *2313–2256* ⌑ *Reservations essential* ▭ *AE, DC, MC, V.*

$$–$$$ ✕ **Avenue.** One of the places to see and be seen in Tsim Sha Tsui, trendy Avenue serves modern European cuisine in a crisp contemporary location overlooking the bustling Golden Mile of Nathan Road. Whitewashed walls and white-marble tile flooring are dramatically accented by unusually large and colorful abstract paintings and murals. Signature dishes include sautéed wild mushrooms, which burst with natural flavor; a refreshing crab-and-avocado salad with lemon mayonnaise; chunky, fresh roast cod; and a luscious crème blur dessert, a variation of crème brûlée, served with strawberries. Last orders for night owls is 10:30 PM. ⊠ *1/F, Holiday Inn Golden Mile, 50 Nathan Rd., Tsim Sha Tsui* ☎ *2315–1118* ☰ *AE, DC, MC, V.*

$$–$$$ ✕ **Felix.** The creation of avant-garde designer Philippe Starck, ultra-fashionable, high-tech Felix—on the top floor of the Peninsula—has breathtaking views of Hong Kong through the floor-to-ceiling glass wall. The food in this restaurant, called a "brasserie for the 21st century," is eclectic, ranging from Mongolian rack of lamb to misoyaki-marinated Atlantic cod and honeyed tempura prawns, but Felix is just as much about the buzz, the cocktail bar, the Crazy Box (its small disco), and even the most celebrated gents' washroom in Asia. ⊠ *28/F, Peninsula Hong Kong, Salisbury Rd., Tsim Sha Tsui* ☎ *2366–6251 or 2315–3188* ⚑ *Reservations essential* ☰ *AE, DC, MC, V.*

$$–$$$ ✕ **Panorama.** A gem of a fine dining room with more affordable prices than most, Panorama has both stunning views of Victoria Harbor and a team of celebrated chefs. A whimsical design element is a live goldfish in a glass bowl at each table. Exquisite Euro-Asian cuisine presents a medley of flavors from both continents with unrivaled flair. Some of the freshest seafood in Hong Kong—plus a new Oyster Bar—makes this an ever-popular choice for fine dining that doesn't break the bank. Both the panfried salmon and the chocolate-and-walnut pudding are menu highlights and have won prizes. The gourmet five-course lunch is a good value at HK$168; the dinner equivalent is HK$480. ⊠ *4/F, New World Renaissance Hotel, 22 Salisbury Rd., Tsim Sha Tsui* ☎ *2734–6660* ☰ *AE, DC, MC, V.*

North American

$–$$ ✕ **Main Street Deli.** Inspired by New York's famous Second Avenue Deli, with a tiled interior to match, Main Street Deli introduced traditional Big Apple neighborhood favorites to Hong Kong and found immediate popularity with visitors and locals alike. The chef personally trained with Second Avenue Deli's owner, Jack Lebewohl. Lunch favorites include hot dogs, bagels, and sandwiches like pastrami on rye, hot corned beef, and turkey with sauerkraut. Brisket, meat loaf, and matzoh-ball soup satisfy homesick New Yorkers. Lemon meringue pie makes an ideal dessert with afternoon coffee. ⊠ *G/F, Langham Hong Kong, 8 Peking Rd., Tsim Sha Tsui* ☎ *2375–1133* ☰ *AE, DC, MC, V.*

Tsim Sha Tsui East

An extension to Tsim Sha Tsui, beyond Chatham Road and south towards the Cross-Harbour Tunnel, this neighborhood is packed with five-star hotels with exquisite restaurants. The closest transit stop is the Tsim Sha Tsui MTR stop.

ECLECTIC ✕ **Café Kool.** This 300-seat international food court has something fun
🕙 **$–$$$** for the whole family, with entertainment by chefs in six "show kitchens"
focusing on cuisines from around the world. Take your pick from the
salad counter; a seafood station; pasta, paella, risotto, and carvery from
the Western kitchen; favorites from all over Asia; tandoories and cur-
ries from the Indian counter; and fresh soufflés, crepes, and even liquid
chocolate from Hong Kong's only chocolate fountain at the dessert sta-
tion. Good-value, all-you-can-eat buffets are served up to midnight for
HK$188 to HK$338. A deli sells take-out food and gourmet gifts.
⊠ *Kowloon Shangri-La, 64 Mody Rd., Tsim Sha Tsui East* ☎ *2733–8753*
▤ *AE, DC, MC, V.*

FRENCH ✕ **Restaurant Margaux.** Reminiscent of a family château in the south of
$$$–$$$$ France, the restaurant focuses on classic cuisine and wine from Bordeaux
and southwest France. It's neither nouvelle nor too trendy, simply re-
laxed, intimate, fine French dining—with a superlative view over Hong
Kong. Dominique Grel oversees the seasonal menu; his beef Rossini with
truffle juice is a masterpiece. The wine list, for which the restaurant has
become known, includes a large selection of Margaux vintages. The three-
course set lunch is an unbeatable value at HK$250. ⊠ *1/F, Kowloon
Shangri-La, 64 Mody Rd., Tsim Sha Tsui East* ☎ *2733–8750* ⟍ *Reser-
vations essential* ▤ *AE, DC, MC, V.*

ITALIAN ✕ **Mistral.** Pizza and pasta are specialties at dark, cozy, candlelit Mis-
$$–$$$ tral, where the large open-plan kitchen is as much an attraction as the
authentic, family-style Italian cooking. It's down-to-earth, inexpensive,
and popular. Freshly made pastas are first-rate; choices range from lin-
guine with vegetables scented with truffle oil to tagliolini with porcini
mushrooms. Nonpasta main courses extend to Tyrolean speck ham and
fresh turbot. ⊠ *Grand Stanford InterContinental Harbour View, 70 Mody
Rd., basement, Tsim Sha Tsui East* ☎ *2731–2870* ▤ *AE, DC, MC, V*
🕙 *Closed Sun.*

★ **$$–$$$** ✕ **Sabatini.** Run by the Sabatini family, who also have restaurants in Rome,
Japan, and Singapore, this small corner of Italy with sponge-painted walls
and wooden furnishings is in the Royal Garden's atrium. It has a cult
following among those who crave authentic Italian cuisine. Linguine Saba-
tini, the house specialty, is prepared according to the original Roman
recipe in a fresh-tomato-and-garlic marinara sauce, served with an array
of luscious seafood. For dessert, try homemade tiramisu or refreshing
wild-berry pudding. ⊠ *3/F, Royal Garden, 69 Mody Rd., Tsim Sha Tsui
East* ☎ *2733–2000* ⟍ *Reservations essential* ▤ *AE, DC, MC, V.*

SPANISH ✕ **Tapas Bar.** International tapas meet New World wines at this upbeat
¢–$$ venue borrowing the Spanish concept of snacking on tasty small dishes,
rather than having one wholesome meal. Chefs work in an open kitchen,
where a tandoor oven ensures freshly baked bread. Typical Spanish tapas
like whitebait, sardines, and chorizo sausage are served, but there are
also dips from around the world, a smorgasbord of olives, sushi-style
tuna, and potato-wrapped shrimp—plus a global oyster selection. The
five-tapas platter with a glass of wine is a good lunchtime value at
HK$118. ⊠ *1/F, Kowloon Shangri-La, 64 Mody Rd., Tsim Sha Tsui East*
☎ *2733–8750* ▤ *AE, DC, MC, V.*

OUTER ISLANDS

Lamma Island

Lamma Island is relatively easy to get to, with ferries leaving Central's pier almost hourly. Yung Shue Wan, where you disembark, has a collection of local seafood restaurants, one or two Western ones, and an odd assortment of shops.

Asian

CANTONESE   ✕ **Han Lok Yuen.** Roast pigeon is the star at Han Lok Yuen. Everyone in Hong Kong makes a pilgrimage here at one time or another to try it, usually during a boat trip. Don't arrive too late, or you might miss out: the pigeon can be sold out by 8 PM on busy weekend nights, when booking in advance is usually essential. The kitchen also turns out an array of typical Chinese dishes to accompany the pigeon. Beautiful sea views make this institution popular with both locals and visitors alike. ⊠ *16–17 Hung Shing Ye, Yung Shue Wan* ☎ *2982–0680* ▭ *AE, DC, MC, V* ⊙ *Closed Mon.*

¢–$$ ✕ **Lancombe.** This Cantonese seafood restaurant is Lamma's best source for no-nonsense food at no-nonsense prices. The huge English/Cantonese menu features seafood, seafood, and more seafood. Try deep-fried squid, garoupa in sweet corn sauce, broccoli in garlic, and beef with black beans. Dishes come in three sizes, but a selection of three or four small ones is sufficient for four people. Take a seat on the terrace out back, where you'll have a view of the sea and distant Peng Chau Island. ⊠ *47 Main St., Yung Shue Wan* ☎ *2982–0881* ▭ *AE, MC, V.*

International

¢–$ ✕ **Toochka.** After exploring Lamma Island, a chilled beer and a curry at Toochka will end your day on a high note. Choose from the extensive menu: salads, pastas, steaks, and the all-time-favorite curries (vegetables, meat, fish—you name it). From the patio, watch island life drift by. ⊠ *44 Main St., Yung Shue Wan* ☎ *2982–0159* ▭ *AE, MC, V* ⊙ *Closed Mon.*

WHERE TO STAY

3

Updated by
Tracey Furniss

ADAPTING TO CHANGE is a Hong Kong specialty. Now that it is a Special Administrative Region of China—instead of a British Crown Colony—visitors from the mainland are the backbone of the tourism industry. Despite a shift in economic fortunes, this epicenter of finance and business still manages to find a way to woo business travelers and tourists alike. As a result, you can expect to find luxury properties continually upgrading their facilities—with health clubs, spas, and pools being standard—along with excellent service and hospitality. In-room, high-speed Internet access is also commonplace.

Considering its size, Hong Kong has more than its fair share of upscale hotels, and more often than not these have magnificent views over Victoria Harbour from either the Hong Kong or the Kowloon side. As they focus increasingly on the business traveler with an expense account, most hotels charge at least US$150 (HK$1,170) a night for rooms of a normal international standard. These may not be in prime locations, but they offer basic and reliable facilities—color TV, radio, telephone, same-day valet laundry service, room service, safe-deposit box, refrigerator and minibars, air-conditioning, and business services. Most hotels also have at least one restaurant and bar, a travel desk, and limousine or car rental. If you pay the full rate, many hotels will offer perks such as limousine pickup at the airport.

However, it's the business services that set Hong Kong apart. Most major hotels have business centers that provide secretarial, translation, courier, telex, fax, Internet, and printing services. Some provide in-room PCs, while others offer support for your own plug-in hardware. Executive floors or clubs have become standard in well-established hotels; these floors typically have extra concierge services, complimentary breakfast and cocktails, express check-in, personalized stationery, butler services, and an area where you can meet with business contacts. Executive rooms also have enhanced business features, such as in-room fax machines, Internet TV, and twin phone lines, though some charge extra for their use. Many hotels have large ballrooms, and most have smaller meeting and conference rooms.

Where to stay in Hong Kong depends on the nature of your trip. Thanks to the three tunnels that run underneath the harbor, the Star Ferry, and the Mass Transit Railway (MTR, or subway), it no longer really matters whether you stay "Hong Kong side" or "Kowloon side"; the other side is only minutes away. The airport rail link will whisk you over the Tsing Ma Suspension Bridge through Kowloon to Central in around 25 minutes. If you want to avoid the main tourist areas, the New Territories and Islands offer a few quieter and cheaper alternatives to Hong Kong Island and Kowloon.

The **Hong Kong Tourist Board** publishes the *Hotel Guide,* which lists rates, services, and facilities for all of its members. The HKTB does not make hotel reservations. The Hong Kong Hotel Association (HKHA) does, and at no extra charge, but only through its reservations office at Hong Kong International Airport.

Accommodations listed in this chapter are grouped by geographical area—Hong Kong Island, Kowloon, and New Territories and the Islands—and neighborhood, and are alphabetical within each price category.

HONG KONG ISLAND

The south side of Hong Kong Island finally has a hotel, the new Le Méridien Cyberport, which is nestled on the waterfront of Telegraph Bay. Built as a high-tech business hub, **Cyberport** also has residential and leisure facilities, including the hotel and a commercial complex. The **Western** district has several hotels that are away from tourist areas amid narrow streets and shops untouched by major redevelopments common in most other areas. It is one of the few places remaining of old Hong Kong. If you need to be near the city's financial hub, you'll prefer the **Central** or **Admiralty** districts, but you'll pay for the convenience and views. Central is as busy as New York City on weekdays, but, except for the Lan Kwai Fong area, it's quiet at night and on weekends. Nearby, Hong Kong's very own SoHo (South of Hollywood Road) in the **Midlevels** has an eclectic mix of restaurants serving everything from Nepalese to modern European cuisine; nearby are a few hotels. **Wanchai**, east of Central, was once a sailor's dream of booze and Suzie Wong types. It still has plenty of nightlife, but office high-rises and the Hong Kong Convention & Exhibition Centre—the territory's most popular venue for large-scale exhibitions and conferences—now draw businesspeople. **Causeway Bay**, farther east, is a brightly lighted shopping district with restaurants, cinemas, and permanent crowds. **Happy Valley** is near the racetrack and Hong Kong Stadium, the territory's largest sports facility. Hotels and restaurants have also sprung up farther east along the MTR line, in residential **North Point** and **Quarry Bay**.

Cyberport

★ **$$$**   Le Méridien Cyberport. Finally, the south side of Hong Kong has a hotel. This relatively small, boutique-style hotel, which opened in April 2004, offers high-tech amenities such as 42-inch plasma TVs and wireless Internet in all rooms, as well as hip bars and restaurants. Rooms are spacious; bathrooms have so-called "rain" showers, which have extra-large showerheads with many holes that rain water down onto you. Each room also has a "soothing corner," where you'll find a stone bowl filled with fresh flower petals, essential oils, and floating candles. Most rooms have sea views, the rest look over the gardens or the pool. ⊠ *100 Cyberport Rd., Cyberport* ☎ *2989–6161* ☏ *2989–6181* ⊕ *www.lemeridien.com* ☞ *169 rooms, 4 suites* ♨ *3 restaurants, room service, in-room data ports, in-room safes, minibars, cable TV with movies and video games, pool, bicycles, bar, lounge, wine bar, shops, babysitting, dry cleaning, laundry service, concierge, Internet, business services, meeting rooms, parking, no-smoking rooms* ▤ *AE, DC, MC, V.*

Western

★ **$$**   Island Pacific Hotel. Designed as a boutique-style hotel, this 29-story property has small rooms, but the windows are large and there are views

Children Most hotels in Hong Kong allow children under a certain age to stay in their parents' room at no extra charge, but others charge for them as extra adults; be sure to find out the cutoff age for children's discounts. The Marco Polo Hongkong Hotel has added a range of amenities to make a child's stay more comfortable including miniature bathrobes, mild shampoos, and rubber ducks. Any of the hotels with large pools and recreational facilities—such as the Peninsula, Ritz-Carlton, Grand Hyatt, Renaissance Harbour View, Salisbury YMCA, and Holiday Inn—would be good choices if you have children in tow.

3

Discounts & Deals Accommodations can be expensive here, but almost no one pays the publicly quoted rate, the so-called rack rate. Travel agents and Internet sites frequently offer huge discounts or package deals that allow you to stay at a fine hotel for a fraction of its full rate. Hotels do their part, too, with such options as discounts and credits for use in their restaurants and bars. Some hotels offer attractive seasonal packages.

Prices Categories for hotel rates are based on the average price for a standard double room in high season for two people. All rates are subject to a 10% service charge and a 3% government tax, which is used to fund the activities of the Hong Kong Tourist Board (HKTB). Most hotels in Hong Kong operate on the European plan, with no meals included. All rooms have private baths unless indicated otherwise. The lodgings we review are the cream of the crop in each price category. We always list the facilities available, but we don't specify whether they cost extra; so when pricing accommodations, always ask what's included and what's not.

WHAT IT COSTS In HK$				
$$$$	$$$	$$	$	¢
FOR 2 PEOPLE over 3,000	2,100–3,000	1,100–2,100	700–1,100	under 700

Prices are for two people in a standard double room in high season.

Reservations You should book your room well in advance for a trip to Hong Kong, especially in March and from September through early December, the high seasons for conventions and conferences. It's always better to arrive with a reservation in hand rather than taking your chances that something good will be available.

of the city or the harbor. The Western Harbour Tunnel, which connects to the airport expressway, is nearby, as is the Hong Kong–Macau Ferry Terminal. A tram stop is outside the hotel, and a ride to Central takes about 10 minutes. Service here is not the best in town and carpets and furnishing look frayed in some rooms, but it is still a good value for the money. ✉ *152 Connaught Rd. W, Western* ☎ *2131–1188* 🖷 *2131–1212* ⊕ *www.islandpacifichotel.com.hk* 🛏 *336 rooms, 7 suites* ⌕ *Coffee* shop, room service, in-room data ports, in-room safes, minibars, cable TV with movies and video games, pool, gym, bar, babysitting, laundry service, Internet, business services, meeting rooms, no-smoking floors ▤ AE, DC, MC, V.

★ $$ 🏨 **Novotel Century Harbourview.** This modern hotel is surrounded by traditional Chinese streets and stores selling antiques, herbal medicines, and bric-a-brac, unchanged from the passage of time. Rooms are small but clean, with either city or harbor views. A free shuttle bus takes you to the Airport Express Hong Kong Station and the HK Convention & Exhibition Centre. Biz Café in the lobby has Internet facilities and is open from early morning for breakfast to late-night for supper and drinks. The rooftop pool and gym have panoramic views. ⊠ 508 Queens Rd. W, Western ☎ 2974–1234 🖷 2974–0333 ⊕ www.centuryhotels.com ⇨ 262 rooms, 12 suites ⏀ Restaurant, coffee shop, room service, in-room data ports, in-room safes, minibars, cable TV with movies, pool, gym, massage, 2 bars, babysitting, laundry service, Internet, business services, meeting rooms, no-smoking floors ▤ AE, DC, MC, V.

Central

$$$$
Fodor'sChoice
★
🏨 **Mandarin Oriental Hong Kong.** A legend worldwide, the Mandarin has served the international elite since 1963, and many world travelers wouldn't consider staying anywhere else in Hong Kong. Eastern antiques adorn the lobby; the comfortable and luxurious guest rooms have antique maps and prints, traditional wooden furnishings, Eastern knickknacks, and glamorous black and gold accents. The top floor houses Vong, a trendy French-Asian fusion restaurant. A harpist plays during high tea in the Clipper Lounge, and a live band performs in the Captains Bar in the evening. ⊠ 5 Connaught Rd., Central ☎ 2522–0111 🖷 2810–6190 ⊕ www.mandarin-oriental.com ⇨ 486 rooms, 55 suites ⏀ 4 restaurants, room service, in-room data ports, in-room safes, minibars, cable TV with movies, indoor pool, gym, health club, hair salon, hot tub, sauna, spa, 3 bars, dry cleaning, laundry service, concierge, Internet, business services, meeting rooms, no-smoking floors ▤ AE, DC, MC, V.

🕙 $$$$
Fodor'sChoice
★
🏨 **Ritz-Carlton, Hong Kong.** Refined elegance and superb hospitality are signatures of the Ritz-Carlton. Gilt-frame mirrors and crystal chandeliers reflect a homey European and Asian blend of furnishings, lush carpeting, and period oil paintings. In your room, complimentary flowers and fruit baskets are replenished daily; you'll also receive a morning newspaper. Other comforts include a bath menu, which includes bath essences for kids, romantics, ladies, or gentlemen brought to your room by the bath butler; there is also a tea and coffee cabinet. Rooms have either harbor or garden views. The upper club floors have a private concierge, lounge, and complimentary refreshments as added services. The main restaurant, Toscana, serves northern Italian cuisine. ⊠ 3 Connaught Rd., Central ☎ 2877–6666, 800/241–3333 in the U.S. 🖷 2877–6778 ⊕ www.ritzcarlton.com ⇨ 187 rooms, 29 suites ⏀ 5 restaurants, room service, in-room data ports, in-room safes, minibars, cable TV with movies, pool, gym, health club, hot tub, massage, sauna, bar, lounge, shop, babysitting, dry cleaning, laundry service, concierge, Internet, business services, meeting rooms, no-smoking floors ▤ AE, DC, MC, V.

Apartment Rentals

If you want a home base that's roomy enough for a family and comes with cooking facilities, consider a furnished rental. These can save you money, especially if you're traveling with a group. Home-exchange directories sometimes list rentals as well as exchanges.

3

In Hong Kong, renting an apartment is really only an alternative if you are planning to stay at least a month since most landlords require a minimum one-month stay. The SoHo area offers several serviced apartments that are convenient to Central offices. In this neighborhood, contact Rich Harvest Property.

International Agents **Hideaways International** ✉ 767 Islington St., Portsmouth, NH 03801 ☎ 603/430–4433 or 800/843–4433 🖷 603/430–4444 ⊕ www.hideaways.com, annual membership $145.

Local Agents **Eaton House** ✉ 380 Nathan Rd., Kowloon ☎ 2710–1800 🖷 2388–6971. **Hong Kong & Shanghai Hotels Ltd.** ✉ 8/F, St. Georges House, 2 Ice House St., Central ☎ 2840–7788 🖷 2845–5526. **Rich Harvest Property** ✉ 299 Queen's Rd., Central ☎ 2805–2223 🖷 2851–9099.

Home Exchanges

If you would like to exchange your home for someone else's, join a home-exchange organization, which will send you its updated listings of available exchanges for a year and will include your own listing in at least one of them. It's up to you to make specific arrangements.

Exchange Clubs **HomeLink International** ✎ Box 47747, Tampa, FL 33647 ☎ 813/975–9825 or 800/638–3841 🖷 813/910–8144 ⊕ www.homelink.org; $110 yearly for a listing, online access, and catalog; $70 without catalog. **Intervac U.S.** ✉ 30 Corte San Fernando, Tiburon, CA 94920 ☎ 800/756–4663 🖷 415/435–7440 ⊕ www.intervacus.com; $125 yearly for a listing, online access, and a catalog; $65 without catalog.

Hostels

No matter what your age, you can save on lodging costs by staying at hostels. The Hong Kong Youth Hostels Association is a full member of the International Youth Hostel Federation (Hostelling International, [HI]). The main hostels, Bradbury Lodge and Ma Wui Hall, are easily accessible by public transport. Both are less than HK$85 per night. In some 4,500 locations in more than 70 countries around the world, Hostelling International (HI), the umbrella group for a number of national youth-hostel associations, offers single-sex, dorm-style beds and, at many hostels, rooms for couples and family accommodations. Membership in any HI national hostel association, open to travelers of all ages, allows you to stay in HI-affiliated hostels at member rates; one-year membership is about $28 for adults (C$35 for a two-year minimum membership in Canada, £14 in the United Kingdom, A$52 in Australia, and NZ$40 in New Zealand); hostels charge about $10–$30 per night. Members have priority if the hostel is full; they're also eligible for discounts around the world, even on rail and bus travel in some countries.

Hostel Information **Bradbury Lodge** ✉ 66 Ting Kok Rd., Tai Mei Tuk Tai Po, New Territories ☎ 2662–5123. **Ma Wui Hall** ✉ Top of Mt. Davis Path, Mt. Davis, Western District, Hong Kong ☎ 2817–5715. **YHA China** ⊕ www.yhachina.com.

Organizations **Hostelling International–USA** ⊠ 8401 Colesville Rd., Suite 600, Silver Spring, MD 20910 ☎ 301/495-1240 🖷 301/495-6697 ⊕ www.hiusa.org. **Hostelling International–Canada** ⊠ 205 Catherine St., Suite 400, Ottawa, Ontario K2P 1C3 ☎ 613/237-7884 or 800/663-5777 🖷 613/237-7868 ⊕ www.hihostels.ca. **YHA Australia** ⊠ 422 Kent St., Sydney, NSW 2001 ☎ 02/9261-1111 🖷 02/9261-1969 ⊕ www.yha.com.au. **YHA England and Wales** ⊠ Trevelyan House, Dimple Rd., Matlock, Derbyshire DE4 3YH U.K. ☎ 0870/870-8808, 0870/770-8868, or 0162/959-2600 🖷 0870/770-6127 ⊕ www.yha.org.uk. **YHA New Zealand** ⊠ Moorhouse City, 166 Moorhouse Ave., level 1, Box 436, Christchurch ☎ 03/379-9970 or 0800/278-299 🖷 03/365-4476 ⊕ www.yha.org.nz.

Admiralty

🖰 **$$$$** 🖻 **JW Marriott Hotel.** This modern, elegant hotel was the first to open at Pacific Place. Its spacious, plant-filled lobby has plenty of natural sunlight, with floor-to-ceiling windows and views of the harbor, and it is a favorite meeting place for businesspeople. Rooms have harbor and mountain views, ample work space, and thoughtful amenities such as irons and ironing boards, complimentary coffee, tea, and mineral water, and high-speed Internet access. Suites have hi-fi systems and CD alarm clocks. There is a well-equipped 24-hour gym and an outdoor pool, and even tai chi lessons every Saturday. Sunday lunch at the Marriott Café has clowns to entertain the children. ⊠ *Pacific Place, 88 Queensway, Central* ☎ *2810–8366, 800/228–9290 in the U.S.* 🖷 *2845–0737* ⊕ *www.marriott.com* 🖢 *602 rooms, 25 suites* 🖰 *4 restaurants, room service, in-room data ports, in-room safes, minibars, cable TV with movies, pool, health club, spa, 3 bars, shop, babysitting, dry cleaning, laundry service, concierge, Internet, business services, meeting rooms, no-smoking floors* ▤ *AE, DC, MC, V.*

★ **$$$** 🖻 **Conrad Hong Kong.** This luxurious business hotel occupies part of a gleaming-white, oval-shape tower rising from Pacific Place, an upscale complex with a multistory mall on the edge of Central. Rooms are spacious and have dramatic views of the harbor and city. All rooms have an iron and ironing board, coffee and tea facilities, and high-speed Internet access. The five executive floors have their own private elevator and lounge and gym. Brasserie on the Eighth is popular for its French fare and views of the park; Nicholini's is one of the city's top spots for Italian cuisine. ⊠ *Pacific Place, 88 Queensway, Central* ☎ *2521–3838* 🖷 *2521–3888* ⊕ *www.conradhotels.com* 🖢 *467 rooms, 46 suites* 🖰 *4 restaurants, room service, in-room data ports, in-room fax, in-room safes, minibars, cable TV with movies, pool, health club, bar, lounge, dry cleaning, laundry service, concierge, Internet, business services, meeting rooms, no-smoking floors* ▤ *AE, DC, MC, V.*

$$$ 🖻 **Island Shangri-La.** The lobby of this deluxe hotel sparkles with more Fodor'sChoice than 780 dazzling Austrian crystal chandeliers hanging from high ceil-★ ings and huge, sunlit windows. A 16-story glass-topped atrium houses the world's largest Chinese landscape painting, *The Great Motherland of China.* Take the elevator up from the 39th floor and see the mainland's misty mountains drift by. Rooms are the largest on Hong Kong

COMING ATTRACTIONS

BEING THE VIBRANT CITY THAT IT IS, Hong Kong always has something developing, just over the horizon. The colonial-era former Marine Police Headquarters on the Kowloon waterfront is being redeveloped into a hotel, though it is not expected to open until sometime in 2007. Not quite as far in the future, the first phase of the new Hong Kong Disneyland will have some 1,000 hotel rooms for those who want to stay close to the park, but the resort won't open until sometime in late 2005 or early 2006. The new Le Meridien Cyberport hotel has already opened on the south side of Hong Kong island, and it is reviewed in this chapter.

Several big luxury hotels were also in the works at this writing, most of which were to open 2005. Here are some of the highlights: **Four Seasons Hong Kong** (⊠ 8 Finance Rd., Central ☎ 3196–8888 pre-opening office ⊕ www.fourseasons.

com), with 386 rooms, will be part of the new International Finance Centre opening on the Hong Kong Island waterfront in 2005.

Landmark Mandarin Oriental (⊠ Pedder St. and Des Voeux Rd., Central ⊕ www. mandarinoriental.com), will open in mid-2005. At the same time, the flagship Mandarin Oriental Hong Kong will close for a major renovation.

Langham Place Hotel (⊠ 555 Shanghai St., Mongkok ☎ 3552–3388 ⊟ 3552-3322 ⊕ www.langhamhotels.com), a high-tech hotel with 665 rooms, opened too late in 2004 to be reviewed in this book; it's a part of the new Langham Place Shopping Centre development in Mongkok.

Island and have magnificent views; all have large desks and all-in-one bedside control panels. Service is friendly and efficient. For very upscale dining there's the French eatery Petrus, or for Chinese food, the Summer Palace. ⊠ *Supreme Court Rd., 2 Pacific Place, Central* ☎ *2877–3838, 800/942–5050 in the U.S.* ⊟ *2521–8742* ⊕ *www.shangri-la.com* ⤶ *531 rooms, 34 suites* ⚘ *4 restaurants, room service, in-room data ports, in-room safes, minibars, cable TV with movies, pool, gym, health club, hair salon, hot tub, massage, sauna, spa, steam room, bar, lounge, shops, babysitting, dry cleaning, laundry service, concierge, Internet, business services, meeting rooms, no-smoking floors* ▭ *AE, DC, MC, V.*

Midlevels

$$ 🏨 **Bishop Lei International House.** Owned and operated by the Catholic
Fodor's Choice   diocese of Hong Kong, this guesthouse is up the Midlevels Escalator
★   at the top of SoHo. Rooms are small but clean and functional, and half have harbor views. Although it's economically priced, there are a fully equipped business center, a workout room, a pool, and a restaurant serving Chinese and Western meals. ⊠ *4 Robinson Rd., Midlevels* ☎ *2868–0828* ⊟ *2868–1551* ⊕ *www.bishopleihtl.com.hk* ⤶ *104 rooms, 101 suites* ⚘ *Restaurant, in-room data ports, in-room safes,*

Where to Stay on Hong Kong Island

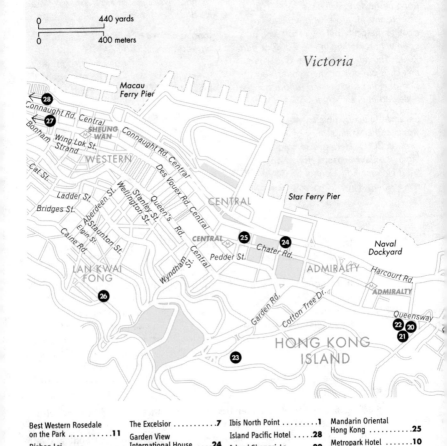

0 ⊢──────┤ 440 yards
0 ⊢──────┤ 400 meters

Victoria

Macau Ferry Pier

Connaught Rd. Central

SHEUNG WAN

Bonham Strand

Wing Lok St.

Connaught Rd. Central

WESTERN

Des Voeux Rd. Central

Cat St.

Ladder St.

Bridges St.

Aberdeen St.

Staunton St.

Elgin St.

Caine Rd.

Stanley St.

Wellington St.

Queen's Rd.

CENTRAL

Star Ferry Pier

CENTRAL

Wyndham St.

Central

Pedder St.

Chater Rd.

Naval Dockyard

LAN KWAI FONG

ADMIRALTY

Harcourt Rd.

ADMIRALTY

Garden Rd.

Cotton Tree Dr.

Queensway

HONG KONG ISLAND

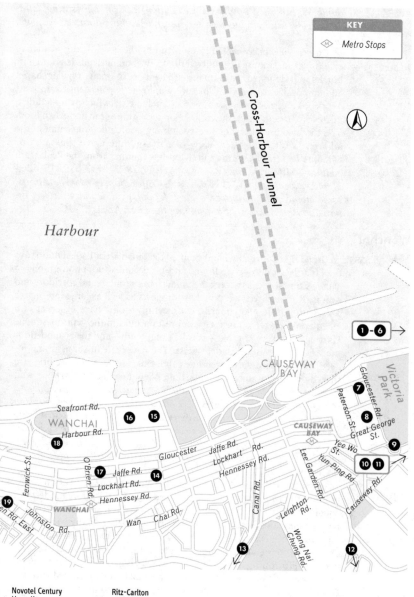

minibars, cable TV, pool, exercise equipment, gym, babysitting, laundry service, Internet, business services, no-smoking floors ▭ *AE, DC, MC, V.*

♻ $ ▦ **Garden View International House.** Run by the YWCA, this attractive
Fodor's Choice   cylindrical guesthouse on a hill overlooks the botanical gardens and har-
★   bor. Its well-designed rooms make excellent use of small irregular shapes
and emphasize each room's picture windows. If you want to do your
own cooking, ask for a room with a kitchenette (which will include a
microwave oven); if not, the coffee shop serves European and Asian food.
You can also use the renovated swimming pool and gymnasium in the
adjacent YWCA. Garden View is a five-minute drive (Bus 12A or
Minibus 1A) from Central and just a few minutes from the Peak tram
station. ✉ *1 MacDonnell Rd., Midlevels* ☎ *2877–3737* 🖷 *2845–6263*
⊕ *www.ywca.org.hk* ⇄ *130 rooms* ♻ *Coffee shop, in-room data ports,
some kitchenettes, minibars, cable TV, pool, gym, laundry service, Internet, business services, no-smoking floors* ▭ *AE, DC, MC, V.*

Wanchai

★ ♻ $$$$ ▦ **Grand Hyatt.** A ceiling hand-painted by Italian artist Paola Dindo tops
the Hyatt's art deco–style lobby, and black-and-white photographs of
classic Chinese scenes accent the modern but rather bland corridors and
rooms. Rooms have sweeping harbor views as well as large interactive
TVs with cordless keyboards; all meeting rooms have ethernet and
video-conference facilities. Grissini restaurant and the Cantonese One
Harbour Road are notable—as is J J's nightclub—and the ground-floor
breakfast buffet is a decadent feast. The new Plateau spa is grand indeed, and suffused with a zen-like calm; extensive outdoor facilities are
shared with the Renaissance Harbour View hotel. ✉ *1 Harbour Rd.,
Wanchai* ☎ *2588–1234* 🖷 *2802–0677* ⊕ *www.hongkong.grand.hyatt.
com* ⇄ *519 rooms, 51 suites* ♻ *4 restaurants, room service, in-room
data ports, in-room safes, minibars, cable TV with movies, driving
range, 2 tennis courts, pool, exercise equipment, gym, health club, hair
salon, spa, bar, lounge, nightclub, babysitting, dry cleaning, laundry service, concierge, Internet, business services, meeting rooms, no-smoking
floors* ▭ *AE, DC, MC, V.*

♻ $$$ ▦ **Renaissance Harbour View.** Sharing the Hong Kong Convention & Ex-
Fodor's Choice   hibition Centre complex with the Grand Hyatt is this more modest but
★   equally attractive hotel. Guest rooms are medium size with plenty of
beveled-glass mirrors that reflect the modern decor. Many rooms have
good harbor views and all have high-speed internet access. Grounds are
extensive and include the largest outdoor hotel pool in town, plus gardens, a playground, and jogging trails, which makes this hotel a good
place to stay if you are with children; these facilities are shared with the
Grand Hyatt. The lobby lounge has a live jazz band in the evening and
is a popular rendezvous spot for locals and visiting businesspeople.
✉ *1 Harbour Rd., Wanchai* ☎ *2802–8888* 🖷 *2802–8833* ⊕ *www.
renaissancehotels.com* ⇄ *807 rooms, 53 suites* ♻ *4 restaurants, room
service, in-room data ports, in-room fax, in-room safes, minibars, cable
TV with movies, driving range, 2 tennis courts, pool, gym, health club,
hair salon, sauna, 2 bars, shops, babysitting, playground, dry cleaning,*

laundry service, concierge, Internet, business services, meeting rooms, no-smoking floors ⊟ *AE, DC, MC, V.*

♨ **$$** ⌖ **Harbour View International House.** This waterfront YMCA property has small but clean—and relatively inexpensive—rooms near the Wanchai Star Ferry Pier. The best rooms face the harbor. The hotel is well placed if you want to attend cultural events in the evening: both the Arts Centre and the Academy for Performing Arts are next door. Opposite Harbour View is the Hong Kong Convention & Exhibition Centre. The 16-story hostel provides free shuttle service to Causeway Bay and the Central Star Ferry. You can use the superb YMCA Kowloon facilities, just a short ferry ride away, for a small fee. ⊠ *4 Harbour Rd., Wanchai* ☎ *2802–0111* 🖷 *2802–9063* ⊕ *www.hvih.com.hk* ⤳ *320 rooms* ♨ *Restaurant, room service, in-room data ports, minibars, cable TV, babysitting, laundry service, concierge, Internet, business services, meeting rooms, no-smoking floor* ⊟ *AE, DC, MC, V.*

$$ ⌖ **Luk Kwok.** This contemporary hotel and office tower designed by Hong Kong's leading architect, Remo Riva, opened its doors in 1989. It replaced the Wanchai landmark of the same name immortalized in Richard Mason's novel *The World of Suzie Wong.* The Luk Kwok's appeal is its proximity to the Hong Kong Convention & Exhibition Centre, the Academy for Performing Arts, and the Arts Centre. Guest rooms, located in the building's 19th to 29th floors, are clean and simple, with contemporary furniture; higher floors have mountain or city views. There's a good Chinese restaurant. ⊠ *72 Gloucester Rd., Wanchai* ☎ *2866–2166* 🖷 *2866–2622* ⊕ *www.lukkwokhotel.com* ⤳ *191 rooms, 5 suites* ♨ *2 restaurants, room service, in-room data ports, in-room safes, minibars, cable TV with movies, health club, lounge, laundry service, Internet, business services, meeting rooms, no-smoking floor* ⊟ *AE, DC, MC, V.*

$$ ⌖ **Novotel Century Hong Kong.** Ideal for conventioneers—a five-minute walk by covered overpass (a lifesaver in the steamy summer heat) from the convention center and the MTR—this 23-story hotel caters to business travelers, offering a well-equipped business center and executive floors. Rooms are modern and have wood furniture. The gym also has an outdoor pool and a golf driving bay. Within the complex are a popular, independently run Shanghainese restaurant, a 24-hour coffee shop (in keeping with Wanchai's reputation for nightlife), and a karaoke lounge. ⊠ *238 Jaffe Rd., Wanchai* ☎ *2598–8888* 🖷 *2598–8866* ⊕ *www.century-hotels.com* ⤳ *497 rooms, 19 suites* ♨ *2 restaurants, room service, in-room data ports, in-room safes, minibars, cable TV with movies, pool, gym, health club, massage, 2 bars, shop, dry cleaning, laundry service, concierge, Internet, business services, meeting rooms, no-smoking floor* ⊟ *AE, DC, MC, V.*

$$ ⌖ **The Wesley.** Built on the site of the old Soldiers & Sailors Home, this 21-story reasonably priced hotel is a short walk from the Hong Kong Convention & Exhibition Centre, the Academy for Performing Arts, and the MTR. Rooms are small but pleasantly furnished, and the more spacious corner "suites" have alcove work areas. No health center or pool is on the premises, but long-stay guests can use the facilities at the Grand Plaza Apartments in Quarry Bay for a discounted fee. A tram stop is right outside the door, and Pacific Place and the bars of Wanchai are close by. ☒ *22 Hennessy Rd., Wanchai* 2866–6688 🖷 2866–6613 ⊕ *www.grandhotel.com.hk* ↶ 251 rooms ⚴ Restaurant, coffee shop, minibars, cable TV, laundry service, concierge, Internet, business services, no-smoking floor ⊟ AE, DC, MC, V.

Causeway Bay

★ ⚙ **$$$** 🏨 **The Excelsior.** This hotel opened in 1973 and remains perennially popular with travelers due in part to its high standard of service. Most rooms are spacious and enjoy splendid sea views, including the yachts and boats moored at the Hong Kong Yacht Club; other rooms have street views. The location is ideal for shopping and dining and is adjacent to Victoria Park. ToTT's Asian Grill & Bar, on the top floor, has East-meets-West cuisine and live music. On a historical note, the hotel sits on the first plot of land auctioned by the British government when Hong Kong became a colony in 1841. ☒ *281 Gloucester Rd., Causeway Bay* 🕿 *2894–8888* 🖷 *2895–6459* ⊕ *www.excelsiorhongkong.com* ↶ *866 rooms, 21 suites* ⚴ *4 restaurants, room service, in-room data ports, in-room safes, minibars, cable TV with movies, 2 tennis courts, health club, hair salon, spa, 2 bars, lounge, shop, dry cleaning, laundry service, concierge, Internet, business services, meeting rooms, no-smoking floors* ⊟ *AE, DC, MC, V.*

★ **$$$** 🏨 **Park Lane.** With an imposing facade reminiscent of something from London's Knightsbridge area, this elegant hotel overlooks Victoria Park and backs onto one of Hong Kong Island's busiest shopping, entertainment, and business areas, Causeway Bay. The beautiful lobby is spacious. Rooms have luxurious marble bathrooms, elegant handcrafted furniture, and marvelous views of the harbor, Victoria Park, or the city. The rooftop restaurant has a panoramic view and serves international cuisine with a touch of Asian flavor. The Premier Club floors add butler service. ☒ *310 Gloucester Rd., Causeway Bay* 🕿 *2293–8888* 🖷 *2576–7853* ⊕ *www.parklane.com.hk* ↶ *759 rooms, 33 suites* ⚴ *2 restaurants, room service, in-room data ports, in-room safes, minibars, cable TV with movies, gym, health club, hair salon, massage, sauna, spa, bar, shop, babysitting, dry cleaning, laundry service, concierge, Internet, business services, meeting rooms, no-smoking floor* ⊟ *AE, DC, MC, V.*

$$$ 🏨 **Regal Hongkong Hotel.** The reception area is small, but service is efficient here. Gilded elevators lead to guest rooms that are decorated in muted earth tones but are made more lively with brightly colored bedspreads, furniture handcrafted by local artisans, and spacious bathrooms with triangular tubs. There are four executive floors. Restaurants include the top-floor Mediterranean Zeffirino's, which has a great view of Victoria Park. The peaceful rooftop pool and terrace also have impressive views. This deluxe hotel is close to the Hong Kong Stadium and the Happy Valley Racetrack, as well as the city's most popular shopping area, Causeway Bay. ☒ *88 Yee Wo St., Causeway Bay* 🕿 *2890–6633, 800/222–8888 in the U.S.* 🖷 *2881–0777* ⊕ *www. regalhongkong.com* ↶ *393 rooms, 32 suites* ⚴ *6 restaurants, room service, in-room data ports, in-room safes, minibars, cable TV, pool,* gym, health club, sauna, spa, bar, lounge, shops, dry cleaning, laundry service, concierge, Internet, business services, meeting rooms, no-smoking floor ☐ AE, DC, MC, V.

$$ 🖾 **Best Western Rosedale on the Park.** This "cyberhotel," the first of its kind in Hong Kong, has lots of high-tech extras. All public areas have computers, and you can rent a printer, computer, or fax for use in your room, where you also have broadband Internet access and a cordless telephone that can be used anywhere on the property. Mobile phones are also available for rent during your stay. Although only the top few floors have park or stadium views, all rooms are bright and comfortable. Next to Victoria Park and only a five-minute walk to the MTR subway, it's a great location for shopping. ⊠ 8 Shelter St., Causeway Bay ☎ 2127–8888 📠 2127–3333 ⊕ www.rosedale.com.hk 🛏 229 rooms, 45 suites ⌂ 2 restaurants, room service, in-room data ports, in-room safes, minibars, cable TV with movies, lounge, babysitting, dry cleaning, laundry service, Internet, business services, meeting rooms, no-smoking floors ☐ AE, DC, MC, V.

★ $$ 🖾 **Metropark Hotel.** At this contemporary hotel with Euro-boutique flair you'll get a prime location and unobstructed views for a fraction of the cost of other hotels. Most rooms have extensive views of Victoria Park next door or the harbor through the floor-to-ceiling windows, and all rooms are equipped with high-speed Internet access. The tiny lobby leads into Vic's, a tapas bar; the trendy Café du Parc has French and Japanese fusion food. Free shuttle buses to and from the Hong Kong Convention & Exhibition Centre and the hub of Causeway Bay run throughout the day. ⊠ 148 Tung Lo Wan Rd., Causeway Bay ☎ 2600–1000 📠 2600–1111 ⊕ www.metroparkhotel.com 🛏 243 rooms, 23 suites ⌂ Restaurant, room service, in-room data ports, in-room safes, minibars, cable TV, pool, gym, sauna, spa, bar, babysitting, dry cleaning, laundry service, Internet, business services, meeting rooms, no-smoking floor ☐ AE, DC, MC, V.

$$ 🖾 **New Cathay Hotel.** Having upgraded its facilities in 2003, this Chinese-managed hotel is close by Victoria Park and the Causeway Bay MTR with bus stops close by that will take you to most areas of Kowloon and Hong Kong. It's also a few minutes from the bustling shopping center of Causeway Bay. The small rooms are plain but have basic amenities such as air-conditioning and TV with soundproof floor-to-ceiling windows and views of the city. An independently run Chinese seafood restaurant is on the top floor. ⊠ 17 Tung Lo Wan Rd., Causeway Bay ☎ 2577–8211 📠 2576–9365 ⊕ newcathay.gdhotels.net 🛏 219 rooms, 3 suites ⌂ Restaurant, coffee shop, room service, in-room safes, minibars, cable TV, dry cleaning, laundry service ☐ AE, DC, MC, V.

Happy Valley

$$ 🖾 **Emperor Happy Valley Hotel.** Catering mainly to business and corporate travelers, this reasonably priced hotel is one of few places to stay in the predominantly residential Happy Valley area. The Emperor is also the best deal in town for horse-racing fans, as it's just a few minutes' walk from the Happy Valley Racetrack. It's also 5 to 10 minutes by taxi from the Causeway Bay shopping area. With a deluxe, European look, the public rooms have regal furnishings, but the corridors are narrow and rooms are small, though clean. ✉ *1A Wang Tak St., Happy Valley* ☎ *2893–3693* 🖷 *2834–6700* ⊕ *www.emperorhotel.com.hk* ⬎ *157 rooms, 1 suite △ 2 restaurants, room service, in-room data ports, in-room safes, minibars, cable TV with movies, bar, laundry service, concierge, Internet, no-smoking floor* ☰ *AE, DC, MC, V.*

North Point

$$ ▦ **City Garden.** Situated in a residential area in North Point and about a five-minute walk to the MTR, this hotel has the advantage of being easily accessible to the Eastern Corridor Expressway, which links Causeway Bay to Taikoo Shing and the eastern-harbor crossing. Small rooms are clean but basic; service is efficient. The hotel caters to Asian tour groups and has a good Cantonese restaurant. ✉ *9 City Garden Rd., North Point* ☎ *2887–2888* 🖷 *2887–1111* ⊕ *www.citygarden.com.hk* ⬎ *613 rooms, 2 suites △ 2 restaurants, room service, in-room data ports, in-room safes, minibars, cable TV with movies, pool, gym, health club, sauna, bar, babysitting, laundry service, Internet, business services, meeting rooms, no-smoking floors* ☰ *AE, DC, MC, V.*

$$ ▦ **Newton Hotel.** In a boxy high-rise that is functional but largely featureless, this hotel has the advantages of proximity to the Fortress Hill MTR station and its surrounding office blocks and a pleasant on-site restaurant-bar with live entertainment. Many claim that the Old Hong Kong Restaurant, in the basement, is one of the better Shanghainese restaurants in town. Rooms are small but adequate. ✉ *218 Electric Rd., North Point* ☎ *2807–2333* 🖷 *2807–1221* ⊕ *www.newtonhk.com* ⬎ *362 rooms, 9 suites △ 2 restaurants, coffee shop, room service, in-room data ports, in-room safes, minibars, cable TV with movies, pool, sauna, bar, lounge, laundry service, Internet, business services, meeting rooms* ☰ *AE, DC, MC, V.*

¢ ▦ **Ibis North Point.** In the increasingly developed eastern harbor-front area, this hotel is well located for business travelers who are working around Quarry Bay, but it's somewhat out of the way for vacationers. However, the prices will be attractive to the budget-minded who want to stay on the Hong Kong side. Many rooms have harbor views, compensating for their small size, and have a full range of functional amenities. ✉ *136–142 Java Rd., North Point* ☎ *2204–6618* 🖷 *2204–6677* ⊕ *www.accorhotels-asia.com* ⬎ *207 rooms, 3 suites △ Restaurant, room service, in-room data ports, in-room safes, minibars, cable TV, pool, lounge, laundry service, Internet, business services* ☰ *AE, DC, MC, V.*

¢ ▦ **South China Hotel Hong Kong.** Managed by a Chinese company and thus naturally attracting groups from mainland China, the hotel is small and functional, and has a large Chinese restaurant and bar. Rooms are small with basic facilities; Internet service is only available in the business center. It's some distance from the North Point MTR and is therefore not the most conveniently placed budget hotel in town, especially if you're planning on doing a lot of sightseeing. However, there are tram and bus stops with frequent service outside the hotel. ✉ *67 Java Rd., North Point* ☎ *2503–1168* 🖷 *2512–8698* ⊕ *www.southchinahotel.com.hk* ⬎ *202 rooms, 1 suite △ 2 restaurants, room service, minibars,* *cable TV with movies, bar, laundry service, Internet, business services, no-smoking floor* ▭ *AE, DC, MC, V.*

Quarry Bay

★ **$$** ▦ **Harbour Plaza North Point.** Despite the name, this hotel, which opened in April 2000, is near the Quarry Bay business district and opposite the Quarry Bay MTR station. Its modern facade stands out amid the old, narrow streets and traditional Chinese shops. Rooms are spacious and bright, with harbor or street views; all bathrooms have showers only. Service is friendly and efficient. A free shuttle bus will take you to the Hong Kong Cultural & Exhibition Centre throughout the day. ✉ *665 Kings Rd., Quarry Bay* ☎ *2187–8888* 🖷 *2187–8899* ⊕ *www.harbour-plaza.com* ⇱ *296 rooms, 270 suites* ⚘ *3 restaurants, room service, in-room data ports, in-room safes, minibars, cable TV with movies, pool, gym, sauna, spa, bar, babysitting, dry cleaning, laundry service, Internet, business services, meeting rooms, no-smoking floors* ▭ *AE, DC, MC, V.*

KOWLOON

Most of Hong Kong's hotels are on the Kowloon Peninsula, which includes the **Tsim Sha Tsui** and **Tsim Sha Tsui East,** neighborhoods and the **Yau Ma Tei** and **Mong Kok** districts, just north of Tsim Sha Tsui. The fabled Golden Mile of shopping on Nathan Road runs through Tsim Sha Tsui, and restaurants, stores, and hotels fill the surrounding backstreets.

Tsim Sha Tsui East is a grid of modern office blocks—many with restaurants or nightclubs—and luxury hotels. This area was created on land reclaimed from the harbor in the 1970s. **Hung Hom,** adjacent to Tsim Sha Tsui East, includes a noisy old residential area and a private-housing complex with cinemas, shops, and new hotels.

North of Tsim Sha Tsui are Yau Ma Tei and Mong Kok, which have older, smaller, more moderately priced hotels. Most of these are on or near Nathan Road and are probably the best bets for travelers on budgets. Excellent bus service and the MTR connect these areas to the center of Tsim Sha Tsui.

Hung Hom

$$$ ▦ **Harbour Plaza Hong Kong.** The opulent Harbour Plaza has one of the
Fodor'sChoice best harbor views in town. The atrium lobby is spacious with good views
★ from lounges on two levels. Rooms are large, comfortable, and contemporary. Dining options include a Japanese *robatayaki* grill restaurant and a fun pub called the Pit Stop. A scenic rooftop pool, a fitness center, and a spa are also on-site. Although it's in the residential area of Whampoa Gardens, hotel shuttles run the 10- to 15-minute trip to Tsim Sha Tsui all day. Close by is the railway station, with trains to China, and a ferry terminal for Hong Kong Island. ✉ *20 Tak Fung St., Hung Hom* ☎ *2621–3188* 🖷 *2621–3311* ⊕ *www.harbour-plaza.com* ⇱ *381 rooms, 30 suites* ⚘ *4 restaurants, room service, in-room data ports, in-*

104 <

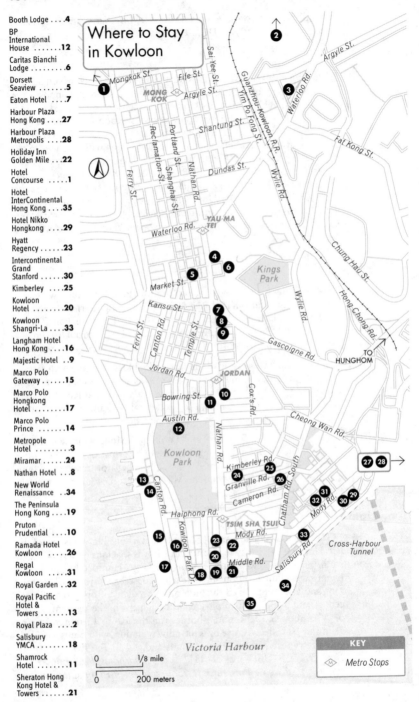

Where to Stay in Kowloon

room safes, minibars, cable TV with movies, pool, health club, hair salon, spa, lounge, pub, shop, babysitting, dry cleaning, laundry service, concierge, Internet, business services, meeting rooms, no-smoking floors 🖭 *AE, DC, MC, V.*

★ **$$** 🏨 **Harbour Plaza Metropolis.** The Harbour Plaza Metropolis, which opened in June 2002, is an ideal place to stay if you are planning to travel by train into China. It is next to the Kowloon–Canton Hung Hom Railway Station, which has a direct link to Shenzhen and Guangzhou. It is also next to the Coliseum, where concerts and sports events take place. A shuttle bus to nearby Tsim Sha Tsui leaves every 20 minutes. Rooms are small and have showers only; most have harbor views. Restaurants include the Patio, which serves Thai food alfresco along with panoramic harbor views. ✉ *7 Metropolis Dr., Hung Hom* 🕾 *3160–6888* 🖷 *3160–6999* ⊕ *www.harbour-plaza.com* 🛏 *687 rooms, 3 suites* ♿ *3 restaurants, in-room data ports, in-room safes, minibars, cable TV with movies, pool, gym, bar, lounge, shop, babysitting, dry cleaning, laundry service, Internet, business services, meeting rooms, no-smoking floors* 🖭 *AE, DC, MC, V.*

Tsim Sha Tsui

★ **$$$$** 🏨 **Hotel InterContinental Hong Kong.** You'll have spectacular harbor views at this luxury hotel formerly known as the Regent. The spacious and modern guest rooms include 24-hour butler service, Italian marble bathrooms with sunken tubs and separate shower stalls, and a TV-based Internet service in all rooms. Suites have harbor views, and some have private terraces with outdoor hot tubs. The spa, open to the public, has luxurious private rooms, each with Jacuzzi, sauna, and steam shower and specialty treatments such as Jet Lag Relief and Oriental Healing. Dining options are top-rate and include Yü for seafood, Yan Toh Heen for Cantonese food, and the Steak House Bar & Grill. ✉ *18 Salisbury Rd., Tsim Sha Tsui* 🕾 *2721–1211, 800/327–0200 in the U.S.* 🖷 *2739–4546* ⊕ *www.ichotelsgroup.com* 🛏 *422 rooms, 92 suites* ♿ *4 restaurants, in-room data ports, minibars, cable TV with movies, pool, gym, health club, hot tub, sauna, spa, steam room, shop, babysitting, dry cleaning, laundry service, concierge, Internet, business services, meeting rooms, no-smoking floors* 🖭 *AE, DC, MC, V.*

$$$$ 🏨 **The Peninsula Hong Kong.** Established in 1928, the Pen is known worldwide for its impeccable taste and old-world style evidenced in its colonial architecture, columned and gilt-corniced lobby, and fleet of Rolls-Royces. Service is attentive and discreet. Spacious rooms, decorated with plush fabrics and Chinese prints, have bedside remotes that operate everything from the lights to the curtains. Sumptuous corner suites have Jacuzzis with views of the skyline. Helicopter transfers and private sightseeing tours take off from the rooftop helipad. Restaurants include Gaddi's, Chinese Spring Moon, and the trendy rooftop Felix. ✉ *Salisbury Rd., Tsim Sha Tsui* 🕾 *2366–6251* 🖷 *2722–4170* ⊕ *www.peninsula.com* 🛏 *246 rooms, 54 suites* ♿ *7 restaurants, room service, in-room data ports, in-room fax, in-room safes, minibars, cable TV with movies, in-room VCRs, pool, gym, health club, hair salon, hot tub, spa, bar, shops, babysitting, dry cleaning, laundry service, concierge, Internet,*

Fodor'sChoice
★

business services, meeting rooms, helipad, no-smoking floors ⊟ *AE, DC, MC, V.*

$$$ ⊡ **Holiday Inn Golden Mile.** On the Golden Mile of Nathan Road, the hub of Kowloon's business and shopping area, is this business-style hotel whose friendly service has ensured its popularity with tourists, business travelers, and locals for more than two decades. The cozy lobby lounge, from which an elegant staircase leads up to the lounge bar, has an East-meets-West theme. The medium-size rooms are designed for comfort and have a sofa and coffee table; the views, however, are not the best in town. The Avenue restaurant serves delicious contemporary European cuisine overlooking the neon sights and sounds of Tsim Sha Tsui's main artery. ⊠ *50 Nathan Rd., Tsim Sha Tsui* ☎ *2369–3111* 🖷 *2369–8016* ⊕ *gold-enmile-hk.holiday-inn.com* ↳ *592 rooms, 8 suites* ⚲ *3 restaurants, room service, in-room data ports, in-room safes, minibars, cable TV with movies, pool, gym, health club, sauna, spa, bar, lounge, shop, babysit-ting, dry cleaning, laundry service, Internet, business services, meeting rooms, no-smoking rooms, no-smoking floors* ⊟ *AE, DC, MC, V.*

$$$ ⊡ **Hyatt Regency.** The hotel's modern facade, top-end shopping arcade, gallery of Asian antiques, and dramatic, marble-and-teak lobby exude glamour. The Buddhist gods of hospitality guarding the spacious lobby's reception area are meant to give you warm blessings and ensure a pleas-ant stay, and to that end, the hotel even has its own feng shui expert with whom you can consult. Rooms are comfortable and soundproofed and well equipped with everything from Internet access to an in-room bar. ⊠ *67 Nathan Rd., Tsim Sha Tsui* ☎ *2311–1234* 🖷 *2739–8701* ⊕ *hongkong.regency.hyatt.com* ↳ *723 rooms, 4 suites* ⚲ *4 restau-rants, coffee shop, room service, in-room data ports, in-room safes, mini-bars, cable TV with movies, 2 bars, shop, babysitting, dry cleaning, laundry service, concierge, Internet, business services, meeting rooms, no-smok-ing rooms, no-smoking floors* ⊟ *AE, DC, MC, V.*

$$$ ⊡ **Langham Hotel Hong Kong.** Formerly the Great Eagle Hotel, this lux-ury hotel's new name aligns it with its sister property in London, the Langham Hilton. The sophisticated lobby has glowing back-lighted onyx pillars reaching up to beautifully painted ceiling murals. On the rooftop is a gym and poolside oasis. Stylish guest rooms mix comfort and elegance with classic European touches. Harbor views, however, are blocked by a high-rise. The Main Street Deli is the only genuine New York deli in town; Asian-attuned palates will love the innovative and delicately presented Chinese dishes at T'ang Court. ⊠ *8 Peking Rd., Tsim Sha Tsui* ☎ *2375–1133* 🖷 *2375–6611* ⊕ *www.langhamhotels.com* ↳ *461 rooms, 25 suites* ⚲ *5 restaurants, room service, in-room data ports, some in-room faxes, in-room safes, minibars, cable TV with movies, pool, gym, sauna, spa, bar, lounge, shop, dry cleaning, laundry service, concierge, Internet, business services, meeting rooms, no-smok-ing floors* ⊟ *AE, DC, MC, V.*

$$$ ⊡ **Marco Polo Gateway.** This 16-story hotel, popular with Japanese tour groups, is in the shopping and commercial area along Canton Road and close to the Tsim Sha Tsui MTR station. The tastefully decorated rooms and suites have large windows and comfortable beds. The most notable restaurant is La Brasserie, serving French provincial cuisine in a typical brasserie style (long bar, dark wood, leather seats, red-checkered tablecloths). The business center is well supplied, and the staff are helpful and well trained. You can use the pool, gym, and spa at the nearby Marco Polo Hongkong Hotel. ⊠ *Harbour City, Canton Rd., Tsim Sha Tsui* ☎ *2113–0888* 🖷 *2113–0022* ⊕ *www.marcopolohotels.com* ⤴ *384 rooms, 56 suites* ⚋ *3 restaurants, room service, in-room data ports, in-room safes, minibars, cable TV with movies, hair salon, bar, shops, babysitting, dry cleaning, laundry service, Internet, business services, meeting rooms, no-smoking floors* ⊟ *AE, DC, MC, V.*

☾ **$$$** 🏨 **Marco Polo Hongkong Hotel.** Next to the Star Ferry and Cultural Centre and part of the wharf-side Harbour City complex, this is the largest, and considered by some to be the best, of three Marco Polo hotels along the same street. Spacious rooms have special touches such as a choice of 11 types of pillows and, for children, miniature bathrobes, mild shampoos, and rubber ducks. The Continental Club floors include 24-hour butler service. All three hotels share the pool, gym, and spa that are at this location. The largest Oktoberfest in town takes place here with more than 1,000 thigh-slapping, beer-swilling, fun-loving participants. ⊠ *Harbour City, Canton Rd., Tsim Sha Tsui* ☎ *2113–0088* 🖷 *2113–0011* ⊕ *www.marcopolohotels.com* ⤴ *621 rooms, 44 suites* ⚋ *6 restaurants, room service, in-room data ports, in-room safes, minibars, cable TV with movies, pool, gym, hair salon, spa, lounge, shops, babysitting, dry cleaning, laundry service, concierge, Internet, business services, meeting rooms, no-smoking floors* ⊟ *AE, DC, MC, V.*

$$$ 🏨 **Marco Polo Prince.** Like its neighboring Marco Polo namesakes in the Harbour City complex (the Hongkong and Gateway), the Prince is convenient to upscale shops, cinemas, and the restaurants and shops of Tsim Sha Tsui. It's also near the China Hong Kong Terminal, where ferries, boats, and buses depart for mainland China. Most small comfortable rooms overlook expansive Kowloon Park, and some suites have views of Victoria Harbour. The Spice Market restaurant serves Southeast Asian buffets and an international menu. You can use the pool, gym, and spa at the Marco Polo Hongkong, a five-minute walk away. ⊠ *Harbour City, Canton Rd., Tsim Sha Tsui* ☎ *2113–1888* 🖷 *2113–0066* ⊕ *www.marcopolohotels.com* ⤴ *345 rooms, 51 suites* ⚋ *4 restaurants, snack bar, room service, in-room data ports, in-room safes, minibars, cable TV with movies, hair salon, bar, shop, babysitting, dry cleaning, laundry service, Internet, business services, meeting rooms, no-smoking floors* ⊟ *AE, DC, MC, V.*

$$$ 🏨 **New World Renaissance.** Part of a large shopping complex, this popular hotel on the Tsim Sha Tsui waterfront has perfect views of Hong Kong Island from its upper club floors, rivaled only by the adjacent Hotel InterContinental Hong Kong, part of the same complex. Long escalators lead from the shopping area to the hotel's large second-floor lobby. The comfortable guest rooms with pleasantly modern touches feel homey and have plenty of space for working and relaxing. Greenery surrounds the outdoor pool, which stays open throughout the year. The Panorama restaurant, one of three in the hotel, has one of the best harbor views in town. ⊠ *22 Salisbury Rd., Tsim Sha Tsui* ☎ *2369–4111* 🖷 *2369–9387* ⊕ *www.marriott.com* ⤴ *501 rooms, 42 suites* ⚋ *3* *restaurants, room service, in-room data ports, in-room safes, minibars, cable TV with movies, pool, gym, health club, hair salon, sauna, spa, lounge, babysitting, dry cleaning, laundry service, Internet, business services, meeting rooms, no-smoking floors* ⊟ *AE, DC, MC, V.*

★ $$$ ▦ **Sheraton Hong Kong Hotel & Towers.** Across the street from the Space Museum at the southern end of the fabled Golden Mile, the Sheraton is contemporary—even avant-garde—with a spacious modern lobby full of arty knickknacks and paintings. Guest rooms, refurbished in 2003, are comfortable yet modern with flat-screen TV, slick glass desktops, and glass washbowls in the bathrooms, which also have a narrow floor-to-ceiling windows overlooking the room and outdoors. There are harbor, city, or courtyard views. Make your way to the rooftop pool and terrace via the exterior glass elevator. The sky lounge has a terrific harbor view, Someplace Else is a popular hangout at happy hour, and the delightful Oyster & Wine Bar is on the top floor. ⊠ *20 Nathan Rd., Tsim Sha Tsui* ☎ *2369–1111* 🖷 *2739–8707* ⊕ *www.sheraton.com* ➲ *686 rooms, 94 suites* ⟁ *5 restaurants, room service, in-room data ports, in-room safes, minibars, cable TV with movies, pool, health club, 3 lounges, shop, babysitting, dry cleaning, laundry service, concierge, Internet, business services, meeting rooms, no-smoking floors* ⊟ *AE, DC, MC, V.*

☾ $$ ▦ **BP International House.** Built by the Boy Scouts Association, this hotel next to Kowloon Park offers an excellent value for the money. A portrait of BP himself, association founder Baron Robert Baden-Powell, hangs in the spacious modern lobby. Hostel-like rooms are small but have regular hotel amenities and panoramic views of Victoria Harbour and clear views of the busiest part of Kowloon. A multipurpose hall hosts exhibitions, conventions, and concerts, and the health club is one of the biggest in town. A major attraction for budget travelers is a self-service coin laundry. ⊠ *8 Austin Rd., Jordan* ☎ *2376–1111* 🖷 *2376–1333* ⊕ *www.megahotels.com.hk* ➲ *524 rooms, 11 suites* ⟁ *2 restaurants, cable TV with movies, health club, hair salon, sauna, spa, dry cleaning, laundry facilities, laundry service, Internet, business services, meeting rooms, parking (fee)* ⊟ *AE, DC, MC, V.*

$$ ▦ **Kowloon Hotel.** The mirrored exterior and the chrome, glass, and marble lobby reflect the hotel's high-tech orientation. Kowloon means "nine dragons" in Cantonese and is the theme here. Triangular windows and a pointed lobby ceiling, made from hundreds of handblown Venetian-glass pyramids, represent dragons' teeth. The Kowloon is the lesser sibling to the adjacent Peninsula hotel, so you can sign for services at the Pen and charge them to your room account here; similarly, all the luxurious facilities of the Peninsula are open to you. Rooms are small, but each has a computer with free Internet service and fax. Airline information is displayed in the lobby *and* in each room. ⊠ *19–21 Nathan Rd., Tsim Sha Tsui* ☎ *2929–2888* 🖷 *2739–9811* ⊕ *www.peninsula.com* ➲ *719 rooms, 17 suites* ⟁ *3 restaurants, room service, in-room data ports, in-room fax, minibars, cable TV with movies, hair salon, shop, babysitting, dry cleaning, laundry service, Internet, business services, meeting room, no-smoking floors* ⊟ *AE, DC, MC, V.*

$$ ▦ **Miramar.** When it opened in 1948, the Miramar was owned by the Spanish Catholic Mission, which intended to use the structure to shel-

ter missionaries expelled from China. As tourism blossomed here, the priests changed their plan and turned the premises into a hotel. At the top of the Golden Mile and across from Kowloon Park, the Miramar has a vast lobby with a dramatic stained-glass ceiling, functional rooms, and smiling service. Rooms are spacious but need decorating; moreover, noise from adjoining rooms and the commotion from busy Nathan Road just outside can be a problem. But you're close to both the Jordan and Tsim Sha Tsui MTR stations. ☒ *130 Nathan Rd., Tsim Sha Tsui* ☎ *2368–1111* 🖷 *2369–1788* ⊕ *www.miramarhk.com* 🛏 *512 rooms, 13 suites* ♺ *3 restaurants, minibars, cable TV with movies, indoor pool, bar, shop, babysitting, dry cleaning, laundry service, Internet, business services, meeting rooms, no-smoking floors* ▭ *AE, DC, MC, V.*

$$ 🏨 **Ramada Hotel Kowloon.** The Ramada is relatively small and tries to use its nonmegalithic size to create a home-away-from-home feeling. A decorative fireplace in the lobby and small but comfortable rooms furnished with natural wood furniture create a cozy and homey environment. The bar attracts young locals for drinks and karaoke. ☒ *73–75 Chatham Rd., Tsim Sha Tsui* ☎ *2311–1100* 🖷 *2311–6000* ⊕ *ramadainternational.com* 🛏 *203 rooms, 2 suites* ♺ *Restaurant, room service, in-room safes, minibars, cable TV with movies, bar, shops, babysitting, laundry service, Internet, business services, meeting room* ▭ *AE, DC, MC, V.*

$$ 🏨 **Royal Pacific Hotel & Towers.** On the Tsim Sha Tsui waterfront, the Royal Pacific is part of the Hong Kong China City complex, which includes the terminal for ferries to mainland China. Guest rooms are arranged in two blocks, the hotel and tower wings. Tower-wing rooms have harbor views and are more luxurious, while hotel-wing rooms have Kowloon street and park views and are smaller but just as attractive, The hotel connects to Kowloon Park by a footbridge and is close to shops and cinemas. ☒ *33 Canton Rd., Tsim Sha Tsui* ☎ *2736–1188* 🖷 *2736–1212* ⊕ *www.royalpacific.com.hk* 🛏 *641 rooms, 32 suites* ♺ *3 restaurants, room service, in-room data ports, in-room safes, minibars, cable TV with movies, gym, health club, sauna, spa, steam room, squash, bar, babysitting, dry cleaning, laundry service, Internet, business services, meeting rooms* ▭ *AE, DC, MC, V.*

$ 🏨 **Kimberley.** On one of the colorful busy streets between Nathan Road and Tsim Sha Tsui East, this hotel has bright, clean—but small—rooms. Its health spa includes masseurs to ease away the aches and pains of shopping. Golf driving nets are available for those who can't kick the habit. The two main restaurants serve Cantonese and Japanese cuisines. ☒ *28 Kimberley Rd., Tsim Sha Tsui* ☎ *2723–3888* 🖷 *2723–1318* ⊕ *www. kimberleyhotel.com.hk* 🛏 *497 rooms, 49 suites* ♺ *3 restaurants, room service, in-room data ports, minibars, cable TV with movies, gym, health club, hair salon, sauna, spa, bar, babysitting, laundry service, Internet, business services, meeting rooms* ▭ *AE, DC, MC, V.*

☾ $ 🏨 **Salisbury YMCA.** This upscale YMCA is Hong Kong's most popular
FodorśChoice and is great value for your money. Next to the Peninsula and opposite
★ the Cultural Centre, Space Museum, and Art Museum, it's in an excellent location for theater, art, and concert crawls. The clean, pastel-color

rooms have harbor views and data ports. The Y also has a chapel, a garden, a conference room with a built-in stage, a children's library, and excellent health facilities, which include a dance studio and even a climbing wall. Restaurants here are both cheap and good. The shops are also affordable. ☒ *41 Salisbury Rd., Tsim Sha Tsui* ☎ *2369–2211* 🖷 *2739–9315* ⊕ *www.ymcahk.org.hk* ↩ *303 rooms, 62 suites* ⌂ *2 restaurants, room service, in-room data ports, in-room safes, minibars, cable TV with movies, indoor pool, gym, health club, hair salon, spa, squash, lounge, shops, babysitting, laundry facilities, business services, meeting room, no-smoking floors* ▭ *AE, DC, MC, V.*

Tsim Sha Tsui East

$$$ 🏨 **Hotel Nikko Hongkong.** Part of the Japanese chain, this luxury harbor-front hotel at the far end of Tsim Sha Tsui East attracts mostly Japanese travelers. The large, split-level atrium depicts a Japanese Garden with water trickling between the greenery. Renovated rooms and bathrooms are comfortable and spacious; nearly 200 rooms have harbor views, and those on the executive floors are equipped with additional facilities such as tea- and coffeemakers and in-room data ports. The Kyoto-inspired restaurant Sagano uses ingredients imported from Japan. ☒ *72 Mody Rd., Tsim Sha Tsui East* ☎ *2739–1111* 🖷 *2311–3122* ⊕ *www. hotelnikko.com.hk* ↩ *444 rooms, 18 suites* ⌂ *4 restaurants, room service, some in-room data ports, in-room safes, minibars, cable TV with movies, pool, gym, health club, sauna, spa, 3 bars, shop, Internet, business services, meeting rooms, no-smoking floors* ▭ *AE, DC, MC, V.*

$$$ 🏨 **Intercontinental Grand Stanford Hong Kong.** More than half the rooms in this luxury hotel have an unobstructed harbor view. The elegant lobby is spacious, the staff is helpful and friendly, and the modern comfortable rooms are decorated in warm earth tones with fine wood fittings and expansive desks. Executive rooms have a direct-line fax machine and a trouser press. The restaurants are well known locally, including Mistral (Italian), Belvedere (regional French), and Tiffany's New York Bar, which celebrates the Roaring 1920s with antique furniture, Tiffany-style glass ceilings, and a live band. ☒ *70 Mody Rd., Tsim Sha Tsui* ☎ *2721–5161* 🖷 *2732–2233* ⊕ *www.grandstanford.com* ↩ *554 rooms, 25 suites* ⌂ *4 restaurants, room service, in-room data ports, in-room safes, minibars, cable TV with movies, pool, gym, health club, sauna, spa, bar, shop, babysitting, dry cleaning, laundry service, Internet, business services, meeting rooms, no-smoking floors* ▭ *AE, DC, MC, V.*

★ **$$$** 🏨 **Kowloon Shangri-La.** Catering mainly to business travelers, this upscale hotel has a 24-hour business center with teleconferencing facilities and, remarkably, the elevator carpets are changed at midnight to indicate the day of the week. The spacious guest rooms all have magnificent harbor or city views. Complimentary newspapers are delivered daily to your room; club rooms have a combination fax/printer/copier/scanner, a DVD, and even a TV in the bathroom. A wireless telephone system allows guests to receive calls throughout the hotel. Attention to detail and outstanding service, in a city where service is already tops, set this hotel apart. ☒ *64 Mody Rd., Tsim Sha Tsui East* ☎ *2721–2111,*

800/942–5050 in the U.S. ☎ *2723–8686* ⊕ *www.shangri-la.com* ↩ *705 rooms, 25 suites* ⚫ *5 restaurants, room service, in-room data ports, in-room safes, minibars, cable TV with movies, indoor pool, gym, health club, hair salon, sauna, spa, bar, lounge, shops, babysitting, dry cleaning, laundry service, concierge, Internet, business services, meeting rooms, no-smoking floor* ═ *AE, DC, MC, V.*

$$$ ▦ **Royal Garden.** A garden atrium with lush greenery and whispering running water rises from the ground floor to the Royal Garden's rooftop. Glass elevators, live classical music, trailing greenery, and trickling streams create a sense of serenity. The spacious comfortable rooms surround the atrium. Rooftop health facilities include an indoor-outdoor pool fashioned after an ancient Roman bath with fountains, a colorful sun mosaic, and underwater music. Its Sabatini restaurant is the sister to the famous Rome dining establishment. ✉ *69 Mody Rd., Tsim Sha Tsui East* ☎ *2721–5215* ☎ *2369–9976* ⊕ *www.theroyalgardenhotel. com.hk* ↩ *374 rooms, 48 suites* ⚫ *4 restaurants, room service, in-room data ports, in-room safes, minibars, cable TV with movies, tennis court, indoor-outdoor pool, gym, health club, hair salon, sauna, spa, bar, pub, dance club, shop, babysitting, dry cleaning, laundry service, concierge, Internet, business services, meeting rooms, no-smoking floor* ═ *AE, DC, MC, V.*

$$ ▦ **Regal Kowloon.** If you're in the mood for a French experience, check in at the Regal. The lobby has an impressive tapestry, and Louis XVI–style furniture graces the guest rooms and one of the lounges. Rooms on the club floors have a more minimalist, modern two-tone appeal than the rest of the hotel would suggest. The French restaurant Maman serves home-style French cooking in a relaxed setting. ✉ *71 Mody Rd., Tsim Sha Tsui East* ☎ *2722–1818* ☎ *2369–6950* ⊕ *www.regalkowloon. com* ↩ *564 rooms, 34 suites* ⚫ *4 restaurants, room service, in-room data ports, in-room safes, minibars, cable TV with movies, gym, health club, hair salon, sauna, spa, 2 bars, lounge, shop, babysitting, dry cleaning, laundry service, concierge, Internet, business services, meeting rooms, no-smoking floor* ═ *AE, DC, MC, V.*

Yau Ma Tei & Mong Kok

Yau Ma Tei and Mong Kok are known for their busy, bustling, noisy street life, bargain shopping, night markets, and cheap and cheerful dining. It's an exciting part of Kowloon if you can handle the crowds which don't seem to dwindle until about 10 PM. Hong Kong is a safe place compared to other major cities in the world, however Mong Kok is crowded and pickpocketing does occur, wallets and mobile phones being the usual items pilfered. Hotels listed are middle range and some of the best for service and value for money in the area. However, keep in mind that rooms are often small and that street noise is sometimes a problem.

★ **$$** ▦ **Eaton Hotel.** In a brick-red shopping and cinema complex in the middle of Nathan Road, the Eaton provides quick access to Hong Kong's bustling after-dark street scene: it's a stone's throw from the Temple Street Night Market. The clean, modern rooms have all the necessities, including fast Internet access and business services. The top floor has a swimming pool and a gym. ⊠ *380 Nathan Rd., Yau Ma Tei* ☎ *2782–1818* 🖷 *2782–5563* ⊕ *www.eaton-hotel.com* 🖘 *458 rooms, 30 suites* ♻ *6 restaurants, room service, in-room data ports, minibars, cable TV with movies, pool, exercise equipment, gym, health club, bar, laundry service, Internet, business services, meeting rooms, no-smoking floor* ⊟ *AE, DC, MC, V.*

$$ 🏨 **Hotel Concourse.** One of Hong Kong's nicer low-to-moderately priced hotels, the Concourse is run by the China Travel Service. It's tucked away from Nathan Road but only a minute's walk from the Prince Edward MTR station in Mong Kok. Rooms are basic and functional, and business services are available. The hotel is well placed for a glimpse of real, day-to-day life in Hong Kong. Loads of simple eateries dot the area, and the night markets are nearby. Most of the streets in Kowloon are busy and noisy and it's no different here, but it is relatively clean and safe. The hotel has both a Chinese and a pan-Asian restaurant. ⊠ *22 Lai Chi Kok Rd., Mong Kok* ☎ *2397–6683* 🖷 *2381–3768* ⊕ *www. hotelconcourse.com.hk* 🖘 *425 rooms, 5 suites* ♻ *2 restaurants, coffee shop, room service, in-room data ports, minibars, cable TV with movies, bar, laundry service, Internet, business services, meeting rooms* ⊟ *AE, DC, MC, V.*

$$ 🏨 **Metropole Hotel.** Just north of Nathan Road's major shopping area, the Metropole is a diner's delight. The on-site Chinese restaurant, House of Tang, is locally renowned for its Szechuanese resident master chefs, who serve authentic Szechuan and Cantonese food. The modern clean rooms have a harmonious mélange of East and West furnishings. The rooftop pool and gym offer a relaxing space to unwind. ⊠ *75 Waterloo Rd., Yau Ma Tei* ☎ *2761–1711* 🖷 *2761–0769* ⊕ *www.metropole. com.hk* 🖘 *479 rooms, 8 suites* ♻ *3 restaurants, room service, in-room data ports, minibars, cable TV with movies, pool, gym, health club, bar, laundry service, Internet, business services, meeting rooms* ⊟ *AE, DC, MC, V.*

$$ 🏨 **Pruton Prudential Hotel.** Rising from a busy corner on upper Nathan Road, above the Jordan MTR station, this hotel is a find if you're on a modest budget. The spacious rooms have views of bustling Nathan Road, with the neon-lighted shop signs and banners. The hotel shares a building with a lively shopping mall and has its own pool. Rooms on the five executive floors have tea- and coffeemakers. ⊠ *222 Nathan Rd., Yau Ma Tei* ☎ *2311–8222* 🖷 *2311–1304* 🖘 *415 rooms, 17 suites* ♻ *Coffee shop, room service, in-room data ports, minibars, cable TV with movies, pool, bar, shop, laundry service, Internet, business services, meeting rooms* ⊟ *AE, DC, MC, V.*

★ **$$** 🏨 **Royal Plaza.** The Royal Plaza is easily accessible from either the adjacent Kowloon–Canton Railway station or the nearby Mong Kok MTR station. As part of the massive Grand Century Place shopping complex, it's a shopper's delight. Rooms, which have views of Lion Rock and Kowloon, are elegant and modern and surprisingly quiet considering the busy location. The hotel itself offers a mix of restaurants, bars, and leisure facilities, including a ballroom and a large pool with underwater music. The garden allows seekers of solitude to contemplate the true meaning of Mong Kok in peace and quiet. ⊠ *193 Prince Edward Rd. W, Mong Kok* ☏*2928–8822* ▤*2628–3383* ⊕*www.royalplaza. com.hk* ⌨*469 rooms, 17 suites* ♨ *3 restaurants, room service, in-room data ports, in-room safes, minibars, cable TV with movies, indoor pool, gym, health club, sauna, spa, bar, laundry service, Internet, business services, meeting rooms* ▤ *AE, DC, MC, V.*

$ 🛏 **Dorsett Seaview.** High-rise buildings now block the Dorsett's sea view, but the location is still a good one if you want to see traditional Hong Kong. Guest rooms are clean but very small; staff are friendly and efficient. The hotel is close to the Yau Ma Tei MTR as well as decent shopping; Shanghai Street is filled with shops selling everything from handmade kitchenware to temple offerings. The restaurant has bargain-priced buffets, especially for lunch. The hotel often gets very busy with tour groups and checkout can be chaotic. ⊠ *268 Shanghai St., Yau Ma Tei* ☏*2782–0882* ▤*2388–1803* ⊕*www.dorsettseaview.com.hk* ⌨*254 rooms, 3 suites* ♨ *Restaurant, room service, minibars, cable TV with movies, bar, lounge, laundry service* ▤ *AE, DC, MC, V.*

$ 🛏 **Majestic Hotel.** This hotel is on the site of the old Majestic Cinema on upper Nathan Road. The lobby is clean and plain, and the sparsely decorated rooms have contemporary furniture; suites have fax machines. Facilities are minimal, with no pool or gym, and only a coffee shop and a bar for dining and imbibing. However, the complex holds shops and a cinema, and plenty of restaurants—running the gamut from Chinese food to Malaysian cuisine—are nearby, as well as the Jordan MTR. ⊠ *348 Nathan Rd., Yau Ma Tei* ☏ *2781–1333* ▤ *2781–1773* ⊕*www. majestichotel.com.hk* ⌨ *387 rooms, 9 suites* ♨ *Coffee shop, room service, in-room data ports, some in-room faxes, minibars, refrigerators, cable TV with movies, bar, cinema, shop, laundry service, Internet, business services, meeting rooms, no-smoking floor* ▤ *AE, DC, MC, V.*

$ 🛏 **Nathan Hotel.** Popular with tour groups from both the East and the West, this busy hotel is near the Jordan MTR and just a stone's throw away from the street-market attractions of Mong Kok and Yau Ma Tei. Rooms are moderately sized and colorful, and include all the basic necessities. ⊠ *378 Nathan Rd., Yau Ma Tei* ☏ *2388–5141* ▤ *2770–4262* ⌨ *185 rooms* ♨ *Restaurant, room service, in-room data ports, minibars, cable TV, bar, shop, laundry service, business services* ▤ *AE, DC, MC, V.*

$ 🛏 **Shamrock Hotel.** One of the oldest budget hotels on Nathan Road, the Shamrock—which opened its doors in the early 1960s—has spruced itself up with refurbished rooms, lobby, and facade. It's just north of Kowloon Park and steps from the Jordan MTR, putting it in the middle of all the 24-hour-a-day Yau Ma Tei action. Rooms are a decent size for the price, and the hotel offers buffet-style dining from its in-house restaurant. ⊠*223 Nathan Rd., Yau Ma Tei* ☏*2735–2271* ▤*2736–7354* ⊕ *www.shamrockhotel.com.hk* ⌨ *128 rooms, 19 suites* ♨ *Restaurant, room service, in-room data ports, minibars, cable TV with movies, laundry service* ▤ *AE, DC, MC, V.*

★ ¢ 🛏 **Booth Lodge.** This pleasant contemporary retreat, which is down a dead-end side street near the Jade Market, is operated by the Salvation Army. But contrary to the image that might conjure up for you, everything in this renovated lodge is clean, bright, and new, from freshly painted walls to starched sheets on the double beds. The lobby is a study in minimalism and may resemble an office, but the Booth is a good value. The coffee shop serves mainly buffets, with a small outdoor balcony offering nice views. The Yau Ma Tei MTR is nearby. ☒ *11 Wing Sing La., Yau Ma Tei* ☏ *2771–9266* 🖷 *2385–1140* ⌨ *54 rooms* ♨ *Restaurant, coffee shop, cable TV, laundry service* ▤ *AE, MC, V.*

¢ 🏨 **Caritas Bianchi Lodge.** Rooms at this clean and friendly hostel, which is operated by the Catholic Diocese of Hong Kong, are simple and modern in their decor and have basic facilities including TVs, minibars, air-conditioning, and private bathrooms. Just around the corner from busy Nathan Road, the lodge is also close to the Jade Market and the nightly Temple Street Market, but it offers peace and quiet due to its dead-end location. ☒ *4 Cliff Rd., Yau Ma Tei* ☏ *2388–1111* 🖷 *2770–6669* ⊕ *www.caritas.org.hk* ⌨ *88 rooms, 2 suites* ♨ *Restaurant, minibars, cable TV, laundry service* ▤ *AE, DC, MC, V.*

THE NEW TERRITORIES & ISLANDS

Although lodging options are limited outside the areas of Hong Kong Island and Kowloon, some are worth considering, especially if you're traveling to or from China on the Kowloon–Canton Railway. You're also closer to the airport out here. Some islands, such as Cheung Chau, do a booming business in rooms for rent, with agents displaying photographs of available rentals on placards along the waterfront opposite the ferry pier.

The New Territories

🕙 **$$** 🏨 **Gold Coast Hotel.** The Gold Coast is Hong Kong's only conference resort, and it can accommodate more than 1,000 people, so check before booking if you want a quiet weekend away. Its vast complex on Kowloon's western harbor front is well connected to the city by public bus, and the hotel runs shuttle buses to the Tsuen Wan MTR and the airport. It is extravagantly decorated inside with acres of marble, miles of wrought-iron balustrades, and several palm-court atriums. All guest rooms are spacious and face the sea. The extensive facilities include a children's play area, a water-sports area, and volleyball and soccer fields. ☒ *1 Castle Peak Rd., Tuen Mun* ☏ *2452–8888* 🖷 *2440–7368* ⊕ *www.goldcoasthotel.com.hk* ⌨ *440 rooms, 10 suites* ♨ *4 restaurants, room service, in-room data ports, minibars, cable TV with movies, putting green, 2 tennis courts, pool, health club, hair salon, spa, beach, boating, archery, soccer, squash, volleyball, bar, babysitting, playground, laundry service, Internet, business services, meeting rooms* ▤ *AE, DC, MC, V.*

$$ 🏨 **Regal Riverside Hotel.** In the foothills of Sha Tin, overlooking the Shing Mun River, this modern hotel is near one of the busiest shopping malls in Hong Kong, the New Town Plaza. Although the guest rooms are in need of renovation, they have uninterrupted river and garden views. The enormous fitness center has myriad facilities including Hong Kong's only sensory-deprivation tank—purported to soothe away the day's pressures.

You can jog or cycle by the riverside or just watch rowers at practice. Shuttle services leave every hour for the New Town Plaza, which is 5 minutes away, and every half hour for Tsim Sha Tsui, which takes about 30 minutes. ⊠ *Tai Chung Kiu Rd., Sha Tin* ☎ *2649–7878* 🖷 *2637–4748* ⊕ *www.regalriverside.com* 🛏 *789 rooms, 41 suites* ⟁ *5 restaurants, room service, in-room data ports, minibars, cable TV with movies, pool, gym, health club, hair salon, sauna, spa, steam room, bar, dance club, shops, babysitting, laundry service, Internet, business services, meeting rooms, no-smoking floor* ▭ *AE, DC, MC, V.*

$$ 🏨 **Royal Park Hotel.** Next to New Town Plaza, the busiest shopping mall in the territory, this 16-story hotel is easily accessed by train and buses (it is about 10 minutes away from the Hung Hom and Tsim Sha Tsui areas by KCR in one direction, and about 20 minutes from Lo Wu border with Shenzhen in the other direction). It's also the nearest hotel to the Sha Tin Racecourse. The lobby is decorated in deep colors, and rooms have bay windows with panoramic views of Sha Tin. ⊠ *8 Pak Hok Ting St., Sha Tin* ☎ *2601–2111* 🖷 *2601–3666* ⊕ *www.royalpark.com.hk* 🛏 *436 rooms, 12 suites* ⟁ *4 restaurants, room service, in-room data ports, minibars, cable TV with movies, tennis court, pool, exercise equipment, gym, lounge, laundry service, Internet, business services, meeting rooms, no-smoking floor* ▭ *AE, DC, MC, V.*

¢ 🏨 **Panda Hotel.** Tsuen Wan in the western New Territories is far from an ideal location for most sightseers, but if you need to be close to the airport or to Shenzhen, then it is a good place to stay at a reasonable price. You can't miss the huge panda mural on the side of this large hotel which has over 1,000 rooms. The interior is reminiscent of Tokyo's Ginza district, with lots of open-plan lounges and ultramodern rooms in warm and natural tones. Some rooms have harbor views. On the premises are a pool, a gym, a range of restaurants, and a department store. Mega Club rooms also have in-room Nintendo and Internet access. Complimentary bus service runs to and from Tsim Sha Tsui and Mong Kok, which takes about 30 minutes, and the MTR is nearby. ⊠ *3 Tsuen Wan St., Tsuen Wan* ☎ *2409–1111* 🖷 *2409–1818* ⊕ *www.megahotels.com.hk* 🛏 *971 rooms, 55 suites* ⟁ *4 restaurants, room service, in-room data ports, minibars, cable TV, pool, gym, health club, Japanese baths, sauna, 2 bars, shop, babysitting, laundry service, Internet, business services, meeting room, no-smoking floor* ▭ *AE, DC, MC, V.*

Cheung Chau Island

¢ 🏨 **Cheung Chau Warwick.** Miles from the fast-paced city, this six-story beachfront nook aims to assure you have a carefree and relaxed stay. A nice pool and a sandy beach take the place of business services and executive floors. An hour by ferry from Hong Kong Island, it's a popular getaway for Hong Kong families, and English is spoken by the staff. There are no cars on the leisurely island, but the hotel is just a 10-minute walk from the pier. The medium-size guest rooms are basic but clean with sea or mountain views. ⊠ *East Bay, Cheung Chau Island* ☎ *2981–0081* 🖷 *2981–9174* 🛏 *71 rooms* ⟁ *2 restaurants, cable TV, pool, beach* ▭ *AE, DC, MC, V.*

Lantau Island

★ $$ 🏨 **Regal Airport Hotel.** Ideal for passengers in transit, this modern hotel is one of the largest airport hotels in the world. It's some distance from the city, but the efficient high-speed rail system can have you on Hong Kong Island in around 25 minutes. It is also connected directly to the passenger terminal by an air-conditioned, moving walkway. Some rooms have terrific views of planes landing from afar; those with balconies overlook the hotel's two swimming pools and have a more resortlike feel. The Grand Ballroom has space for up to 1,000 people and has simultaneous translation, video-conferencing capability, and a built-in stage. ✉ *Chek Lap Kok International Airport, Lantau Island* ☎ *2286–8888* 🖷 *2286–8686* ⊕ *www.regalhotel.com* 🛏 *1,100 rooms, 25 suites* ⚄ *7 restaurants, coffee shop, room service, in-room data ports, in-room safes, minibars, cable TV with movies, indoor-outdoor pool, exercise equipment, gym, bar, 2 lounges, shop, dry cleaning, laundry service, Internet, business services, meeting rooms, no-smoking floors* ▭ *AE, DC, MC, V.*

$ 🏨 **Silvermine Beach Hotel.** This bay-side resort in Mui Wo steers entirely clear of Hong Kong's sound and fury. It's an hour by ferry from Hong Kong Island, then a five-minute walk from the pier. A pool is open in summer, and a tennis court, gym, and sauna are open year-round. Guest rooms are spacious and have tea- and coffee-making facilities. Public buses or taxis outside the hotel can take you to the airport as well as some of the island's attractions. ✉ *D. D. 2, Lot 648 Silvermine Bay, Mui Wo, Lantau Island* ☎ *2984–8295* 🖷 *2984–1907* ⊕ *www.resort.com.hk* 🛏 *128 rooms, 2 suites* ⚄ *2 restaurants, cable TV, tennis court, pool, exercise equipment, gym, sauna, steam room, meeting rooms* ▭ *AE, DC, MC, V.*

NIGHTLIFE & THE ARTS

4

BEST NEIGHBORHOOD TO LET LOOSE
Lan Kwai Fong ⇨p.119

CINEMA CHIC
Palace IFC ⇨p.131

BEST DRINK WITH A VIEW
Felix, in the Peninsula Hotel ⇨p.122

INNOVATIVE MODERN DANCE
City Contemporary Dance Company ⇨p.129

EVERY GESTURE IS MEANINGFUL
Chinese Opera,though undoubtedly an
acquired taste ⇨p.128

HOSTESSES WITH THE MOSTEST
Club BBoss ⇨p.124

Updated by
Eva Chui
Loiterton

A RIOT OF NEON, heralding frenetic after-hours action, announces Hong Kong's nightlife districts. Hectic workdays make way for an even busier nighttime scene. Clubs and bars fill to capacity, evening markets pack in shoppers looking for bargains, restaurants welcome diners, cinemas pop corn as fast as they can, and theaters and concert halls prepare for full houses. Hong Kong entertainment runs the gamut, encompassing sophisticated piano bars, elegant lounges, superstrobe discos, rowdy pubs, smoky jazz dens, hostess clubs, and classy bars.

All premises licensed to serve alcohol are supposedly subject to stringent fire, safety, and sanitary controls, although at times this is hard to believe, given the overcrowding at the hippest places. Wise travelers should think twice before succumbing to the city's raunchier hideaways. If you stumble into one, check out cover and hostess charges *before* you get too comfortable. Pay for each round of drinks as it's served (by cash rather than credit card), and never sign any blank checks. Hong Kong is a surprisingly safe place, but as in every tourist destination the art of the tourist rip-off has been perfected. If you're unsure, visit places signposted as members of the Hong Kong Tourist Board (HKTB). You can pick up the association's free membership listing (that is, approved restaurants and nightspots) at any HKTB information office.

Take note, too, of Hong Kong's laws. You must be over 18 to buy alcohol. Drugs, obscene publications, and unlicensed gambling are ostensibly illegal. There is some consumer protection, but the generally helpful police, many of whom speak English, expect everyone to know the meaning of *caveat emptor* (let the buyer beware).

Note that many of Hong Kong's smarter nightspots are in hotels. Fast-paced, competitive Hong Kong is a world of change where buildings seem to vanish overnight and fads emerge weekly; don't be surprised if some places have altered their look, changed their name, or closed altogether since this book went to press. Also, many clubs have a "members-only" policy, but don't let this deter you. Usually this just means that you must pay a cover charge, while members do not. Note, too, that although most clubs and discos levy a cover charge, this fee usually includes a complimentary drink.

NIGHTLIFE

The most comprehensive nightlife listings are in *HK Magazine,* a free weekly newspaper distributed each Friday to many restaurants, stores, and bars. The nightlife coverage in *BC Magazine* is almost as extensive. Another good source of nightlife information is the *South China Morning Post.*

Bars

Hong Kong has its share of licensed designer bars that provide some diversion from the staid pubs. Whether it's because of the transient nature of the city or hardworking lifestyles that leave little time for relationships, there's a rampant singles scene here, with lots of people out looking for that special someone or even that special someone just for the night.

Lan Kwai Fong & Vicinity

Fodor'sChoice ★ Most Westerners and a growing number of locals meet in crowded comfort in the Lan Kwai Fong area, a hillside section around Central's D'Aguilar Street that has many appetizing bistros and a large selection of bars. When people tire of Lan Kwai Fong itself, there are plenty more bars just around the corner.

Alibi. Sophisticated guys and dolls flock to this cool bar (with fine dining upstairs) that's wall to wall with bodies most nights. If there's one place to dress to impress, this is it. ⊠ *73 Wyndham St., Central* ☎ *2167–8989.*

Après. This bar is so named because management says the steep street it opens onto could double as a ski slope. Although it's highly unlikely that the tropical Hong Kong weather will ever allow for snow, you can still enjoy a drink alfresco style here. ⊠ *79 Wyndham St., entrance off Pottinger St., upper basement, Central* ☎ *2524–7722.*

★ **California.** Singles mix happily at the ultramodern bar, which stays open late most nights and after several years as a trendsetter is still one of the hottest places to be seen. ⊠ *32–34 D'Aguilar St., Lan Kwai Fong* ☎ *2521–1345.*

Club 64. Writers, artists, travelers, and the occasional banker gravitate toward the unpretentious environs of this bar, where you can get a reasonably priced drink in a humble and cozy, if a little run-down, setting. ⊠ *12–14 Wing Wah La., Lan Kwai Fong* ☎ *2523–2801.*

D'Apartment. Step into the library, lounge room, or even bedroom in the ultrahip basement "apartment," which opened in early 2004. The tiny library is dimly lighted and stacked with real books, but there's no chance of dozing off with the music blaring in the next "room." The bedroom has a lush bedlike sofa to laze on, and, don't worry, there are no neighbors to complain about the loud racket. ⊠ *California Entertainment Bldg., 34–36 D'Aguilar St., basement, Lan Kwai Fong* ☎ *2523–2002.*

★ **Fringe Club.** The arts-minded mingle in a historic redbrick building that also houses the members-only Foreign Correspondents Club. The Club is the headquarters for Hong Kong's alternative arts scene and normally stages live music twice a week. ⊠ *2 Lower Albert Rd., Central* ☎ *2521–7251.*

Insomnia. The 24/7 haze is so crowded with perfumed women and suited men on weekend nights you have to fight your way to the back to the bathrooms. If you stay up at the front bar, by the arched windows, you might have some breathing room. ⊠ *38–44 D'Aguilar St., Lan Kwai Fong* ☎ *2525–0957.*

La Dolce Vita. The tiny bar—beneath its sister restaurant **Post 97** and next to its other sibling **Club 97**—often spills onto the pavement. With a sleek interior and a crowd to match, this chic haven for the name-dropping masses is a place to be seen. ⊠ *9 Lan Kwai Fong, Lan Kwai Fong* ☎ *2810–9333.*

Le Jardin. For a gregariously cosmopolitan vibe, this trendy bar has a lovely outdoor terrace overlooking a not-so-lovely alley. ⊠ *1/F, 10 Wing Wah La., Lan Kwai Fong* ☎ *2526–2717.*

CloseUp

LAN KWAI FONG

A CURIOUSLY L-SHAPE COBBLESTONE LANE in Central is the center of nightlife and dining in Hong Kong. Lan Kwai Fong, or just "the Fong," is a must-go-to spot that really shines after the sun sets. You can have a predinner drink at any number of bars, enjoy some of the territory's finest dining, and then pop into a nightclub to boogie the night away.

For such a small warren, Lan Kwai Fong has an incredibly broad range of nightlife to offer, with more than 20 bars, restaurants, and clubs within just a few blocks. Since most of the ground-floor establishments spill out onto the pavement, there's an audible buzz about the place, an atmosphere not matched elsewhere in Hong Kong. Whether it's corporate financiers celebrating their latest million-dollar deals at California, La Dolce Vita, or Oscars, or more humble office workers having drinks with their buddies at Le Jardin or Insomnia, there's quite literally something here for everyone.

The same "something for everyone" motto extends to the plethora of upmarket eateries in the Fong. For Asian taste buds there are Chinese, Thai, Japanese, and Vietnamese restaurants, while European flavors are on offer at French and Italian establishments. If your wallet's feeling a little light from your latest shopping expedition, take heed of the excited waiters waving to potential customers along nearby Wing Wah Lane. Here you'll find rowdy Indian, Thai, and Malaysian restaurants that serve piping-hot dishes at reasonable prices.

Lan Kwai Fong used to be a hawkers' place before the World War I I. Its modern success is largely due to Canadian expatriate Allan Zeman, an eccentric figure who has been dubbed the "King of Lan Kwai Fong" by the local media. He opened his first North American–style restaurant here 20 years ago; today he not only owns dozens of other restaurants and bars, but also the buildings they're in. He claims to have about 100 restaurants, and although he doesn't actually own them all, he acts as the landlord for most of them. The Fong is now simply a hobby for Zeman, whose business empire includes everything from property development to fashion.

New Year's Eve on December 31 is undoubtedly the busiest time for Lan Kwai Fong. Thousands of people line the tiny area to celebrate and party. You'll notice a strong police presence moving the human traffic through the streets and keeping an eye out for any troublemakers. While it's reassuring to have a watchful eye over the festivities, the police presence is actually to prevent another tragedy. As a massive throng ushered in a new year in the early 1990s, 21 people were crushed when the huge crowds went out of control. The accident shocked the territory and left a black mark on the authorities. Now when large crowds are anticipated—usually New Year's Eve, Christmas Eve, and, interestingly, Halloween—the police carefully monitor the number of people entering the area.

Call it progress or a type of survival-of-the-strongest evolution, but the trendy area has opened as many establishments as it has closed. New spots are constantly in development, or old places are under refurbishment. Regardless of the changes, Lan Kwai Fong is always alive with scores of people and places to be merry.

— Eva Chui Loiterton

SoHo

Hong Kong is proud of its own *très* chic SoHo, a small warren of streets between Central and Midlevels. This area is filled with commensurately priced cosmopolitan restaurants ranging from Middle Eastern and Portuguese to Vietnamese and Italian, as well as a handful of bars.

Barco. One of many small drinking holes popping up in SoHo, this bar is cozy, with a small lounge area and a courtyard in the back. ✉ *42 Staunton St., SoHo* ☎ *2857–4478.*

Staunton's Wine Bar & Cafe. Adjacent to Hong Kong's famous outdoor escalator is this hip bistro-style café and bar. Partly alfresco, it's the perfect place to people-watch; it attracts crowds at night to drink and by day to sip coffee or take in a meal. It's also a Sunday-morning favorite for nursing hangovers over brunch. ✉ *10–12 Staunton St., SoHo* ☎ *2973–6611.*

V 13. Affectionately known by locals as the Vodka Bar, V 13 teems with locals and expats who enjoy hearty libations. Once the bartenders start pouring the vodka, they don't stop until they reach the rim. Then they add the tonic. ✉ *13 Old Baily St., SoHo* ☎ *8208–1313.*

Wanchai & Happy Valley

Wanchai nightlife has cleaned up its act and is no longer the seedy area that *The World of Suzie Wong* inspired. While hostess bars are still found here, they now share the streets with hip and cool bars.

★ **Brown.** Much like a New York neighborhood restaurant and bar, Brown is comfy and homey for those who need to wind down from a hectic day (either working or shopping). Spacious high ceilings give the space an airy feel, and there are sink-down-and-chill sofas at the back. The small courtyard is a favorite for weekend brunches. ✉ *18A Sing Woo Rd., Happy Valley* ☎ *2891–8558.*

★ **1/5.** Walk upstairs through the narrow, mirrored ceiling corridor to enter a large, dimly lighted bar with triple-height ceilings and brown velour lounge areas. Located in the hip Star Street area, this bar is the location of choice for those who want an alternative to Lan Kwai Fong and SoHo. ✉ *1/F, Starcrest Bldg., 9 Star St., Wanchai* ☎ *2520–2515.*

Tango Martini. Shaken or stirred is what this martini bar is all about. A stylish and sophisticated lounge, this joint also has an adjoining restaurant. ✉ *3/F, Empire Land Commercial Centre, 81–85 Lockhart Rd., Wanchai* ☎ *2528–0855.*

Tsim Sha Tsui

Central and Wanchai are undoubtedly the king and queen of nightlife in Hong Kong. However, if you're staying in a hotel or having dinner on *the other side,* that is, Kowloon, a fun place in Tsim Sha Tsui is an out-of-the-way strip called Knutsford Terrace.

Bahama Mama's. You'll find tropical rhythms at the Caribbean-inspired bar, where world music plays and the kitsch props include a surfboard over the bar and the silhouette of a curvaceous woman showering behind a screen over the restroom entrance. ✉ *4–5 Knutsford Terr., Tsim Sha Tsui* ☎ *2368–2121.*

Balalaika. Vodka is served in a minus -20°C (-36°F) room at this Russian-theme bar, but don't be alarmed at the freezing temperature—they provide you with fur coats and traditional Russian fur hats. Take your pick from the 15 varieties of vodka from five different countries. ⊠ *2/ F, 10 Knutsford Terr., Tsim Sha Tsui* ☎ *2312–6222.*

Hotel Bars

Sophisticated and elegant cocktail bars are the norm at Hong Kong's luxury hotels. Some offer live music (usually Filipino trios with a female singer; occasionally international acts) in a gleaming setting with a small dance floor. Hong Kong's happy hours typically run from late afternoon to early evening, most places offering two drinks for the price of one. Request a window seat when making reservations.

Hong Kong Island

Captain's Bar. This bar in the Mandarin Oriental is where the smart, Cohiba-smoking set meets to discuss the day's business or to enjoy a post-meeting drink. ⊠ *G/F, Mandarin Oriental Hotel, 5 Connaught Rd., Central* ☎ *2522–0111.*

Talk of the Town. At the Excelsior's bar, also known as ToTT's, you're treated to a 270-degree vista of Hong Kong harbor. ⊠ *34/F, The Excelsior, 281 Gloucester Rd., Causeway Bay* ☎ *2837–6786.*

★ **Vong.** A small but wonderfully elegant bar with excellent service, Vong specializes in martinis. Try the lychee concoction while admiring the view of Kowloon. The popular bar is also a restaurant. ⊠ *25/F, Mandarin Oriental Hotel, 5 Connaught Rd., Central* ☎ *2522–0111.*

Kowloon

The Bar. Feeling pampered is your pleasure at the Peninsula's lobby bar. Society watchers linger here; sit to the right of the hotel entrance to better observe the crème de la crème. *Peninsula hotel* ⊠ *Salisbury Rd., Tsim Sha Tsui* ☎ *2920–2888.*

Chin Chin. The Hyatt Regency's bar appeals to the executive set. ⊠ *Hyatt Regency, 67 Nathan Rd., Tsim Sha Tsui* ☎ *2311–1234.*

Fodor's Choice **Felix.** This bar, high up in the Peninsula hotel, is a must for visitors; it
★ not only has a brilliant view of the island, but the impressive bar and disco were designed by the visionary Philippe Starck. Don't forget to check out the padded disco room. ⊠ *28/F, The Peninsula Hong Kong, Salisbury Rd., Tsim Sha Tsui* ☎ *2920–2888.*

Gripps. With spectacular harbor views from the ocean-liner level and a central bar modeled after a high-class London pub, the bar in the Marco Polo Hongkong Hotel draws the executive set. More recently though, many mainland businessmen and tourists flock to the hotel due to its location in the heart of Kowloon. ⊠ *6/F, Marco Polo Hongkong Hotel, Harbour City, Canton Rd., Tsim Sha Tsui* ☎ *2113–0088.*

Hotel InterContinental Hong Kong. Even though the hotel's name and management have changed (it was formerly the Regent), the lobby lounge here is still a place to see and be seen, but the uninterrupted views of Hong Kong island may compete for your attention. ⊠ *Hotel Inter-Continental Hong Kong, 18 Salisbury Rd., Tsim Sha Tsui* ☎ *2721–1211.*

Sky Lounge. Ride the bubble elevator to this bar high up in the Sheraton in time for sunset, and you won't be disappointed. ⊠ *18/F, Sheraton Hong Kong Hotel & Towers, 20 Nathan Rd., Tsim Sha Tsui* ☎ *2369–1111.*

Discos

Hong Kong's discos are diverse in style and clientele, not to mention price, so there's something to suit everyone. The thriving youth culture is best exemplified in these houses of dance, where young folks prance about in the latest fashions. Cover charges are high by U.S. standards; entrance to the smarter spots is usually HK$100 or more (much more on the eves of major holidays), though this usually entitles you to one or two drinks. If you prefer dance parties to discos, look for posters in Lan Kwai Fong and Wanchai that scream about the latest international DJ (usually very well known) arriving in town to play for one night only. Some bars and restaurants also hold weekly or monthly club nights, where music ranges from drum-and-bass to happy house.

Big Apple Pub & Disco. The dance floor gets going in the wee hours—and keeps going. There is a sleaze factor here, but when it's late late, who cares? ⊠ *Basement, 20 Luard Rd., Wanchai* ☎ *2529–3461.*

Club Ing. As its name suggests, this spot is about slipping into a pair of dancing shoes and hitting the floor. Those wishing to party the night away will not be disappointed because the party generally goes on into the wee hours. ⊠ *Renaissance Harbour View hotel, 1 Harbour Rd., Wanchai* ☎ *2824–0523.*

Joe Bananas. One of the mainstays of Wanchai nightlife, this club's reputation for all-night partying and general good times remains unchallenged. This disco-cum-bar strictly excludes the military and people dressed too casually: no shorts, sneakers, or T-shirts (the only exception is the Rugby Sevens weekend when even Joe can't turn away the thirsty and carefree swarm). Arrive before 11 PM to avoid the queue. ⊠ *23 Luard Rd., Wanchai* ☎ *2529–1811.*

Neptune Disco II. This is another late-night haunt for the dance-till-you-drop set. ⊠ *98–108 Jaffe Rd., Wanchai* ☎ *2865–2238.*

Rick's Cafe. Rick's is practically a disco institution, and despite being one of the oldest, remains popular. If you arrive after midnight on a weekend, be prepared to stand in line. ⊠ *53–59 Kimberly Rd., Luna Ct., Tsim Sha Tsui* ☎ *2311–2255.*

Hostess Clubs

These are clubs in name only. Hong Kong's better ones are multimillion-dollar operations with hundreds of presentable hostess-companions of many races. Computerized time clocks on each table tabulate companionship charges in timed units; the costs are clearly detailed on table cards, as are standard drink tabs. The clubs' dance floors are often larger than those at discos, and they have one or more live bands and a scheduled lineup of both pop and cabaret singers. They also have dozens of luxuriously furnished private rooms, with partitioned lounges and the

LATE-NIGHT BITES

When the late-night pub-crawl rumbles strike, go to *Al's Diner* (✉ *39 D'Aguilar St., Lan Kwai Fong* ☎ *2869–1869)*, which is open until 4 AM, serving up hamburgers and fry-ups, along with good bagels and coffee, all to the tunes of "everything except hip-hop and disco" according to the management, in a neon-lit, chrome-plated diner space. If you have a bit of a frat-boy spirit, try a vodka-spiked Jell-O shot or, for the ultra-insane, a tequila Jell-O shot with the worm.

A perennial late-supper favorite is **Post 97** (✉ *1/F, 9 Lan Kwai Fong, Lan Kwai Fong* ☎ *2810–9333)*, where the kitchen is open until 2 AM on Friday and Saturday. The consistently good all-day menu ranges from focaccias and salads to chicken wings (a very popular snack) and hearty breakfast items. Grab a window seat to peer down at the other late-night revelers of Lan Kwai Fong.

ubiquitous karaoke setup. Local and visiting businessmen adore these rooms—and the multilingual hostesses; business is so good that the clubs are willing to allow visitors *not* to ask for companionship. The better clubs are on a par with music lounges in deluxe hotels, though they cost a little more. Their happy hours start in the afternoon, when many have a sort of tea-dance ambience, and continue through to mid-evening. Peak hours are 10 PM to 4 AM. However, many hostess-oriented clubs, whether modest or posh, are also prostitution fronts.

Fodor'sChoice ★ **Club BBoss.** This is Hong Kong's grandest and most boisterous hostess club, tended by a staff of more than 1,000. Executives—mostly locals—provide the entertainment. If your VIP room is too far from the entrance, you can hire an electrified vintage Rolls-Royce and purr around an indoor roadway. Be warned that this is tycoon territory—a bottle of brandy can cost HK$18,000. ✉ *Mandarin Plaza, Tsim Sha Tsui East* ☎ *2369–2883.*

Club Kokusai. As its name applies, this place appeals to visitors from the Land of the Rising Yen. ✉ *81 Nathan Rd., Tsim Sha Tsui* ☎ *2367–6969.*

New Era. Along the harbor is the former Club Deluxe, which has undergone a much needed face-lift, opening up the dance floor and lounge area. Wannabe pop stars or visitors simply wishing to stretch their vocal cords can karaoke the night away. ✉ *East Wing, New World Centre, level 3, Tsim Sha Tsui* ☎ 2721–0277.

Jazz & Folk Clubs

Ned Kelly's Last Stand. Come to this Aussie-managed haven in Kowloon for pub meals and, oddly enough, Dixieland jazz. Arrive before 10 PM to get a comfortable seat. ✉ *11A Ashley Rd., Tsim Sha Tsui* ☎ *2376–0562.*

The Wanch. Wanchai's unpretentious alternative to the topless bar scene has live local folk and rock performances. The Hong Kong–theme interior (remember *Love Is a Many Splendored Thing*?) is worth a visit in itself. ⊠ *54 Jaffe Rd., Wanchai* ☎ *2861–1621*.

Nightclubs

Although nightclubs are similar in some ways to discos, the ones listed here tend to be smaller and more intimate than their high-octane megaplex cousins.

★ **C Club.** The upwardly mobile and occasional Hong Kong minor celebrity party here. There's a large dance floor, a flashy bar, and plenty of nooks to lounge in. But be warned: no sneakers, no shorts, no jeans. And weekends command a HK$200 door charge, which doesn't include the normally standard free drink. Ouch! ⊠ *32–34 D'Aguilar St., basement, Lan Kwai Fong* ☎ *2526–1139*.

Club 97. With a sorely needed revamp completed, this club continues to be a glitzy nightspot that draws mobs of beautiful people. It started out as a members-only club, a rule that has since been disregarded. ⊠ *9–11 Lan Kwai Fong, Lan Kwai Fong* ☎ *2186–1819*.

★ **dragon i.** The latest establishment where the glamour set prances, poses, and preens, dragon i is owned by local party boy and social celebrity Gilbert Yeung. The club's entrance is marked by an enormous birdcage (filled with real budgies and canaries) made entirely of bamboo poles. Have a drink on the wonderful alfresco deck by the doorway or step inside the rich, red playroom, which doubles as a restaurant in the early evening. A trip to the bathroom will find arguably the biggest cubicles in Hong Kong, with floor-to-ceiling silver tiles and double-height mirrored ceilings. ⊠ *Upper G/F, The Centrium, 60 Wyndham St., Central* ☎ *3110–1222*.

★ **Drop.** Although it has been around for a few years, this A-list club is still a favorite. Drop is where international celebrities party when they're in town—and party until the sun rises. It may take some effort to find, but that only adds an air of exclusivity to the speakeasy-like location. Excellent and unique martinis are Drop's forte. ⊠ *On Lok Mansion, 39–43 Hollywood Rd., basement (entrance off Cochrine St.), Central* ☎ *2543–8856*.

Propaganda. Off a quaint but steep cobblestone street, this is one of the most popular gay clubs in the territory. (It's known as P P to the locals, Props to the expatriate lot.) The art deco bar area is stylish, with elegant booths and tables surrounded by soft lighting; at the other end of the aesthetic spectrum, the dance floor has lap poles on either side for go-go boys who willingly flaunt their wares. Crowds don't arrive until well after midnight, and the entrance fee of HK$160 incurred on Friday and Saturday nights includes one standard drink. ⊠ *Lower G/F, 1 Hollywood Rd., Central* ☎ *2868–1316*.

Pubs

Lively pubs proliferate in Hong Kong. Some serve cheap drinks in a modest setting, while others are pricier and more elegant. They help ease homesickness for British expats by serving up fish-and-chips while airing rugby and football matches. Trivia quiz games have taken many of the

Hong Kong pubs by storm. Pub-hopping in Wanchai is best enjoyed by the energetic and the easy-to-please—or those trying to immortalize Suzie Wong.

Carnegies. Bar-top dancing to classic rock tunes is not unusual at this rowdy late-night hot spot that's usually bursting at the seams. ✉ *53–55 Lockhart Rd., Wanchai* ☎ *2866–6289.*

Chasers. You wouldn't think that a spot fitted with genuine English antiques including chairs, lamps, and prints, would be as groovy as it is, but with live pop music most evenings it draws a regular and bustling crowd. ✉ *2–3 Knutsford Terr., Tsim Sha Tsui* ☎ *2367–9487.*

★ **Delaney's.** Both branches of the pioneer of Hong Kong Irish pubs have interiors that were made in Ireland and shipped to Hong Kong, and the mood is as authentic as the furnishings. There are Guinness and Delaney's ale (a specialty microbrew) on tap, corner snugs (small private rooms), and a menu of Irish specialties, plus a happy hour that runs from 5 to 9 PM daily. ✉ *71–77 Peking Rd., basement, Tsim Sha Tsui* ☎ *2301–3980* ✉ *G/F, 1 Capital Pl., 18 Luard Rd., Wanchai* ☎ *2804–2880.*

Dickens Bar. For a reasonably priced hotel drinking hole, try the Excelsior's basement pub, which offers live music and football games via satellite TV. ✉ *281 Gloucester Rd., basement, Causeway Bay* ☎ *2837–6782.*

Dublin Jack. Drink Guinness and Irish ales while watching the latest football games. This pub just off the Midlevels outdoor escalators stands out with a fetching, bright-red exterior. ✉ *37 Cochrine St., Central* ☎ *2543–0081.*

Globe. Straddling the more upmarket Lan Kwai Fong and SoHo, the Globe is one of the few laid-back places in the area to knock back a beer or two with down-to-earth folks. ✉ *39 Hollywood Rd., Central* ☎ *2543–1941.*

Horse & Groom. It may be down-at-the-heels, but this is certainly a true pub, with regulars who seem to have become part of the furniture. ✉ *161 Lockhart Rd., Wanchai* ☎ *2507–2517.*

Just "M." The guess is that this curiously named pub stands for either "men" (but don't mistake it for a gay bar) or "money," but the owners playfully refuse to give up the goods. The minimalist industrial design gives it a laid-back feel, and the small mezzanine level has large black couches to sink into. ✉ *Shop 5, Podium Plaza, 5 Hanoi Rd., Tsim Sha Tsui* ☎ *2311–9188.*

Ned Kelly's Last Stand. An institution, Ned Kelly's has Aussie-style beer tucker (pub grub), and rollicking live jazz in the evening. ✉ *11A Ashley Rd., Tsim Sha Tsui* ☎ *2376–0562.*

Old China Hand Hand. This pub has been here since time immemorial, and the interior suffers accordingly, but the authentic vibe is intact. It's something of an institution for those wishing to sober up with greasy grub after a long night out. ✉ *104 Lockhart Rd., Wanchai* ☎ *2865–4378.*

Rick's Cafe. A local hangout, this restaurant-pub is decorated à la *Casablanca,* with potted palms, ceiling fans, and posters of Bogie and Bergman. ✉ *53–59 Kimberly Rd., Luna Ct., Tsim Sha Tsui* ☎ *2311–2255.*

Wine Bars

Juliette's. Tiny and classy, Juliette's is a cozy spot for chuppie (Hong Kong's Chinese yuppies) couples and corporate types relaxing after a busy day's trading. ⊠ *6 Hoi Ping Rd., Causeway Bay* ☎ *2882–5460.*

Le Tire Bouchon. If you are planning an intimate encounter, try this little restaurant and wine bar, where fine wines by the glass accompany tasty bistro meals. ⊠ *45A Graham St., Central* ☎ *2523–5459.*

THE ARTS

The most comprehensive calendar of cultural events is *HK Magazine,* a free weekly newspaper distributed each Friday to many restaurants, stores, and bars. You can also read daily reviews in the City section of the *South China Morning Post.* The free monthly newspaper *City News* lists City Hall events.

Tickets

URBTIX outlets are the easiest places to buy tickets for most arts performances in the city; you'll find branches at the Hong Kong Arts Centre in addition to City Hall and the Cultural Centre. ⊠ *Hong Kong Cultural Centre, 10 Salisbury Rd., Tsim Sha Tsui* ☎ *2734–2009* ⊠ *Hong Kong Arts Centre, 2 Harbour Rd., Wanchai* ☎ *2582–0232* ⊠ *City Hall, 5 Edinburgh Pl., near the Star Ferry, Central* ☎ *2921–2840.*

Performance Venues

Hong Kong Island

City Hall. Classical music, theatrical performances, films, and art exhibitions are presented in this complex's large auditorium, recital hall, and theater (the popular dim sum restaurant on the top floor is where former president Bill Clinton enjoyed a typical Chinese lunch). ⊠ *5 Edinburgh Pl., near the Star Ferry, Central* ☎ *2921–2840.*

Hong Kong Academy for Performing Arts. This arts school has two major theaters, each seating 1,600 people, plus a 200-seat studio theater and a 500-seat outdoor theater. Performances include local and international theater, modern and classical dance, and concerts. ⊠ *1 Gloucester Rd., Wanchai* ☎ *2584–8500.*

★ **Hong Kong Arts Centre.** Several floors of auditoriums, rehearsal halls, and recital rooms spotlight both local and visiting groups. It also has several floors of art galleries. ⊠ *2 Harbour Rd., Wanchai* ☎ *2582–0200.*

★ **Hong Kong Fringe Club.** Some of Hong Kong's most innovative entertainment and art exhibits play here. Shows range from the blatantly amateurish to the dazzlingly professional. Entertainment also includes good jazz, avant-garde drama, and many other events. The large, glass-fronted entrance facing the street houses some great professional and amateur artwork and photography exhibits. ⊠ *2 Lower Albert Rd., Central* ☎ *2521–7251* ⊕ *www.hkfringeclub.com.*

Queen Elizabeth Stadium. Though it's basically a sports stadium, this 3,500-seat venue frequently presents ballets and orchestral and pop concerts. ⊠ *18 Oi Kwan Rd., Wanchai* ☎ *2591–1346.*

Kowloon

Hong Kong Coliseum. This 12,000-plus-seat stadium presents everything from basketball to ballet, from skating polar bears to local and international pop stars. ⊠ *9 Cheong Wan Rd., at Hung Hom railway station, Hung Hom* ☎ *2355–7234.*

Hong Kong Cultural Centre. This conference and performance facility contains the Grand Theatre, which seats 1,750, and a concert hall, which seats 2,100. The center is used by both local and visiting artists for operas, ballets, and orchestral concerts. ⊠ *10 Salisbury Rd., Tsim Sha Tsui* ☎ *2734–2009.*

University Hall. Baptist University owns this modern auditorium, which usually hosts pop concerts but also offers dance and symphony concerts. The odd headline act plays here, such as the legendary Tom Jones, but the space usually caters to local talent, which is worth checking out. ⊠ *224 Waterloo Rd., Kowloon Tong* ☎ *3411–5182.*

The New Territories

Sha Tin Town Hall. Attached to New Town Plaza, an enormous shopping arcade, this impressive building is a five-minute walk from the KCR station at Sha Tin. Its cultural events include dance, drama, and concert performances. ⊠ *1 Yuen Wo Rd., Sha Tin* ☎ *2694–2509.*

Tsuen Wan Town Hall. It's off the beaten path, but this auditorium gets a constant stream of local and international performers. Acts include everything from the Warsaw Philharmonic to Chinese acrobats. The hall seats 1,424 and probably has the best acoustics of any performance space in Hong Kong. ⊠ *72 Tai Ho Rd., Tsuen Wan* ☎ *2414–0144.*

Chinese Opera

★ There are 10 **Cantonese opera** troupes headquartered in Hong Kong, as well as many amateur singing groups. These groups perform "street opera" in, for example, the Temple Street Night Market almost every night, while others perform at temple fairs, in City Hall, or in playgrounds under the auspices of the Urban Council. Visitors unfamiliar with the form are sometimes alienated by the strange sounds of this highly complex and extremely sophisticated art form. Every gesture has its own meaning; in fact, there are 50 gestures for the hand alone. Props attached to the costumes are similarly intricate and are used in exceptional ways. For example, the principal female often has 5-foot-long pheasant-feather tails attached to her headdress; she shows anger by dropping the head and shaking it in a circular fashion so that the feathers move in a perfect circle. Surprise is shown by what's called "nodding the feathers." One can also "dance with the feathers" to show a mixture of anger and determination. Orchestral music punctuates the singing. It's best to attend with a local acquaintance, who can translate the gestures, since the stories are so complex that Wagner and Verdi librettos begin to seem basic in comparison.

The highly stylized **Peking opera** employs higher-pitched voices than Cantonese opera. Peking opera is an older form, more respected for its classical traditions; the meticulous training of the several troupes visiting Hong Kong from the People's Republic of China each year is well regarded. They perform in City Hall or at special temple ceremonies. The Hong Kong Cultural Centre provides the latest programs and flyers.

Dance

Fodor'sChoice ★ **City Contemporary Dance Company.** The flagship of modern dance in Hong Kong presents innovative programs with local themes at various venues both indoors and outdoors. ☎ *2326–8597* ⊕ *www.ccdc.com.hk.*

Hong Kong Ballet. Hong Kong's first professional ballet company and vocational ballet school is Western oriented in both its classical and its contemporary repertoires. The company performs at schools, auditoriums, and festivals. ☎ *2573–7398* ⊕ *www.hkballet.com.*

Hong Kong Dance Company. Since 1981, the company has been promoting the art of Chinese dance and choreographing modern works with historical themes. The 30-odd members are experts in folk and classical dance. Sponsored by the Urban Council, they perform about three times a month throughout the territory. ☎ *3103–1888* ⊕ *www.hkdance.com.*

Film

Hong Kong reigns as the film capital of Asian martial-arts/triad-theme movies. Unlike the shoot-'em-ups of Hollywood films, the camera work in martial-arts flicks emphasizes the ricochet choreography of physical combat. The international success of the critically acclaimed *Crouching Tiger, Hidden Dragon* and heavy influence on the more recent *Kill Bill* is testament to the industry's emerging importance in world cinema.

If you want to experience a true Hong Kong Canto-flick, you'll have plenty to choose from. If a Jackie Chan or Chow Yun-Fat film is in release, you can be sure nearly every cinema in town will be showing it. Other movies are mostly B-grade, centering on the cops-and-robbers and slapstick genres; locals love these because they star popular (and very attractive) Hong Kong actors. Wong Kar Wai, Ann Hui, John Woo, and Ang Lee, all international award–winning filmmakers, have helped draw attention to Hong Kong film with their visionary and dynamic direction. For show times and theaters, check the listings in *HK Magazine* and the *South China Morning Post.*

★ **Broadway Cinematheque.** If you're looking for more than just a visual feast (that is, you want to see an art-house feature), visit this theater. The train-station design of this art house has won awards; the departure board displays foreign and independent films (local films are rare). Here you can read the latest reel-world magazines from around the globe in a minilibrary. A shop sells current and vintage film paraphernalia, and there's a coffee bar as well. To get here, use the Temple Street exit at the Yau Ma Tei MTR. ☒ *Prosperous Garden, 3 Public Square St., Yau Ma Tei* ☎ *2388–3188 for ticket reservations* ⊕ *www.cinema.com.hk.*

Cine-Art House. The quaint, two-theater cinema screens art-house and foreign films. Definitely bring your own shawl. ☒ *G/F, Sun Hung Kai Centre, 30 Harbour Rd., Wanchai* ☎ *2317–6666* ⊕ *www.cityline.com.*

CloseUp

MARTIAL ARTS GO HOLLYWOOD

ALTHOUGH A CULT FAVORITE **AROUND THE GLOBE,** martial-arts films in Hong Kong are no less than a phenomenon—their actors no less than superstars. Walk into a Hong Kong shop, visit a tourist office, step into an office atrium, and who do you see? Jackie Chan. Not the man, but his image. A life-size, cutout figure of the humorous martial-arts superstar with a thousand-watt smile.

Chan has been called a "physical genius" and "the world's greatest action star." After years of international fame and accolades, this ultraflexible stuntman extraordinaire finally broke into the American market with Rumble in the Bronx in the mid-1990s. Two years later, Chan solidified his fame in the West with his first exclusively U.S. production, Rush Hour.

But in Hong Kong he's been a god, a crutch during economic hard times, when he was routinely asked to step in, support, sing praise, and raise the spirits of the people, as he is at this writing in the Hong Kong Tourist Board's marketing campaign for Hong Kong. He's the man who's guaranteed to draw the crowds every time his latest movie is released. When he's on the silver screen, Hong Kongers know they can kick back and forget about their troubles for a while.

Of course Chan is not the first, or only, martial-arts golden son of Hong Kong. Recent heroes include John Woo, who created such bullet-ridden cult classics as A Better Tomorrow, The Killer, and Hard-Boiled. He was also responsible for launching Chow Yun-Fat's movie career. Chow Yun-Fat, who was born on the small island of Lamma and moved to Hong Kong in 1965, is the ultratough, muscular martial artist who worked with Woo on A Better Tomorrow, which propelled both men into the limelight of the action-movie genre. Both men are also known for the slick Hollywood flick The Replacement Killers, which Woo produced and Chow Yun-Fat starred in; but Yun-Fat's name is now most associated with his graceful fighting prowess in the international hit Crouching Tiger, Hidden Dragon.

Although their Hollywood films do well in the United States, both Chow Yun-Fat and Jackie Chan are equally famous in the Hong Kong film industry for their locally filmed slapstick and heroic bloodshed films. Like the godfather of the genre, Bruce Lee, both are more than just hometown boys made good—they're international stars.

But it was Lee who broke the ground and still shines as the martial artist to live up to in life and on the screen. Martial artists still talk about Lee and his muscular physique and Lee and his style.

Just after moving to America in the 1960s, Lee was challenged to a fight by Cantonese experts in Oakland's Chinatown because he was teaching Chinese "secrets" to non-Chinese individuals. This was perceived as treason among some members of the martial-arts community. Lee won the challenge, and nowadays students around the world study such techniques. In part they can thank Lee for their schooling.

Unlike other areas in the region, Hong Kong isn't a city where you're likely to get into a bar fight with a local who thinks he is Jackie Chan or Bruce Lee. But you are likely to see some of the cheesiest, funniest, most artistically and athletically amazing movies here if you just pop into a local movie theater. It's a Hong Kong experience without parallel.

★ **Hong Kong Arts Centre Theatre.** This theater screens some of the best independent, classic, documentary, animated and short films from around the world as well as local productions, often with themes focusing on a particular country, period, or director. ⊠ *2 Harbour Rd., Wanchai* ☎ *2582–0200* ⊕ *www.hkac.org.hk.*

★ **Palace IFC.** Large, sink-into red leather seats and ushers in tuxedos make this brand-new boutique cinema seem more like a Broadway theater than a mini-multiplex. Five screens show new releases, foreign and independent films, as well as classic celluloid such as *Gone With the Wind* and *West Side Story.* But what really sets Palace apart from the rest is the "Shawl Loan" for those who get a little chilly—Hong Kong cinemas are notoriously frigid. There's also a bookshop and café, where visitors can discuss afterwards whether Rhett really did give a damn. ⊠ *IFC Mall, 8 Finance St., level 1, Central* ☎ *2388–6268* ⊕ *www.palaceifc.cinema. com.hk.*

Orchestras

Hong Kong Chinese Orchestra. Created in 1977 by the Urban Council, this orchestra performs exclusively Chinese works. It consists of bowed strings, plucked instruments, wind, and percussion. Each work is specially arranged for each concert. ☎ *3185–1600* ⊕ *www.hkco.org.*

★ **Hong Kong Philharmonic Orchestra.** Almost 100 musicians from Hong Kong, the United States, Australia, and Europe perform everything from classical to avant-garde to contemporary music by Chinese composers. Past soloists have included Vladimir Ashkenazy, Rudolf Firkusny, and Maureen Forrester. Performances are usually held Friday and Saturday at 8 PM in City Hall or in recital halls in the New Territories. ☎ *2721–2030* ⊕ *www.hkpo.com.*

Theater

Chung Ying Theatre Company. This professional company of Chinese actors stages plays—most of them original and written by local playwrights—mainly in Cantonese. The group also organizes exchanges with theater companies from overseas, often inviting international directors to head productions. Performance venues vary. ☎ *2521–6628* ⊕ *www.chungying.com.*

Zuni Icosahedron. The best-known avant-garde group in Hong Kong stages multimedia drama and dance, usually in Cantonese, at various locations. ☎ *2893–8419* ⊕ *zuni.org.hk.*

SPORTS &
THE OUTDOORS

5

Updated by
Tim Metcalfe

SWEAT IN HONG KONG spills beyond the floors of the stock exchange and dance clubs. You can work up a sweat studying martial arts from karate to tae kwon do or by joining local Hong Kongers hiking in the mountains, sailing beyond Victoria Harbour into the South China Sea, golfing with coworkers, and playing tennis with friends on weekends. You can also join the hordes of men and women who rise when the roosters crow to perform their ritual morning tai chi in public parks before they head off for a light breakfast of dim sum.

If you're in town during the horse-racing season, don't miss the spectacle when gambling-mad punters stake a huge part of their incomes on stallions and mares. Rugby and soccer tournaments draw enthusiastic—if often drunken—fans, and the annual dragon boat races are highly entertaining. Check weekly activity schedules at a **Hong Kong Tourist Board (HKTB)** information booth for listings of spectator-sport events. Although most activities require a little advance planning, they're well worth the effort.

Perhaps because of its British legacy, Hong Kong has long been known as a club-oriented city: whether you're into golf, sailing, squash, or tennis, you'll find that members-only clubs have the best facilities. Several clubs have reciprocal privileges with clubs outside Hong Kong. The Hong Kong Jockey Club offers members of such affiliates free entry to its members' enclosure during racing season (though not use of club recreational facilities). Visitors with reciprocal privileges at the Hong Kong Golf Club are allowed 14 free rounds of golf each year. Other clubs with reciprocal policies are the Hong Kong Yacht Club, Hong Kong Cricket Club, Kowloon Cricket Club, Hong Kong Football Club, Hong Kong Country Club, Kowloon Club, Hong Kong Club, and Ladies' Recreation Club.

Before you leave home, check with your club to see if it has an arrangement with a club in Hong Kong. If so, you'll need to bring your membership card, a letter of introduction, and often your passport when you visit the affiliated establishment in Hong Kong. Call when you arrive to book facilities, or ask your hotel concierge to make arrangements.

Beaches

Hong Kong is not known for its beaches, but it's surrounded by hundreds of them and has a thriving sunbathing culture. About 40 of the beaches around Hong Kong and its outlying islands are "gazetted"—cleaned and maintained by the government, with services that include lifeguards, floats, and swimming-zone safety markers.

The scenery is often breathtaking, but pollution is occasionally a problem, so don't swim if a red flag—indicating either pollution or an approaching storm—is hoisted. The red flag flies often at Big Wave Bay (on the south side of Hong Kong Island) because of the rough surf.

Swimming is extremely popular with Hong Kongers, which means locals pack most beaches on summer weekends and public holidays. The more popular beaches, such as Repulse Bay, are busy day and night throughout summer.

Beaches out in Sai Kung Country Park are by far the most spectacular, but also the most remote. Almost all other beaches can be reached by bus or taxi, which will cost around HK$150 or more, depending on where you're staying. Beaches on outlying islands connect to Central by the Hong Kong Ferry, and are often a short walk from the pier.

Hong Kong Island

Big Wave Bay, Hong Kong's most accessible surfing beach, lives up to its name and is frequently closed for swimming as a result. The beach has kiosks, barbecue pits, a playground, changing rooms, showers, and toilets. From Shau Ki Wan, take Bus 9 to the roundabout; walk about 20 minutes along the road, which is usually lined with cars on weekends.

At **Deep Water Bay** the action starts at dawn every morning, all year long, when members of the Polar Bear Club go for a dip. The beach is packed in summer, when there are lifeguards, swimming rafts, and safety-zone markers, plus a police reporting center. Barbecue pits, showers, and restrooms are open year-round. A taxi from Central will take about 20 minutes. You can also take Bus 6A from the Exchange Square Bus Terminus; for a scenic route, take Bus 70 from Exchange Square to Aberdeen and change to Bus 73, which passes the beach en route to Stanley.

Repulse Bay has changing rooms, showers, toilets, swimming rafts, swimming safety-zone markers, and playgrounds. Several Chinese restaurants dot the beach, and kiosks serve light refreshments. The Lifesaving Club is at the east end and resembles a Chinese temple, with large statues of Tin Hau, goddess of the sea, and Kwun Yum, goddess of mercy. Take Bus 6, 6A, 64, 260, or 262 from Exchange Square, or Bus 73 from Aberdeen.

Shek O, not far from Big Wave Bay, is almost Mediterranean in aspect. A wide beach with shops and restaurants nearby, it has refreshment kiosks, barbecue pits, lifeguards, swimming rafts, playgrounds, changing rooms, showers, and toilets. The views are magnificent as the bus begins its descent toward the heart of the small village. In the center of town there are several outdoor dining areas, serving everything from Thai to Cantonese. Take the MTR from Central to Shau Ki Wan (there is a bus from Central to Shau Ki Wan, but it takes between one and two hours), then Bus 9 to the end of the line.

Stanley Main, a wide sweep of sand, is popular with the windsurfing crowd and has a refreshment kiosk, swimming rafts, changing rooms, showers, and toilets, plus a nearby market packed to the rafters, where you should bargain—in a friendly but confident manner. It also hosts the annual dragon boat races, usually held in June, in which friendly teams paddle out into the sea, turn around, and, at the sound of the gun, race ferociously back to the beach. It's a great day out, but head out early to claim a spot along the beach, as it gets chaotically crowded. There are several English pubs and Southeast Asian restaurants along the main strip. Take a taxi from Central (about 45 minutes); Bus 6, 6A, 6X or 260 from Exchange Square; or Bus 73 from Aberdeen.

Turtle Cove, isolated but scenic, has lifeguards and rafts in summer, barbecue pits, a refreshment kiosk, changing rooms, showers, and toilets. From Central take the MTR to Sai Wan Ho and change to Bus 14; get off at Tai Tam Road after passing the dam of Tai Tuk Reservoir.

The New Territories

Expansive Sai Kung Peninsula has some of Hong Kong's most beautiful beaches, and many of these are easily reached by public transportation. Here are the three most popular:

Hap Mun Wan (Half Moon Bay) is a gem of a beach, with brilliant, golden sand. On a grassy island near Sai Kung Town, it can only be reached by sampan. Sampans depart from Sai Kung waterfront, beside the bus station. If you're sharing a sampan with other passengers, remember the color of the flag on the roof: that's the color you need for your return ferry. Shared sampans cost HK$40. Amenities at the beach include a refreshments kiosk, barbecue pits, and toilets. Take the MTR to Choi Hung, then Minibus 1 to Sai Kung.

Sha Ha's waters are shallow, even far from shore, and ideal for beginning windsurfers. The Kent Windsurfing Centre is here. Facilities include refreshment kiosks, a coffee shop, a pub, and a Chinese restaurant at the Beach Resort. Take the MTR to Choi Hung, then Minibus 1 to Sai Kung. It's a 10-minute walk along the shore to Sha Ha.

Silverstrand is always crowded on summer weekends. Though a little rocky in spots, it has soft sand and all the facilities, including changing rooms, showers, and toilets. Take the MTR to Choi Hung, then Bus 92 or a taxi to Silverstrand.

The Outer Islands

A day trip to one of Hong Kong's islands is a terrific way to spend some time outside the city. Many Hong Kongers make a point of going to visit on the weekend—it's an opportunity to breathe fresh air. If you take a morning ferry to Lamma, Lantau, or Cheung Chau, you can combine a beach trip with a sightseeing tour of the island. Ferry schedules are available at the piers. The faster ferries are marked as such, usually run every other ferry, and will cut 15 to 30 minutes from your transport time.

Cheung Sha is a popular beach on Lantau, only a short taxi or bus ride from the Silvermine Bay ferry pier. Its mile-long sandy expanse is excellent for swimming. All the standard facilities—from bathrooms to snack stands—are available. Take the ferry from Central to Silvermine Bay. Buses meet the ferry every half hour on weekdays and Saturday; on Sunday and holidays buses leave when full.

Hung Shing Ye, on Lamma Island, is popular with young locals. It is known as Power Station Beach because a massive plant is clearly visible from the beach, but that doesn't deter sunbathers, who materialize whenever the rays smile down. There are showers, toilets, changing rooms, barbecue pits, and a kiosk, but no swimming rafts. Take the ferry from Central to Yung Shue Wan and walk through the village, then over a low hill.

Lo So Shing, on Lamma Island, is popular with families. It's an easy hike on a paved path from the fishing village of Sok Kwu Wan. Facilities include a kiosk, barbecue pits, swimming rafts, changing rooms, showers, and toilets. Lamma is known as a hippy enclave, and there are some interesting shops selling trinkets from all over Asia, although mostly from Indonesia and Thailand. Take the ferry from Central to Sok Kwu Wan, then walk for 20 to 30 minutes.

Tung Wan is the main beach on Cheung Chau Island. On weekends its wide sweep of golden sand is so crowded with sunbathers that it's barely visible. You'll see it from the ferry as you approach the dock—at one end of the beach is the Warwick Hotel. Plenty of restaurants along the beach offer refreshments, seafood, and shade. There are no private cars allowed on this island, so the air is noticeably cleaner. Amenities include changing rooms, showers, and toilets. Take the ferry from Central to Cheung Chau Ferry Pier and walk five minutes through the village to the beach.

Cricket

★ Each November, as Hong Kong basks in its most delightful climate of the year, the city hosts its second-most-important international sporting event, the **Hong Kong Cricket Sixes,** which has now returned to its spiritual home at the quaint, intimate Kowloon Cricket Club (KCC), a short stroll from the Jordan MTR and Tsim Sha Tsui. Don't worry if you are not a cricket fan, or indeed have no idea at all about the game. It's not conventional cricket lasting all day, or even five days, but a six-a-side version with each match between top cricketing countries like England, Australia, India, Pakistan, Sri Lanka, and South Africa lasting only about 25 minutes. The two-day event is fun, fast-paced, and thrilling—with the bonus of appearances by some of the world's best players. This being Hong Kong, it goes without saying that vast quantities of beer and wine are consumed—along with pizzas, hot dogs, burgers, and curries. Like the International Rugby Sevens, the Sixes is virtually a compulsory date on Hong Kong's sporting calendar. Tickets (around HK$450 for both days) can be purchased in advance from the Hong Kong Cricket Association, but you can usually buy them at the gate. ⊠ *Kowloon Cricket Club, 10 Cox's Rd., Jordan* ☎ *2367–4141 for club, 2504–8101 for tickets* ⊕ *www.hkca.cricket.org.*

Golf

Locals generally head to Hong Kong's only public course at Kau Sai Chau or to nearby Shenzhen, which is across the border in mainland China, to play golf; however, you need a Chinese visa to play in Shenzhen without spending an arm and a leg. Hong Kong's top clubs will also allow you to play their courses, but don't expect much change from US$200.

Clearwater Bay Golf and Country Club in the New Territories permits overseas visitors to play golf on its 18-hole course on weekdays with tee-off times between 9:30 and 11:30 AM as long as you book three days in advance. It's best to take a taxi if you are going here. ⊠ *139 Tai Aumum*

Rd., Clearwater Bay ☎ *2719–1595, 2335–3885 for booking office* 🖃 *Green fee HK$1,400 with golf cart.*

Deep Water Bay Golf Course, the most convenient course to play if you're staying on Hong Kong Island, or even Tsim Sha Tsui for that matter, can be deceptive. Though it's only 9 holes—played twice as a par 56 with two tees for each pin—it represents a tough challenge. With 16 par 3s and two par 4s, almost every shot is at the flag. As a test of your short game, with no margin for error, it can't be beaten. It's a members' club (some of Hong Kong's richest businessmen play here), owned by the Hong Kong Golf Club, but visitors with handicap cards are admitted on weekdays, and it's casual enough to allow you to play in trainers. Deep Water Bay is just 20 minutes from Central via Bus 6, 64, or 260, or you can take a taxi. ⊠ *19 Island Rd., Deep Water Bay* ☎ *2812–7070* 🖃 *Green fee HK$450; club rental HK$100.*

Discovery Bay Golf Club, on Lantau Island, has an 18-hole course open to visitors on Monday, Tuesday, and Friday between 7:30 and 11:45 AM. You must reserve two days in advance. Take the Discovery Bay ferry from the Star Ferry Terminal in Central, then catch the bus to the course (call the club for up-to-date bus information). ⊠ *Discovery Bay* ☎ *2987–7273* 🖃 *Green fee HK$1,400; club rental HK$160; golf-cart rental HK$190; shoe rental HK$50; ½-hr lesson HK$400.*

The oldest club in the territory, the Hong Kong Golf Club, owns the **Fanling Golf Course** and hosts the annual Hong Kong Open, an Asian PGA event. Visitors with handicaps can play on its three 18-hole courses at Fanling, in the New Territories, weekdays from 7:30 AM to 2 PM. Check with your local club for reciprocal membership as the HKGC has worldwide connections. Take the KCR to Fanling, then a taxi to the club. ⊠ *Just off Fanling Hwy., Fanling* ☎ *2670–1211 for bookings, 2670–0647 for club rentals* 🖃 *Green fee HK$1,400 for 18 holes; club rental HK$250; ½-hr lesson HK$300.*

Fodor'sChoice **Hong Kong Jockey Club, Kau Sai Chau,** Hong Kong's only public golf course,
★ is by far its cheapest and most popular. Overseas visitors pay a marginal premium on green fees, but the cost is well worth it. Both the more difficult North Course and the less-taxing but still challenging South Course are superb tests of accuracy amid breathtaking scenery on an island 20 minutes by dedicated ferry from the delightful fishing port of Sai Kung. Booking is advisable, especially on weekends, on these Gary Player–designed gems, but unbooked "walk-ons" for lone golfers are usually possible on weekdays. Take the MTR to Choi Hung and then Bus 92 or 96R, or Minibus 1 to Sai Kung Town, where you can catch the golf-course ferry to Kau Sai Chau; the ferry departs the Sai Kung waterfront every 20 minutes. ⊠ *Kau Sai Chau* ☎ *2791–3380 automated booking line, 2791–3390 help line* 🖃 *Combined green fee and ferry ticket: HK$550 for South Course, HK$600 for North Course; club rental HK$160; shoe rental HK$35.*

Tuen Mun Golf Centre, a public golf center in the Western New Territories, has 100 driving bays and a practice green, but there is no course. Take the MTR to Tsuen Wan station and then Bus 66M or 66P to Tuen

CloseUp

SMOOTH MOVES

WHEN YOU ARRIVE in Hong Kong, chances are you'll be suffering from jet lag. If you wake up at 4AM raring to go, you can wander down to any public park and watch some of the more than 100,000 Hong Kongers who practice tai chi each morning.

Just before dawn it's not unusual to see young businessmen and retired grandparents practicing tai chi: slowly stretching, breathing deeply, and moving in ways most Western teenagers can't manage. There's no better advertising for tai chi than seeing an octogenarian balance on one leg, with the other outstretched and held high for a long moment before gracefully swinging into another pose that requires balance, coordination, and strength.

The art of tai chi consists of slow, steady, flowing movements with moderate postures—suitable for people of all ages, flexibility, and fitness levels to practice. It offers physical and mental benefits and may give you insights into the philosophical path followed by thousands throughout the centuries. While that may be common knowledge, few people know that tai chi is also a subtle, sophisticated, and scientific method of self-defense.

The founder of tai chi was Chang San Feng, a Taoist, who was born in AD 1247. His accomplishments were such that titles and honors were showered on Chang, and a magnificent mansion was built for him on Wutan Mountain as a special gift from the provincial governor. News of his fame reached the ears of the Emperor himself.

One of the greatest tai chi masters was Yang Lu Chan (1799–1872) who served as the chief combat instructor to the Imperial Guard during the Ching Dynasty. His fighting ability earned him the nickname "Invincible Yang."

To follow in their footsteps you need to study under an accomplished master. Only a good master can correctly demonstrate techniques, identify faults, and give proper advice and guidance that will help you progress. You will also experience a more calming feeling when studying under an accomplished master.

If you want to try tai chi while you're in Hong Kong, contact the Hong Kong Tourist Board (HKTB). Under the guidance of a tai chi master, you can learn simple breathing and relaxation exercises. Free classes are offered at Hong Kong Park every Tuesday, Friday, and Sunday from 8:15 to 9:15 AM.

Mun, then take a taxi to the golf course. ⊠ *Lung Mun Rd., Tuen Mun* ☎ *2466–2600* ✍ *HK$12 per bay; HK$12 per club; HK$12 per hr per 30 balls* ⊙ *Daily 8 AM–10 PM.*

Health Clubs

Most Hong Kong health clubs require membership; the person behind the desk will look at you blankly if you try to explain that your health club at home might have a reciprocal arrangement. The majority of first-class hotels have health clubs on their premises, and California Fitness Center, New York Fitness, and Seasons Sport Club—all on Hong Kong Island—will let you enter for a reasonable short-term rate.

California Fitness Center sells guest passes for HK$150 per day or HK$450 per week. This gym has an excellent master yoga instructor, Master Kamal, who travels throughout Asia teaching yoga, meditation, and relaxation. If you're into yoga, call any of the branches to find out where and when he's teaching. ⊠ *1 Wellington St., Central* ☎ *2522–5229* ✉ *99 Percival St., Causeway Bay* ☎ *2577–0004* ✉ *88 Gloucester Rd., Wanchai* ☎ *2877–7070.*

Alongside the Midlevels outdoor escalator, **New York Fitness** sells a one-week pass for HK$500. ⊠ *32 Hollywood Rd., Central* ☎ *2543–2280.*

Seasons Sport Club charges HK$100 for a weekday visit before 5 PM, HK$150 after 5 and on weekends. ⊠ *3/F, Asia Pacific Finance Tower, 3 Garden Rd., Central* ☎ *2521–4541.*

Hiking

Most visitors to Hong Kong do not come for the lush lowlands, bamboo and pine forests, rugged mountains with panoramas of the sea, and secluded beaches, but nature is never very far from the skyscrapers of Central and Tsim Sha Tsui. In fact, about 40% of Hong Kong is protected in 23 parks, three marine parks, and one marine reserve. A day's hike (or two days if you're prepared to camp out) takes a bit of planning, but you'll see the best of Hong Kong. You'll seem farther than you really are from the buildings below, which appear almost insignificant from this perspective.

Don't expect to find the wilderness wholly unspoiled, however. Few upland areas escape Hong Kong's relentless plague of hill fires for more than a few years at a time. Some are caused by dried-out vegetation; others erupt from small graveside fires set by locals to clear the land around ancestors' eternal resting spots. Partly because of these fires, most of Hong Kong's forests, except for a few spots in the New Territories, support no obvious wildlife other than birds—and mosquitoes. Bring repellent.

Gear

Basic necessities include sunglasses or hat, bottled water, day pack, and sturdy hiking boots. Wear layered clothing; weather in the hills tends to be very warm during the day and colder toward nightfall. The cliff sides get quite windy. Of course, if you're planning to camp, carry a sleeping bag and tent. If you arrive in Hong Kong and need some basics, there are several options.

Although it doesn't sell the same range of camping equipment, backpacks, sleeping bags, and clothes you'd find in the United States or in the United Kingdom, **Great Outdoor Clothing Company** (⊠ 2/F, Silvercord Bldg., 30 Canton Rd., Tsim Sha Tsui ☎ 2730–9009) will do in a pinch.

Timberland (⊠ Shop 212, Pacific Place, 88 Queensway, Admiralty ☎ 2868–0845) sells hiking boots, backpacks, and appropriate clothing.

Probably comparable to your favorite camping store back home, **World Sports Co. Ltd.** (⊠ 2/F, 83 Fa Yuen St., Mong Kok ☎ 2396–9357) caters to your every outdoor need with a very helpful staff. It stocks everything from pocketknives and wool socks to gas burners and tents.

Maps

Before setting off for the wild, pick up guides such as *Hong Kong Hikes* from any bookstore. You can purchase hiking trail maps at the **Government Publications Centre** (⊠ Pacific Place, Government Office, G/F, 66 Queensway, Admiralty ☎ 2537–1910). Ask for blueprints of the trails and the Countryside Series maps. The HM20C series comprises handsome four-color maps, but it's not very reliable.

Trails

You can hike through any of the territory's country parks and around any of the accessible outlying islands. Here are some short one-day hikes and two camping treks on the most popular trails.

Fodor'sChoice
★
Dragon's Back, one of Hong Kong's most popular trails, crosses the "rooftop" of Hong Kong Island. Take the Peak Tram from Central up to the Peak, and tackle as much or as little of the range as you feel like—there are numerous exits "downhill" to public-transport networks. Surprisingly wild country feels a world away from the urban bustle of Hong Kong below, and the panoramas of Victoria Harbour on one side, with South Island and outlying islands on the other, are the most spectacular you will find anywhere, especially on a clear day. You can follow the trail all the way to the delightful seaside village of Shek O, where you can relax over an evening dinner before returning to the city by minibus or taxi. The entire trip takes the better part of an unforgettable day.

Lantau Island is a popular hiking destination. First catch public transport to the world's largest seated Buddha at Po Lin Monastery—one of Hong Kong's most famous tourist attractions. The Lantau Island ferry departs regularly from Central for the quaint village of Mui Wo, and the monastery is a scenic bus ride away (take the bus marked PO LIN MONASTERY), close to the summit of Lantau Peak, Hong Kong's second-highest mountain. From a vantage point with stunning views of Shek Pik Reservoir and the South China Sea, a hiking path meanders down to the Taoist Kwun Yam Temple, named after the goddess of mercy. The trail goes for 7 km (4½ mi), and takes about 3½ hours to hike; it's about 2½ hours to the monastery.

The trail to **Lion Rock,** one of Hong Kong's most spectacular summits, is also the most convenient to access from Kowloon. The hike passes through dense woodland with bamboo groves along the Eagle's Nest Nature Trail and up open slopes to Beacon Hill for 360-degree views over hills and the city. The contrasting vistas of green hills and the city's hustle and bustle are extraordinary. There's a climb up the steep rough track to the top of Lion Rock, a superb vantage point for appreciating Kowloon's setting between hills and sea. The trail ends at Wong Tai Sin Taoist Temple, one of Hong Kong's most famous temples, where you can have your fortune told. To start, catch the MTR to Choi Hung (15 minutes from Tsim Sha Tsui) and a 10-minute taxi ride up Lion Rock. From Wong Tai Sin, return by MTR.

Fodor'sChoice
★ The **MacLehose Trail,** named after an ex-governor of Hong Kong, is the course for the annual charity MacLehose Trailwalker, a grueling 97-km (60-mi) event. Top teams finish in an astonishing 15 hours, but the average hiker can only tackle relatively short sections of the trail in one day; otherwise, allow two days from beginning to end. This splendidly isolated path through the New Territories starts at Tsak Yue Wu, beyond Sai Kung, and circles High Island Reservoir before breaking north. Climb through Sai Kung Country Park to a steep section of the trail, up the mountain called Ma On Shan. Turn south for a high-ridge view, and walk through Ma On Shan Country Park. From here you walk west along the ridges of the mountains known as the "Eight Dragons," which gave Kowloon its name. After crossing Tai Po Road, the path follows a ridge to the summit of Tai Mo Mountain, at 3,161 feet above sea level the tallest mountain in Hong Kong. Continuing west, the trail drops to Tai Lam Reservoir and Tuen Mun, where you can catch public transport back to the city. To reach Tsak Yue Wu, take the MTR to Choi Hung and then Bus 92 or 96R, or Minibus 1 to Sai Kung Town. From Sai Kung Town, take Bus 94 to the country park.

Wilson Trail is 78 km (48 mi) long, from Stanley Gap on Hong Kong Island to Nam Chung in the northeastern New Territories. You have to cross the harbor by MTR at Quarry Bay to complete the entire walk. The trail is smoothed by steps paved with stone, and footbridges aid with steep sections and streams. Clearly marked with signs and information boards, this popular walk is divided into 10 sections, and you can easily take just 1 or 2 (figure on 3 to 4 hours a section); traversing the whole trail takes about 31 hours. It begins at Stanley Gap Road, on the south end of Hong Kong Island, and takes you through rugged peaks that have a panoramic view of Repulse Bay and the nearby Round and Middle islands. This first part, Section 1, is only for the very fit. Much of the trail requires walking up steep mountain grades. For an easier walk, try Section 7, which begins at Sing Mun Reservoir and takes you along a greenery-filled, fairly level path that winds past the eastern shore of the Sing Mun Reservoir in the New Territories and then descends to Tai Po, where there's a sweeping view of Tolo Harbour. Other sections will take you through the monkey forest at the Kowloon Hill Fitness Trail, over mountains, and past charming Chinese villages.

Horse Racing

Horse racing is the nearest thing in Hong Kong to a national sport. It is a multimillion-dollar-a-year business, employing thousands of people and drawing crowds that approach insanity in their eagerness to rid themselves of their hard-earned money. Even if you're not a gambler, it's worth going to one of Hong Kong's two tracks just to experience the phenomenon. The "sport of kings" is run under a monopoly by the Hong Kong Jockey Club, one of the most politically powerful entities in the territory. Profits go to charity and community organizations. The racing season runs from September through June. Some 65 races are held at one or the other of the two courses—on Saturday or Sunday afternoon at Sha Tin and Wednesday night at Happy Valley—which must rank as one of the world's great horse-racing experiences. The HKTB organizes tours to the club and track. Costs range from HK$245 to HK$490 and can include transfers, lunch, and tips on picking a winner. Alternatively, you can watch the races from the public stands, where the vibe is lively and loud—this is highly recommended for a truly local experience, and the cost is only HK$10. Both courses have huge video screens at the finish line so that gamblers can see what's happening every foot of the way.

Fodor'sChoice **Happy Valley Racetrack** on Hong Kong Island, is one of Hong Kong's ★ most beloved institutions. Racing is on Wednesday evenings and the atmosphere is electric. The track is a five-minute walk from the Causeway Bay MTR, or you can take a taxi. ⊠ *Hong Kong Jockey Club, 1 Sports Rd., Happy Valley* ☎ *2966–8111 or 2966–8364.*

★ **Sha Tin Racecourse,** in the New Territories, is newer than Happy Valley; in fact, it's one of the most modern racecourses in the world. Racing is on Saturday or Sunday afternoon, and it is the venue for all of Hong Kong's championship events. The easiest way to get here is by taxi, or you can catch the MTR to Kowloon Tong and transfer to the KCR train, which stops at the track on race days. A walkway from the station takes you directly to the racetrack. ⊠ *Tai Po Rd., next to Racecourse KCR station, Sha Tin* ☎ *2966–6520.*

Junking

Dining on the water aboard large pleasure craft—which also serve as platforms for swimmers and water-skiers—is a boating style unique to Hong Kong. Junking has become so popular that there is now a fairly large junk-building industry producing highly varnished, plushly appointed, air-conditioned junks up to 80 feet long. After a day out on a junk, sailing by the shimmering lights of Hong Kong Island on the ride back into town is spectacular.

These floating rumpus rooms serve a purpose, especially for denizens of Hong Kong Island who suffer from "rock fever" and need to escape for a day on the water. Also known as "gin junks" because so much alcohol is consumed, these junks are commanded by "weekend admirals." If anyone so much as breathes an invitation for junking, grab it.

You can also rent a junk. The pilot will take you to your choice of the following outer islands: Cheung Chau, Lamma, Lantau, Po Toi, or the islands in Port Shelter, Sai Kung.

Jubilee International Tour Centre (✉ Far East Consortium Bldg., 121 Des Vouex Rd., Central ☎ 2530–0530) is an established charter outfit recommended by the HKTB.

Simpson Marine Ltd. (✉ Aberdeen Marina Tower, 8 Shun Wan Rd., Aberdeen ☎ 2555–7349) is an established charter operator whose crewed junks can hold 35 to 45 people. Prices begin at HK$2,800 for an eight-hour day trip or a four-hour night trip during the week, HK$4,500 on summer weekends. The price goes up on holidays. You need to reserve in advance; half of the fee is required upon receipt of a signed contract, the remaining half at least five days prior to departure.

Paragliding

The **Hong Kong Paragliding Association** will recommend an instructor, then, weather permitting, you can soar over Hong Kong at an altitude rarely experienced by the populace. Paragliders are usually sighted over the scenic Shek O Peninsula. If you just want to watch, you can spy take-offs and landings from the hike along Dragon's Back. ✉ *Union Commercial Bldg., 12–16 Lyndhurst Terr., Room 202, Central* ☎ *2543–2901.*

Rugby

FodorśChoice ★ One weekend every spring (usually in March), Hong Kong hosts **International Rugby Sevens,** more popularly known as "the Sevens," at the Hong Kong Stadium (take the MTR to Causeway Bay and then exit F, or take a taxi). The entire city, swelled with rugby supporters from across the planet, goes wild. It's a serious party event; in fact, it's one of Hong Kong's wildest parties of the year, so don't be afraid to sport fancy dress or take the kids. Purchasing tickets (around HK$550 for both days) in advance through your overseas travel agent is advisable, but you can usually acquire them at the entrance. One word of warning: if you attend the Sevens once, you might get addicted and find yourself coming back year after year. *Hong Kong Rugby Football Union* ✉ *Sports House, 1 Stadium Path, Room 2001, Causeway Bay* ☎ *2504–8300.*

Scuba Diving

Bunn's Divers Institute (✉ 38–40 Yee Woo St., Causeway Bay ☎ 2574–7951) runs outings for qualified divers to areas like Sai Kung. The cost of a day trip runs HK$700 and includes two dive sessions, one in the morning and another in the afternoon. You'll need to bring your own lunch.

Skating

The **Glacier** is a part of Festival Walk, an extensive entertainment complex in Yau Yat Tsuen, next to the Kowloon Tong KCR station. The Glacier is the largest ice-skating rink in Hong Kong. You can rent figure skates that fit larger feet (up to a man's 11½). ✉ *Festival Walk,*

Kowloon Bay ☎ 2265–8888 ⊠ *HK$50 weekdays, HK$60 weekends; skate rentals HK$50* ⊘ *2-hr sessions Mon.–Sat. 10–10, Sun. 1–10.*

Cityplaza II on Hong Kong Island has a first-class ice-skating rink, **Ice Plaza.** During the week this rink allows you to skate for an unlimited number of sessions provided you don't leave the rink, but on weekends you are limited to a single 1½- to 2-hour session. Rental skates are mostly in children's sizes. The rink is near Quarry Bay; to get there take the MTR to Taikoo Shing. ⊠ *Cityplaza II, 1111 Kings Rd., Taikoo Shing* ☎ *2885–4697* ⊠ *HK$40 morning session, HK$50 afternoon session; skate rentals HK$50* ⊘ *Weekdays 8–noon and 12:30–10 PM; Sat. 7–9 AM, 12:30–2, 3–5, 5:30–7:30, and 8–10; Sun. 7–noon, 12:30–2:30, 3–5, 5:30–7:30, and 8–10.*

Squash

The Hong Kong Urban Council runs many public squash courts in the territory and provides a **central booking service.** You can reserve courts up to 10 days in advance, and should do so as early as possible. Bring a passport for identification. Most courts are open daily from 7 AM to 10 or 11 PM and cost HK$27 for 30 minutes, HK$54 for an hour. The Urban Council can give directions, or you can contact the court directly for directions or reservations.

Harbour Road Indoor Games Hall (⊠ 27 Harbour Rd., Wanchai ☎ 2827–9684, 2927–8080 or 2922–8008 for central booking service).
Hong Kong Squash Centre (⊠ Cotton Tree Dr. across from Peak Tram Terminal, Central ☎ 2521–5072, 2927–8080 or 2922–8008 for central booking service).
Laichikok Park (⊠ 1 Lai Wan Rd., Kowloon ☎ 2745–2796, 2927–8080 or 2922–8008 for central booking service).
Victoria Park (⊠ Hing Fat St., Causeway Bay ☎ 2570–6186, 2927–8080 or 2922–8008 for central booking service).

Tennis

Most hotels have tennis courts, but if yours doesn't, there are some public tennis courts in Hong Kong. Unfortunately, they're usually booked far in advance. To reserve one you'll need identification, such as a passport, and you must reserve in person and pay in advance. Most courts open daily from 7 AM to 10 or 11 PM and cost HK$42 in the daytime and HK$57 in the evening. If you want to try to play without a reservation, try during the day on Monday through Friday; courts are almost invariably booked for weekends.

Bowen Road Courts (⊠ 7 Kennedy Rd., Wanchai ☎ 2528–2983) has 4 courts.
Hong Kong Tennis Centre (⊠ Wongneichong Gap, Happy Valley ☎ 2574–9122) has 17 courts.
Kowloon Tsai Park (⊠ 13 Inverness Rd., Kowloon Tong ☎ 2336–7878) has 8 courts.

Victoria Park (✉ Hing Fat St., Causeway Bay ☎ 2570–6186) has 14 courts, plus an additional 8 courts on King's Road. These back courts are quieter. Of all of the public tennis courts in Hong Kong, Victoria Park's are the easiest to get to, simply because you just have to tell a taxi driver "Victoria Park Tennis Courts." You can book Centre Court—and pretend you are a pro—if you like, it's just an HK$10 additional fee.

Waterskiing

Patrick's Waterskiing (✉ Stanley Main Beach, Stanley ☎ 2813–2372) is run by the friendly, laid-back man himself. Patrick will take you to the best waters in the Stanley Beach area and give you pointers on your waterskiing or wakeboarding technique. The fee—HK$700 per hour—includes a range of equipment and life jackets. To rent a speedboat, equipment, and the services of a driver, contact the **Waterski Club** (✉ Pier at Deep Water Bay Beach, Deep Water Bay ☎ 2812–0391) or ask your hotel for the names and numbers of other outfitters. The cost is usually about HK$580 per hour.

Windsurfing

Windsurfing has grown dramatically in popularity since Hong Kong's Lee Lai-shan sailed off with a women's Olympic gold medal at the 1996 Summer Olympic Games in Atlanta, inspiring a generation of youngsters to take up the sport, which is further popularized on ESPN and MTV. Now windsurfing centers at Stanley Beach on Hong Kong Island, Sai Kung, and Tung Wan Beach (Lee's home on Cheung Chau Island), will gladly start you on the path to glory with some lessons. You can take lessons or rent a board at the **Kent Windsurfing Centre** (✉ Sha Ha ☎ 2813–2372). To reach Sha Ha, take the MTR to Choi Hung, then Minibus 1 to Sai Kung. It's a 10-minute walk along the shore to Sha Ha.

Patrick's Waterskiing (✉ Stanley Main Beach, Stanley ☎ 2813–2372) offers a full-day course for HK$880; the more experienced can rent windsurfing boards for HK$70–HK$120 a day.

SHOPPING

6

Updated by
Tracey Furniss

HIGH RENTS, unstable economies in Hong Kong and the rest of the region, and a tendency for manufacturers to open outlets elsewhere in the world have put a damper on the megabargains for which Hong Kong was once known. The lack of sales tax, however, helps to keep prices lower than those in Shanghai or Beijing, though this will only last for a few more years as the Hong Kong government plans to introduce a sales tax by 2007. You will find that clothing, computers, and many electronic goods cost only slightly less than in the United States. However, there are some real bargains out there; you just have to know when and where to look. For now, stores are fully stocked and busy, and at this writing, the SARS outbreak, which kept major shopping malls and streets deserted for more than a couple of months in 2003, is but a distant memory.

We've divided this chapter into two handy sections for mastering the art of shopping in Hong Kong: the first is divided into regions, the second into categories. To many Hong Kongers, especially women, shopping is a sport. When Hong Kong women shop, they don't go out to buy a blouse or a pair of trousers, they go out to *shop*. They scout areas and scour markets, carrying designer shopping bags advertising previous scores. If you ask one of these shopaholics where to buy a specific item, the answer will not be a specific shop, but a whole section of town. If you want to shop as the experts do, you should learn the best shopping neighborhoods. The Western tendency, however, is to shop for specifics. Given the time constraints on short visits to Hong Kong, sometimes this style of shopping is unavoidable, which is why the second half of the chapter is divided into categories of potential purchases such as carpets or women's clothing.

Many major boutiques are in malls or shopping complexes in the basements of office buildings and hotels. It might seem incongruous to mallcrawl in Hong Kong—the land of bargain alleys and outdoor markets—but the advantage is air-conditioning and big-name designers all piled on top of one another. Still, some of the best deals are found in the local boutiques and in the freestanding designer shops. If you're coming to Hong Kong just to shop, you should plan your visit for the end-of-season sales (January through February and July through August), when prices are slashed anywhere from 50% to 90% in major department stores and boutiques.

Although shopping in Hong Kong can be a thrilling adventure, you need to be careful. Parallel imports—when a company orders wholesale goods directly from the country of manufacture, bypassing official wholesalers based in Hong Kong—are legal here, but because the seller has purchased goods meant for sale in a particular country, the buyer must beware as warranties may not cover your area of the world. For example, if a store purchases cell phones bound for Argentina directly from the Korean manufacturer, the phones' warranties won't be valid in the United States. You may be saving with the purchase but spending more on repairs if something goes wrong. Electronics shops selling the ever-popular photographic and hi-fi gear in Tsim Sha Tsui have a fearsome—and, regrettably, well-earned—reputation. Watch out for absurd discounts (to get you in the door), the switch (after you've paid, they pack a cheaper model), and the heavy, and sometimes physical, push to get you to buy a more expensive item than you want.

It is not uncommon for jewelers in the mid-price range to offer you a discount of 10% to 20% if you look at a few items and seem moderately interested. Be wary if a salesperson tries to drop the price much lower; you might go home to find you've purchased an inferior or defective item.

Know, too, that in spite of the credit-card decals on the door (every card you could possibly imagine and more), most stores will insist on cash or add 3% to 5% to the total if you pay by credit card. Shopping at stores with the Hong Kong Tourist Board (HKTB) decal on the window buys you some protection since the shop belongs to the organization, but if you have trouble, head for the police, the Consumer Council, or the HKTB itself.

Shopping Tours

If you're really determined to shop 'til you drop, **Asian Cajun Ltd.** (⊠ 4/F, 12 Scenic Villa Dr., Pokfulam ☎ 2817–3687) leads customized shopping tours for visitors seeking good buys in antiques, art, jewelry, designer clothes, and specialty items. Escorted tours, which include hard-to-find shops and private dealers, are US$130 per hour for a small group of up to four people but do not include the cost for transportation, and there is a minimum of three hours per tour. If you are looking for a fun day out in the New Territories visiting lesser-known factories, then **Guided Shopping Expeditions** (☎☎ 2592–9940), run by Sandra Hawghton, will take you to brass-ware, porcelain, and candle factories; antique furniture warehouses; and fashion and lingerie outlets. The cost will range from HK$350 to HK$500 per person for the daylong tour, with a minimum of 8 to 10 people. Discounts can be negotiated and shipping arranged.

MAJOR SHOPPING AREAS

Hong Kong Island

Hong Kong Island shopping districts are listed here from west to east. All of them are easily accessible by MTR stations. Visiting them all in one day is conceivable but would likely be exhausting. Try working in two or at most three regions per shopping day.

Western District

The Western District is one of the oldest and most typically Chinese areas in Hong Kong. (Take the MTR to Sheung Wan or the tram to Western Market.) Here you'll find craftsmen making mah-jongg tiles, opera costumes, fans, and chops (seals carved in stone with engraved initials); Chinese-medicine shops selling ginseng, snake musk, shark's fin, and powdered lizards; rice shops and rattan-furniture dealers; and cobblers, tinkers, and tailors. You'll also come across alleyways where merchants have set up stalls filled with knickknacks and curios.

The streets behind **Western Market** are some of the best places to soak up some of Hong Kong's traditional Chinese feeling, though the goods available in the market itself can be found elsewhere. Wing Lok Street and Bonham Strand West are excellent browsing areas, with shops selling herbs, rice, bird's nests, tea, and Chinese medicines. Heading uphill, don't miss the stalls selling bric-a-brac on Ladder Street, which angles down from Queen's Road in Central to Hollywood and Caine roads. Hollywood Road is lined with Chinese antiques and collectibles; it turns into Wyndham Street in Central.

Two of Hong Kong's largest Western-style department stores, **Sincere** and Wing On, are technically in Central but you will pass them as you are walking from Western to Central along Des Voeux Road.

need a break?

Visit **She Wong Yuen** (✉ 89–93 Bonham Strand, Western ☎ No phone) for a taste of snake's-gall-bladder wine. Snake soup is popular in Hong Kong in winter months. If you are uninterested in partaking of snake's gall bladder or anything else snake, try some ginseng or Chinese herbal tea. There are plenty of old-style Chinese shop fronts in the Western Market area. One recommendable place is **Tung Fung Tai Ginseng** (✉ G/F, 188 Queen's Rd., Western ☎ 2517–1230).

Central District

Otherwise known as Hong Kong's financial and business district, Central has an extraordinary mixture of designer boutiques, department stores, and narrow lanes full of vendors selling inexpensive clothing and knockoffs of designer goods.

Many exclusive shops are housed in Central's major office buildings and shopping complexes such as the **Landmark,** on Des Voeux Road, **Prince's Building,** on Chater Road, and the **Galleria at 9 Queen's Road,** all of which are connected by elevated walkways. If couture labels are what you're after, don't miss shopping here. While absorbing the piped-in music, golden hues, and spacious settings of these interconnected shopping arcades, you will find Christian Dior, the internationally renowned fashion designer; Coach, makers of fine leather handbags, purses, and belts; giftware from Lalique; and a whole range of designer boutiques.

In **Shanghai Tang** you'll find fine silk Mandarin jackets for men and women, as well as an exciting collection of silks and cashmeres in brilliant colors.

If you're familiar with British stores, you'll recognize **Marks & Spencer** (better known as Marks & Sparks); however, you may find the prices here aren't much better than you will find in England. In the **Jardine House,** at Connaught Place, across from the Central Post Office, check out the Oxfam Hong Kong shop in the basement. Even if you are not a secondhand shopper, it's worth a look for all the designer labels selling for a fraction of their original retail cost.

You can hunt for bargains on clothing, shoes, woolens, handbags, and accessories in the stalls that fill **East and West Li Yuen streets,** between Queen's Road and Des Voeux Road. Watch out for pickpockets in these

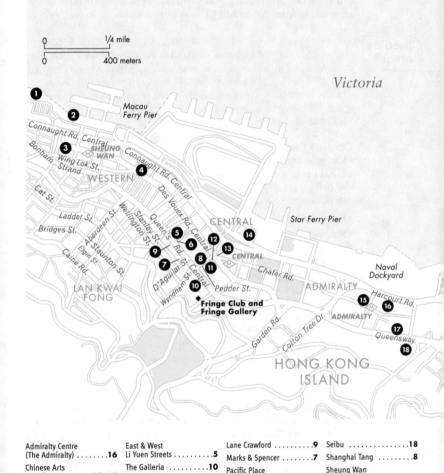

Shopping on Hong Kong Island

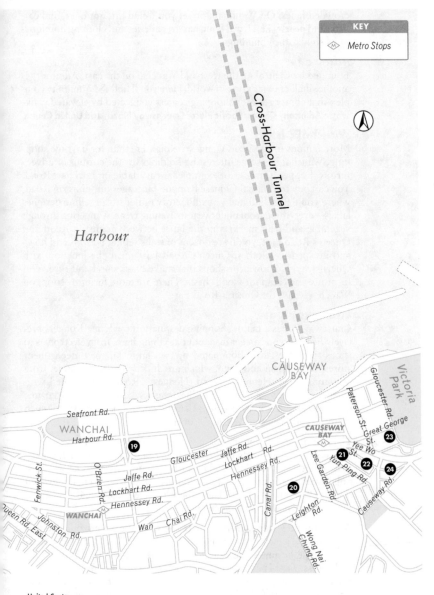

KEY

◈ Metro Stops

Cross-Harbour Tunnel

Harbour

CAUSEWAY BAY

Victoria Park

Seafront Rd.

WANCHAI
Harbour Rd.

19

Gloucester Rd.

Jaffe Rd.

Lockhart Rd.

Hennessey Rd.

CAUSEWAY BAY

Paterson St.

Gloucester Rd.

Great George St.

Yee Wo St.

23

21

22

24

Fenwick St.

O'Brien Rd.

Jaffe Rd.

Lockhart Rd.

Hennessey Rd.

Canal Rd.

Lee Garden Rd.

Yun Ping Rd.

Causeway Rd.

20

Leighton Rd.

Queen Rd. East

Johnston Rd.

WANCHAI

Wan Chai Rd.

Wong Nai Chung Rd.

crowded lanes. On Wyndham Street you'll find art, antiques, and carpets, and nearby Lan Kwai Fong has art galleries and clothing boutiques in its small office buildings.

Admiralty

Bounded by Central on the west and Wanchai on the east, Admiralty is another mall-crawler's dream world. Here you'll find the Admiralty complex that comprises four shopping centers connected by elevated walkways: **Admiralty Centre, Pacific Place, Queensway Plaza,** and **United Centre.**

Wanchai District

More famous for its Suzie Wong–style nightlife than for daytime shopping, Wanchai has some interesting holdings for the curious or adventurous shopper. Tattoos, for example, are available on Lockhart Road. You can buy traditional Chinese bamboo birdcages on Johnston Road, where you'll also find many small factory outlet stores selling designer labels—everything from underwear to evening wear. Wandering through vegetable and fruit markets in the lanes between Johnston Road and Queen's Road East, you'll see dozens of stalls selling buttons and bows and inexpensive clothes. Queen's Road East (near the junction with Queensway) is known for shops that make blackwood and rosewood furniture and camphor-wood chests. There are more furniture shops on Wanchai Road, off Queen's Road East.

Causeway Bay

Causeway Bay is a major shopping destination for Hong Kongers precisely because you can get just about anything here, from electronics to shoes to clothes. It is dominated by two large Japanese department stores, Mitsukoshi and Sogo, which are directly across the street from one another on Hennessy Road. Hennessy Road is also filled with smaller shops selling jewelry, watches, stereos, cameras, and electronic goods. Parallel Lockhart Road has several good shoe stores selling such major brands as Nine West and Rockport.

The boutiques of Vogue Alley, at the intersection of Paterson and Kingston streets, spotlight the best of Hong Kong's own fashion designers. Just behind the Excelsior hotel is **Windsor House,** toward Victoria Park opposite the Park Lane Hotel on Gloucester Road, with a mall plus two floors of computer supplies. The **Chinese Resources Center (CRC)** has a vast selection of goods made in China.

Behind the Sogo department store (away from the waterfront) are two other interesting streets. Jardine's Bazaar has stacks of Chinese restaurants, while Jardine's Crescent is an alley of bargain-basement clothes and accessories. The latter is a traditional destination for inexpensive apparel and geared toward Chinese shoppers, so you're not likely to find larger, Western sizes. At the end of the alley, there's a bustling "wet market" (so called because the vendors are perpetually hosing down their produce), where Chinese housewives shop for fresh produce and for fresh chickens, which are slaughtered on the spot.

The streets around the megamall **Times Square,** on Matheson Street, have some of the most interesting boutiques in Hong Kong. These shops go in and out of business with some frequency, and they cater to Hong Kong women's sizes (tiny); if you fit the clothes, however, you're likely to find some real one-of-a-kind deals.

Eastern District

If you're shopping with or for children, you might want to shop in the Eastern District, which includes the North Point, Quarry Bay, and Shaukiwan neighborhoods. The best shopping is in Quarry Bay's huge **Cityplaza,** which houses Hong Kong's largest department store, UNY, as well as more than 400 shops (including toy stores), an ice-skating rink, and a bowling alley.

Stanley

Most people visit here for the sole purpose of bargain-hunting at **Stanley Market.** You should allot at least a half day for this market; and if you dine here, it can be an all-day outing. The area around Main Street has a trendy, artsy vibe, with beachfront restaurants and an open-air shopping complex. The colonial building on the beachfront is Murray House, which originally stood in Central and was dismantled brick by brick and rebuilt on the waterfront of Stanley Bay. It dates back to 1844 and now houses a selection of restaurants. On the way to Stanley Market, stop at Repulse Bay's shopping arcade, in which several stores sell fine reproductions of traditional Chinese furniture.

Kowloon

Kowloon is where you'll find the famous Nathan Road filled with bright neon lights on every building. Locals usually don't shop on Nathan Road and tourists usually get ripped off here. But when it comes to outdoor markets, Kowloon draws the locals and the in-the-know tourists who are willing to bargain for their bargains. In addition to good sales at outdoor vending areas such as the Temple Street Night Market and the Ladies' Market, cultural shopping experiences abound in places such as the Bird Garden or the Jade Market.

Visiting all the outdoor markets in Kowloon in one day may be exhausting. You're better off picking three sites you want to spend some time in rather than rushing through them all.

Tsim Sha Tsui District

Known for its Golden Mile of shopping along Nathan Road, Tsim Sha Tsui is popular for its hundreds of stereo, camera, jewelry, cosmetics, fashion, and souvenir shops. Branching off Nathan Road are narrow streets lined with shops crowded with every possible type of merchandise. Explore Granville Road, with its embroidery and porcelain shops and clothing factory outlets (not as plentiful as they were a few years ago, but still worth a look for serious bargain hunters), and Mody Road, for souvenir shops. Peking Road has the largest CD, VCD, and DVD store in Hong Kong, and nearby Star House, next to the Star Ferry, has a quality computer center selling everything from laptops to desktops, software, and computer accessories.

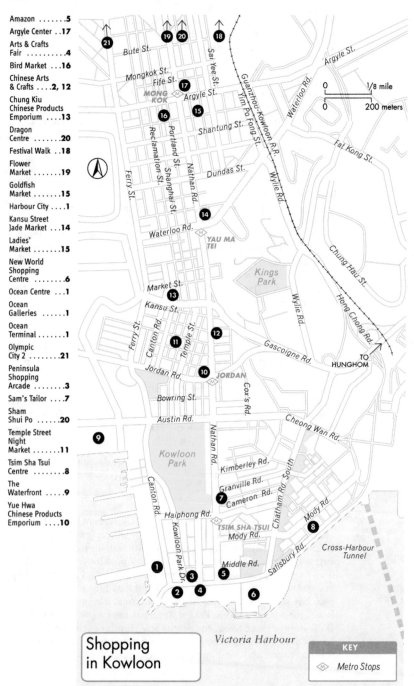

Shopping
in Kowloon

Victoria Harbour

KEY

◈ Metro Stops

The shopkeepers on Nathan Road are known to take advantage of unsuspecting shoppers. It's best to be absolutely sure of the quality and price you should be paying before shopping on Nathan Road. Stick to the places listed in this chapter or those displaying HKTB stickers.

Chinese Arts & Crafts has a fairly wide and good-quality selection of silk embroidered clothing, porcelain, and gems.

At **HMV** you can buy reasonably priced CDs, VCDs, and DVDs. At **Joyce Boutique** you can find chic housewares and clothes by such designers as Issey Miyake and Prada. **Yue Hwa Chinese Products Emporium** has household products, clothes, and a popular medicine counter.

Harbour City, next to the Star Ferry Pier, is the largest shopping complex in Hong Kong, and one of the largest in the world; if you can't find it here, it probably doesn't exist. **The Peninsula Hong Kong**'s shopping arcade houses boutiques selling luxury clothing and accessories.

The **Waterfront** is a new area of Tsim Sha Tsui built on reclaimed land on the waterfront beyond the Harbour City complex. The high-rise apartments loom over TST and cannot be missed. The Kowloon Station on the airport MTR line is here. The shopping scene here is dominated by several floors of factory-outlet shops. Although it is a small shopping center, it is worth checking out for big year-round discounts on designer products. Deals on everything from shoes, household goods, luggage, handbags, casual sportswear, children's designer wear, designer evening wear and suits for men, with labels such as Arnold Palmer, Polo Ralph Lauren, DKNY, Levi's, Disney, Polo Kids, Reebok, Nike, Lancel, Coach, among others. The sizes range from small to larger Western sizes.

Tsim Sha Tsui East

This area of hotels, shops, and offices east of Chatham Road is accessible via minibus from the Kowloon Star Ferry. Fifteen different shopping plazas are clustered here, including Wing On Plaza, **Tsim Sha Tsui Centre,** Empire Centre, Houston Centre, South Seas Centre, and Energy Plaza. Prices are reasonable, but unless you're the equivalent of an Asian size (about an American size 4) you may have trouble finding clothing here. However, the lively atmosphere makes up for the lack of size diversity.

Hung Hom District

Travel east of Tsim Sha Tsui East to Hung Hom, the center of Hong Kong's jewelry and textile industries, for a tremendous selection of bargains in both designer boutiques and factory outlets. Man Yue Street is a good nexus.

West Kowloon to Mong Kok

The harbor reclamation work in Tai Kok Tsui next to Yau Ma Tei has given way to beautiful new residential and shopping areas near the Western Harbour Tunnel. North of Jordan Road, Tsim Sha Tsui's bright lights and big-city world give way to tenements and overcrowding. You could visit this area in conjunction with Nathan Road. But if you're planning a day of hunting and gathering, skip Nathan Road shops and start here, where street signs revert to Chinese, retirees gather to play checkers and mah-jongg in the park, and outdoor markets abound. You can find great deals as well as fakes, pickpockets, and hawking shopkeepers with no-return policies—truly a place to enjoy the bargaining and the chaos of it all. However, the biggest draw to Mong Kok in the future may be the new upscale Langham Place shopping mall, which is directly accessed from the Mong Kok MTR Station.

Sham Shui Po

Two stops from Mong Kok on the MTR is Sham Shui Po, a labyrinth of small streets teeming with outdoor flea markets and wholesale shops, where you can buy anything from electronics to computers to clothing. Favored by locals, whole streets are devoted to fabrics, buttons, laces, and ribbons; other streets are filled with gadgets and parts for gadgets. There is a computer center with very competitive prices, though the machines often come without a warranty. You'll even find a shopping mall with a roller coaster here.

New Territories

Kowloon proper ends at Boundary Street, which in the 19th century served as the border with China and was marked by bamboo poles. As development progresses, Kowloon and the New Territories continue to blend together. The key difference is that the farther out you travel from Kowloon, the less densely populated the area becomes. High-rises still abound in many pockets, but they give way to trees, rolling hills, and seaside views as you move out from the city proper. Most of the shopping experience in this region is in malls—the best of which are the **Maritime Square** mall on Tsing Yi Island and the enormous **New Town Plaza** mall in Sha Tin.

SHOPPING CENTERS & MALLS

Hong Kong Island

Fodor'sChoice ★ **The Admiralty.** This gigantic shopping complex is actually comprised of four shopping centers connected by elevated walkways: Admiralty Centre, Pacific Place, Queensway Plaza, and United Centre. **Admiralty Centre** has reasonably priced optical shops and men's tailors, a chop maker, and an excellent carpet shop. Glitzy **Pacific Place** is perhaps the most popular shopping mall in Hong Kong, with four floors of upscale shops and restaurants. Its flagship Japanese department store, Seibu, has upmarket products; Lane Crawford, another upscale emporium, also has a branch here. You'll find that in most cases the most expensive stores are on the top floors and the prices go down as you descend. For a break in your shopping, stop by at the multiplex cinema, which screens international releases, or dine at one of the dozens of restaurants. The Marriott, the Island Shangri-La, and the Conrad hotels are all connected to this shopping plaza. **Queensway Plaza** is dominated by smaller boutiques selling mainly locally made clothes and shoes, and these boutiques are worth checking out if you want one-of-a-kind buys without having to scour the street markets. The **United Centre** houses several furniture shops,

CENTRAL & WESTERN DISTRICTS BLITZ TOUR

START WITH THE STREETS BEHIND **Western Market** for a traditional Chinese experience, where spices, herbs, and aphrodisiacs are sold amid old, walk-up buildings. Mah-jongg shops, tea sellers, and packed dim sum restaurants abound.

Then head up the main thoroughfare, Des Voeux Road. Both **Wing On** and **Sincere** sell everything from household items to clothing. Farther along Des Voeux Road you come to Pedder Street, where the **Landmark** shopping mall houses high-end boutiques such as Louis Vuitton and Fendi. Next door, in the Central Building, there is a branch of **Moiselle**, where you will find elegant women's suits and evening wear. Also in the Central Building is **HMV**, on the first floor, which is a good stop for CDs and DVDs. Do not leave this area without visiting **Shanghai Tang**, opposite the Landmark on Pedder Street, for upscale

Chinese fashions. Upstairs in the same building are some warehouse stores with discounted designer labels.

From here, cross Queen's Road by the Hong Kong & Shanghai Bank, on the corner of Pedder Street, and walk up the hill on D'Aguilar Street to Lan Kwai Fong, where you may find a wide range of restaurants, coffee shops, and bars for refreshments. Check out the discount designer clothes in the **Grand Progress Building** in Lan Kwai Fong. If you head up to Hollywood Road and work your way back towards Western, you will find many art galleries, carpet shops, and antiques stores. This should take you at least a morning, but if you are still game for more shopping, head down hill to Central's Star Ferry Terminal, and cross over to the Kowloon side.

— Tracey Furniss

---

but it's worth visiting just for Tequila Kola, which sells upscale, hand-crafted bedroom sets, couches, fabrics, and gifts. ✉ *Queensway, Central* Ⓜ *Admiralty.*

Cityplaza. One of Hong Kong's busiest shopping centers, Cityplaza is popular with families because of its ice-skating rink, multiplex theater, bowling alley, and weekly cultural shows. Many shops carry children's clothing, with labels such as Les Enfants, Crocodile, Peter Pan, and Crystal. Its selection of more than 400 shops includes plenty of clothing stores for men and women and a number of toy stores. ✉ *1111 Kings Rd., Taikoo Shing, Quarry Bay* Ⓜ *Taikoo Shing.*

The Landmark. One of Central's most prestigious shopping sites, the Landmark houses Celine, Loewe, Gucci, Joyce Boutique, Hermès, and other designer boutiques. There are also art galleries and fine jewelry shops. A pedestrian bridge links the Landmark with shopping arcades in Jardine House, the Prince's Building, the Mandarin Oriental Hotel, and 9 Queen's Road. ✉ *Pedder St. and Des Voeux Rd., Central* Ⓜ *Central.*

Shun Tak Centre. Attached to the Macau Ferry Terminal, this shopping center has a selection of boutiques selling clothing, handbags, toys, and novelties. If you're waiting for the Macau Ferry, have a look around;

otherwise, a special trip is not required since most of the stores here are chains that can be found all over Hong Kong. ⊠ *200 Connaught Rd., Western* Ⓜ *Sheung Wan.*

★ **Times Square.** This gleaming mall packs in most of Hong Kong's best-known stores, including Lane Crawford and Marks & Spencer, into 12 frenzied floors. An indoor atrium hosts entertainment ranging from heavy-metal bands to fashion shows to local movie-star appearances; there are also a cinema complex and a dozen or so eateries. At the first basement level are City Super, a popular Japanese supermarket and international food court, and two excellent bookstores. ⊠ *1 Matheson St., Causeway Bay* Ⓜ *Causeway Bay.*

Western Market. This Victorian, redbrick building was built in 1906 and originally used as a produce market. The first two floors are filled with shops selling crafts, toys, jewelry, collectibles, and fabrics, but it's certainly not worth a special trip. You can find these goods elsewhere in town. However, it is worth visiting the Grand Stage Chinese restaurant/ballroom on the top floor for lunch, dinner, or high tea; you can experience authentic Chinese food and afterwards do some ballroom dancing to a live band belting out the cha-cha and tango in an atmospheric Edwardian and Chinese art deco setting. The surroundings behind Western Market are full of old-style Chinese stores, especially along Wing Lok Street and Bonham Strand West; opposite, on the harbor front, is a night market that is open during the daytime on weekends and public holidays. That's when it's worth the trouble to come out here. ⊠ *Des Voeux Rd., Sheung Wan* Ⓜ *Sheung Wan.*

Kowloon

Amazon. This underground shopping center between the Hotel Inter-Continental Hong Kong and the Space Museum (you enter from the promenade on Nathan Road next to the Peninsula hotel or outside the InterContinental) is just the place to go when it's pouring rain. The shopping selection is limited, but the Teddy Bear Kingdom, which has a teddy bear museum, an amusement center, and a shop where you can make your own bear, is a good distraction for children. ⊠ *12 Salisbury Rd., Tsim Sha Tsui* Ⓜ *Tsim Sha Tsui.*

Dragon Centre. People go to Sham Shui Po for the outside markets, cheap computer components, and computer software, but if you have children with you, this shopping mall is a good place to drop them off for a day of fun, since there is an ice rink, indoor roller coaster, and games hall. For shopping there are the usual chain-store outlets and local boutiques, a supermarket, fast-food restaurants, and small stalls in the corridors selling knicknacks and trinkets. You can find some bargains here. ⊠ *37K Yen Chow St., Sham Shui Po* Ⓜ *Sham Shui Po.*

Fodor'sChoice **Festival Walk.** The fanciest mall in Hong Kong is very easy to reach, al-
★ beit slightly off the beaten path, in the mainly residential area of Kowloon Tong. A large Marks & Spencer and a large Esprit serve as anchors, but Armani Exchange, Calvin Klein, Vivienne Tam, Moiselle, Mandarina Duck, not to mention the boutiques of local Hong Kong designers, are what draw the elite crowds. The mall also has the largest ice rink in Hong Kong as well as a multiplex cinema, perfect if you're shopping with kids

KOWLOON BLITZ TOUR

F YOU AREN'T STAYING on the Kowloon side, take the Star Ferry over. This is the beginning of your tour, regardless of where you're staying. You will find Star House on the left side as you exit the Star Ferry Terminal. **Chinese Arts & Crafts,** where you can buy silks, jade, porcelain, and the best of Chinese art, is here. On the second floor is **Star Computer City,** a source for reasonably priced computer software and hardware in a more spacious setting compared to other computer centers in town. On the third floor is a large bookstore with reasonably priced magazines and books. Heading back down the ground level, turn into Ocean Terminal, which is the oldest part of the Harbour City complex. On the right is the Hong Kong Hotel with a huge **Lane Crawford** department store; this is the most prestigious department store in town, and you can buy brand-named cosmetics, handbags, clothing, shoes, bedding, and elegant household products. If you walk to the left of the entrance and

straight down one wing of the complex, you will find many stores selling children's clothing and baby accessories, including a large Toys "R" Us.

If you walk straight ahead from the Star Ferry exit and keep walking on Canton Road, you will be heading towards the Gateway and the China Ferry Terminal. There are many high-end boutiques along the way, including **Joyce Boutique** and DKNY, and the more reasonably priced **Marks & Spencer. CD Warehouse,** where you can buy DVDs and VCDs as well as CDs, is in the Gateway, and nearby is a great supermarket and deli, City Super, next to which is a good bookstore. On the third floor of the Ocean Terminal are many shops selling Asian crafts, carpets, home furnishings, and electronics, including a branch of **Fortress.** One of the great things about shopping in Harbour City is that there is nearly everything under one roof and you need not get hot and bothered in summer months.

— Tracey Furniss

who want a respite from the sometimes scorching hot weather. ✉ *80 Tat Chee Ave., Kowloon Tong* Ⓜ *Kowloon Tong.*

★ **Harbour City.** The largest shopping complex in Hong Kong is also one of the largest in the world; if you can't find it here, it probably doesn't exist. Harbour City, which is next to the Star Ferry Terminal, houses **Ocean Centre,** Ocean Galleries, **Ocean Terminal,** the **Gateway,** and the Marco Polo group of hotels (the Hongkong, Gateway, and Prince hotels). At last count there were some 50 restaurants and 600 shops, including 36 shoe stores and 31 jewelry and watch stores. The complex contains a vast Toys "R" Us and a large branch of Marks & Spencer. A giant observation wheel, like the London Eye, is scheduled to open by 2006. ✉ *Canton Rd., Tsim Sha Tsui* Ⓜ *Tsim Sha Tsui.*

New World Shopping Centre. This harbor-front shopping center (next to the New World Hotel) has four floors of fashion and leather boutiques, jewelry stores, restaurants, optical shops, tailors, stereo stores, arts and crafts shops, as well as the Japanese Tokyu department store. ✉ *18 Salisbury Rd., Tsim Sha Tsui* Ⓜ *Tsim Sha Tsui.*

Olympian City 2. One of Hong Kong's newest shopping malls is above Olympic Station. There's a great food court on the ground floor, and most restaurants have alfresco dining, which is a rarity in Hong Kong.

Shops—a selection of the usual suspects—surround a three-story atrium. A multiplex cinema shows Chinese and Western films. ✉ *Olympian City, Tai Kok Tsui* Ⓜ *Olympic Station.*

The Peninsula Hong Kong Shopping Arcade. In the landmark hotel, this shopping arcade is chockablock with upscale designer boutiques—including branches of Shanghai Tang, Prada, Christian Dior, Versace, and the men's tailor Gieves & Hawkes of London's Savile Row. All shops are on the mezzanine, ground floor, and basement. ✉ *Salisbury Rd., Tsim Sha Tsui* Ⓜ *Tsim Sha Tsui.*

Tsim Sha Tsui Centre. This is one of many shopping malls in the Tsim Sha Tsui East area selling mostly local fashions in local sizes. You'll find branches of U2 and Giordano, both of which have shops all over Hong Kong. There are also several shops selling jewelry and watches, furniture and bedding, DVDs and VCDs, and books. It is worth a browse around if you are in the area along with the adjoining Empire Centre, but otherwise it's not worth a special trip since none of the stores stands out. ✉ *66 Mody Rd., Tsim Sha Tsui East* Ⓜ *Hung Hom KCR or Tsim Sha Tsui MTR.*

The Waterfront. Built above the Kowloon Station on the Airport Express MTR line, this small mall is worth a visit since it specializes in designer fashions and accessories that are at off-season and/or warehouse prices. You'll usually find that most everything is 80% or more off regular retail prices. The good news is, you can also find Western sizes (above U.S. size 10 for women), which are otherwise hard to find in Hong Kong. Other products sold here include shoes, handbags, children's clothes and accessories, luggage, sporting goods, watches, and some electrical goods. You'll also find a food gallery and free Internet-browsing terminals. The best time to shop is during the week as weekends get very busy. ✉ *1 Austin Rd. W, Tsim Sha Tsui* Ⓜ *Kowloon Station.*

New Territories

Maritime Square. Maritime Square is the largest shopping mall on newly developed Tsing Yi Island, with 200 shops, restaurants, and a multiplex cinema. In keeping with its name, the interior is decorated with a maritime theme, and there is a good view of the Tsing Ma Bridge. The Old Market inside the mall sells souvenirs and trinkets of old China, and there is an old-style Chinese teahouse nearby. It is above the Tsing Yi MTR and makes it a good place to shop for airport transit passengers as it is only 12 minutes away from Chek Lap Kok on the Airport Express. ✉ *33 Tsing King Rd., Tsing Yi* Ⓜ *Tsing Yi.*

★ **New Town Plaza.** One of Hong Kong's largest malls, the New Town Plaza has more than 350 shops and restaurants anchored by the Japanese department store Seibu. A huge multiplex cinema draws crowds on weekends. Kids may be interested in Snoopy World, which is on the outside podium area next to the Town Hall; it is a small park area with a Snoopy theme. The mall is connected to several other smaller malls and a hotel via a series of walkways and is adjacent to the Sha Tin KCR station. ✉ *18 Sha Tin Centre St., Sha Tin* ☎ *2699–5992* Ⓜ *Sha Tin KCR.*

DEPARTMENT STORES

Chinese

Hong Kong's many Chinese-product stores offer some of the most unusual and spectacular buys in the territory—sometimes at better prices than in the rest of China. Whether you're looking for pearls, gold, jade, silk jackets, fur hats, Chinese stationery, or just a pair of chopsticks, you can't go wrong with these stores. Most are open seven days a week but are crowded on sale days and at lunchtime on weekdays. The shopkeepers are expert at packing, shipping, and mailing goods abroad, if not so well schooled in the finer art of pleasant service.

★ **Chinese Arts & Crafts.** This is a particularly good bet for well-priced fabrics, white porcelain, silk-embroidered clothing, jewelry, and carpets. A specialty item here is the large globe with lapis oceans and landmasses inlaid with semiprecious stones, all for a mere HK$70,000. ⊠ Shop 230, Pacific Place, Admiralty ☎ 2827–6667 for information ⊠ China Resources Bldg., 26 Harbour Rd., Wanchai ⊠ Star House, 3 Salisbury Rd., Tsim Sha Tsui ⊠ Nathan Hotel, 378 Nathan Rd., Tsim Sha Tsui.

Chinese Resources Center (CRC). You'll find a vast selection of goods made in China here, including casual clothing, fancy traditional garb, furniture, teapots, and household appliances ranging from rice cookers to televisions. ⊠ 488 Hennessy Rd., Causeway Bay ☎ 2577–0222 ⊠ G/F, 92 Queen's Rd., Central ⊠ Argyle Centre, 65 Argyle St., Mong Kok.

Chung Kiu Chinese Products Emporium. Specializing in arts and crafts, this store also has a good selection of traditional Chinese clothing and fine silk lingerie. ⊠ 528–532 Nathan Rd., Yau Ma Tei ☎ 2782–1131.

Fodor'sChoice ★ **Shanghai Tang Department Store.** In addition to the brilliantly hued—and expensive—displays of silk and cashmere clothing, you'll find custommade suits starting at around HK$5,000, including fabric from a large selection of Chinese silks. You can also have a *cheongsam* (a sexy slit-skirt silk dress with a Mandarin collar) made for HK$2,500–HK$3,500, including fabric. Ready-to-wear Mandarin suits and unisex kimonos are all in the HK$1,500–HK$2,000 range. Among the Chinese souvenirs are novelty watches with mah-jongg tiles or dim sum instead of numbers. There's a second location inside The Peninsula Hong Kong. ⊠ 12 Pedder St., Central ☎ 2525–7333 ⊠ Shop ML1-3, The Peninsula Hong Kong, Salisbury Rd., Tsim Sha Tsui ☎ 2537–2888.

★ **Yue Hwa Chinese Products Emporium.** This store carries a broad selection of Chinese goods such as traditional clothing, statues, tea sets, and embroidered materials. There's also a popular medicine counter. ⊠143–161 Nathan Rd., Tsim Sha Tsui ☎ 2739–3888 ⊠ 54–64 Nathan Rd., Tsim Sha Tsui ☎ 2368–9165 ⊠ 301–309 Nathan Rd., Yau Ma Tei ☎ 2384–0084 ⊠ 1 Kowloon Park Dr., Tsim Sha Tsui ☎ 2317 5333.

Other Department Stores

Joyce Boutique. This local retailer has a concept approach—the hushed interior and beautifully displayed upscale merchandise are meant to reflect the tastes of the owner, local businesswoman and socialite Joyce Ma. In addition to the latest in Western designer fashions for women and men, Joyce sells unique household items. ✉ *New World Tower, 16 Queen's Rd., Central* ☎ *2810–1120* ✉ *Pacific Place, 88 Queensway, Admiralty* ☎ *2523–5944* ✉ *Shops G106 & G205, Harbour City, Tsim Sha Tsui.*

★ **Lane Crawford.** The most prestigious Western-style department store in Hong Kong has prices to match. The Central branch is the largest. Special sales here can be exhausting because everyone pushes and shoves to find bargains. There are also branches in Pacific Place, Harbour City, and Times Square. ✉ *70 Queen's Rd., Central* ☎ *2118–3388* ✉ *3 Canton Rd., Tsim Sha Tsui* ☎ *2118–3428.*

Marks & Spencer. The famed British retailer has good-quality clothing in Western (i.e., large) sizes as well as a British specialty food market. Many of the large malls have a branch of this popular store. ✉ *28 Queen's Rd., Central* ☎ *2921–8321.*

Seibu. The most upscale of the Japanese department stores in Hong Kong has several branches. In addition to Japanese products, the stores carry Western brands such as Clarks sandals, Timberlands boots, and Clinique cosmetics. ✉ *Pacific Place, 88 Queen's Way, Admiralty* ☎ *2971–3333* ✉ *G/F, Windsor House, 311 Gloucester Rd., Causeway Bay* ☎ *2890–0333.*

Sincere. This store sells clothing and household goods made in China as well as imported items ranging from frying pans to jelly beans. You'll also find the full range of makeup counters you'd find in any U.S. department store. Prices tend to be very reasonable. The Sincere Company, which is more than 100 years old, is run by the third generation of the Ma family, grandchildren of the founder Ma Ying-piu. Sincere was the first store in Hong Kong to give paid days off to employees, the first to showcase newly arrived imported merchandise in store windows, the first to hire women in sales positions—beginning with the founder's wife and sister-in-law—and the first to establish a fixed-price policy backed up by the regionally novel idea of issuing receipts. ✉ *173 Des Voeux Rd., Central* ☎ *2544–2688* ✉ *73 Argyle St., Mong Kok* ☎ *2394–8233.*

MARKETS & BAZAARS

Each Hong Kong district has an Urban Council–run market selling fresh fruit, vegetables, meat, seafood, and live chickens (chickens are slaughtered out in the open here). Surrounding the markets are small stores selling every imaginable kitchen and bathroom appliance, as well as clothes and even electronics.

Around heavy pedestrian areas you'll find illegal hawkers with a wide variety of cheap goods, but beware—constantly on the lookout for the police, vendors may literally run off with their goods. If so, get out of their way! In summer they often materialize in Tsim Sha Tsui in front of the Hyatt, around Granville and Mody roads, and at the Star Ferry Terminal.

Street bazaars and markets embody some of the best things about Hong Kong shopping—bargains, local color, and an almost audible buzz of excitement. Famous Cat Street—the curio haunt in Upper Lascar Row, running behind Central and Western—is now full of small, high-quality Chinese antiques shops, but in the street outside you'll still see plenty of hawkers selling inexpensive jewelry, opium pipes, Mao buttons, and assorted paraphernalia.

Kowloon has the Ladies Market, outside the Mong Kok MTR station, with outdoor stalls full of women's clothes. If you rummage around long enough, you might find a designer item at a rock-bottom price.

The famous Hong Kong Night Market in Sheung Wan made a comeback in 2003 after a decade-long absence, and it is in the same place, next to the Hong Kong–Macau Ferry Terminal. For those who remember the original market, it was a must-visit spot to pick up souvenirs, toys, and cheap novelties. It was also where you could try sugarcane drinks and eat at authentic outdoor *dai pai dongs* (which are somewhere between sidewalk café and wheeled food cart) with the locals.

On Sunday at the Cultural Centre Piazza, by the harbor front in Tsim Sha Tsui, and also at Hong Kong Park, Kowloon Park, Lai Chi Kok Park, and Victoria Park, there are arts and crafts fairs with stalls selling handmade products with a local flair. You'll find artwork, jewelry, clothing, and other knickknacks, not to mention the instant portrait artists. Each stall holder is chosen by a panel of judges who look to enhance Hong Kong artists and small businesses.

Arts & Crafts Fair. Small stalls from local cottage industries sell handicrafts, and portrait artists are at hand to capture your likeness each Sunday and on public holidays from 2 PM to 7 PM. ⊠ *Hong Kong Cultural Centre Piazza, Salisbury Rd., Tsim Sha Tsui.*

Flower Market. This open-air market in Mong Kok is a collection of street stalls selling cut flowers and potted plants, with a few outlets specializing in plastic plants and silk flowers. The area takes on an excited hum in the week leading up to the Chinese new year. ⊠ *Flower St. near Prince Edward MTR station, Mong Kok.*

Goldfish Market. Goldfish are considered auspicious in Hong Kong, and aquariums have to be positioned in the right place in the house in order to bring good luck to the family. They are commonplace in Hong Kong households, and this market is a favorite local source. You can see a large variety of goldfish and aquarium supplies here. The market is open between 10 and 6 daily. ⊠ *Tung Choi St., Mong Kok.*

Jardine's Bazaar and Jardine's Crescent. These markets are on two small streets parallel to each other facing the Causeway Bay MTR (Exit F). Open between noon and 10 PM, they offer bargains on the usual clothes, children's clothing, and bags. The surrounding local boutiques are also worth a look for local and Japanese fashions, though the sizes are small. ⊠ *Jardine's Bazaar, Causeway Bay.*

Kansu Street Jade Market. Jade in every form, color, shape, and size is for sale here, as well as jewelry and trinkets made from other kinds of minerals and semiprecious gems, including pearls. The market is full of traders conducting intriguing deals and keen-witted sellers trying to lure tourists. Some items are reasonably priced, but unless you know a lot about jade, don't be tempted to buy something pricey. Some of the so-called "jade" sold here is actually aventurine, bowenite, soapstone, serpentine, and Australian jade—all inferior to the real thing. The market is open daily from 10 to 4. ⊠ *Kansu St. off Nathan Rd., Yau Ma Tei.*

Ladies' Market. The same clothing you find in the Temple Street Night Market is on sale here, except that it's also open during the day, from noon to 11 PM daily. Despite the name, there is a fairly large selection of men's and children's as well. To reach the market, take the Nelson Street exit from the Mong Kok MTR station, and walk two blocks east to Tung Choi Street. ⊠ *Tung Choi St., Mong Kok.*

Sheung Wan Gala Point Market. This busy night market has opened at the same site as the original Hong Kong night market, which closed in the early 1990s. It is all back with some extras, such as live entertainment—including some traditional Chinese dramas—on weekends and a game zone for children. There are more than 250 stalls and 30 outside eateries. The bright lights will guide you in the right direction. Notice the lights on the fence surrounding the market; they depict a well-known Chinese fable and are changed every few months. The nearest MTR is Sheung Wan; once you exit, head toward the Hong Kong–Macau Ferry Terminal. The market is open weekdays from 6 PM to 2 AM, on weekends and public holidays from 11 AM to 2 AM, but the best time to visit is between Tuesday and Sunday after 7 PM. Although the market is open Monday, a lot of stall holders take that night off, so you may be disappointed. The overhead walkway along the harbor front between the Star Ferry and the Hong Kong–Macau Ferry Terminal is the best way to get there. ⊠ *Gala Point, Sheung Wan.*

★ **Stanley Village Market.** The Stanley Village Market is not quite the bargain trove it used to be, but you can still find some good buys in sportswear and casual clothing if you comb through the stalls. Stanley Village Market is also a good place to buy linens. Dozens and dozens of shops line a main street so narrow that awnings from each side meet in the middle. Stores open early, around 10 AM but close between 5 and 6. The market is most enjoyable on weekdays, when it's less crowded. To get to Stanley, take Bus 6, 6A, or 260 from the Central Bus Terminus on Hong Kong Island, or Bus 260 from the Star Ferry; in Kowloon, take Bus 973 from Tsim Sha Tsui. **Allan Janny Ltd.** (⊠ 17 Stanley New St.) has antique furniture and porcelain. **China Town** (⊠ 39 Stanley Main St.) has well-priced cashmere sweaters, but remember you get what you pay for as far as quality is concerned. **Sun & Moon Fashion Shop** (⊠ 18A–B Stanley Main St.) sells casual wear, with bargains on such familiar names as L. L. Bean, Yves St. Laurent, and Talbots (keep in mind that some of these are factory seconds). **Tong's Sheets & Linen Co.** (⊠ 55–57 Stanley St.) has sheets, tablecloths, and brocade pillow covers, as well as silk kimonos and pajamas. ⊠ *Stanley.*

Temple Street Night Market. This market is filled with a colorful collection of clothes, handbags, electrical goods, gadgets, and all sorts of household items. By the light of lamps strung up between stalls, hawkers try to catch the eyes of shoppers by flinging clothes up from their stalls.

Cantonese opera competes with pop music, and a constant chatter of vendors' cries and shoppers' haggling fills the air. Adding to the color here are the fortune-tellers, opera singers, and, occasionally, the odd magician or acrobatic performer who has set up shop in the street. The market stretches for almost a mile and is one of Hong Kong's liveliest nighttime shopping experiences. You can go as early as 5 PM and leave by 10 PM; the best time to come is about 8 PM. You can hire a local guide to take you; ask at your concierge desk about tours. Some of the surrounding neighborhoods may be unsafe at night. ⊠ *Mong Kok* Ⓜ *Jordan.*

SPECIALTY SHOPPING

Antiques

China has laws against taking items more than 120 years old out of the country, but Hong Kong's antiques dealers can, at least officially, sell whatever they want to. So ancient porcelain, textiles, and specialty furniture are still available. Everyday furniture and pottery are not considered national treasures and are not affected by the export laws.

Auction Houses

Hong Kong auctions are interesting even if you don't go in with a particular goal. Watch for auction announcements in the classified section of the *South China Morning Post*.

Christie's. The prestigious international house carries very fine and expensive pieces. ⊠ *16–20 Chater Rd., Central* ☎ *2521–5396.*

Lammert Brothers. This house caters to locals and usually offers up less expensive goods. ⊠ *Union Commercial Bldg., 12–16 Lyndhurst Terr., mezzanine, Central* ☎ *2545–9859.*

Sotheby's. The well-respected international house caters to a clientele for whom money is no object. ⊠ *4–4A Des Voeux Rd., Central* ☎ *2822–8100.*

Victoria Auctioneers. This Hong Kong house carries both reasonably priced and high-end art and furniture. ⊠ *16/F, Century Sq., 1–13 D'Aguilar St., Central* ☎ *2524–7611.*

Shops

HOLLYWOOD & WYNDHAM Hollywood Road and Wyndham Street, which are actually one long lane running from Central to Western, are undeniably the best places for poking about in shops and stalls selling antiques from many Asian countries. Treasures are hidden away among a jumble of old family curio shops, sidewalk junk stalls, slick new display windows, and dilapidated warehouses. You will also find great furniture here.

C. L. Ma Antiques. You'll find Ming Dynasty–style reproductions, especially large carved chests and tables made of unlacquered wood. ⊠ *43–55 Wyndham St., Central* ☎ *2525–6665.*

Dynasty Furniture Co. The specialty here is *netsukes* (small statues) skillfully carved out of tagua, a rain-forest nut that looks a lot like ivory. ⊠ *68A Hollywood Rd., Central* ☎ *2369–6940.*

CloseUp

A SHOPPER'S PARADISE

NO MATTER WHY YOU COME to Hong Kong, and whether or not you're a shopper by nature, it's highly unlikely that you'll leave here without having bought something. Hong Kong does a roaring trade in bargain-priced luggage simply because so many travelers run out of space in their suitcases.

There are good reasons for this: Hong Kong's status as a free port, where everything other than alcohol, tobacco, perfumes, cosmetics, cars, and some petroleum products comes in without import duty; access to a skilled and still relatively inexpensive labor force just across the border in China; and the highly competitive retail business, the result of a local free-trade policy that encourages shopkeepers to try to undercut one another.

What else makes Hong Kong special? Because it's small and heavily populated, Hong Kong has had to grow upward and downward rather than outward. There are shops and small businesses in all sorts of unexpected places—a boutique might be up a back staircase of a scruffy building in the alleyway, in the basement of a lighting shop, or on the 13th floor of an office building. Space is limited and precious in Hong Kong, so don't confine yourself to the main roads if you're really bargain-hunting. This is the land of free trade; shopping around is a prerequisite to any successful purchase.

The pressure from salespeople can be exasperating. If you're just browsing, make this very clear; don't be pushed into a purchase. While you're looking around, note ballpark prices and descriptions on the shop's business card. Always ask for discounts—you might get deeper ones for multiple purchases. Expect 10% to 50% off; you'll likely get larger discounts in the outdoor markets. Everywhere, except in Japanese department stores and some of the larger boutiques, discounts abound.

Don't be shy. Bargain. This is the accepted and expected way of conducting business all over Asia. Don't take the salesman's word for it when he assures that his price is the "very best": shop around. Once you have a good idea how much you should pay, go back to the shop of choice first thing the next morning. Remind the salesperson that you are the first customer; it's a superstition that works in your favor. Local shopkeepers believe if they sell to the first customer who walks into their store, they will have a good business day.

If you plan to shop in the outdoor stalls and alleys, don't dress up; being well dressed will not help your bargaining position. Inspect the goods you buy very carefully; many are seconds. When you buy clothing, inspect the actual item handed to you; if you've chosen it based on a hanging sample, you might end up taking home a different, seriously flawed item. Having made your selection and struck the right price for it, you're ready for the exchange of money. Although credit cards and traveler's checks are widely accepted, surcharges are common, so you may get a better price if you pay cash. Make sure you get the worldwide guarantee that carries the name or logo of the relevant sole agent in Hong Kong, and, for electronics, make sure there's a service center in your home country. Also, make a point of checking the item that you're paying for to make sure that it's the same item that you've seen displayed for purchase. Lastly, get a fully itemized receipt for any major purchase.

Whether you're drifting about in the comfort of an air-conditioned shopping mall, exploring the factory outlets of Hung Hom, or poking through alleys and backstreets, you're getting a look at the life and guts of Hong Kong. It's as much a cultural experience as a shopping expedition, and that's the best bargain of all.

Eastern Dreams. This store sells antique and reproduction furniture, screens, and curios. It's open by appointment only. ⊠ *47A Hollywood Rd., Central* ☎ *2544–2804* ✉ *4 Shelley St., Central* ☎ *2524–4787*.

Honeychurch Antiques. Honeychurch is known especially for antique silver jewelry from Southeast Asia, China, and England. ⊠ *29 Hollywood Rd., Central* ☎ *2543–2433*.

Schoeni Art Gallery. Japanese, Chinese, and Thai antiques are sold here, including Chinese silverware, such as opium boxes, and rare Chinese pottery. There's another branch on Old Bailey Street. ⊠ *27 Hollywood Rd., Central* ☎ *2542–3143*.

Teresa Coleman. This store carries antique embroidered pieces, including magnificent must-see kimonos. ⊠ *79 Wyndham St., Central* ☎ *2526–2450*.

Tibetan Gallery. Here you'll find antique *thangkas* (meditation paintings), incense holders, and prayer rugs, all from Tibet. ⊠ *55 Wyndham St., Central* ☎ *2530–4863*.

True Arts & Curios. This cluttered shop has good buys in embroidered items (including tiny slippers meant for bound feet), silver, porcelain, and snuff bottles. ⊠ *89 Hollywood Rd., Central* ☎ *2559–1485*.

Wing Tei. The especially helpful owner, Peter Lee, who speaks very good English, sells wonderful porcelain plates as well as curios, furniture, and wood carvings. ⊠ *190-F Hollywood Rd., Central* ☎ *2547–4755*.

Yue Po Chai Antique Co. One of Hollywood Road's oldest shops has a vast and varied stock. ⊠ *G/F, 132–136 Hollywood Rd., next to Man Mo Temple, Central* ☎ *2540–4374*.

Zitan Oriental Antiques. This shop sells antique furnishings only from mainland China. Look for traditional wood wedding beds or intricately carved armoires. ⊠ *G/F, 43–55 Wyndham St., Central* ☎ *2523–7584*.

CAT STREET Cat Street (or Upper Lascar Row), once famous for its thieves' market of secondhand stolen goods, now has almost as many small antiques shops as Hollywood Road itself. They're lined up behind the outdoor stalls selling old—or at least old-looking—jewelry, curios, and assorted bits of junk.

Cat Street Galleries. The ground-floor cluster of shops sells porcelain and furniture. ⊠ *38 Lok Ku Rd., Sheung Wan* ☎ *2541–8908*.

China Art. You'll find fine furnishings here, mostly from the Suzhou area of China. The store owner leads tours roughly once a month to its warehouse in southern China. ⊠ *15 Upper Lascar Row, Sheung Wan* ☎ *2542–0982*.

OTHER AREAS **Altfield Gallery.** This store carries furniture, fabrics, and collectibles from all over Asia. ⊠ *248–249 Prince's Bldg., 10 Chater Rd., Central* ☎ *2537–6370*.

Charlotte Horstmann and Gerald Godfrey. This is a good source for wood carvings, bronze ware, and furniture. ⊠ *Ocean Terminal, Tsim Sha Tsui* ☎ *2735–7167*.

Art

Like other major cosmopolitan cities around the world where the monied class is looking for aesthetic investment, Hong Kong has a lively contemporary gallery scene, much of it concentrating on the best work coming out of China and Southeast Asia.

Galleries

Asian Art News, a bimonthly magazine, sold at bigger newsstands for HK$50, is a good guide to what's happening in galleries around the region. If you want a firsthand look at the latest trends in Asian art, plan to spend a day gallery-hopping in Central and in Lan Kwai Fong.

Alisan Fine Arts Ltd. This was one of the first galleries in Hong Kong to promote Chinese artists living abroad. It shows contemporary art with an East-meets-West flavor. ⊠ *Prince's Bldg., Central* ☎ *2526–1091.*

Fringe Gallery. Part of the Fringe Club, this is a showcase for young, not-yet-famous Hong Kong artists, both Chinese and expat. ⊠ *2 Lower Albert Rd., Central* ☎ *2521–7251.*

Galerie La Vong. The works of today's leading Vietnamese artists, many of whose creations reveal an intriguing combination of French impressionist and traditional Chinese influences, are the focus here. ⊠ *13/F, 1 Lan Kwai Fong, Central* ☎ *2869–6863.*

Galeriasia. The gallery promotes artists from Asia, with exhibits from Burmese and Vietnamese artists. ⊠ *6/F, 1 Lan Kwai Fong, Lan Kwai Fong* ☎ *2529–2598.*

Hanart TZ Gallery. This gallery shows contemporary Chinese artists from the mainland, Taiwan, Hong Kong, and abroad. ⊠ *Room 202, 2/F, Henley Bldg., 5 Queen's Rd., Central* ☎ *2526–9019.*

Plum Blossoms Gallery. Chinese and Western art, along with antique textiles and Tibetan carpets, are on display and for sale here. ⊠ *1 Hollywood Rd., Central* ☎ *2521–2189.*

Sandra Walters. The public showroom displays late-19th-century to contemporary Western and Chinese art, but you need to call for an appointment. ⊠ *501 Hoseinee House, 69 Wyndham St., Central* ☎ *2522–1137.*

Schoeni Art Gallery. You'll find a dramatic mix of abstract, realist, and political paintings by contemporary mainland-Chinese artists here. Once a year Schoeni mounts a show of European masters. There's another branch on Hollywood Road. ⊠ *Upper G/F, 21–31 Old Bailey St., Central* ☎ *2525–5225.*

Wattis Fine Art. Wattis specializes in 18th- to 20th-century European paintings and the work of contemporary artists living in Hong Kong, both Chinese and expat. ⊠ *2/F, 20 Hollywood Rd., Central* ☎ *2524–5302.*

Zee Stone Gallery. The gallery displays a combination of contemporary Chinese paintings and antique Tibetan silver and carpets. It sells Chinese furniture as well. ⊠ *Yu Yuet Bldg., 43–55 Wyndham St., Central* ☎ *2810–5895.*

Framers

It may be worth having your artwork framed in Hong Kong, as prices are much lower than in Europe and the United States, but be sure to consider the cost of shipping if the framed art is too big to carry onto a plane. The following framers are reputable and centrally located:

Arts + Frame. You'll find European-style frames for pictures and mirrors that can be customized to suit your tastes. ⊠ *G/F, 56 Lyndhurst Terr., Central* ☎ *3104–1139*.

Wing Ching Frame Maker. Choose frames for your photos from a wide selection of styles and colors at sensible prices. ⊠ *G/F, 22 Lyndhurst Terr., Central* ☎ *2815–8301*.

Beauty & Cosmetics

Aveda Environmental Lifestyle Store. Aveda sells animal- and environment-friendly makeup and bath and beauty products. ⊠ *Shop 003, Ocean Centre, Harbour City, Tsim Sha Tsui* ☎ *2110–0881*.

Clarins. This spa is the place to go when you're ready for a little relaxation. The amazing staff here excels in facials, massages, and other body treatments. All of the gentle Clarins products are available for sale, too. ⊠ *7/F, The Peninsula Hong Kong, Salisbury Rd., Tsim Sha Tsui* ☎ *2315–3271*.

Mannings. You'll find this chain of drug and beauty stores throughout the city. It sells everything from shampoo and lotions to emery boards and cough medicine. ⊠ *Entertainment Bldg., 30 Queen's Rd., Central* ☎ *2868–4388* ⊠ *Haiphong Mansion, 101 Nathan Rd., Tsim Sha Tsui* ☎ *2369–2011*.

Sa-Sa Cosmetics. These stores can be found throughout town. They sell discounted cosmetics, from cheap glittery styles to designer lines. You can find some great perfume sales on the likes of Calvin Klein One or Ralph Lauren perfume; the prices are nearly always lower than those offered at international airport duty-free shops. ⊠ *G/F, 14 Kai Chiu Rd., Causeway Bay* ☎ *2895–3302* ⊠ *200 Nathan Rd., Jordan* ☎ *2317–1820*.

Cameras, Lenses & Binoculars

Many of Hong Kong's thousands of camera shops are clustered in the Lock Road–lower Nathan Road area of Tsim Sha Tsui, in the backstreets of Central, and on Hennessy Road in Causeway Bay. If in doubt about where to shop for such items, stick to HKTB-noted shops. (Pick up the HKTB shopping guide at any of the board's visitor centers.) All reputable dealers should give you a one-year worldwide guarantee. If you want to buy a number of different items in one camera shop (most also stock binoculars, calculators, radios, and other electronic gadgets), you should be able to bargain for a good discount. You may find good bargains at unauthorized (but legal) dealers, but these shops will most likely not provide a guarantee.

Always be on the lookout for con jobs, as tourists are frequent targets. Quite often merchandise is physically switched so that you select one type of camera only to discover back in your hotel room that you've been given another. Another ploy is to lure you in with word of a great deal, tell you that particular model is out of stock, and begin an aggressive campaign to sell you a more expensive model. **Don't be rushed; compare prices in several shops.** If a shop will not give you a written quote, you don't want to do business with them. Be advised that paying by credit card may increase the final bill by 3% to 5%, even though most card companies prohibit the practice.

Photo Scientific Appliances. This shop is where local photographers come for their equipment. Expect good prices on both new and used cameras, lenses, video cameras, and accessories. ⊠ *6 Stanley St., Central* ☎ *2522–1903.*

Williams Photo Supply. This reliable dealer stocks a range of products for your photography needs. ⊠ *341 Prince's Bldg., 10 Chater Rd., Central* ☎ *2522–8437.*

Carpets & Rugs

Regular imports from elsewhere in China and from Iran, India, Pakistan, Afghanistan, and Kashmir make carpets and rugs a reasonable buy in Hong Kong. Plenty of carpets are also made locally. Though prices have increased since the late 1990s, carpets are still cheaper in Hong Kong than in Europe and the United States. Yue Hwa China Products Company and Chinese Arts & Crafts provide some of the best selections and price ranges.

Chinese Carpets

★ **Tai Ping Carpets Ltd.** Ta Ping is highly regarded for locally made carpets, especially custom-made rugs and wall-to-wall carpets. The store takes 2½ to 3 months to make specially ordered carpets; you can specify color, thickness, and even the direction of the weave. Tai Ping's occasional sales are well worth attending; check the classified section of the *South China Morning Post* for dates. Opening times are Monday to Saturday 10 to 6:30, and Sunday noon to 5:30. ⊠ *Shop 213-218, Prince's Bldg, 10 Chater Rd., Central* ☎ *2522–7138.*

Other Asian Carpets

On Upper Wyndham Street, in Central, several shops sell Central Asian, Persian (Iranian), Turkish, Indian, Pakistani, Tibetan, and Afghan rugs—just don't expect miraculously low prices. Note: American citizens *are* allowed to import Persian rugs into the United States.

Chine Gallery. The specialty here is Mongolian rugs and carpets. ⊠ *42A Hollywood Rd., Central* ☎ *2543–0023.*

Mir Oriental Carpets. One of the most appealing of the Wyndham shops, it has great service and a large stock. New selections arrive frequently. ⊠ *52 Wyndham St., Central* ☎ *2521–5641.*

Oriental Carpet. The store has a large stock of carpets from Iran, Pakistan, Afghanistan, and China (Persian designs only). The staff is extremely helpful and friendly. ⊠ *41 Wyndham St., Central* ☎ *2523–9502.*

Oriental Carpets Gallery. You'll find a large selection of hand-knotted carpets and rugs from Iran, Afghanistan, Pakistan, and Russia here. ⊠ *G/ F, 44 Wyndham St., Central* ☎ *2521–6677.*

CDs, DVDs & VCDs

There are plenty of small stores throughout Hong Kong that sell CDs, DVDs, and VCDs; however, you have to be careful you are buying authentic versions and not pirated copies, which are usually of poor quality. And if you think the prices are too good to be true, they usually are. Some good deals can be had when buying CDs, which are often cheaper by about HK$20 than those in the major chains as they are locally distributed. The smaller shops usually sell only local DVDs for Region 3 (the United States and Canada are in Region 1, the United Kingdom is in Region 2). Therefore, it is recommended that you go to one of the many major chains, such as HMV, Hong Kong Records, or CD Warehouse, where an international selection of movies and music are on offer and staff speak good English and can help you buy the right format for your country. However, prices are usually more expensive than those in the countries of origin, which are often the United States or the United Kingdom. You may want to buy some good Kung Fu movies or other Hong Kong action movies, which are usually subtitled, but be sure to ask the staff about the format of the DVD. VCDs, popular in Asia and significantly cheaper than DVDs, do not have the picture quality of DVDs—on screen they appear more of the quality of a VHS tape—but they are usually region-free, meaning they can be played in your computer or DVD player no matter where you live, and Chinese-language films are usually subtitled in English. Prices of VCDs can be as little as the equivalent of US$2 but go up to US$8 for popular new releases.

CD Warehouse. This major store has a good selection of CDs, DVDs, and VCDs, both from China and from abroad. ⊠ *Shop 322, Harbour City, Tsim Sha Tsui* ☎ *2175–0866.*

HMV. This U.K.-based chain has a wide selection of local and international music covering everything from rap to classical and Cantopop to Japanese music. A huge selection of DVDs and VCDs are here as well, ranging from U.S. and U.K. movies and television shows to local movies. VCDs are a lot cheaper than DVDs; however, the format is not popular in the United States or United Kingdom. International magazines are sold here at the best prices in town, but they still cost a lot more than in their countries of origin. ⊠ *57 Peking Rd., Tsim Sha Tsui* ☎ *2302–0122* ⊠ *1/F, Central Bldg., 1–3 Pedder St., Central* ☎ *2739–0268.*

Hong Kong Records. You'll find a good selection of local CDs and DVDs along with some international selections. ⊠ *Shop 252, Pacific Place, 88 Queensway, Admiralty* ☎ *2845–7088* ⊠ *Shop L102, Festival Walk, Kowloon Tong* ☎ *2265–8328.*

Ceramics

For a full selection of ceramic Chinese tableware, visit the various Chinese department stores, which also have fantastic bargains on attractively designed vases, bowls, and table lamps. Inexpensive buys can also be had in the streets of Tsim Sha Tsui, the shopping centers of Tsim Sha Tsui East and Harbour City, the Kowloon City Market, and the shops along Queen's Road East in Wanchai.

Antiques & Reproductions

Sheung Yu Ceramic Arts. This shop carries good reproductions. ⊠ *Vita Tower, 29 Wong Chuk Hang Rd., Aberdeen* ☎ *2845–2598.*

Yue Po Chai Antique Co. Yue Po Chai is the best place for antique ceramic items. ⊠ *G/F, 132–136 Hollywood Rd., next to Man Mo Temple, Central* ☎ *2540–4374.*

Factory Outlets

Ah Chow Factory. You can score real deals at this popular factory outlet. Take the MTR to the Laichikok station and follow exit signs to Leighton Textile Building/Tung Chau West. ⊠ *Block B, 7/F, Hong Kong Industrial Centre, 489–491 Castle Peak Rd., Laichikok* ☎ *2745–1511.*
Overjoy Porcelain. This store has good bargains. Take the MTR to the Kwai Hing station, then grab a taxi. ⊠ *1/F, 10–18 Chun Pin St., Kwai Chung, New Territories* ☎ *2487–0615.*

Clothing

Children's

Plenty of stores in Hong Kong sell Western-style ready-to-wear children's clothing. Ocean Terminal has a large new area on the ground floor dedicated to children's wear and accessories. You can also shop for adorable traditional Chinese-style clothing for tots in two clothing alleys in Central—Li Yuen Street East and West.

Crocodile Garments Ltd. With locations all over town, Crocodile sells Western-style children's clothes. ⊠ *Ocean Terminal, Tsim Sha Tsui* ☎ *2735–5136.*
Marleen Molenaar Sleepwear. After many years in the fashion industry, Marleen Molenaar has her own label selling high-quality children's pajamas and sleepwear. Her showroom is open mornings only from 8 to noon. ⊠ *10/F, Winner Bldg., 27–39 D'Aguilar St., Central* ☎ *9162–0350.*
Mothercare. This British store carries both baby clothing and maternity wear. ⊠ *Windsor House, 311 Gloucester Rd., Causeway Bay* ☎ *2882–3468* ⊠ *Prince's Bldg., Central* ☎ *2523–5704* ⊠ *Ocean Terminal, Tsim Sha Tsui* ☎ *2735–5738.*

European Designer Boutiques

Even when the Hong Kong economy is on a downturn and consumer spending is low, the designer stores still flourish. Nearly every name is here, from Armani to Versace, and designer stores are in every major shopping mall in town. Luxury goods in Hong Kong cost up to 20% less than those in the States and Canada, and the prices are possibly the best outside Europe. Tourists and big spenders from surrounding Asian countries, including China and Japan, flock here to buy these designer goods since Hong Kong prices are easily the best in Asia—even outside of sale times. You may also want to check out the boutiques of some local high-end designers, who are making an impact in the region.

Anne Klein. Clothes, shoes, and bags in the designer's sophisticated but simple, elegant style are on sale here. ⊠ *Shop 271–2 Harbour City, Canton Rd., Tsim Sha Tsui* ☎ *2730–8020.*
Burberry. The company sells its distinctive plaid design on everything from trench coats to miniskirts. ⊠ *The Landmark, Pedder St. and Des Voeux Rd., Central* ☎ *2868–3511* ⊠ *Sheraton Hong Kong Hotel & Towers, 20 Nathan Rd., Tsim Sha Tsui* ☎ *2368–6303.*

Chanel. Originally known for classic coutures like the "little black dress" and women's tailored suits and hats, the company has revived in recent years under the design leadership of Karl Lagerfeld by tapping into a younger market. The Chanel brand also appears on watches and jewelry. You'll find the signature break-the-bank pieces that some women can't live without at these boutiques. ⊠ *Prince's Bldg., 10 Chater Rd., Central* ☎ *2810–0978* ⊠ *The Peninsula Hong Kong, Salisbury Rd., Tsim Sha Tsui* ☎ *2368–6879.*

Christian Dior. Dior offers high-end fashion for design-conscious shoppers. ⊠ *The Landmark, Pedder St. and Des Voeux Rd., Central* ☎ *2869–8333.*

Dolce & Gabbana. You usually have to be ultraslim to wear D&G clothing, which is cutting-edge and sexy. This store sells the fashions plus shoes and accessories for both men and women. ⊠ *Shop 233, The Landmark, Pedder St. and Des Voeux Rd., Central* ☎ *2845–4636.*

Escada. This pricey store is the perfect place to find elegant but versatile day-to-evening wear, sports and casual wear, and accessories for women. ⊠ *Pacific Place, 88 Queen's Way, Admiralty* ☎ *2845–4321.*

Fendi. The chic handbag purveyor also carries shoes, furs, and other accessories for men and women. ⊠ *The Landmark, Pedder St. and Des Voeux Rd., Central* ☎ *2524–5668* ⊠ *Pacific Place, 88 Queensway, Admiralty* ☎ *2918–0771* ⊠ *Sheraton Hong Kong Hotel & Towers, 20 Nathan Rd., Tsim Sha Tsui* ☎ *2367–0781.*

Gieves & Hawkes. The famous London Savile Row men's store has tailored suits and casuals, which are classics. ⊠ *Shop 2, St. Georges Bldg., 2 Ice House St., Central* ☎ *2526–1020.*

Giorgio Armani. The Italian designer's named boutiques carry glamorous evening wear along with casual wear for men and women. ⊠ *Shop 07–12 Times Square, Russell St., Causeway Bay* ☎ *2506–2018.*

Gucci. This world-renowned Italian company sells couture fashions as well as ready-to-wear clothing, watches, classic bags, and shoes which are a must-buy for the fashion-conscious. ⊠ *Shop 2, GW2, The Peninsula Hong Kong, Salisbury Rd., Tsim Sha Tsui* ☎ *2368–7300.*

Hermès. The company's chic, classic silk and leather accessories and bags are available here. ⊠ *The Galleria, 9 Queen's Rd., Central* ☎ *2525–5900* ⊠ *The Peninsula Hong Kong, Salisbury Rd., Tsim Sha Tsui* ☎ *2368–6739.*

Louis Vuitton. Everyone still lines up for the handbags and leather accessories, but increasingly people also come here for contemporary clothing in modern fabrics. ⊠ *The Landmark, Pedder St. and Des Voeux Rd., Central* ☎ *2366–3731* ⊠ *The Peninsula Hong Kong, Salisbury Rd., Tsim Sha Tsui* ☎ *2366–3731.*

Prada. The designer's slimmed-down, trendy Italian clothes, shoes, and bags are local favorites with men and women. The somewhat less pricey line Miu Miu caters to a younger market. ⊠ *Shops 111 and 210, Lee Gardens, 33-37 Hysan Ave., Causeway Bay* ☎ *2907–3525.*

Versace Collections. The local stores sell the entire line of sexy and colorful, high-end Italian designs, which range from formal evening wear to casual. ⊠ *Pacific Place, 88 Queen's Way, Admiralty* ☎ *2522–8329* ⊠ *Shop 106–113 Times Square, Russell St., Causeway Bay* ☎ *2506–2281.*

Hong Kong Designers

Some popular, high-end local designers are making a regional, if not global, impact on the fashion world. The main flagship stores cater to the high-end market, but some secondary labels are aimed at a younger, more casual crowd. Sizes are mostly small but some suits and jackets can be up to a women's size 14.

★ **Lu Lu Cheung.** Renowned for her elegant, feminine, and exquisite workmanship, Lu Lu Cheung designs casual wear, suits, and evening wear, targeting 20- to 35-year olds. Her secondary line is called 21Lu. ⊠ *G309, Zone A, Harbour City, Canton Rd., Tsim Sha Tsui* ☎ *2117–0682.*

★ **Moiselle.** Moiselle has won awards from the Hong Kong Fashion industry for creativity and best use of materials. These trendy and sophisticated pieces are must-buys for the fashion-conscious elite in Hong Kong. The secondary label, iMaroon, is priced a bit more down to earth. ⊠ *Shop 5-6, G/F, Central Bldg, Pedder St., Central* ☎ *2810–9811* ⊠ *Shop 323–325, Times Square, 1 Matheson St., Causeway Bay* ☎ *2265–8282.*

Vivienne Tam. Outside of Hong Kong, Tam is one of the best-known Hong Kong designers, renowned for her East-meets-West elegant designs. More recently, her Red Dragon line has begun to reach out to a less wealthy set. ⊠ *Shop 209, Pacific Place, 88 Queensway, Admiralty* ☎ *2918–0238.*

Tailor-Made Clothing

Along with Hong Kong's multitude of ready-to-wear-clothing stores, you can still find Chinese tailors to make suits, dresses, and evening gowns. However, for even less-expensive options, consider a trip to Shenzhen in south China for tailor-made clothing. All tailors keep records of clients' measurements so that satisfied customers can make repeat orders by mail or telephone. Keep a copy of the original measurements in case you need to change them.

For a suit, overcoat, or jacket, give the tailor plenty of time—at least three to five days—and allow for a minimum of two proper fittings plus a final one for finishing touches. Shirts can be made in a day, but you'll get better quality if you allow more time.

Tailors in hotels or other major shopping centers may be more expensive, but they are convenient, dependable, and more accustomed to Western styles and fittings.

Have a good idea of what you want before you go to the tailor. Often the best plan is to take a suit you want copied. Go through the details carefully, and make sure they're listed on the order form, together with a swatch of the material ordered (the swatch is essential).

When you pay a deposit (which should not be more than 50% of the final cost), make sure the receipt includes all relevant details: the date of delivery, the description of the material, and any special requirements.

FOR MEN **A-Man Hing Cheong Co., Ltd.** This tailor is known for European-cut suits and custom shirts and has a list of distinguished clients. ⊠ *Mandarin Oriental Hotel, 5 Connaught Rd., Central* ☎ *2522–3336.*

Ascot Chang Co. Ltd. The specialty here since 1949 has been custom-made shirts for men. ⊠ *Shop 130, Prince's Bldg., 10 Chater Rd., Central*

☎ 2523–3663 ✉ *The Peninsula Hong Kong, Salisbury Rd., Tsim Sha Tsui* ☎ 2366–2398 ✉ *Hotel Inter-Continental Hong Kong hotel arcade, 18 Salisbury Rd., Tsim Sha Tsui* ☎ 2367–8319.

David's. David's is an excellent shirtmaker. ✉ *Mandarin Oriental Hotel, 5 Connaught Rd., Central* ☎ 2524–2979 ✉ *Wing Lee Bldg., 33 Kimberley Rd., Tsim Sha Tsui* ☎ 2367–9556.

Jimmy Chen Co. Ltd. Come here for suits, shirts, and whatever else you need. ✉ *The Peninsula Hong Kong, Salisbury Rd., Tsim Sha Tsui* ☎ 2722–1888.

★ **Sam's Tailor.** Sam's is one of the most famous of all Hong Kong's custom tailors, having outfitted everyone from European royal families to American and British politicians and, of course, your average tourist looking for a bargain. It serves women as impeccably as it serves men. ✉ *Shop K, Burlington Arcade, 94 Nathan Rd., Tsim Sha Tsui* ☎ 2721–8375.

W. W. Chan & Sons. Chan is known for top-quality classic cuts and has bolts and bolts of fine European fabrics. They will also make alterations for the lifetime of the suit, which should be about 20 years. Tailors also travel to the United States several times a year to fill orders for their customers; if you have a suit made here and leave your address, they'll let you know when they plan to be visiting. ✉ *Burlington House, 92–94 Nathan Rd., Tsim Sha Tsui* ☎ 2366–9738.

FOR WOMEN Hong Kong tailors do their best work on tailored suits, coats, and dresses, performing less well with more fluid styles or knit fabrics. Tailors are the place to order a traditional Chinese cheongsam. As for patterns, you can bring in an item to be copied or choose a style from one of the tailor's catalogs; you can also bring in a photo from a magazine or, if you're skilled with pencil and paper and sure of what you want, bring in a sketch.

A good tailor has a wide selection of fabrics, but you can also bring in your own. Visit Chinese Arts & Crafts for beautiful Chinese brocades. The Western Market has fabrics on the second floor, but the quality is not the best in the world. In fact, many people bring material to Hong Kong for the express purpose of the highest quality custom tailoring. If you don't want to lug material to Hong Kong, the best place to buy the finest silks is at Shanghai Tang; just be prepared for the expensive prices. One detail often overlooked by the customer is buttons; your tailor will probably provide buttons made of the suit fabric at no extra charge.

Bobby's Fashions. This women's tailor is a favorite of local expats. ✉ *Mirador Mansion, 3A Carnarvon Rd., Tsim Sha Tsui* ☎ 2724–2615.

Irene Fashions. Irene is the women's division of W. W. Chan, the noted men's tailor. ✉ *Burlington House, 92–94 Nathan Rd., Tsim Sha Tsui* ☎ 2367–5588.

Jimmy Chen Co. Ltd. This company makes suits, dresses, evening dress, outerwear, you name it. ✉ *The Peninsula Hong Kong, Salisbury Rd., Tsim Sha Tsui* ☎ 2722–1888.

Linva Tailors. Linva is one of the best of the old-fashioned cheongsam tailors. Prices begin at around HK$2,200 (including fabric and labor) and go up, up, and up if you want special brocades or beautifully embroidered fabrics. ⊠ *38 Cochrane St., Central* ☎ *2544–2456*.

Mode Elegante. This company is known for its high-fashion suits for the executive woman. ⊠ *The Peninsula Hong Kong, Salisbury Rd., Tsim Sha Tsui* ☎ *2366–8153*.

Shanghai Tang. Shanghai Tang can make conservative or contemporary versions of the cheongsam. Men can also have a Chinese *tang* suit made to order. Here, you will also find perhaps the finest silks in all of Hong Kong. ⊠ *12 Pedder St., Central* ☎ *2525–7333*.

Clothing Factory Outlets

Hong Kong used to be the factory-outlet center of the world, the place where European and American labels were manufactured and the overruns sold at near-wholesale prices. Those days are long gone, but because many garments manufactured elsewhere in China and in other developing countries still come through Hong Kong's duty-free port, you can find samples and overruns in the territory's many outlets. Calvin Klein, Donna Karan, Gap, and the Limited lines are easiest to find. Discounts generally run a mere 20% to 30% off retail, but if you comb through everything, more often than not you'll bag at least one fabulous bargain. A word of caution, however: check garments carefully for damage, poor stitching, mis-sizing and fading. Outlets do not accept returns.

Pedder Building

The **Pedder Building** (⊠ 12 Pedder St., Central), just a few feet from a Central MTR exit, contains five floors of small shops. The number of shops offering discounts of around 30% off retail—and sometimes more—seems now to be growing, after a few years of an upscale trend. **Blanc de Chine** (☎ 2524–7875) has beautiful Chinese clothes, in styles similar to those at the more famous Shanghai Tang but in subtler colors, plus reproductions of antique snuffboxes as well as silver mirrors and picture frames. **Labels Plus** (☎ 2521–8811) has some men's fashions as well as women's daytime separates. **La Place** (☎ 2868–3163) has youthful fashions, Prada bags, and a large selection of Chanel jackets at about 20% off retail. **Shopper's World–Safari** (☎ 2523–1950) has more variety than most outlets and a small upstairs department with men's fashions.

Lan Kwai Fong Area

The small area of Central called Lan Kwai Fong is a good place to outlet-shop. Ask passersby for directions if you have trouble finding this neighborhood; its three streets—including the one called Lan Kwai Fong—are tucked away, but locals know its nightlife well. Amid the outlet shops, which are by and large on upper floors of the office buildings in this neighborhood, you will also find first-floor boutique shops that sell the latest trends. Each shop will have the same style, in a cookie-cutter slave-to-fashion monotony, but the advantage is you can get good buys if you like the look. You simply have to say to the shop owners, "But it's cheaper next door!" and they will haggle a reasonable price with you.

Anna's Collection. Anna's sells casual clothing, swimwear (up to size 16), and Italian shoes for women that fit American sizes 7 to 11. The outside entrance to this building is under the huge neon Carlsberg sign. ☒ *3/F, Grand Progress Bldg., 15–16 Lan Kwai Fong, Lan Kwai Fong* ☏ *2501–4955.*

Evelyn B Fashion. Next door to and co-owned by the owner of Anna's Collection, this shop sells business wear, cocktail dresses, and full gowns. ☒ *3/F, 7/F, and 8/F, Grand Progress Bldg., 58–62 D'Aguilar St., Lan Kwai Fong* ☏ *2523–9506.*

IN Fashion. You'll find career wear and casual clothes by Ann Taylor, Laura Ashley, Next, Talbots, and an occasional item designed for Nordstrom, as well as designer ball gowns. ☒ *9A Grand Progress Bldg., 15–16 Lan Kwai Fong, Lan Kwai Fong* ☏ *2877–9590.*

Ricky's. From time to time, you can find Emanuel Ungaro, Episode, Donna Karan, Tahari, Jaeger, Ellen Tracy, and Just Cotton here. ☒ *1/F, Lyndhurst Tower, Lyndhurst Rd., Central* ☏ *2869–4348.*

Zeno Fashions. This store stocks mostly career wear, from labels such as Ellen Tracy, Emmanuel Ungaro, Krizia, and Banana Republic. ☒ *Block B, Man Cheung Bldg., 15–17 Wyndham St., Central* ☏ *2868–4850.*

Other Outlets

★ **Diane Freis Factory Outlet.** This outlet offers discounts of around 30% on Hong Kong–based designer Diane Freis's day-wear concoctions and elaborate cocktail dresses. Ask your concierge about transportation; it's usually easier to take a taxi to Kwun Tong, but you can take the MTR to Kwun Tong Station and walk. The store is open weekdays from 9:30 to 5:30, Saturday from 9:30 to 12:30. ☒ *3/F, World Interest Bldg., 8 Tsun Yip La., Kwun Tong* ☏ *2362–1760.*

★ **Dickson Warehouse.** This building has two floors of outlet stores selling household, audiovisual, luggage, shoes, bags, children's clothing, and men and women's smart and casual clothing from labels such as Timberland, DKNY, Ellen Tracy, Disney, and Polo Ralph Lauren. Discounts are usually 70% to 90% off retail prices. Open hours are weekdays from 11 to 8, weekends and public holidays from 11 to 9. ☒ *1 Austin Rd. W, in the Kowloon MTR station, Tsim Sha Tsui* ☏ *2626–0298.*

Fair Factor. You'll find plenty of uninteresting items here, but you may be rewarded with some real finds—such as items by Gap, Adrienne Vittadini, Villager, and Victoria's Secret for a mere HK$50 to HK$100. ☒ *44 Granville Rd., Tsim Sha Tsui* ☏ *No phone.*

★ **The Joyce Warehouse.** This place has taken local shopaholics by storm: it's an outlet for women's and men's fashions from the ritzy Joyce Boutiques in Central, Pacific Place, and Tsim Sha Tsui, with labels by such major designers as Jil Sander and Giorgio Armani. Prices for each garment are reduced by about 10% each month, so the longer the piece stays on the rack the less it costs. The outlet is open Tuesday through Saturday from 10 to 6 and Sunday from noon to 6. Take Bus 90 from Exchange Square and get off at Ap Lei Chau; the trip takes about 25 minutes, with buses running every 23 minutes; once there, it's easiest to get a taxi to Horizon Plaza, about a 4-minute ride. ☒ *21/F, Horizon Plaza, 2 Lee Wing St., Ap Lei Chau* ☏ *2814–8313.*

Pot Pourri/Nova Palm. This outlet has Talbots, Emanuel Ungaro, and Fenn Wright & Manson. ⊠ *10B Long To Bldg., 654 Castle Peak Rd., Tsuen Wan* ☎ *2525–1111.*

TSL Jewelry Showroom. This place has fairly good prices on diamonds and other precious stones in unique settings, and there's an on-site workshop where you can see the jewelry being made. ⊠ *Wah Ming Bldg., 34 Wong Chuk Hang Rd., Aberdeen* ☎ *2873–2618.*

Computers & Computer Games

All the big names in computer technology are available in Hong Kong; whether you need to buy the latest in hardware or software or accessories, you will find it here. There are many computer centers around Hong Kong, but make sure you buy from a recommended dealer; look for the quality sign of the Hong Kong Tourist Board in the shop window—it guarantees quality service with product warranties and no shady dealings or parallel imports, which are so common in Hong Kong.

Prices of computer products are slightly less than in the United States or Canada, and computer games average US$25 to US$30. The variety of video games is wider due to the selection of Sony Playstation and Dreamcast imports from Japan, which are popular here. The real computer bargains are the locally assembled versions of the most popular brands. Several malls specialize in computers, peripherals, and electronic equipment, each containing hundreds of shops ranging from small local enterprises to branches of the international brand names. The individual shops usually don't have retail phone numbers.

A favorite haunt for local computer buffs is the Windsor House computer mall in Causeway Bay. There are three floors of computer products with the widest selection of Mac and PC computer games, video games, laptops, desktops, and accessories. This is a reputable center with competitive prices.

Star Computer City in Tsim Sha Tsui has one whole floor dedicated to computers. The Apple Shop is here as well as the Compaq Service Center. The Software Collection has a variety of software to choose from. The selection of shops is limited here, but it is worth browsing around as sometimes bargains can be found.

Wanchai Computer Centre on Hennessy Road is a good place to buy parts for the techno-buffs who are interested in assembling their own computers—this is a popular pastime with locals. You can negotiate prices here. The average computer will cost around US$400 depending on whether you want the most up-to-date hardware and processor, and also on which additional peripherals you choose. Your computer can be put together by a computer technician in less than a day if you are in a hurry; otherwise, two days is normal.

If you plan to buy, make sure the machine will work on the voltage in your country—a PC sold in Hong Kong works on 220 volts, while the identical machine in the United States works on 110 volts. Servicing is another major concern since the homemade computers rarely have warranties.

★ **Fortress.** Fortress has good deals on printers and accessories. You won't have a wide choice of computers, but at least you will get a guarantee that enables you to bring it back if it doesn't work. ⊠ *718–720 Times Square, 1 Matheson St., Causeway Bay* ☎ *2506–0031* ⊠ *Ocean Terminal, Deck 3, Harbour City, Canton Rd., Tsim Sha Tsui* ☎ *2735–8628.*

Mongkok Computer Center. This labyrinth of small shops and narrow corridors is somewhat claustrophobic, but it has many good deals on computers and software. Ask for a warranty and check the details carefully. ⊠ *8–8A Nelson St., Mong Kok* ☎ *2781–1109.*

Star Computer City. Look here for name-brand computers and peripherals. ⊠ *2/F, Star House, Salisbury Rd., Tsim Sha Tsui* ☎ *2736–2083.*

STD (Far East) Ltd. This reputable store sells name-brand computers and software. ⊠ *1/F, 67 Bedford Rd., Tai Kok Tsui* ☎ *No phone.*

Wanchai Computer Centre. You'll find honest-to-goodness bargains here on computer goods and accessories in the labyrinth of shops. ⊠ *130 Hennessy Rd., Wanchai* ☎ *No phone.*

★ **Windsor House Computer Plaza.** There is a wide selection of name brands and also some good deals on hardware and software. ⊠ *10/F–12/F, Windsor House, 311 Gloucester Rd., Causeway Bay* ☎ *2895–6796.*

Furniture & Furnishings

Hong Kong has seen a tremendous boom in the home-decor market in the past decade, and manufacturers of furniture and home furnishings have been quick to increase production. Rosewood furniture is a very popular buy in Hong Kong, as are several other specialty woods. A number of old-style shops specialize in the rich-looking blackwood furniture that originated in southern China at the turn of the 20th century; look for chairs, chests, couches, and other pieces at the west end of Hollywood Road, near Man Mo Temple. Queen's Road East and nearby Wanchai Road are good sources for camphor-wood chests, as is Canton Road in Kowloon.

Reproductions are common, so "antique" furniture should be inspected carefully. Traits of genuinely old pieces are: a mature sheen on the wood, slight gaps at joints as a result of natural drying and shrinking of the wood, signs of former restorations, and signs of gradual wear, especially at leg bottoms. Keep in mind, too, that blackwood, rosewood, and teak must be properly dried, seasoned, and aged to prevent pieces from cracking in climates that are less humid than Hong Kong's. Even in more humid areas, the dryness of winter heating systems can be harmful.

Definitely look on Wyndham Street and Hollywood Road, but also consider window-shopping in Hong Kong but buying in Macau. Prices in Macau are often considerably cheaper for the exact same item sold in Hong Kong; most Macau stores will ship to Hong Kong for free and elsewhere for a reasonable fee.

★ **Banyan Tree.** This company has furniture and bric-a-brac, both old and new, from Europe, India, and Southeast Asia. Its warehouse outlet has some discounted items; a Chinese birdcage for example, sells here for

HK$700, while lesser-quality birdcages go for more than HK$800 at Stanley Market. You can arrange to visit Banyan Tree's warehouse by calling its office (☎ 2506–0033). You won't get a discount if you buy from the warehouse, but you will have the chance to see—and buy—pieces that have just arrived. ⊠ *Prince's Bldg., Central* ☎ *2523–5561* ⊠ *Repulse Bay Shopping Arcade, Repulse Bay* ☎ *2592–8721* ⊠ *Ocean Terminal, Harbour City, Tsim Sha Tsui* ☎ *2730–6631* ⊠ *Warehouse Outlet, 18/F, Horizon Plaza, 2 Lee Wing St., Ap Lei Chau* ☎ *2555–0540.*

Cathay Arts. Cathay is one of many rosewood-furniture dealers in the Harbour City complex at Tsim Sha Tsui. ⊠ *Ocean Centre, Tsim Sha Tsui* ☎ *2730–6193.*

Choy Lee Co. Ltd. In Wanchai's great furniture retailing and manufacturing area, Choy Lee is the most famous, selling everything from full rosewood dining sets in Ming style to furniture in French, English, and Chinese styles. Custom-made orders are accepted. ⊠ *1 Queen's Rd. E, Wanchai* ☎ *2527–3709.*

Horizon Plaza. You'll find several furniture outlets here, including Shambala, G.O.D. Warehouse, Tequila Kola, Resource Asia, E&H, Antique Express, Inside, Banyan Tree, Dynasty Antiques, and Elmwood. ⊠ *2 Lee Wing St., Ap Lei Chau.*

Tequila Kola. Tequila Kola has reproductions of antique wrought-iron beds, one-of-a-kind furniture, home accessories, and jewelry from various corners of Asia. It's like a cross between IKEA and an Asian boutique. *Main showroom* ⊠ *United Centre, Admiralty* ☎ *2520–1611.*

Gifts

If you're stuck for a gift idea, think Chinese. How about an embroidered silk kimono or a pair of finely painted black-lacquer chopsticks? Or a Chinese chop, engraved with your friend's name in Chinese? These are available throughout Hong Kong. For chop ideas, take a walk down Man Wa Lane, in Central near the Wing On department store.

For those who live in cold climates, wonderful *mien laps* (padded silk jackets) are sold in the alleys of Central or in the various shops featuring Chinese products. Another unusual item for rainy weather—or even as a decorative display—is a hand-painted Chinese umbrella, available very inexpensively at Chinese Arts & Crafts and China Products Company. Chinese tea, packed in colorful traditional tins, is sold in the teahouses in Bonham Strand and Wing Lok Street in Western. A bit more expensive, but novel ideas, are padded tea baskets with teapot and teacups, and tiered bamboo food baskets, which also make good sewing baskets.

Handicrafts & Curios

China's traditional crafts include lanterns, temple rubbings, screen paintings, paper cuttings, seal engravings, and wooden birds.

Banyan Tree. This furniture company has lots of knickknacks from all over Asia. The main store and other locations carry a pricey but attractive selection of items. ⊠ *Prince's Bldg., Central* ☎ *2523–5561.*

Kinari. This store sells crafts and antiques from all over Southeast Asia. ✉ *Anson House, 61 Wyndham St., Central* ☎ *2869–6827.*

Mountain Folkcraft. You'll find a varied collection of fascinating curios here. To reach the store from Queen's Road Central, walk up D'Aguilar Street past Wellington Street, then turn right onto Wo On Lane. ✉ *12 Wo On La., Central* ☎ *2525–3199.*

Vincent Sum Designs Ltd. The specialties here are Indonesian silver, crafts, and batiks. ✉ *15 Lyndhurst Terr., Central* ☎ *2542–2610.*

Welfare Handicrafts Shop. This store stocks a good collection of inexpensive Chinese handicrafts for both adults and children. This is also an excellent place to find interesting greeting cards. Many of the galleries have photos of their paintings made into cards that are sold here. All profits go to charity. ✉ *Shop 1, Jardine House, 1 Connaught Pl., basement, Central* ☎ *2524–3356* ✉ *Salisbury Rd., next to the YMCA, Tsim Sha Tsui* ☎ *2366–6979.*

Jewelry

Jewelry is the most popular item with foreign shoppers in Hong Kong. It is not subject to any local tax or duty, so prices are normally much lower than in most other places. Turnover is fast, competition is fierce, and the selection is fantastic.

Settings for diamonds and other gems will also cost less here than in most Western cities, but check your country's customs regulations, as some countries charge a great deal more for imported set jewelry than for unset gems. Hong Kong law requires all jewelers to indicate on every gold item displayed or proffered for sale both the number of carats and the identity of the shop or manufacturer—make sure these marks are present. Also, check current gold prices, which most stores display, against the price of the gold item you are thinking of buying. For factory outlets, see the HKTB's *Factory Outlets for Locally Made Fashion and Jewellery.* Also consider the Chinese department store Chinese Resources Center (CRC). Terrific bargains are available here, particularly on jade and pearls.

Gems

DIAMONDS **Diamond Importers Association.** As one of the world's largest diamond-trading centers, Hong Kong sells these gems at prices at least 10% lower than world market levels. When buying diamonds, remember the four "C's: color, clarity, carat (size), and cut. Shop only in reputable outlets—those recommended by someone who lives in Hong Kong or listed in the Hong Kong Tourist Board's shopping guide (available at HKTB visitor centers). Call the association for information or advice. ☎ *2523–5497.*

JADE Hong Kong's most famous stone, jade comes not only in green but in shades of purple, orange, yellow, brown, white, and violet. Although you'll see trinkets and figurines purported to be made of jade throughout Hong Kong, high-quality jade is rare and expensive. Historically, the Chinese believe that jade brings luck. Hence, it's traditionally worn as a charm around the neck, as an amulet or as a bracelet, or even as a statue to keep in your home. Translucency and evenness of color and texture determine jade's value; translucent, deep-emerald-green Emperor's jade is the most expensive. Be careful not to pay jade prices for green stones such as aventurine, bowenite, soapstone, serpentine, and Australian jade. Many of the pieces for sale at the **Kansu Street Jade Market** are made of these impostors, but the endless sea of stalls brimming with trinkets of every size, shape, and color makes a visit worthwhile. If you are wary of spending any money on Kansu Street, visit a reputable dealer.

Chow Sang Sang. Chow Sang Sang has 17 smaller branches around town in addition to this main branch, and each sells jade necklaces, bracelets, and brooches in traditional Chinese designs. ⊠ *229 Nathan Rd., Tsim Sha Tsui* ☎ *2730–3241.*

Chow Tai Fook. With 15 branches all over town, Chow Tai Fook is a good place to shop for fine jade. ⊠ *29 Queen's Rd., Central* ☎ *2523–7128.*

PEARLS Pearls, often a good buy in Hong Kong, should be checked for color against a white background. Shades include white, silvery white, light pink, darker pink, and cream. Cultured pearls usually have a perfectly round shape, semibaroque pearls have slight imperfections, and baroque pearls are distinctly misshapen. Check for luster, which synthetics never have. Freshwater pearls from China, which look like rough grains of rice, are inexpensive and look lovely in several twisted strands. Jewelry shops with a good selection of pearls include the following:

K. S. Sze & Sons. This store is known for its fair prices on pearl necklaces and other designs. ⊠ *Mandarin Oriental Hotel, 5 Connaught Rd., Central* ☎ *2524–2803.*

Po Kwong. Specializing in strung pearls from Australia and the South Seas, Po Kwong will add clasps to your specifications. ⊠ *82 Queen's Rd., Central* ☎ *2521–4686.*

Trio Pearl. Trio has beautiful one-of-a-kind designs in pearl jewelry. ⊠ *The Peninsula Hong Kong, Salisbury Rd., Tsim Sha Tsui* ☎ *2367–9171.*

Jewelers

Chan Che Kee. The specialty here is fist-size 14- to 18-carat gold Chinese zodiac animals, a unique gift. Smaller versions can be worn as charms. Other stores on Pottinger Street also carry these animals. ⊠ *18 Pottinger St., Central* ☎ *2524–1654.*

China Handicrafts & Gem House. This store specializes in loose gemstones. ⊠ *25A Mody Rd., Tsim Sha Tsui East* ☎ *2366–0973.*

Just Gold. With 14 other branches, Just Gold specializes in delicate gold jewelry, a favorite with the Hong Kong Chinese. Prices rarely go past HK$5,000. ⊠ *47 Queen's Rd., Central* ☎ *2869–0799* ⊠ *27 Nathan Rd., Tsim Sha Tsui* ☎ *2312–1120.*

Kai-Yin Lo. The fabulous modern jewelry here has a distinct Asian influence. ⊠ *Pacific Place, Admiralty.*

The Showroom. You'll find creative pieces using various gems and diamonds here. ⊠ *Room 1203, 12/F, Central Bldg., Pedder St., Central* ☎ *2525–7085.*

Leather Bags & Belts

Italian bags, belts, and briefcases are popular status symbols in Hong Kong, but you'll pay top dollar for them. Locally made leather bags are clearly of inferior quality—the leather isn't as soft, and the feel isn't nearly as luxurious as that of fine European leather. But if you're looking for bargains, check out the locally produced designer knockoffs on Li Yuen streets East and West, in Central, and in other shopping lanes. The leather-garment industry is a growing one, and although most of the production is for export, you can find some good buys in the factory outlets of Hung Hom, Kowloon. Medium-quality bags and belts from the local manufacturer Goldlion are sold at Chinese Arts & Crafts.

For top-name international products, visit department stores such as **Lane Crawford, Wing On,** and **Sincere** and the Japanese stores in Causeway Bay, Mitsukoshi, and Sogo; all carry leather by such names as Nina Ricci, Cartier, Lancel, Il Bisonte, Comtesse, Guido Borelli, Caran d'Ache, Franco Pugi, and Christian Dior. You may, however, find the prices higher than they are at home.

Linens, Silks & Embroideries

Pure silk shantung, silk and gold brocade, silk velvet, silk damask, and printed silk crepe de chine are just some of the exquisite materials available in Hong Kong at reasonable prices. China Products Company, Chinese Arts & Crafts, and Yue Hwa Chinese Products Emporium have the best selections. Ready-to-wear silk garments, from mandarin coats and cheongsams to negligees, dresses, blouses, and slacks, are good buys at Chinese Arts & Crafts.

Irish linen, Swiss cotton, Thai silk, and Indian, Malay, and Indonesian fabric are among the imported cloths available here. Vincent Sum Designs Ltd. specializes in Indonesian batik; there's also a small selection at Mountain Folkcraft. Thai silk is about the same price in Hong Kong as it is in Bangkok.

The best buys from China are hand-embroidered and -appliquéd linen and cotton. You'll find a magnificent selection of tablecloths, place mats, napkins, and handkerchiefs in the China Products Company and Chinese Arts & Crafts stores and in linen shops in Stanley Market. Try, too, the various shops on Wyndham and On Lan streets in Central. When buying hand-embroidered items, be certain the edges are properly overcast, and beware of machine-made versions being passed off as handmade.

Martial Arts Supplies

There are hundreds of martial-arts schools and supply shops in Hong Kong, especially in the areas of Mong Kok, Yau Ma Tei, and Wanchai, but they're often hidden away in backstreets and up narrow stairways.

Kung Fu Supplies Co. The most convenient place to buy your drum cymbal, leather boots, sword, whip, double dagger, studded wrist bracelet,

Bruce Lee *kempo* gloves, and other kung-fu exotica is this store. ⊠ *188 Johnston Rd., Wanchai* ☎ *2891–1912.*

Optical Goods

Hong Kong has a vast number of optical shops. Soft contact lenses, hard lenses, and eyeglass frames—in all the latest styles and of the highest quality—are sold in leading optical shops. The prices are lower than those in Europe, but not lower than chain-store prices in the United States.

Optical Shop. The many branches of this reliable optical store can be found throughout Hong Kong. Eye tests using the latest equipment are given free of charge. *Main branch* ⊠ *117 Prince's Bldg., 10 Chater Rd., Central* ☎ *2523–8385.*

Shoes

The best place to buy shoes in Hong Kong is on Wong Nai Chung Road, in Happy Valley, next to the racetrack. Here a variety of shops sell inexpensive locally made shoes; Japanese-made shoes; and copies of European designer shoes, boots, and bags. If you have small feet, these shops can offer excellent buys; if you wear a women's size 8 or larger, you'll probably have trouble finding shoes that fit well. The merchants are also particularly good at making shoes and bags, covered with silk or satin, to match an outfit. If you leave your size information, you can make future purchases through mail order. Top-name Italian and other European shoes are sold in Hong Kong's department stores and shopping centers, but prices for designer shoes will be similar to those back home—or higher.

Kow Hoo Shoe Company. This is the place to go for great cowboy boots in knee-high calfskin. ⊠ *1/F, Prince's Bldg., Central* ☎ *2523–0489.*
Luen Fat Shoe Makers. This company custom-makes shoes for both men and women and is renowned for its skill in copying specific styles at reasonable prices. ⊠ *19–21B Hankow Rd., Tsim Sha Tsui* ☎ *2376–1180.*
Mayer Shoes. Mayer has an excellent selection of styles and leathers for men and women. ⊠ *Mandarin Oriental Hotel, 5 Connaught Rd., Central* ☎ *2524–3317.*

Sporting Goods

Hong Kong is an excellent place to buy sports gear, thanks to high volume and reasonable prices.

Bunns Diving Equipment. The biggest dive shop in Hong Kong has a large selection and good prices. ⊠ *38-40 Yee Woo St., Causeway Bay* ☎ *2574–7951* ⊠ *217 Sai Yee St., Mong Kok, Kowloon* ☎ *2380–5344.*
Marathon Sports. With another dozen stores on both sides of the harbor, Marathon carries a good selection of equipment and clothing for tennis players and golfers. ⊠ *Tak Shing House, Theatre La., 20 Des Voeux Rd., Central* ☎ *2810–4521* ⊠ *Pacific Place, Admiralty* ☎ *2524–6992.*
Po Kee Fishing Tackle Company. Po Kee has everything the fisherman needs. ⊠ *6 Hillier St., Central* ☎ *2730–4562.*

World Top Sports Goods Ltd. This large Kowloon sporting goods store sells a comprehensive selection of equipment. ✉ *49 Hankow Rd., Tsim Sha Tsui* ☎ *2376–2937.*

Stereo Equipment

Hennessy Road in Causeway Bay has long been the center for stereo gear, although many small shops on Central's Queen Victoria and Stanley streets and on Tsim Sha Tsui's Nathan Road sell a similar selection of goods. Be sure to compare prices before buying, as they can vary widely. Make sure also that guarantees are applicable in your own country. It helps to know exactly what you want, since most shopkeepers don't have the space or inclination to let you test and compare sound systems. Some major manufacturers do, however, have individual showrooms where you can test equipment before buying; the shopkeeper will be able to direct you. Another tip: though most of the export gear sold in Hong Kong has fuses or dual wiring that can be used in any country, it pays to double-check.

Fortress. Part of billionaire Li Ka-shing's empire, Fortress sells electronics with warranties, a safety precaution that draws the crowds. You can spot the shops by looking for the big orange sign. ✉ *718–720 Times Square, 1 Matheson St., Causeway Bay* ☎ *2506–0031* ✉ *Ocean Terminal, Deck 3, Harbour City, Canton Rd., Tsim Sha Tsui* ☎ *2735–8628.*

Tea

Cha (Chinese tea) falls into three categories: green (unfermented), black (fermented), and oolong (semifermented). The various flavors include jasmine, chrysanthemum, rose, and narcissus. Loong Ching green tea and jasmine green tea are among the most popular, and are often sold in attractive tins that make inexpensive and unusual gifts. If you wanted to buy a large variety of tea, you could probably do so in the Western district, Hong Kong's most famous tea area. Walk down Queen's Road West and Des Voeux Road West and you'll see dozens of tea merchants and dealers. You can also buy packages or small tins of Chinese tea in Western tea shops or at various Chinese-product stores and leading supermarkets, such as Park 'n' Shop and Wellcome.

Cheng Leung Wing. This long-standing tea purveyor is in the heart of the tea district. ✉ *526 Queen's Rd. W, Sheung Wan* ☎ *No phone.*
Fook Ming Tong Tea Shop. Here is a dreamland for the sophisticated tea shopper. Other branches are at Mitsukoshi and Sogo stores in Causeway Bay, Ocean Terminal, Harbour Centre, and Tsim Sha Tsui. You can get superb teas in beautifully designed tins or invest in some antique clay tea ware. ✉ *The Landmark, Pedder St. and Des Voeux Rd., Central* ☎ *2521–0337.*
Tea Zen. This store offers a large selection of teas in a simple setting. ✉ *G/F, House for Tea Connoisseurs, 290 Queen's Rd., Sheung Wan* ☎ *2544–1375.*

TVs, DVD Players & VCRs

Color TV systems vary throughout the world, so it's important to be certain the TV set, DVD player, or videocassette recorder you find in Hong Kong has a system compatible with the one in your country. Hong Kong, Australia, Great Britain, and most European countries use the PAL system; the United States uses the NTSC system; and France and Russia use the SECAM system. Before you buy, tell the shopkeeper where you'll be using your TV, DVD player, or VCR; you'll generally be able to get the right model without a problem. Fortress is a good choice for electronics. It's possible to buy a region-free DVD player in Hong Kong that will play DVDs from anywhere in the world—including those based on the United Kingdom's PAL system—but buy from a reputable dealer and ask to make sure that your player will work once you get it home.

Watches

You'll have no trouble finding watches in Hong Kong. Street stalls, department stores, and jewelry shops overflow with every variety, style, and brand name imaginable, many with irresistible gadgets. Just remember Hong Kong's remarkable talent for imitation. A super-bargain gold "Rolex" may have hidden flaws—cheap local mechanisms, for instance, or "gold" that rusts. Stick to officially appointed dealers carrying the manufacturers' signs if you want to be sure you're getting the real thing. When buying an expensive watch, check the serial number against the manufacturer's guarantee certificate and ask the salesperson to open the case to check the movement serial number. If the watch has an expensive band, find out whether it comes from the original manufacturer or is locally made, as this will dramatically affect the price (originals are much more expensive). Always obtain a detailed receipt, the manufacturer's guarantee, and a worldwide warranty.

City Chain Co. Ltd. With locations all over Hong Kong, City Chain has a wide selection of watches for various budgets, including Swatch. ✉ *Shops 609 and 610, Times Square, 1 Matheson St., Causeway Bay* ☎ *2506–4217.*

SIDE TRIP
TO MACAU

7

GET AWAY FROM IT ALL
Westin Resort ⇨*p.213*

BEST PORTUGUESE CUISINE
A Lorcha ⇨*p.210*

BEST PLACE TO REFLECT
A-Ma Temple ⇨*p.200*

MOST PICTURESQUE SQUARE
Largo do Senado ⇨*p.192*

CHEAP & DELICIOUS ITALIAN
Pizzeria Toscana ⇨*p.210*

HAS THE MONOPOLY ON CHARM
Pousada de São Tiago ⇨*p.214*

A SLICE OF PARIS IN MACAU
Robuchon a Galera ⇨*p.209*

Updated by
Eva Chui
Loiterton

IF YOU ASK PEOPLE in Hong Kong what they think of Macau, the former Portuguese colony an hour away by jet foil, they'll probably concede that it has good food and wine, maybe a little gambling, but not much else. This obscurity is highly undeserved. To see what makes Macau special, you have to walk through the Old Town square and up a small hill to where two narrow, winding alleys called Travessa de Don Quixote and Travessa de Sancho Pança meet at a corner marked by a Buddhist temple. Such cultural juxtapositions are commonplace in Macau. At every turn in this intriguing, densely populated city of 450,000 you'll see evocative street names, baroque buildings, and sidewalk cafés that reflect long, intimate ties to Europe. The connection changed but did not break when Macau was handed to China in December 1999, ending almost 450 years of Portuguese rule.

It is the Buddhist temple, with its swaying red lanterns and faint scent of joss sticks, that reminds you that, for all the Portuguese influence here, you're in Asia, not Europe. The people, the culture, the way of life: all are predominantly Chinese—or, more accurately, a uniquely Macanese fusion of East and West. Macau's cuisine is legendary within the region, drawing on both Chinese cooking techniques and flavors from throughout Portugal's onetime globe-spanning empire. Historic architecture also exhibits mixed traditions; a pink colonial building might house a traditional Chinese herbal medicine shop.

Above all, Macau's unique culture is seen in the faces of the Macanese themselves, in particular the thousands of Eurasian families who consider themselves neither Portuguese nor Chinese but something in between. Some can trace the intermarriage of their ancestors back a century or two, and in many ways they form the bridge between Macau's two identities. Many of the mixed-blood Macanese are from old, established families, and count among their numbers Stanley Ho—Macau's biggest taipan, whose business interests include the boat that brings you here from Hong Kong, the hotel you stay in (if it's the Lisboa, Sintra, or one of a host of others), and the casino where you gamble.

And it is gambling that essentially keeps Macau afloat, providing almost half the government's tax revenues and countless jobs. The casinos rely mainly on Chinese bettors, as most Westerners find them drab compared to, say, Las Vegas. However, this situation may change, as 20 new Las Vegas–style casinos—themed gambling palaces that are notable for their glamour as well as their gambling—are planned at this writing, including the Las Vegas Sands, which opened in May 2004. Hidden below Macau's calm, communal surface are gambling's inevitable sister industries: pawn shops, cabarets, and prostitution. Fortunately, this seedy side of Macau is almost invisible unless you set out to find it.

Macau's past was very different. Settled in 1557 by the Portuguese, Macau was Europe's first colony in east Asia, and for a time its richest. For a century it thrived as the main intermediary in the trade between Asia and the rest of the world: ships filled with Chinese silk and tea, Japanese crafts, Indian spices, African ivory, Brazilian gold, and European technological inventions all sought refuge in Macau's small harbor.

7

Architecture

Architecture in Macau is not merely a matter of having a few old buildings: it represents the visual legacy of almost 450 years of European rule and cultural exchange. Wisely, Macau hasn't gone the way of Hong Kong. Vibrantly colored baroque churches sit cheek-by-jowl with Chinese merchant shops and Buddhist temples. But the government faced the classic problem of having a collection of traditional buildings too beautiful to tear down but too decrepit to use. Fortunately, it hit upon an innovative solution: build modern buildings within the walls of old ones. The results are most visible on Largo do Senado, Macau's Old Town square, where the colorful, carefully restored facades hide modern, fully functioning interiors. Not all of Macau has survived unscathed: the Outer Harbour district, near the ferry terminal (and thus your first impression on arrival), is particularly unlovely, and the Avenida da Praia Grande, once one of the most romantic seaside walks in all of Asia, now fronts two drab artificial ponds enclosed by reclaimed land.

Casinos

You can easily visit Macau and never set foot in a casino, but the city wouldn't survive without them. Sociedade de Turismo e Diversoes de Macau (STDM), the syndicate that runs the casinos, provides more than 40% of the government's total tax revenues and still makes enough to earn a hefty profit. Historically, Macau's casinos have tended to be sparsely decorated, unglamorous places, where the serious business of losing money is not disturbed by free drinks or entertainment. The Hong Kong and mainland Chinese who crowd around the tables don't seem to mind, as they're indulging a passion largely barred to them at home. The arrival of Las Vegas–style casinos—such as the Las Vegas Sands, which opened in May 2004, and the forthcoming Venetian, expected sometime in 2006—may herald a change in the gambling scene and has effectively ended Stanley Ho's four-decade monopoly franchise, so the face of gambling in Macau is looking up.

Dining

Macau makes much of its position at the crossroads of East and West, but nowhere is that more evident than in the distinctive local cuisine. After conquering Macau in the 16th century, the Portuguese imported foods from the rest of their empire, which extended from Brazil and Mozambique to Goa and Malacca. You can see the results of this exchange today in uniquely Macanese dishes such as prawns *piri-piri,* which fuses shrimp sautéed in a wok with a fiery red pepper from Mozambique; or "African chicken," baked in a sauce of tomatoes, coconut, curry, and saffron (it's more subtle than it sounds). You'll also find traditional Portuguese restaurants serving the best *caldo verde* (a filling blend of kale and potatoes) and stewed rabbit this side of Lisbon. There are even a few bakeries that make the Portuguese specialty *bolo de arroz* (a sort of rice muffin with a hint of lemon), always wrapped in its signature blue-and-white ribbon of wax paper and delicious with a morning coffee.

Wandering Having few monumental sights, Macau doesn't lend itself to heavily planned itineraries but is, instead, best seen spontaneously, by catching a glimpse down an alley and just following it. What you discover en route to your destination will probably be the most memorable—the little Mediterranean café down a blind alley, or the Chinese antique-furniture store hidden behind a street stall. The history of Macau is literally embedded in the urban landscape, and the only way to unearth it is to wander with a keen eye.

Portuguese dominance over global trade didn't last long, however. Early in the 17th century the Dutch emerged as the most powerful empire in Southeast Asia, repeatedly attacking Macau without successfully capturing it. But it was the rise in the mid-19th century of Portugal's former ally, Great Britain, that finally ended Macau's prosperous role as an entrepôt. The British victory over China in the Opium War of 1841 led to the founding of Hong Kong, which—with its deep-water port, free-trade rules, and British protection—forever changed the balance of power in the region.

Today Macau is very much the poor relation to wealthy Hong Kong, but in the last few decades it has rebuilt a position (in tandem with its neighbor, the booming Chinese Special Economic Zone of Zhuhai) as an exporter of textiles, toys, furniture, and electronics. And for all its status as a relative backwater, Macau is no stranger to Hong Kong–style property speculation and handover frenzy, a fact that will become obvious the moment you step off the ferry. The Portuguese administration launched a staggering number of public works in the period preceding the handover: an international airport, a cultural center, several massive land-reclamation projects, a modern bridge to China, the construction of two artificial lakes along the Praia Grande and a related offshore highway, numerous sculpture installations, and too many ugly office buildings to count. Whether this flurry of activity was an effort by the Portuguese to get money out of the colony before the Chinese took over (as many locals think) or part of a bold vision of Macau's future, the effect has been to give wide swaths of the city the feel of a boomtown. In an effort to boost its image, Macau is now attempting to reinvent itself as much more than a seedy gambling den, and marketing itself as a family holiday destination.

Indeed, the Portuguese departure from Macau was so sordid—scarred by rumors of widespread corruption and wasteful public spending—that most Macau residents (unlike their Hong Kong counterparts) welcomed Chinese rule, hoping it would bring with it a return to law and order. And thus far, to China's credit, it has. As a result, probably the most obvious impact of the handover has been the reduction in the size of the Portuguese expatriate community, many of whom returned home once their comfy government jobs disappeared. Some remain, of course, as do most of the mixed-blood Macanese, but since all Macau residents were given the option of taking a Portuguese (and thus, European Union) passport, they may elect to leave if the situation changes. If that happens, we may look back on Macau in the 20th century much as we now look at Córdoba or Toledo before the Christian Reconquest: an improbable convergence of peoples, languages, and cultures that will never be replicated. For now, though, there is much in Macau to persuade people to stay: despite all the soulless construction in the newer areas, the city remains, at heart, a tranquil, romantic place, with a community that reflects its special history.

EXPLORING MACAU

Almost all of the territory's residents live in peninsular Macau, but the drab yet spacious high-rise developments on Taipa Island are fast becoming popular with those used to cramped old buildings. Nearby Coloane however, has yet to lose its charm to such modernity. On today's maps, huge tracts of land (especially along the Outer Harbour and between Taipa and Coloane) are marked off with diagonal lines, indicating areas that have been reclaimed from the sea—these tend to be brutally functional and, for the traveler, largely uninteresting. Thus, the historic areas are mostly in the interior rather than on the coast, occupying the parts of peninsular Macau that have been above water for more than 20 years. Largo do Senado, the Old Town square, is still the center, and you can take interesting walks through the skein of small streets running north to the Kun Iam Temple and south to the A-Ma Temple. Because the streets are so irregular, getting lost is common (indeed, part of the pleasure), even though streets are generally well marked.

Numbers in the text correspond to numbers in the margin and on the Macau and Taipa & Coloane Islands maps.

Downtown Macau

Most visitors to Macau arrive at the ferry terminal, which offers easy access to buses and taxis (just exit the terminal and turn right) but is a 40-minute walk from the town center. Alas, the district you see first— the Outer Harbour—is one of Macau's least charming, and the only nearby sights of real interest are the Grand Prix Museum and the Wine Museum, both in the Macau Forum. You'll do better to go straight to the historic area around Avenida Almeida Ribeiro (more commonly known by its Chinese name, Sanmalo) and circle back to see the museums before you return to Hong Kong.

a good walk

Avenida Almeida Ribeiro (Sanmalo) runs from the Avenida da Praia Grande, on the eastern shore, to the Inner Harbour, on the west. Starting at the eastern end, the buildings are a mix of glass-and-marble towers and old merchants' shops, their ground floors modernized but their upper floors still intriguing. The weathered neon Coca-Cola and Fanta signs are particularly striking. The handsome gray-stone building on the right as you walk west is the **General Post Office ❶ ▶**, and the historic town square is called the **Largo do Senado ❷**. The buildings around the square have all been carefully restored and form an explosion of pastels. The most important is the Senate, **Leal Senado ❸**, on the south side; also interesting are the whitewashed House of Charity, which is called **Santa Casa da Misericordia ❹**, and the church of **São Domingos ❺**. The main tourist office is in the yellow **Ritz Building** ⑥. Continue down San-malo, past jewelers and pawn shops, and turn left on Travessa do Mas-tro to reach **Rua da Felicidade** ⑦, once a red-light district and now lovingly restored as a traditional China Coast merchants' street. You can either follow Rua da Felicidade to the end or return to Sanmalo to get to the Inner Harbour, which teems with workers unloading ships and ducking in and out of decaying warehouses.

TIMING   This walk does not cover much distance, so you could complete it in about an hour, but there's so much to discover just off the route that two or three hours is a better estimate. An exhibit in Leal Senado might distract you even further.

What to See

▶ ❶ **General Post Office.** Built in 1931, this GPO is the newest of the old build-ings on Largo do Senado, with an attractive stone facade that comple-ments its colorful neighbors. Like most historic buildings in Macau, it's been restored with an eye toward practicality and still functions as a post office and telephone center. ⊠ *Largo do Senado at Av. Almeida Ribeiro* ☎ *396–8516.*

❷ **Largo do Senado** (Senate Square). The heart of old Macau and one of the most charming squares in Asia, the Largo is surrounded by an exquisite collection of brilliantly colored colonial buildings. It's paved with black and white stone tiles arranged in a Portuguese-style wave pat-tern and furnished with benches, plants, and a fountain. Residents ap-propriated the space immediately, and it now functions as a town square should: as a communal meeting place where old women gather to gos-sip and children run free. At night the buildings are lighted by spotlights, and the square becomes even more alluring, as locals of all generations meet and socialize. ⊠ *Av. Almeida Ribeiro.*

Fodor$Choice
★

❸ **Leal Senado** (Loyal Senate). A superb example of colonial architecture, the Loyal Senate anchors the southern end of Largo do Senado. It was built in the late 18th century to house the Senate of leading citizens—which was, at the time, far more powerful than the governors, who usu-ally served their appointed time and then promptly returned to Portugal. Today the Senate has both elected and appointed members and acts as the municipal government, with its president holding the same power as a mayor. Inside the building, a beautiful stone staircase leads to wrought-iron gates that open onto a charming garden. Note the blue-and-white tile work (such tiles are called *azulejos*), a typical Portuguese craft originally perfected by the Moors of North Africa. The attractive garden in the back has cast busts of two great Portuguese men of let-ters: the 16th-century poet Luis de Camões and the 19th-century writer João de Deus. The foyer and garden are open during business hours, and there are frequent art and historical exhibitions in the foyer and gallery.

On the second floor of the Leal Senado is the **Macau Central Library**, a superb copy of the classic Portuguese library in Mafra. It holds what may be the world's best collection of books in English about China—many were inherited from the British- and American-managed Chinese Customs House. The library also has rare books from the early days of

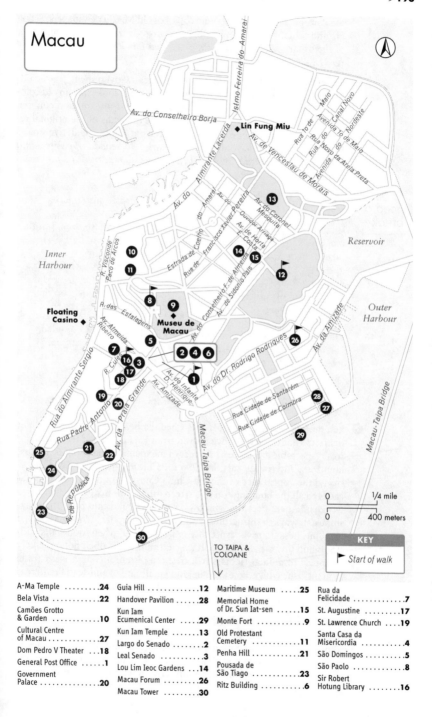

Macau

Inner Harbour

Floating Casino ◆

Av. do Conselheiro Borja

Lin Fung Miu ◆

Reservoir

Outer Harbour

Museu de Macau

TO TAIPA & COLOANE

KEY

▶ Start of walk

0 ¼ mile

0 400 meters

the Portuguese empire and bound copies of old Macau newspapers. Scholars and others are welcome to browse or study; there's also a nice view of the square. ⊠ *Largo do Senado at Rua Dr. Soares, 2/F* ☎ *558–049* 🖨 *318–756* ⊙ *Daily 2–8.*

6 **Ritz Building.** Formerly the home of the Macau Government Tourist Office, this is a grand building that from the outside looks like an old colonial three-story building. It now houses a tourist information counter. Once you step inside, you realize that only the walls of the original remain; a modern building stands within the old, squeezing in five stories where there were once only three. ⊠ *Largo do Senado opposite Santa Casa da Misericordia* ☎ *397–1120* ⊕ *www.macautourism.gov.mo* ⊙ *Daily 9–6.*

> **need a break?**
>
> For a slightly out-of-the-ordinary refreshment, step into the **Leiteria i Son milk bar** (☎ 573–638) at Largo do Senado 7—look for the small cow sign overhead. The decor is cafeteria-style spartan, but the bar whips up frothy glasses of fresh milk from its own dairy and blends them with all manner of juices: papaya, coconut, apricot . . . there's even a mysterious "steamed milk in two films" (a kind of hot custard with a milk film on top). But the highlight is the series of almost pornographic photos of cows, their udders on the verge of bursting.
>
> For a Macanese-style break, head to the delightful **O Barril 2** (⊠ 14A/B Travessa de São Domingos ☎ 370–533) on a quaint side street off the Largo do Senado (turn right at the McDonald's). The café serves, among other delights, fresh orange juice, coffee, and an assortment of yummy pastries for a few patacas, including crunchy cat's tongue biscuits (like ladyfingers but crunchier) and apricot tarts.

7 **Rua da Felicidade.** This street was once the heart of Macau's red-light district. That trade has since moved from Rua da Felicidade, leaving it to a respectable existence as a street of inexpensive guesthouses, tailors, laundries, and restaurants. In 1996 the Cultural Institute of Macau restored the appearance of the old China Coast and fitted traditional facades to all the buildings on this street—the result is stunning, with red wooden lattices over the windows, retractable red canopies, and gray-stone gateways to shrine-filled courtyards. The updated look has helped local business flourish, especially in the evening, when food stalls with stools and tiny tables emerge. It's a charming area, albeit not one likely to appeal to animal-rights advocates: the restaurants do a brisk trade in giant fish, which lie motionless in small tanks, and feathered creatures, which are cooped up in cages until mealtime. ⊠ *Off Av. Almeida Ribeiro at Travessa do Mastro.*

4 **Santa Casa da Misericordia.** Founded in 1569, Portugal's Holy House of Mercy is the oldest Christian charity on the China Coast. This handsome baroque building with a blindingly white facade houses its headquarters. Look inside if you can (it's not normally open to the public), as the interior was rebuilt in an attractive modern style that contrasts starkly with the timeless exterior. The Casa's offices administer homes for the elderly, kitchens for the poor, clinics, and a leprosarium; its president is by tradition the Senate president. A reception room on the second floor (also generally closed to the public) contains paintings of benefactress Marta Merop and Macau's first bishop, Dom Belchior, along with the latter's cross and skull. ⊠ *Largo do Senado next to the GPO.*

❺ São Domingos. Following an ambitious restoration, St. Dominick's is once again the most beautiful church in Macau. The stunning cream-and-white nave leads to a filigreed altar intricately carved in the Mannerist style. São Domingos was originally a convent founded by Spanish Dominican friars in 1587, but was rebuilt as a church in the 17th century. When convents were banned in Portugal in 1834, this church became a repository for sacred art. The works are now on display in the museum on the first to third floors, accessible via a small staircase to the right of the altar. Indeed, the church itself has had a stormy history: in 1644 a Portuguese officer was murdered at the altar by a mob during mass; in 1707 the church was besieged by the governor's troops when the Dominicans sided with the pope against the Jesuits on the question of whether ancestor worship should be permitted among Chinese Christian converts. After three days the soldiers broke down the doors and briefly imprisoned the priests. ⊠ *Rua de São Domingos at Largo do Senado.*

The Old Citadel

The most remarkable early buildings in Macau were on or around the centrally located **Monte Hill,** and those that have survived are eloquent reminders of Portugal's golden age. If you're intending to visit several of Macau's museums, a good investment is the Museum Pass—it's valid for five days and includes entry to the Museum of Macau, the Macau Museum of Art, the Lin Zexu Museum, the Maritime Museum, and the Grand Prix and Wine museums. The 25-pataca pass is available from any of the above-listed museums or from the Macau Government Tourist Office at the Macau Ferry Terminal.

a good walk

Approach the old citadel from the Largo do Senado by following the black-and-white tiles. Take Rua da São Domingos, to the right of the church, then turn left on Rua da Palha—look for the design of concentric circles in the paving. This street runs into Rua de São Paulo and leads you to the dramatic freestanding facade of **São Paulo** ❽ ☞. Go up the steps to take in the view of Macau, then descend to visit the Museum of Sacred Art, then cross the road to view the remains of the **Monte Fort** ❾, which holds the Museum of Macau. Return down the stone staircase and turn right onto Rua de São Paulo. After you pass the antiques and souvenir shops, you'll arrive at the Praça Luís Camões Park, where you can people-watch in the **Camões Grotto & Garden** ❿ and relax in the shade of giant banyan trees. Finally, go next door to visit the graves of early-American and British pioneers in China now buried in the **Old Protestant Cemetery** ⓫.

TIMING   The walk should take about two hours without allowing time for stops. Allot another hour for museum exploration.

What to See

⑩ Camões Grotto & Garden. Macau's most popular public park is frequented from dawn to dusk by tai chi enthusiasts, young lovers, students, and men huddled over Chinese chessboards with their caged songbirds nearby. The garden houses the Orient Foundation and was originally the private grounds of the Camões Museum, which later became the headquarters of the British East India Company. In 1785 it was used by French cartographer La Perouse as a small observatory aimed at China. The garden was taken over by the city in 1886 and a heroic bronze bust of Camões, Portugal's greatest poet and 16th-century Macau resident, was installed in a rocky niche. Nearby, a wall of stone slabs is inscribed with poems by various contemporary writers praising Camões and Macau. At the entrance to the grotto a bronze sculpture honors the friendship between Portugal and China. Some rooms in the Orient Foundation contain historical and art exhibits; the basement houses an art gallery. ✉ *13 Praça Luis de Camões* ☎ *554–699* ⊕ *www. macautourism.gov.mo* ✉ *Free* ☉ *Gardens, daily dawn–dusk; house, weekdays 10:30–12:30 and 3:30–5:30.*

★ ⑨ Monte Fort. On the hill overlooking St. Paul's, this renovated fort was built by the Jesuits in the early 17th century and, in 1622, became the site of Macau's most legendary battle. At the time, the Dutch, jealous of Portugal's power in Asia, were attempting to invade Macau, which was guarded by a small force of soldiers, priests, and African slaves. As the Dutch closed in on Monte Fort, a lucky cannon shot (fired by one of the priests) hit the enemy's powder supply. In the ensuing confusion the Dutch were driven back to sea. Soon after the victory, the first full-time governor of Macau evicted the Jesuits from the fort, and for the next 150 years it served as the residence and office of Macau's governors. The interior buildings were destroyed by fire in 1835, but the great walls remain, along with the cannon. The fort has since become a popular park and is a soothing place to sit, enjoy the breeze, and survey the city.

Museu de Macau (Museum of Macau). Brilliantly constructed within the base of Monte Fort, the museum is the ideal place to learn about the rich cultural layering that shaped the development of Macau. The exhibition begins with a comparison, dating back to the 16th century, of the dress, religious icons, ships, and writing instruments of Macau's two dominant civilizations: China and Portugal. This theme of exchange—rather than competition—runs through the rest of the museum, where there are displays of Chinese and Portuguese architectural facades, markets, traded goods, sacred art, and printing presses. The cumulative effect is very powerful: East and West have been meeting (and learning from each other) for far longer than many imagine. ✉ *Praceta do Museu de Macau, base of Monte Fort* ☎ *357–911* ⊕ *www.macautourism. gov.mo* ✉ *15 patacas* ☉ *Tues.–Sun. 10–6.*

⑪ Old Protestant Cemetery. Through the cream-color entrance to the right of the Camões Garden lies the tranquil resting place of more than 150 Americans and British, whose tombstones recall the triumphs and troubles of Westerners in 19th-century China. Some of the names are familiar:

Captain Henry Churchill, great-granduncle of Sir Winston; Joseph Adams, grandson of John Adams, the second U.S. president; and Robert Morrison, who translated the Bible into Chinese. It is for Morrison that the small whitewashed chapel on the grounds was named. This was the first Protestant church on Chinese soil and dates from the early 1800s (although it was rebuilt in 1922). The Chinese characters in the stained-glass window translate to: "In the beginning there was the Word." When the sun is down an electric light illuminates the window. ⊠ 22 *Praça Luis Camões* ☉ *Daily 9–6.*

▶ ❽ **São Paulo.** The church of St. Paul, which occupies an imposing site at the top of a long flight of steps, has long since been adopted as Macau's symbol, even though the only thing that remains of the once spectacular structure is its facade. Built under the direction of the Jesuits by exiled Japanese Christians and local craftsmen between 1602 and 1627, St. Paul's has always been tied to the struggle to preserve a Christian presence in Asia. The story of the church is told on its carved-stone facade and in the excavated crypt, which contains the tomb of the church's founder, Alessandro Valignano, and the bones of Japanese and Indo-Chinese martyrs. St. Paul's also served as part of the first Western-style university in Asia, attended by such scholars as Matteo Ricci and Adam Van Schall, who studied here before going to the emperor's court in Peking. The college, along with the body of the church and most of Monte Fort, was destroyed in the disastrous fire in 1835. Behind the facade, in an underground site beneath the onetime body of the church, is the **Museum of Sacred Art,** which holds statues, crucifixes, chalices, and other sacramental objects dating from the 17th through the 18th century and borrowed from local churches. The 17th-century paintings by exiled Japanese artists depict the crucified martyrs of Nagasaki and the Archangel Michael in the guise of a samurai. ⊠ *Rua de São Paulo at Largo da Companhia* ☎ *358–444* ⊕ *www.macautourism.gov.mo* ⊠ *Free* ☉ *Daily 9–6.*

Restoration Macau

One of the most endearing aspects of Macau is the fact that traditional Chinese temples and gardens—many of them restored in the last few decades—continue to flourish in the modern, European-influenced heart of the city.

a good tour

Begin with a taxi ride to **Guia Hill** ⑫ ▶ for an overview of the city, then walk around the hill to take the cable car to Avenida de Sidonio Pais—alternatively, you can reach the avenue by walking down the steps that lead through the Flora Gardens. Turn right (north) on Sidonio Pais and then left (west) to get to the **Kun Iam Temple** ⑬, on Avenida do Coronel Mesquita, where the first Sino-American treaty was signed. If you're up for the walk, continue along the avenue until you pass Mong Ha Hill and then turn right (north) on Avenida do Almirante Lacerda, which becomes Avenida de Barbosa (on your left you'll see the Canidrome, where greyhound dog races are run three or four nights a week), to find the little-visited temple Lin Fung Miu, with its statue of the opium-burning Commissioner Lin. From there, catch a taxi to the charming **Lou Lim Ieoc Garden** ⑭. Exit left from the gardens and then take your second left to find the neo-Moorish **Memorial Home of Dr. Sun Iat (Yat)-sen** ⑮, which is between Rua de Antonio Basto and Rua de Leoncio Ferreira, across from the police station. Nearby on Avenida do Conselheiro Ferreira de Almeida is the Dutch quarter with a series of restored red-and-ocher 1920s mansions now housing the government archives, the public library, and the Health Department.

TIMING This tour should take around four hours, depending on how long you linger in the gardens and temples.

What to See

▶ ⑫ **Guia Hill.** Studded with modern homes, a convent, and a hospital, Guia (Guide) Hill is topped with a fort that dates from the 1630s. It also has the oldest lighthouse on the China Coast (built in 1865) and a small white-stone chapel built in 1707. Inside the chapel are crumbling frescoes that depict an unorthodox mix of Christian angels and Chinese dragons. One of the old guardhouses is a café, and there is also a small tourist information office. From the fort you can see all of Macau, its islands, the airport, and the surrounding Chinese seascape—a much easier way to catch a glimpse of China than making the trek up to Portas do Cerco. ⊠ *Est. do Engenheiro Trigo* ☏ *569–808* ⊕ *www.macautourism.gov. mo* ☉ *Daily 9–1 and 2:15–5:30.*

⑬ **Kun Iam Temple.** This Buddhist temple dedicated to the goddess of mercy was founded in the 13th century. The present 17th-century buildings are richly filled with carvings, porcelain figurines, statues, old scrolls, antique furniture, and ritual objects—note the three exquisite statues of Buddha that grace the entry chamber. The temple is best known among Western visitors as the place where the first Sino-American treaty was signed by the viceroy of Canton and the United States envoy, Caleb Cushing, on July 3, 1844. The temple has a large number of funeral chapels, with offerings of paper cars, airplanes, luggage, and money that are burned in order to accompany the souls of the dead. ⊠ *Av. do Coronel Mesquita at Rua do Almirante Costa Cabral* ☏ *No phone* ⊕ *www.macautourism. gov.mo* ☉ *Daily dawn–dusk.*

---

off the beaten path

LIN FUNG MIU – The Temple of the Lotus, dedicated to both Buddhist and Taoist deities, was built in 1592 and used for overnight lodging by Mandarins traveling between Macau and Canton (now Guangzhou). It's best known for the facade's 19th-century clay bas-reliefs depicting mythological and historical scenes, and for an interior frieze of colorful writhing dragons. One famous visitor was Commissioner Lin Zexu, who spent some hours here soon after burning the foreign traders' opium in 1839. His statue stands in the courtyard, outside a small museum that describes his battle against the opium traders. ⊠ *Av. do Artur Tamagnini Barbosa at Est. do Arco* ☏ *No phone* ⊕ *www.macautourism.gov. mo* ☉ *Daily dawn–dusk.*

⑭ **Lou Lim Ieoc Gardens.** This classic Chinese garden, modeled on those of old Suzhou, was built in the 19th century by a wealthy Chinese merchant named Lou. With the decline of the Lou family fortunes early in the 20th century, the house was sold and turned into a school. The gardens had fallen into ruin before the city restored them in 1974. Now they're a haven of tranquillity in an increasingly hectic city. Enclosed by a wall, the gardens are a miniaturized landscape, with miniforests of bamboo and flowering bushes, a mountain of sculpted concrete, and a small lake filled with lotuses and golden carp. A traditional nine-turn bridge (to deter evil spirits, which can move only in straight lines) zigzags across the lake to a colonial-style pavilion with a wide veranda. The pavilion is used for exhibitions and concerts. ✉ *Est. de Adolfo Loureiro at Av. do Conselheiro Ferreira de Almeida* ☎ No phone ⊕ *www.macautourism.gov.mo* 💹 *1 pataca, free Fri.* ☉ *Daily dawn–dusk.*

⓯ **Memorial Home of Dr. Sun Iat-sen** (Dr. Sun Yat-sen). Father of the 1911 Chinese revolution, Sun lived in Macau from 1892 to 1894 while working as a physician. The memorial home was built in the 1930s in a strange mock-Moorish style and was occupied by some of his family members following his death. It was renovated by Sun admirers from Taiwan—hence the preponderance of Taiwanese flags hanging about. It now contains interesting photographs, books, and souvenirs of Sun and his long years of exile in different parts of the world. ✉ *1 Rua Ferreira do Amaral, between Rua de Antonio Basto and Rua de Leoncio Ferreira* ☎ *574–064* ⊕ *www.macautourism.gov.mo* 💹 *Free* ☉ *Wed.–Mon. 10–5.*

Peninsular Macau

Macau's narrow, hilly peninsula is one of the oldest districts in the city and is full of colonial churches, landmark hotels, restaurants, and shopping streets. It's bordered on the east by the Avenida da Praia Grande and the Avenida da República, both tree-shaded promenades on a bay from which land is now being reclaimed to make way for a downtown area to replace Largo do Senado with restaurants, cafés, and shops along the man-made lakes. (This was once a favorite place for residents to stroll, fish, or play chess.) On the west side, the Inner Harbour's Rua do Almirante Sergio and Rua das Lorchas still retain the bustle of an Asian port with their traditional Chinese shop houses—ground floors occupied by ships' chandlers, net makers, ironmongers, and shops selling spices and salted fish.

a good walk

Begin at the Leal Senado and take the steep Rua Dr. Soares, which climbs up to the left. Branch left on Calçada Tronco Velho and you'll arrive in the peaceful Largo do Santo Agostinho where you can visit the little-known **Sir Robert Hotung Library** ⓰ ⮞ in the former home of one of the most prominent Macanese families. On the same square are the church of **St. Augustine** ⓱ and the **Dom Pedro V Theater** ⓲. The Rampa do Teatro will lead you down to Rua Central. Continue to the right, and on the block-long Rua de São Lourenço you'll find **St. Lawrence Church** ⓳. Take the Travessa do Padre Narciso down to the Praia Grande, and the **Government Palace** ⓴ will be on your left. Go right along the waterfront—less picturesque than it once was, due to the huge land-reclamation project—and make a detour up Calçada do Bom Parto to **Penha Hill** ㉑ for some great views. On the way back to the waterfront you'll pass the **Bela Vista** ㉒, once the city's most luxurious hotel and now the home of the Portuguese consul general. Continue along Avenida da República and stop for a drink on the terrace of the **Pousada de São Tiago** ㉓, a boutique hotel built into an old fortress; just offshore is the black, monolithic *Monument of Understanding,* a massive arched sculpture rising out of the bay, celebrating Sino-Portuguese friendship. Walk around the tip of the peninsula to the **A-Ma Temple** ㉔ and finish with a visit to the unique **Maritime Museum** ㉕.

TIMING This walk should last most of the day, with a leisurely lunch at an Inner Harbour or Praia Grande restaurant, drinks at the São Tiago, and plenty of time in the museum and temple. If you're brisk, however, you can cover it in four or five hours.

What to See

★ ㉔ **A-Ma Temple.** Properly called Ma Kok Temple but known to everyone as A-Ma, this is thought to be the oldest building in Macau, dating from sometime in the Ming Dynasty (1368–1644). Its origins are obscure, but it was here when the Portuguese first landed in Macau. The rocks are inscribed with red calligraphy telling the story of A-Ma (also known as Tin Hau); a favorite goddess of fishermen, she is purported to have saved a humble junk from a storm. One of the many Chinese names for this area was A-Ma Gau (Bay of A-Ma), and the Portuguese transformed this name into Macau. The temple is the territory's most picturesque, with ornate prayer halls and pavilions among the giant boulders of the waterfront hillside. ⊠ *Largo do Pagode da Barra opposite the Maritime Museum* ☉ *Daily dawn–dusk.*

㉒ **Bela Vista.** The Bela Vista was built in the 1870s as the private home of a prosperous merchant, but became the city's grandest hotel around the turn of the 20th century. It had a brief golden age but then followed Macau's waning fortunes into a long, steady decline. In the 1990s, the building was magnificently resurrected by local architects Bruno Soares and Irene O, who transformed it into a luxurious eight-suite hotel that reclaimed its rightful place in the city's social universe. Sadly, it closed to the public after the handover to China and now serves as the official residence of the Portuguese consul general. ⊠ *8 Rua do Comendador Kou Ho Neng.*

⑱ **Dom Pedro V Theater.** The oldest Western theater on the China Coast, the Dom Pedro V was built in 1859 in the style of a European court theater. It was in regular use until World War II, and since its renovation by the Orient Foundation it now hosts concerts, plays, and recitals once again. You can sometimes look inside when performances are not scheduled, though the rather bare interior may come as a disappointment after the striking green-and-white facade. ⊠ *Largo do Santo Agostinho at Rampa do Teatro* ☎ *554–691 for Orient Foundation.*

⑳ **Government Palace.** This pink-and-white colonial building on the Avenida da Praia Grande has deep verandas and a handsome portico. For a long time it was Lisbon's seat of power in Macau, housing the offices of the governor and his cabinet, but with the departure of the Portuguese it has lost some of its symbolic importance, although it still retains its architectural grace. It is not open to the public. ⊠ *Av. da Praia Grande between Travessa do Padre Narciso and Travessa da Paiva.*

★ ❷⑤ **Maritime Museum.** Ideally placed on the waterfront **Barra Square**, this gem of a museum has been a favorite since it opened in 1987. The four-story building resembles a sailing ship and contains one of the foremost maritime museums in Asia. The adjacent dock was restored as a pier for a tug, a dragon boat, a sampan, and working replicas of a South China trading junk and a 19th-century pirate-chasing *lorcha* (a wooden sailing ship). Inside the museum is a breathtaking series of detailed models of local and foreign ships, with illustrations of how each one catches fish or captures the wind. There are also light-box charts of great voyages by Portuguese and Chinese explorers, a relief model of 17th-century Macau, the story of the A-Ma Temple in slide-show style, navigational aids such as a paraffin lamp once used in the Guia Lighthouse, and all manner of interactive touch screens and videos. The museum also operates a 30-minute pleasure junk (10 patacas extra per person) around the Inner and Outer harbors daily except Tuesday and the first Sunday of the month. ⊠ *Largo do Pagode da Barra opposite A-Ma Temple* ☎ *595–481* ⊕ *www.museumaritimo.gov.mo* ✉ *10 patacas* ☾ *Wed.–Mon. 10–5:30.*

❷① **Penha Hill.** The Beverly Hills of Macau, Penha Hill is home to the Macanese rich and wealthy. It's here you'll find **Bishop's Palace** chapel, which overlooks the entire city and islands and has some of the best views of Macau from its courtyard. Dominating the view is the ultramodern Macau Tower soaring 1,115 feet above the city and best viewed at dusk on a clear night. The chapel is dedicated to the patroness of seafarers and was originally built in 1622. The current structure (along with the adjacent palace, which is closed to the public) was completely rebuilt in 1837. ⊠ *Est. de D. João Paulino* ☾ *Daily 9–5:30.*

❷③ **Pousada de São Tiago.** There's no more tranquil place to linger over a drink than on the terrace of this Portuguese inn. Built into the ruined foundations of a 17th-century fort, the hotel has a magnificent view of the harbor and mainland China. ⊠ *Fortaleza de São Tiago da Barra, Av. da República* ☎ *378–111* ⊕ *www.saotiago.com.mo.*

①⑦ **St. Augustine.** This church dates from 1814 and feels like a real colonial outpost: grand but slightly worn, with a high wood-beam ceiling and a drafty interior. The stone altar has a recessed scene of Christ on his knees bearing the cross, with small crucifixes in silhouette on the hill behind him. The statue, called *Our Lord of Passos*, is carried through the streets on the first day of Lent. ⊠ *Largo do Santo Agostinho and Calçada do Tronco Velho.*

①⑨ **St. Lawrence Church.** What is arguably Macau's most elegant church stands in a pleasant garden, shaded by palm trees. Always a fashionable place, it looks the part with elegant wood carvings, an ornate baroque altar, and stunning crystal chandeliers. Concerts are held here during the Macau International Music Festival each October. ⊠ *Rua de São Lourenço at Travessa do Padre Narciso* ✉ *Free* ☾ *Tues.–Sun. 10–6, Mon. 1–2.*

▶ **⑯ Sir Robert Hotung Library.** In a small garden hidden behind wrought-iron gates, this was once the private home of the Hotung family. The ground floor is a functioning library, and on the second floor you'll find a traditional-style study (ask someone to open the door if it's locked) with classical Chinese furniture, scrolls, family portraits, and large cabinets filled with old texts. The smell of lacquered wood and musty books is intoxicating—so, too, is the way the light on the enclosed balcony shimmers on a sunny day. ⊠ *3 Largo do Santo Agostinho* 🔳 *Free* ☉ *Mon.–Sat. 1–7.*

New Macau

The newly developed districts along the Outer Harbour may have been built on an inhuman scale that is more functional than charming, but they also house most of the city's most important contemporary cultural institutions.

a good tour

Take a taxi to the **Macau Forum ㉖** ▶, near the base of Guia Hill, to visit the **Wine Museum,** with its focus on Portuguese regional wines, and the superb **Grand Prix Museum,** which is interesting even to those not particularly fanatical about cars. From the Forum take a taxi to the **Cultural Centre of Macau ㉗,** which often has excellent exhibitions. Next to the Centre is what remains of the **Handover Pavilion ㉘,** and from there, you can walk along the water on Avenida Dr. Sun Yat-sen to reach the **Kun Iam Ecumenical Center ㉙,** which has a lovely view out to Taipa Island. Another short taxi ride will take you to the shiny modern **Macau Tower ㉚,** which has open and indoor observation decks for panoramic views of the islands.

TIMING This tour should take about four hours, although some may want to spend that long in the Grand Prix and Wine museums alone.

What to See

㉗ Cultural Centre of Macau. This building, easily identifiable by the giant swooping curve gracing the roof, serves as an all-purpose cultural forum, hosting dance, music, theater, and films. Some shows are free but most require tickets, with opening hours depending on the event. Next door is the **Macau Museum of Art** which has eclectic art, photography, and interactive installation exhibitions and is definitely worth a visit; it's free on Sunday. ⊠ *Av. Xian Xing Hai* 🕾 *791–9814* ⊕ *www.ccm.gov.mo* 🔳 *Museum 5 patacas, free Sun.* ☉ *Museum Tues.–Sun. 10–6:30.*

㉘ Handover Pavilion. Built in haste for the 1999 handover, the pavilion—or rather what's left of it—is merely four white columns. The pavilion was slated for dismantling after the handover, but the public outcry—over its historic importance and, conversely, the epic waste of money involved—kept it open. However, soon after, the building was found to be structurally unsound and deemed unsafe for visitors. ⊠ *Av. Xian Xing Hai.*

㉙ Kun Iam Ecumenical Center. This elegant 65-foot-high bronze statue of the Buddhist goddess of mercy was designed by Portuguese architect Cristina Rocha Leiria. It rests on an artificial islet and houses an ecumenical center that aims to spread the peaceful teachings of Buddhism, Taoism, and Confucianism. It also has a small exhibition space. So far, however, it has sown mostly strife. The center was installed just before the handover amid much local grumbling about the exorbitant cost and supposed Portuguese efforts to fleece the territory before leaving town. To make matters worse, it fails to adhere to the appropriate feng shui principles, which would have the statue facing out to sea rather than toward land. ⊠ *Av. Dr. Sun Yat-sen* 🕾 *No phone* ⊕ *www.macautourism. gov.mo* ☉ *Sat.–Thurs. 10–6.*

➤ **26** **Macau Forum.** This multipurpose facility has a 4,000-seat stadium for sports events and pop concerts and a 350-seat auditorium for operas and plays. The adjoining Tourism Activities Centre—usually known by its Portuguese initials, CAT—contains the Grand Prix and Wine museums. ⊠ *Rua Luís Gonzaga Gomes.*

The **Grand Prix Museum** tells the story of the races that were first run in Macau in 1953 and today are on par with Monaco's famed race. It's a required stop for all racing fans, with an exquisite collection of winners' cars, among which pride of place is given to Eduardo de Carvalho's gorgeous Triumph TR-2 "long door," which won the first Grand Prix. In the background you hear the suitably frenzied voices of English announcers, and around you are videos, photos, and memorabilia. 🕾 *798–4126* ⊕ *www.macautourism.gov.mo* 🎫 *10 patacas* ☉ *Wed.–Sun. 10–6.*

The **Wine Museum** lovingly illustrates the history of wine making with photographs, maps, paintings, antique wine presses, Portuguese wine fraternity costumes, and 750 different Portuguese wines. The cellar's oldest bottle is an 1815 Porto Garrafeira, and because the museum had a problem with theft when it first opened, all the valuable bottles are kept in a locked chamber. Admission includes a glass of wine in the tasting area, and there is a small shop that sells a variety of wines and port. 🕾 *798–4108* ⊕ *www.macautourism.gov.mo* 🎫 *15 patacas* ☉ *Wed.–Mon. 10–6.*

🏝 **30** **Macau Tower.** The shiny cocktail stick of a building stands 1,115 feet tall—staggering for this island's standards and among the tallest structures in the world. The Observation Lounge gives you an eagle's-eye view of Macau, and the glass floor allows you to see the city beneath your feet (literally). The revolving restaurant serves buffet lunch and dinner; the sleek 180 Lounge serves high tea and is a great place for evening drinks. A J Hackett (the New Zealand company that practically gave birth to bungee-jumping) runs an Adventure Zone using the mammoth structure as its playground. Thrill seekers can climb to the top of the Tower's mast—338 feet above the observation deck. The tamer Skywalk allows you to walk outside around the main observation deck on a metal walkway with or without handrails. Ironwalk and Ironwalk X require you to climb and balance on the tower's superstructure, along bridges, steel cables, and nets. For kids there's a carousel, bungee trampoline, and large open plaza at the base of the tower. Owned by casino tycoon Stanley Ho (who else?), the tower is at the southwestern tip of the Macau peninsula, on a narrow strip of land that separates the Pearl River from the man-made Nam Van Lakes. ⊠ *Largo da Torre de Macau* ☎ *933–339, 2283–2626 Shun Tak Travel in Hong Kong, 9888–858 A J Hackett* ⊕ *www. macautower.com.mo* ✉ *Main observation deck 45 patacas, outdoor observation deck 35 patacas, both decks 70 patacas; mast climb 777 patacas–1,100 patacas, depending on the day and number of persons; Skywalk 100 patacas–120 patacas; Ironwalk 50 patacas–80 patacas; Ironwalk X 100 patacas–120 patacas* ⊘ *Weekdays 10–9, weekends 9–9.*

Taipa Island

Although the Portuguese presence on Macau peninsula dates from the mid-1500s, they did not occupy Taipa until the mid-1800s, when it was actually two separate islands. Taipa remained a military garrison and pastoral retreat—albeit one that was also home to a number of fireworks factories—until the 1970s, when it was linked to the city by a bridge. Since then it has evolved in two different directions: parts retain the quiet, charming feel of village life while others have been transformed into a local version of Hong Kong, with block after block of soulless high-rise apartment buildings. Highlights of Taipa's past are the village's narrow alleys and many restaurants and the seafront promenade of the Taipa House Museum; the newer areas have the Macau Jockey Club and the airport.

a good walk

Take a bus or taxi over one of the bridges to **Taipa Village** ㉛ ▶ and explore the narrow lanes. Then, take the main Rua Direita Carlos Eugenio to Calçada do Carma and walk up to the small square in front of the Church of Our Lady of Carmel. Continue down to the old seafront to visit the **Taipa House Museum** ㉜. To see other parts of Taipa, take a bus or taxi to the Hyatt Regency hotel and walk around the back road, Estrada de Almirante Joaquim Marques Esparteiro, to the **Pou Tai Un Temple** ㉝.

TIMING   The walk around Taipa Village and the house museum can take as little as one hour, but a visit to Taipa is incomplete without lunch at one of its many restaurants.

What to See

㉝ **Pou Tai Un Temple.** This temple is famed for its restaurant, which serves a large selection of fresh, reasonably priced vegetarian dishes. Thanks to donations from devotees, it has a series of prayer halls, including an impressive yellow-tile pavilion, and a statue of Kun Iam, the Buddhist goddess of mercy. ⊠ *Est. de Almirante Joaquim Marques Esparteiro, behind Hyatt Regency.*

㉜ **Taipa House Museum.** This area has long been one of the most charming stretches of Macau: five colonial mansions along a tree-lined cobblestone path look out over the ocean. Initially, only one of the mansions was open to the public, but following renovation work, three others are now accessible. Unfortunately, the interiors were gutted, leaving unexpectedly large exhibition spaces (showing Chinese artifacts, Portuguese folk costumes, and an illustrated history of the islands) that do little to recreate the feel of colonial domestic life. The fifth mansion has been fit-

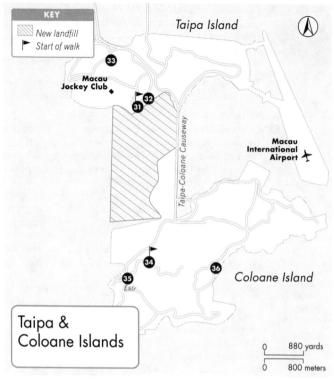

KEY

New landfill

Start of walk

Taipa Island

Macau Jockey Club

Taipa-Coloane Causeway

Macau International Airport

Coloane Island

Estr.

Taipa & Coloane Islands

| 0 | 880 yards |
| 0 | 800 meters |

ted out for a Macanese restaurant, but at this writing, the government was still looking for a restaurateur to occupy the space. Just up the hill is the small boxy Church of Our Lady of Carmel, and across a lovely pebbled courtyard is an antiquated *biblioteca* (library). ⊠ *Taipa Praia off Largo do Carmo* 🖂 *5 patacas, free Sun.* ☉ *Tues.–Sun. 10–6.*

▶ **31 Taipa Village.** Despite the addition of modern homes and conveniences such as banks, this tight maze of streets and shops retains much of the feel of an old China Coast fishing village. There are small, well-kept temples and restored colonial buildings that house the municipal council for the islands. Occasionally you can still see racks of fish lying out in the sun to dry. But the village is, today, most treasured for its numerous restaurants, which in good weather spill out of the two- and three-story shop houses and fill the quiet back alleys.

Coloane Island

The 3-km (2-mi) causeway that once separated Coloane from Taipa has been bridged by a massive land-reclamation project. But the larger, less populated island of Coloane still retains a distinctive feel, with a village that's quieter and more intimate than the comparatively bustling Taipa. Coloane is also popular for its parks, beaches, and golf club.

Take a bus or taxi to **Seac Pai Van Park** any day but Monday to see the aviary, the forest, and the natural-history museum. Continue by bus along Estrada de Seac Pai Van to Coloane Village and visit the **Chapel of St. Francis Xavier**. Continue on to **Hac Sa Beach**, a black-sand beach adjoining the marvelous bluff-side Westin Resort.

TIMING Try to spend a day on Coloane, taking it easy with the walk and stopping for a leisurely lunch. The walk alone takes about three hours.

What to See

Chapel of St. Francis Xavier. This charming little village chapel, with a blue-and-white facade and bell tower, was once the site of a Christian mission established to educate the local Chinese. It was built in 1928 to house a reliquary containing an arm bone of the eponymous saint (other body parts were kept in Goa and Rome) who died on an island south of Macau while waiting to enter China. Since then the relic has been moved, as have the bones of Japanese and Vietnamese martyrs once enshrined here. The square outside is paved with colored Portuguese tiles, landscaped with gardens, and marked by a monument commemorating the local defeat of a pirate band in 1910—Macau's last encounter with old-style buccaneers. ⊠ *Largo do Sto. Francisco Xavier, Coloane Village.*

need a break?

Lord Stow's Bakery (⊠ Coloane Village square ☎ 882–534) is an institution in Macau. Andrew Stow's famous *pasteis de nata* or Portuguese egg tarts—rich, creamy custard filling in a perfect pastry cup—are like mouthfuls of heaven. When Andrew Stow and wife Margaret separated, Margaret set up her own bakery and café in Macau. **Margaret's Café e Nata** (⊠ Gum Loi Bldg. on a side street off Av. D. João IV ☎ 710–032) has egg tarts that are just as excellent as those of her former husband.

Hac Sa Beach. This black-sand beach is the biggest and best in Macau. Despite its ocher color, created by the silt carried by the Pearl River from the delta, the water is clean and safe for swimming and water sports. It draws a crowd in summer, many of whom grill food at the barbecue pits in the nearby picnic area. Also nearby is **Fernando's,** the one Macau restaurant known to everyone in Hong Kong. ⊠ *Praia da Hac Sa, Est. de Hac Sa.*

Seac Pai Van Park. Also known as Coloane Park and located on the west coast of the island, this is one of Macau's most interesting natural preserves, though parts of it have been paved over to provide visitor facilities. Its walk-in aviary has more than 200 species of birds, including the rare Palawan peacock and the crested white pheasant. Nearby are a playground, a pond with black swans, the Balichão restaurant, a picnic area, and a nature trail around the hillside. At the end of the nature trail is an enormous **statue of A-Ma** carved out of white jade and weighing 500 tons. It's the largest white-jade statue in the world and was installed to celebrate the handover of Macau from the Portuguese to the Chinese. It faces north to protect the city. The park also has a small **Museum of Nature and Agriculture**, which contains traditional farm implements, clay statues illustrating rice cultivation, and displays of traditional herbal medicines. ✉ *Est. de Seac Pai Van* ☎ *No phone* ⊕ *www.macautourism.gov.mo* ✍ *Free* ☉ *Park, Tues.–Sun. 9–5:45; museum, Tues.–Sun. 10–4.*

WHERE TO EAT

Macau is legendary in the region for the diversity of its cuisine, which reflects the range of influences on its long history. There are a number of excellent Chinese restaurants, particularly Cantonese and Chiu Chow; but since there is no shortage of those in the neighboring countries, Macau has earned its reputation for its more distant cuisines of which Portuguese is the most common. Most restaurants serve the beloved *bacalhau* (salt cod), either baked, boiled, grilled, deep-fried with potato, or stewed with onion, garlic, and eggs. You'll also find Portuguese sardines, country soups such as *caldo verde* and *sopa alentejana,* and various rabbit dishes. Some kitchens prepare baked quail, curried crab, and the delectable Macau sole, as well as giant prawns in spicy sauce, one of Macau's special dining pleasures. There are also dishes drawn from throughout Portugal's once-mighty empire: from Brazil come *feijoadas,* stews of beans, pork, spicy sausage, and vegetables; and from Mozambique comes African chicken, baked or grilled in fiery piri-piri (a type of chili pepper).

The Macanese have their own signature cuisine that is, like the city, a blend of East and West. For years this food was difficult to find outside private homes, but a few restaurants (such as Balichão and Litoral) have filled this gap. One of the most distinctive Macanese ingredients is *balichão,* a flavorful shrimp paste for which every family traditionally had its own recipe. Another Macanese staple is *minchi,* a blend of ground pork or beef sautéed with onion, garlic, a bit of soy, and diced potatoes.

After Chinese, Portuguese, and Macanese cuisine, there are a few superb Italian and French places. Regardless of cuisine, however, almost every restaurant in Macau has at least a bottle or two of delicious Portuguese wine—usually a hearty red from the Dão region or the slightly sparkling *vinho verde*. Some Western restaurants have wine lists as long as small phone books.

Prices for both food and wine are, on the whole, very reasonable, and a drinkable Portuguese wine often costs little more than a bottle of mineral water. However, expect to pay much more for Chinese specialty dishes such as abalone, bird's nest, and shark's fin soup. Outside Chinese restaurants, the service trade is almost completely run by Filipinos, so ordering in English is rarely a problem—indeed, many Macanese have to order in English to make themselves understood. Meals are on a southern European schedule: that is, long, leisurely affairs with lunch from 1 to 3 and dinner after 8, though it's usually possible to eat earlier. Dress is casual, and most restaurants are open daily year-round with perhaps a few days off around Chinese New Year (in late January or early February). Reservations are rarely necessary except at the very finest restaurants, and even then only on weekends. The tourist-office brochure "Eating Out in Macau" has an exhaustive listing of local dining spots. Almost all restaurants will add a 10% service charge; when this happens, round up the bill and leave a bit extra. Tip about 10% in restaurants where there is not a service charge.

	WHAT IT COSTS In patacas				
	$$$$	$$$	$$	$	¢
AT DINNER	over 300	200–300	100–200	60–100	under 60

Prices are for a main course at dinner and do not include the customary 10% service charge.

Chinese

$–$$$ ✕ **Four Five Six.** Lovers of Shanghainese food flock here for the house specialties: lacquered duck, braised eel, and chicken broiled in rice wine, plus steamed crabs in winter. The atmosphere is generally cheerful, noisy, and welcoming. ⊠ *Hotel Lisboa, Lisboa Tower, Av. da Amizade, mezzanine* ☎ *388–474 or 388–407* ▭ *AE, DC, MC, V.*

$–$$$ ✕ **Portas do Sol.** Despite its Portuguese name, this is a great place for a Chinese dim sum lunch. Shanghainese pork buns, chicken feet, rice-flour rolls, dumplings with shark's fin or minced beef—just pick a few that sound good and you won't be disappointed, plus you can add more as you go along. Desserts tend to be very sweet Chinese favorites, such as sago pudding and double-boiled papaya with snow fungus, which is less interesting than you'd think. The restaurant also has a large selection of traditional Chinese delicacies, including sautéed crab with salty egg yolk and deep-fried duck fillet with minced prawn. ⊠ *Hotel Lisboa, Av. da Amizade* ☎ *377–666* ▭ *AE, MC, V.*

$–$$ ✕ **Chinese Restaurant.** A delightful open kitchen with stacks of steaming baskets greets you at this popular dim sum spot. You've never had shrimp dumplings this big before—king prawns are used—or this incredibly fresh tasting. Also good are the rice rolls, crispy roast pork, and dessert mini egg tarts. If you can't get enough at lunchtime, dim sum is also served at night, along with dishes such as sautéed scallops with XO sauce and the perennial favorite, sweet and sour pork. ⊠ *Hyatt Regency, 2 Est. de Almirante Joaquim Marques Esparteiro, Taipa Island* ☎ *831–234* ▭ *AE, DC, MC, V.*

$–$$ ✕ **Chiu Chau.** This is probably the best—and certainly the most sumptuous—restaurant in Macau serving the Chiu Chow cuisine of Chaozhou (formerly known as Swatow), in eastern Guangdong. Many Hong Kong and Thai Chinese (i.e., many of Macau's gamblers) are Chiu Chow, and they love this rich cuisine, with its thick, strong shark's fin soup, chicken in hot *chinjew* sauce (made from herbs and peppercorns), oyster omelet, and crab in chicken sauce. ⊠ *Hotel Lisboa, Av. de Lisboa* ☎ *712–549* ▭ *AE, DC, MC, V.*

$–$$ ✕ **Long Kei.** One of the oldest and most popular Cantonese restaurants in Macau, Long Kei has a huge menu. Daily specials are printed only in Chinese, so ask the waiter to translate. Like all good Chinese restaurants in this part of the world, this one is noisy and chaotic, and makes no attempt at glamour or sophistication. The focus is the food, and it rarely disappoints; be sure to sample the shrimp toast. ✉ *7B Largo do Senado* ☎ *573–970* ▭ *AE, DC, MC, V.*

¢–$$ ✕ **Lua Azul.** An upscale sophisticated alternative to standard dim sum restaurants, Lua Azul is filled with well-to-do families, young and old. Mixing traditional booths and round tables with subtle lighting and a contemporary interior, the restaurant bustles with friendly and efficient waiters. Don't miss the deep-fried shrimp balls with piping-hot soup inside. Dishes change monthly, but the staple dim sum remains. The dinner menu specializes in Huai Yang cuisine. If you plan to visit over the weekend, be sure to make a reservation. ✉ *Level 3, Largo da Torre de Macau* ☎ *988–8700* ▭ *AE, DC, MC, V.*

Continental

$–$$ ✕ **Os Gatos.** The setting is the main reason to dine here, since the restaurant is part of the Pousada de São Tiago, a traditional Portuguese inn built into a 17th-century fortress. The large outdoor terrace has huge linen umbrellas and patio furniture, while the interior has hand-carved mahogany furniture and blue-and-white wall tiles. The food, though enjoyable, is not quite the equal of the setting. The menu is heavy on Italian dishes, with others from Portugal, Provence, and Greece. Specialties include seafood paella, baked crab with saffron and sage, and chicken piri-piri. ✉ *Pousada de São Tiago, Av. da República* ☎ *968–686* ▭ *AE, DC, MC, V.*

French

$$$–$$$$ ✕ **Robuchon a Galera.** For a truly fine dining experience and a slice of
Fodor'sChoice Paris in the heart of Macau, this restaurant from French celebrity chef
★ Joël Robuchon is a must. The luscious gold-and-royal-blue interior is exquisitely detailed. Elaborate presentations are the norm; among the signature dishes are a heavenly mille-feuille of tomato and crabmeat, duck breast with turnips and foie gras, and lamb au jus served with creamy potato puree. Finish with a choice from the sophisticated cheese trolley, or dig into the warm molten chocolate cake. The wine list is as thick as an encyclopedia and is reputed to be the most extensive in Asia. ✉ *Hotel Lisboa, Lisboa Tower, Av. de Lisboa, 3/F* ☎ *377–666* ⟐ *Reservations essential* ▭ *AE, DC, MC, V.*

Italian

$$–$$$ ✕ **Mezzaluna.** Consistently good, hearty Italian fare has always drawn businessmen and government officials to this sunny restaurant. The menu changes monthly, but staples such as the wood-fired pizzas and pastas are constant. Especially good is the linguine with baby lobster in basil cream sauce that has a lovely hint of chili. The Mezzaluna Plate for two is full of yummy bites including roasted butternut squash with rosemary, Parma ham, and home-dried tomatoes. Treat yourself with a tiramisu and espresso to finish off your meal. Although the restaurant was undergoing a substantial renovation at this writing, the menu was expected to remain the same. ✉ *Mandarin Oriental, 956–1110 Av. da Amizade* ☎ *567–888* ▭ *AE, DC, MC, V.*

★ **$-$$** ✕ **Pizzeria Toscana.** Don't be put off by the "pizzeria" in the name or the strange location in the middle of a parking lot opposite the ferry terminal: this is one of the best restaurants in the city, owned by a Macanese family with roots in Pisa. Try the *bresaola involtini* (air-cured beef with shredded Parmesan) or the delicate salmon carpaccio to start; then move on to grilled king prawns in a garlic-and-tomato sauce or tortellini with porcini mushrooms. The owner is one of the biggest wine importers in the region, and the wine list is superb. There's also the quaint Toscana café (run by different management) in the heart of the old quarter Travessa de São Domingos, which serves a slightly smaller menu. ⊠ *Av. da Amizade opposite the ferry terminal* ☎ 726–637 ▤ *AE, DC, MC, V.*

Macanese-Portuguese

$-$$$ ✕ **Flamingo.** Soft lighting and slow-moving ceiling fans give a romantic ambience to this restaurant in two colonial-style rooms in the Hyatt Regency. It's also possible to dine alfresco around the large koi pond, where ducks swim freely. Ironically, braised duck with tomatoes, white wine vinegar, and thickened duck blood is a specialty here. Also good is the crab cooked either Chinese style, with ginger and spring onions, or Macanese style, preserved in a bean-curd sauce and braised with curry spices and onion. The menu changes regularly, but signature dishes remain. The service is attentive and comes with a smile. ⊠ *Hyatt Regency, 2 Est. de Almirante Joaquim Marques Esparteiro, Taipa Island* ☎ 831–234 ▤ *AE, DC, MC, V.*

$-$$$ ✕ **Military Club.** When the exclusive Military Club restored its headquarters (which date from 1870) in the late 1990s, it appeared that the beautiful dining hall might remain off-limits to the public. While the bar and tearoom are for members only, the dining hall, thankfully, has been opened to all and is well worth a visit. The languid old-world atmosphere is a rare treat, and the extensive Portuguese menu—with such specialties as partridge pie, cold stuffed crab, grilled venison, and a range of egg puddings—is excellent. ⊠ *975 Av. da Praia Grande* ☎ 714–000 ▤ *AE, MC, V.*

$-$$ ✕ **Afonso III.** After some years at the Hyatt Regency, Afonso decided to open his own place and cook the way his grandmother did. The result is this modest café in the heart of downtown, with a small cozy downstairs decorated in wood and stucco and a larger, less intimate upstairs. The food is nothing complicated—just simple hearty Portuguese dishes served up to homesick expatriates who work nearby. Most choose the daily specials, which usually include codfish, braised pork, and beef stew prepared as nowhere else in Macau. The wine list is equally unusual, and the prices are low. ⊠ *11A Rua Central* ☎ 586–272 ▤ *No credit cards* ☺ *Closed Sun.*

★ **$-$$** ✕ **A Lorcha.** Ask people in town to name their favorite Portuguese restaurant, and odds are they'll mention A Lorcha. It's not a fancy place, but they get everything just right. The menu leans towards traditional stalwarts such as *bacalhau* (salt cod), grilled seafood, or meat, but the dishes are always prepared with quality ingredients and lots of care; be sure to ask what is fresh that day. This is also a good place to try typical Macanese desserts such as cool mango pudding and *serradura* (a very sweet, rich cream and biscuit pudding). ⊠ *289 Rua do Almirante Sergio* ☎ *313–195* ⌕ *Reservations essential* 🖃 *AE, DC, MC, V* ⊘ *Closed Tues.*

¢–$$ ✕ **Fernando's.** You may have to look long and hard to find this country-style Portuguese restaurant next to Hac Sa Beach; the entrance looks like that of a typical Chinese café. Your guiding light is the fact that everyone from Hong Kong comes here, and the owner aggressively promotes the place with tourists. It has a pleasant open-air setting (covered with a roof) and serves satisfying seafood that's not altogether worthy of the hype. Fernando personally reigns over the dining room, and he is without a doubt the restaurant's greatest selling point. ⊠ *Hac Sa Beach 9, Coloane* ☎ *882–531* ⌕ *Reservations essential* 🖃 *No credit cards.*

★ ¢–$$ ✕ **Litoral.** One of the most popular local restaurants, Litoral serves Portuguese and Macanese dishes that are relatively humble but invariably delicious. Be warned that the Portuguese favor cuts of meat for which you need to acquire a taste: pig's ear and ox tripe, to name just two. From time to time the owner removes some dishes—such as the braised duck in a complex sweet-soy sauce—from the menu; it's worth asking if it's available. The braised pork with shrimp paste is a must. For dessert, try the *bebinca de leite,* a coconut-milk custard, or the traditional egg pudding, *pudim abade de priscos.* ⊠ *261 Rua do Almirante Sergio* ☎ *967–878* 🖃 *AE, MC, V.*

¢–$$ ✕ **Miramar Restaurante.** Opposite the Westin Resort on Hac Sa Beach, Miramar is a gem of a restaurant with an uninterrupted view of the sea. The no-frills spot is large and airy, and you can dine indoors, on the terrace, or in the garden. The restaurant serves generous portions of tasty Portuguese and Macanese food delivered by a friendly staff. Highlights are the local dishes, including *bacalhau* (salt cod), African chicken (served in a peppery coconut broth), and delicious honey-marinated pork spareribs. It's quite difficult to find this restaurant, but the quiet location makes it worth a special trip. ⊠ *Zona Norte da Praia de Hac Sa, Coloane* ☎ *882–623* 🖃 *MC, V* ⊘ *Closed Dec–Feb.*

¢–$$ ✕ **O Porto Interior.** The focus at this restaurant, named for its location on the Inner Harbour (but separated from the water by warehouses), is on beautifully presented upmarket Macanese dishes. The daily set menu is one of the best deals in town. It's the design, however, that makes the place so special. The elegant two-story facade has colonnades and Iberian arches; inside, the walls are covered with azulejos and intricately carved wooden grilles. To enter, you cross a marble bridge. ⊠ *259 Rua do Almirante Sergio* ☎ *967–770* 🖃 *AE, DC, MC, V.*

¢–$$ ✕ **Sol Nascente.** This modest restaurant on the main road at the entrance to Taipa Village has proved a real winner. It's furnished simply, with homemade chairs and a nice mural to illustrate the name ("Rising Sun"), but what's special is the menu. You're bound to find clams in coriander sauce; mussels stuffed with bread crumbs, spring onions, and garlic; Goan prawn curry; and beef rice with chestnuts, as well as the usual Macanese favorites—most everything for 90 patacas or less. Wine is available for as little as 60 patacas a bottle, and the servers are friendly and helpful. ⊠ *Av. Dr. Sun Yat-sen, Edificio Chun Leong Garden, G/F, Taipa Island* ☎ *836–288* 🖃 *AE, DC, MC, V.*

¢–$ ✕ **Praia Grande.** The Praia Grande used to have the most lovely view of the harbor but now faces not-so-lovely reclaimed land. Nevertheless, the simple interior at this classic Portuguese restaurant—white arches, terracotta floors, and wrought-iron furniture—still makes it a pleasant place to dine. The menu presents such imaginative fare as Portuguese dim sum, African chicken (in a peppery coconut broth), mussels in white wine, and clams *cataplana* (in a stew of pork, onions, tomatoes, and wine). The esplanade, with a serving kiosk and umbrella-shaded tables, is ideal for drinks and snacks. ✉ *10A Lobo d'Avila, at Ave. da Praia Grande* ☎ *973–022* ▭ *AE, MC, V.*

Thai

¢–$$ ✕ **Naam.** The Mandarin Oriental's soothing Thai restaurant, which is surrounded by a lovely tropical garden and free-form swimming pool, is popular with business folk as well as with ladies who lunch, so be sure to make a reservation. Start off with the delicate *yam som-o* (herbed pomelo salad with chicken and prawns) or aromatic *tom kha gai* (herbed coconut soup with chicken). Interesting main courses include *pla-ga pong nueng manow* (steamed sea bass with chilies, lime, and garlic) and the time-honored favorite *moo phad bai ga praow* (spicy pork with chilies and hot basil leaves). Finish off with melt-in-your-mouth *kluey thod krub bai toey* (deep-fried banana with pandanus sauce). ✉ *Mandarin Oriental, 956–1110 Av. da Amizade* ☎ *567–888* ▭ *AE, DC, MC, V.*

WHERE TO STAY

Although Macau's landmark colonial hotel, the luxurious Bela Vista, is now the residence of the first Portuguese consul general, the territory still has an impressive range of lodging options for such a small city. The most charming are the *pousadas,* such as the São Tiago, a modern hotel within an old Portuguese fort; others, such as the Mandarin Oriental, are modern and blissfully efficient. Only the cheaper and more modest guesthouses occupy old buildings in the historic heart of the city, but even the Westin, on the distant island of Coloane, is just a 15-minute taxi ride from the main square—and heaven knows it compensates, with extensive sports facilities, including access to a golf course and a black-sand beach.

In general, hotels listed in the higher price categories ($$$ and $$$$) are of international standard, with swimming pools and health clubs, meeting rooms, fine restaurants, elaborately designed public areas, business centers, and guest rooms with all the modern comforts and conveniences. Those in the $$ category are efficient, clean, and comfortable, with air-conditioning, color TV (showing English and Chinese programs from Hong Kong as well as the local channel), room service, and restaurants; they cater primarily to gamblers, regular Hong Kong visitors, and budget tour groups. Hotels in the ¢ and $ categories tend to be old and spartan and are used mostly by mainland Chinese travelers, so their staffs generally speak little English. They are, however, usually clean and inexpensive and sometimes even offer private bath and TV.

You can assume that rooms in all but the lowest price categories will have private baths.

Bear in mind that Macau relies heavily on weekend traffic, so reservations are difficult to come by on Saturday night. You can save up to 40% off the published rate (and have the hotel virtually to yourself) by coming to Macau during the week; even Friday night is usually 30% cheaper than Saturday night.

WHAT IT COSTS In patacas				
$$$$	**$$$**	**$$**	**$**	**¢**
FOR 2 PEOPLE over 1,800	1,000–1,800	500–1,000	200–500	under 200

Prices are for two people in a standard double room on a typical Saturday night, not including 10% service charge and 5% tax.

★ **$$$$**   ⊞ **Mandarin Oriental.** The Mandarin has always been luxurious—with an opulent lobby, beautifully appointed rooms, and service that is second to none—but the enormous spa makes it irresistible. After a grueling day of sightseeing, pop into the sauna and then ease into the heat of the hot tub before heading outdoors to the large tropical swimming pool. You'll then be ready to retire to your spacious room with its plush bed and large bathroom. Amid such pleasures, it's easy to forget that the office towers and frenzied traffic of urban Macau lie just beyond the hotel's entrance. ⊠ *956–1110 Av. da Amizade* ☎ *567–888, 2881–1988 in Hong Kong, 800/526–6566 in the U.S.* 🖷 *594–589* ⊕ *www.mandarinoriental.com* ⤇ *407 rooms, 28 suites* ⅋ *4 restaurants, café, room service, in-room data ports, in-room safes, minibars, refrigerators, cable TV with movies, 2 tennis courts, 2 pools, gym, 2 hot tubs (1 outdoor), massage, sauna, spa, squash, bar, casino, children's programs (ages 3–12), dry cleaning, laundry service, Internet, business services, meeting rooms* ⊟ *AE, DC, MC, V.*

$$$$ ⊞ **Westin Resort.** The Westin is designed for those primarily interested
Fodor'sChoice   in getting away from it all. Occupying a magnificent site on a headland
★   overlooking the black-sand beach of Hac Sa, the resort is surrounded by open water and total silence. From the moment you enter the lobby the pace slows to that of a tropical island. The comfortable rooms are large and the terraces even larger, while the sports and recreational facilities are the best in Macau—you'll even have course and clubhouse privileges at the Macau Golf & Country Club, accessible directly from the hotel. ⊠ *Hac Sa Beach, Coloane* ☎ *871–111 or 2803–2002, 800/ 228–3000 in Hong Kong* 🖷 *871–122* ⊕ *www.westin-macau.com* ⤇ *200 rooms, 8 suites* ⅋ *4 restaurants, room service, in-room data ports, in-room safes, minibars, cable TV with movies, driving range, 18-hole golf course, miniature golf, 8 tennis courts, 2 pools (1 indoor), health club, 2 hot tubs (1 outdoor), massage, bicycles, badminton, squash, 2 bars, shops, babysitting, Internet, business services, meeting rooms, car rental, no-smoking rooms* ⊟ *AE, DC, MC, V.*

$$$ ⊞ **Hotel Lisboa.** Though hectic, the Lisboa is an unexpectedly appealing place to stay. Its exterior has become a popular symbol of Macau: a gaudy mustard-and-white confection with a roof of giant balls on spikes that is said to resemble a roulette wheel. The lobby is more tasteful, though still a little ostentatious. The rooms, especially in the Lisboa Tower, come as a delightful surprise: large, comfortable, wedge-shape spaces with opulent furnishings that have been decorated with a thoughtful and restrained hand. Geographically speaking, the Lisboa is like Rome: all roads (and many buses) lead here, making this an exceptionally convenient option. ⊠ *Av. da Amizade* ☎ *577–666, 2559–1028 or 800/969–130 in Hong Kong* 🖷 *567–193* ⊕ *www.hotelisboa.com* 🛏 *830 rooms, 79 suites* ♨ *18 restaurants, coffee shop, pizzeria, pool, sauna, bar, casino, theater* 🖃 *AE, DC, MC, V.*

$$$ 🏨 **Hotel Ritz.** This handsome hotel is a series of low-rise blocks built into the hillside opposite the Bela Vista, so many of its rooms have balconies that look out over the Outer Harbour—and, unfortunately, the construction that goes along with the Nam Van Lakes project. The huge, marble-clad, chandelier-lighted lobby opens onto a café, a French restaurant, and a large health center. The restaurant Lijinxuan, which serves dishes from many parts of China, is opulent, with enormous chandeliers and masses of gilded wood. Guests often include VIPs from the mainland and upscale tour groups from Japan. ⊠ *7–13 Rua Comendador Kou Ho Neng* ☎ *339–955, 2739–6993, 2540–6333, 2367–3043 in Hong Kong* 🖷 *317–826* ⊕ *www.ritzhotel.com.mo* 🛏 *144 rooms, 18 suites* ♨ *3 restaurants, café, miniature golf, 2 tennis courts, indoor pool, gym, hair salon, hot tub, sauna, steam room, squash, bar, Internet, business services* 🖃 *AE, DC, MC, V.*

★ $$$ 🏨 **Pousada de São Tiago.** The São Tiago has the monopoly on charm among Macau's hotels. It was ingeniously built into a 17th-century Portuguese fortress that once guarded the southern tip of the peninsula, and the entrance alone is worth a visit, with a staircase that runs through an old lichen-covered tunnel through which water seeps in soothing trickles. Rooms are decorated with unusual mahogany furnishings and azulejos that lend atmosphere. Views from most guest rooms and dining terraces take in the harbor and mainland China beyond. The only shortcoming is that service can be a little lethargic. ⊠ *Av. da República* ☎ *378–111, 2739–1216 in Hong Kong* 🖷 *552–170, 2739–1198 in Hong Kong* ⊕ *www.saotiago.com.mo* 🛏 *20 rooms, 4 suites* ♨ *Restaurant, room service, minibars, cable TV, pool, bar, dry cleaning, laundry service* 🖃 *AE, DC, MC, V.*

$$–$$$ 🏨 **Beverly Plaza.** Located on the reclaimed land behind the Lisboa, this hotel is managed by the China Travel Service and is a fairly standard China-run operation, with disco and karaoke, a large Chinese banquet room, and a Western coffee shop. The hotel shop sells bargain-priced stereos, television sets, microwave ovens, and other goods that local Chinese buy for their relatives in China and ship home. The rooms are clean, air-conditioned, and are equipped with hot-water flasks for tea and coffee. Devoid of frills, it's still fairly comfortable and a good budget option. ⊠ *70 Av. Dr. Rodrigo Rodrigues* ☎ *782–288, 2739–6993 in Hong Kong* 🖷 *780–701* ⊕ *www.beverlyplaza.com* 🛏 *300 rooms* ♨ *3 restaurants, coffee shop, patisserie, minibars, cable TV, indoor pool, hair salon, hot tub, massage, sauna, bar, nightclub, video game room, shop, business services, meeting rooms* 🖃 *AE, DC, MC, V.*

$$–$$$ ⊞ **Emperor.** Formerly the "New World" Emperor, this hotel in the Outer Harbour district shortened its name in 2003. Situated near casinos and the wharf, it's a good value with reasonably attractive rooms furnished with potted plants, desks, TV consoles, and pastel drapes and bedspreads. There's a fine Cantonese restaurant and a nightclub with disco and karaoke, and the lobby bazaar sells clothes and accessories. ⊠ *51 Rua de Xangai* ☎ *781–888* 🖶 *782–287* ⊕ *www.emperorhotel. com.mo* 🛏 *239 rooms, 33 suites* ♨ *2 restaurants, room service, minibars, cable TV with movies, sauna, bar, dance club, nightclub, shop, babysitting, dry cleaning, laundry service, business services* ☰ *AE, DC, MC, V.*

$$–$$$ ⊞ **Hotel Royal.** The Royal has an excellent location, on a small hill with fine views of Guia, the city, and the Inner Harbour. The marble-clad lobby has a marble fountain, a lounge, and some fine shops, and the basement hides sports facilities and a karaoke bar. Upstairs are the glass-roofed swimming pool and two restaurants: the Vasco da Gama for Portuguese-Continental and a coffee shop. The hotel runs shuttle buses to the casinos. ⊠ *2–4 Est. da Vitoria* ☎ *552–222, 2543–6426 in Hong Kong* 🖶 *563–008* ⊕ *www.hotelroyal.com.mo* 🛏 *365 rooms, 15 suites* ♨ *2 restaurants, room service, minibars, cable TV with movies, indoor pool, health club, squash, bar, shop, dry cleaning, laundry service, no-smoking rooms* ☰ *AE, DC, MC, V.*

$$–$$$ ⊞ **Hotel Sintra.** This location is arguably the best of any hotel, within easy walking distance of both the old quarter and the bustling surrounding areas. In 2002 a major renovation was completed, giving all rooms a much-needed face-lift, adding large beds and comfy goose-down duvets. The hotel mainly attracts businesspeople, who don't care that the room's lake views are obstructed by ugly office blocks. The restaurant claims to serve the best steak in town. ⊠ *58–62 Av. Dom João IV* ☎ *710–111, 2546–6944 in Hong Kong* 🖶 *510–527* ⊕ *www.hotelsintra.com* 🛏 *228 rooms, 12 suites* ♨ *Restaurant, room service, some in-room data ports, some in-room safes, minibars, refrigerators, cable TV, sauna, shops, dry cleaning, laundry service, business services, meeting rooms, no-smoking floor* ☰ *AE, DC, MC, V.*

$$–$$$ ⊞ **Hyatt Regency & Taipa Island Resort.** The Hyatt was the originator of the resort concept in Macau, but in the last few years it has been trumped by its rivals—the newer Mandarin, which is closer to downtown, and the Westin, which is much more secluded and special. Nevertheless, the Hyatt is a pleasant place to stay, though the last major renovation was in 1997. The resort has superb facilities, including a health spa, a huge outdoor swimming pool, and a hot tub that looks like a modern take on the Turkish bath. The Hyatt is particularly popular with Hong Kong families. ⊠ *2 Est. de Almirante Joaquim Marques Esparteiro, Taipa Island* ☎ *831–234, 2559–0168 in Hong Kong, 800/633–7313 in the U.S.* 🖶 *830–195* ⊕ *www.macau.hyatt.com* 🛏 *308 rooms, 18 suites* ♨ *3 restaurants, coffee shop, minibars, cable TV with movies, 4 tennis courts, pool, health club, hair salon, bicycles, 2 squash courts, 2 bars, casino, children's programs (ages 5–12)* ☰ *AE, DC, MC, V.*

$$–$$$ ⊞ **Kingsway Hotel.** This moderately priced hotel on the Outer Harbour has small rooms, but all have IDD phones, minibars, and in-house movies. The casino caters mostly to gambling junketeers from Southeast Asia. ⊠ *Rua Luis Gonzaga Gomes* ☎ *702–888, 2548–0989 in Hong Kong* 🖷 *702–828* ⊕ *www.hotelkingsway.com.mo* 🛏 *410 rooms* ♢ *2 restaurants, minibars, cable TV with movies, sauna, casino* ⊟ *AE, DC, MC, V.*

$$-$$$ ⊡ **New Century Hotel.** Between the university and the Hyatt Regency, this opulent hotel tends to appeal more to mainland Chinese than to Westerners, who may find the shininess of all the decorations a little over the top. The atrium lobby really is breathtaking, however, and the huge pool terrace has splendid views of the city and Taipa. Rooms are somewhat more tastefully furnished, and there's a wide range of dining options, including a wooden deck with Caribbean-style cabanas for parties. The Prince Galaxie is an excellent entertainment center, with a pub, a disco, and karaoke rooms. ⊠ *Est. de Almirante Joaquim Marques Esparteiro, Taipa Island* ☎ *831–111, 2581–9863 in Hong Kong, 800/908–738 in the U.S.* 🖷 *832–222* ⊕ *www.newcenturyhotel-macau.com* 🛏 *526 rooms, 28 apartments* ♢ *4 restaurants, room service, refrigerators, cable TV with movies, 2 tennis courts, pool, health club, billiards, bowling, Ping-Pong, squash, bar, pub, casino, dance club* ⊟ *AE, DC, MC, V.*

$-$$$ ⊡ **Hotel Grandeur.** Owned and operated by China Travel Service, this hotel in the Outer Harbour is where you'll find Rotunda, Macau's first revolving restaurant, with great views and nightly entertainment. Each room has a window bay with a table and chairs, and furnishings are brightly floral. The hotel is an efficient, businesslike place, without the grand lobby favored by most other hotels; but you can relax in its indoor pool and health club. The Grandeur caters to Japanese and mainland tour groups as well as Hong Kong businesspeople and some Western tourists. ⊠ *199 Rua de Pequim* ☎ *781–233, 2857–2846 in Hong Kong* 🖷 *781–211, 2546–4920 or 800/933–385 in Hong Kong* ⊕ *www.hotelgrandeur.com* 🛏 *338 rooms, 35 suites* ♢ *3 restaurants, minibars, cable TV, indoor pool, gym, hair salon, hot tub, massage, sauna, steam room, bar, Internet, business services, meeting rooms* ⊟ *AE, DC, MC, V.*

$$ ⊡ **Hotel Presidente.** The Presidente has an excellent location a block from the Lisboa casino, on the Outer Harbour Road between the ferry terminal and the bridge to Taipa Island. The hotel's modern rooms are comfortable and have soft lighting. It has an agreeable lobby lounge, European and Chinese restaurants, the best Korean food in town, and a disco. This hotel is very popular with Hong Kongers. ⊠ *Av. da Amizade* ☎ *553–888, 2857–1533 in Hong Kong* 🖷 *552–735* ⊕ *www.hotelpresident.com.mo* 🛏 *312 rooms, 4 suites* ♢ *3 restaurants, room service, minibars, cable TV with movies, hot tub, massage, sauna, steam room, dance club, meeting room* ⊟ *AE, DC, MC, V.*

$ ⊡ **Central.** In the heart of town just off the Old Town square, this was once the tallest building in the city. It was also the home of Macau's only legal casino—and doubled as a brothel. All that is long gone, and it's now a budget hotel with clean, basic rooms. ⊠ *26–28 Av. Almeida Ribeiro* ☎ *373–888* 🖷 *332–275* 🛏 *160 rooms* ⊟ *AE, MC, V.*

NIGHTLIFE

According to old movies and novels about the China Coast, Macau was a city of opium dens, wild gambling, international spies, and slinky ladies of the night. While this image is not far from the truth today (albeit shorn of any romantic mystique), it's kept so well hidden that most visitors will be unaware such an underbelly exists. The tacky hostess nightclubs, karaoke lounges, and so-called sauna parlors that abound are popular with Asian men. Unfortunately, nightlife that does not involve gambling or live girls is hard to come by here; many travelers find themselves simply enjoying long dinners that run late into the night. The city has tried to develop the Outer Harbour waterfront into a cluster of pubs and music bars with mixed success.

Mona Lisa Theater. The Lisboa's *Crazy Paris Show* was first staged in the late 1970s and has become a popular fixture. The stripper-dancers are artists from Europe, Australia, and the Americas, and they put on a highly sophisticated and cleverly staged show. They shed their clothes, but the performance is not lewd; in fact, half the audience is likely to be made up of female tourists. The acts change every few months. Tickets are available at hotel desks, Hong Kong and Macau ferry terminals, and the theater itself. ⊠ *Hotel Lisboa, Av. da Amizade, 2/F* ☏ *577–666 Ext. 3193, 800/938–366 in Hong Kong* 🎫 *205–260 patacas* ⊙ *Shows, Sun.–Fri. at 8 and 9:30, Sat. at 8, 9:30, and 11.*

Nightclubs & Pubs

Many nightspots are staffed with hostesses from Thailand, the Philippines, or Russia and are merely thinly veiled covers for the world's oldest profession. The legitimate clubs that do exist tend not to survive for very long. Check with the Macau Government Tourist Office to find out about interesting spots that are currently open.

Pubs and music bars open and close with astonishing speed and are mostly known only to locals by word of mouth. You can inquire at the tourist office or, better still, spot the coolest-looking person on staff at your hotel and ask where they go out at night. For some time the government has been promoting the area on the reclaimed land near the Hotel Lisboa as Macau's own Lan Kwai Fong—after Hong Kong's popular nightlife district. Although the comparison to Hong Kong is still a bit of a stretch, there is finally a critical mass of bars, live music spots, and restaurants. It's somewhat desolate during the day and on most weeknights, but the area comes alive on Friday and Saturday. The main street here is Avenida Marginal Baia Nova, known as "The Docks" to expatriates, and most of the hot spots are gathered on the southwestern block. There are a few that stand out in the crowd.

Celluloid is the theme at the aptly named **Casablanca** (⊠ Av. Dr. Sun Yat Sen ☏ 751–281), where homages are paid to Marcello Mastroianni and Hong Kong director Wong Kar Wai's *Chungking Express* via large posters. It's opulently fitted out with deep-plush red velvet curtains and chairs. **The Embassy** (⊠ Mandarin Oriental, 956–1110 Av. da Amizade ☎ 567–888) bar is reminiscent of foreign correspondent clubs around the world. Portraits of ex–consuls general and indigenous souvenirs from their countries hang somberly on the walls. For live Latin American, jazz, or the occasional pop music, depending on the night, head to the **Green Spot** (⊠ Emperor Hotel, Rue de Xangai, lobby ☎ 788–666 or 781–888). The spacious mint-color lounge was opened by popular Hong Kong singer Maria Cordeiro, who is originally from Macau (she also owns the Green Spot in Hong Kong). Reservations are recommended for a table on the weekends. Evoking South American mystique is the loungy **Rio Café** (⊠ Av. Dr. Sun Yat Sen ☎ 751–306), fitted out with large leafy plants and fiery orange-and-red decor.

Casinos

Since the late 1950s, Stanley Ho has had a monopoly on the gambling scene in Macau—he owned *all* of Macau's casinos. However, things are on the move, as three more casino-operating concessions have been won (one by Mr. Ho himself, the other two by consortiums that have connections to Las Vegas). Plans are underway to revamp the seedy image of gambling and to create resort-style entertainment venues offering conference halls, hotels, theaters, restaurants, shopping malls, and the like. The first of these Las Vegas–style casinos, the Las Vegas Sands, opened in May 2004 next to the Mandarin Oriental; the most eagerly awaited, however, is the Venetian from the same group; it is expected to open in Cotai, a new development area between Coloane and Taipa islands, in March 2006. Las Vegas entrepreneur Steve Wynn has his own casino plans in the works, but hasn't yet broken ground on his project. The busiest and largest casino is the two-story operation in the Lisboa, where the games are roulette, blackjack, baccarat, *pacapio,* and the Chinese games called fan-tan and "big and small." There are also hundreds of slot machines, which the Chinese call "hungry tigers."

At this writing, there are a dozen casinos in Macau, and the main ones are in several major hotels, including the **Hotel Lisboa, Mandarin Oriental, New Century, Kingsway Hotel**, and **Hyatt Regency & Taipa Island Resort.** The **Las Vegas Sands** (⊠ Av. de Amizade and Av. Dr. Sun Yat Sen ☎ 883–388) is the first of Macau's Las Vegas–style casinos and dwarfs the adjacent Mandarin Oriental. The gold reflective windows give it a sense of glitz and glamor, long missing from the Macau gambling scene. The **Palacio de Macau** (⊠ Av. de Amizade, at the Outer Harbour ☎ 346-701) is more popularly known as the Floating Casino. The **Pharoah's Palace** (⊠ Landmark Plaza, Av. da Amizade ☎788–111) is an independent casino.

Gambling in Macau

The solid mass of players in the casinos might look rather unsophisticated, but they are as knowledgeable as any gamblers in the world. They are also more single-minded than most, eschewing alcohol and all but essential nourishment while at the tables. (Small bottles of chicken essence are much in evidence.) And they are extremely superstitious, which leads to gambles that may confuse Westerners.

There are few limitations to gambling in Macau. No one under 18 is allowed in, but identity cards are not checked. Although there are posted betting limits, high rollers are not discouraged by such formalities. A credit card can get you cash in either patacas or Hong Kong dollars from the automatic teller machines, and there are also 24-hour currency exchanges. Bets are almost always placed in Hong Kong dollars. There are a few games that might not be familiar:

Baccarat has become a big-status game for well-heeled gamblers from Hong Kong, who brag as much about losing a million as about winning one. The baccarat tables occupy their own special corners and are usually surrounded by an admiring, envying crowd. Bets usually begin at HK$1,000 and go up to HK$30,000. In Macau the player cannot take the bank, and the fixed rules on drawing and standing are complex, making this completely a game of chance.

Big and Small is a traditional game in which you bet on combinations of numbers for big or small totals determined by rolled dice. The minimum bet is HK$50.

Fan-tan is an ancient Chinese game that has somehow survived Western competition—"somehow," because it's so incredibly simple. A pile of porcelain buttons is placed on the table, and the croupier removes four at a time until one, two, three, or four are left. Players wager on the result, and some are so experienced they know the answer long before the game ends.

Pacapio has replaced the similar game of keno. Players choose between 4 and 25 numbers from 1 to 80. Winning numbers are chosen by computer and appear every half hour or so on screens in the Lisboa and the Jai Alai Stadium.

Pai kao has been a popular Chinese game since the 19th century. It's played with dominoes and a revolving banker system, both of which make it all but impossible for novices to understand. The minimum bet is either HK$100 or HK$200.

Roulette is based on the European system, with a single zero, but has some American touches. Players buy colored chips at an American-style table, and bets are collected, rather than frozen, when the zero appears. Roulette has been steadily losing popularity and is now played only in the Lisboa and Mandarin Oriental casinos. The minimum bet is HK$50.

SPORTS & THE OUTDOORS

For most regular visitors to Macau, the sporting life means playing the casinos, but there are plenty of other sports here, albeit often with gambling on the side. The Macanese are keen on team sports and perform quite creditably in soccer and field hockey. In addition to traditional annual events, such as the Grand Prix auto race, there are international championships in volleyball and table tennis (a.k.a. Ping-Pong, which, played professionally, is a completely different animal from the game you played in your basement). Major indoor events, such as the World

Volleyball Championships, are held in the **Macau Forum,** while the venue for outdoor events is the **Taipa Stadium.** Participatory sports activity has increased, with some excellent routes for joggers and more fitness facilities in hotels.

Dragon Boat Racing

This newest of international sports derives from the ancient Chinese dragon boat festivals, during which fishing communities competed, paddling long, shallow boats with dragons' heads and tails in honor of Chu Yuen, a poet and scholar who drowned himself to protest official corruption. At the time, almost 2,000 years ago, his friends took boats into the water and pounded their oars and beat drums to scare away the fish who would have eaten the poet's body. The festival and races have been revived in many parts of Asia, with teams competing from Hong Kong, Japan, Singapore, Thailand, Malaysia, and Macau, plus crews from Australia, the United States, Europe, and China's Guangdong Province. The races are held alongside the waterfront, which provides a natural grandstand for spectators. The Dragon Boat Festival takes place on the fifth day of the fifth moon (usually sometime in June) and is attended by a flotilla of fishing junks decorated with silk banners and by fishing families beating drums and setting off firecrackers.

Go-Cart Racing

On reclaimed land opposite Coloane Park is Macau's go-cart track, the **Kartodromo,** where you can hire a vehicle for go-cart racing. It's great fun, and on weekends most Hong Kong visitors come here to let off some steam. Otherwise the track is basically headquarters for local go-cart enthusiasts and there are floodlights for night racing. ⊠ *Seac Pai Van, Coloane* ☎ *882–126* ⌨ *100 patacas for 10 mins, 180 patacas for 20 mins* ☾ *Sun.–Thurs. 10:30 AM–7:30 PM, Fri. and Sat. 10 AM–9:30 PM.*

Golf

The **Macau Golf & Country Club,** affiliated with the Westin Resort, is beside Hac Sa Beach. The 18-hole, par-71 course is built into the wooded headland above the hotel; an elevator from the hotel leaves you a few yards from the first tee. The clubhouse has a pro shop, a pool, a sauna, massage rooms, steam baths, and restaurants. The Westin offers golf packages that includes one-night accommodation and 18 holes are worth checking out for keen golfers. Only hotel guests and members of affiliated clubs can play. ☎ *871–188* ⌨ *Greens fees for 18 holes: HK$700 weekdays, HK$1,400 weekends.*

Greyhound Racing

The dogs are very popular with both residents and Hong Kong gamblers, who flock to races in the scenic, open-air **Macau Canidrome,** near the old Chinese border. Most dogs are imported from Australia; some come from Ireland and the United States. The 10,000-seat stadium has rows and rows of betting windows and stalls for food and drink. Multimillion-dollar purses are not unheard of, and special events, such as Irish Nights, are held frequently. Races start at 8 PM (there are usually eight) and finish at about 11 PM. ✉ *Av. do Artur Tamagnini Barbosa at Av. General Castelo Branco* 🎟 *Public stands 2 patacas, members' stand 5 patacas, 6-seat box 80 patacas* 🕐 *Tues., Thurs., and weekends at 8 PM.*

Horse Racing

The **Macau Raceway,** originally built as Asia's first trotting track, occupies 50 acres of reclaimed land near the Hyatt Regency hotel. Trotting did not catch on with local gamblers, so the Macau Jockey Club was formed and the facility converted—with no expense spared—into a world-class racecourse, with grass and sand tracks, floodlighting, and the most sophisticated computerized betting system available. The five-story grandstand can accommodate 15,000 people, 6,000 of them in air-conditioned comfort; members have boxes where gourmet meals can be catered. There are several public restaurants, bars, a small casino, and a huge electronic screen to show the odds, winnings, and races in progress. Races are held throughout the year on weekends (usually in the afternoon) and midweek (at night), timed not to clash with events at the Hong Kong Jockey Club. The Hotel Lisboa runs free bus service to the racecourse. Ask your hotel desk for more details. ✉ *Est. Governador Albano de Oliveira* 🎟 *20 patacas* 🕐 *Race usually Wed. and Sat. at 7:30 from late Sept.–late Aug.*

Ice-Skating

☺ The **Future Bright Amusement Park** has a small, crowded ice-skating rink and a highly qualified teaching staff. The park also houses a bowling alley, a food court, a video arcade, and a children's playground. Don't bother calling ahead unless you speak Chinese. ✉ *Praça Luis de Camões* ☎ *953–399* 🎟 *40 patacas, including skate rental for unlimited time between 10 AM and 10:30 PM* 🕐 *Daily 9 AM–10 PM.*

Motor Racing

The **Macau Grand Prix** takes place the third or fourth weekend of November. From the beginning of the week, the city is pierced with the sound of supercharged engines testing the 6-km (4-mi) Guia Circuit, which follows the city roads along the Outer Harbour to Guia Hill and around the reservoir. The route is as challenging as that of Monaco, with rapid gear changes demanded at the right-angle Statue Corner, the Doña Maria bend, and the Melco hairpin.

The Grand Prix was first staged here in 1953, and the standard of performance has now reached world class. Today cars achieve speeds of 224 kph (140 mph) on the straightaways, with the lap record approaching 2 minutes, 20 seconds. The premier event is the Formula Three Championship, with cars competing from around the world in what is now the official World Cup of Formula Three racing, where winners qualify for Formula One licenses. There are also races for motorcycles and production cars.

Room reservations for the week of the Grand Prix should be made months in advance, and anyone not interested in motor racing should avoid coming to Macau that weekend. Tickets are available from tourist offices or from agents in Macau and Hong Kong.

SHOPPING

At first glance, Macau is a poor country cousin to Hong Kong in the retail business. So why bother to shop here at all? First, the shopping areas are much more compact and navigable. Second, the sales staffs are on the whole more pleasant and relaxed here, even if their command of English is less impressive. And most important, many goods are cheaper. Like Hong Kong, Macau is a duty-free port for almost all items; but commercial rents, unlike those in the former British territory, are reasonable, and wages are low, reducing the overhead and hence the prices shopkeepers need to charge.

Except for family-run businesses, which take a short holiday after the Chinese New Year, Macau's shops are open 365 days a year. Opening hours vary according by type of shop, but usually extend into mid-evening, around 8 or so. Most shops accept major credit cards, except for those items with the deepest discounts. Friendly bargaining is expected and is done by asking for the "best price," which produces discounts of 10% or more. Discounts larger than that on expensive items should be treated with suspicion. Macau has its share of phony antiques, fake name-brand watches, and other rip-offs. Be sure to shop around, check the guarantee on name brands (sometimes fakes come with misspellings—Rolax, anyone?), and get receipts for expensive items.

Macau's major shopping districts are its main street, Avenida Almeida Ribeiro (commonly known by its Chinese name, Sanmalo); Mercadores and its side streets; Cinco de Outubro; and Rua do Campo. Shop names reflect Macau's dual heritage; for example, Pastelarias Mei Mun (pastry shops), Relojoaria Tat On (watches and clocks), and Sapatarias João Leong (shoes). For the best selection of traditional Chinese furniture, scroll paintings, porcelain, figurines, fans, dragon robes, lacquerware, and other collectibles, troll the area around St. Paul's, particularly Rua do São Antonio and Rua de São Paulo.

Antiques

The days of discovering treasures from the Ming among the Qing (pronounced *Ching*) chinoiserie in Macau's antiques shops are long gone, but there are still plenty of old and interesting pieces laying about. Collectors of old porcelain can find some well-preserved bowls and other simple Ming ware once used as ballast in trading ships. Prices for such genuine items run into the hundreds or thousands of dollars. Far cheaper are the ornate vases, stools, and dishes from the late Qing period (concurrent with England's Victorian era). This style of pottery is still very popular among the Chinese, and a lot of so-called Qing is faithfully reproduced today in China, Hong Kong, and Macau. Many of these copies are excellent and hard to distinguish from their antique cousins.

Interesting antique furniture is the focus of a store called **Asian Artifacts** (✉ 25 Rua dos Negociantes, Coloane Village ☎ 881–022), on a side street in Coloane Village. The owner keeps her shop and its extension filled with valuable old tables, screens, chests, and wardrobes as well as some high-quality reproductions. In keeping with the name of the street, which translates to "negotiating street," be sure to barter. Good service is the reason why **Hong Hap** (✉ 170 Cinco de Outubro) has earned an excellent reputation from antiques shoppers over the years. Quality antiques can be found at **Wing Tai** (✉ 1A Av. Almeida Ribeiro).

Clothing

Many Macau stores sell casual and sports clothes for men and women at bargain prices. Most items are made here in Macau and carry brand-name labels—in some cases these are fakes, but more often they're genuine overruns or rejects from local factories that are licensed manufacturers for Yves Saint Laurent, Cacharel, Van Heusen, Adidas, Banana Republic, Abercrombie & Fitch, Gloria Vanderbilt, and many others. You can also buy padded jackets, sweaters, jogging suits, windbreakers, and a wide range of clothes for children and infants at very low prices. The best shopping areas are on **Rua do Campo** and around **Mercadores.** For the very best bargains, visit the street markets of **São Domingos** (off Largo do Senado), **Rua Cinco de Outubro,** and **Rua da Palha.** There are also a growing number of designer and name-brand boutiques, such as the two-story **Emporio Armani** at 61 Avenida Almeida Ribeiro, where prices are usually much lower than in Hong Kong. Credit cards are accepted at most larger shops.

Crafts

Many traditional Chinese crafts are made in Macau. The best places to watch the craftspeople at work are on Tercena and Estalagens streets; these old streets are lined with three-story shop houses with open-front workshops on the ground floor, living quarters and offices above. Some shops produce beautifully carved chests and furniture made of mahogany, camphor wood, and redwood, some inlaid with marble or mother-of-pearl; others make bamboo birdcages with tiny porcelain bowls to go in them, door plaques thought to bring luck, and family altars. To find these two small streets, turn left off the path to St. Paul's church at the intersection of Rua da Palha and Rua São Paulo and then take your first right. Follow the cream and black paving tiles that the government uses to indicate the route to many of Macau's major sights. Macau also produces lacquer screens, modern and traditional Chinese pottery, and ceremonial items such as lion-dance costumes, giant incense coils, and temple offerings.

Department Stores

The Japanese department store **New Yaohan** (✉ Av. da Amizade), next door to the Jai Alai Stadium, offers a one-stop arena for everything from linen tablecloths to clothing, jewelry, housewares, shoe repair, a bakery, a fully stocked food hall, and several dining options. Other popular stores are the two branches of **Nam Kwong** (✉ 95 Av. Almeida Ribeiro ✉ 9 Ria Pequim), which specialize in products made in China.

Furniture

Most Hong Kong visitors come to Macau for two things: to eat and to buy furniture. Chinese-style furniture from Macau is less expensive than in Hong Kong, and most shops waive the delivery charge if shipping to Hong Kong. After visiting a half dozen stores, you'll start recognizing the same pieces over and over, so it's good to scour several shops first and compare prices rather than buy the first item you fall in love with. Shopkeepers are all very helpful, but remember to barter: if you're interested in more than one piece, you will likely receive a discount. Most shops can arrange international shipping. **Lucky Castle** (✉ 14-A/B Rua de Santo Antonio) specializes in intricately carved wooden art screens and panels. The owner, Johnny, uses the store as a workshop, so you may see him crafting and polishing screens for windows, doors, or wall hangings. The large **Mobilia de Long Ngai** (✉ 46–48A R/C Rua De São Paulo) has two floors stacked with items such as wedding cabinets (now used mainly as TV and video consoles) and CD drawers. Writing desks, bed bases, chests, and rocking chairs are just a few of the large variety of items on offer at **Wa Fat Trade Company** (✉ 11 R/C Rua De São Paulo).

Jewelry

Macau's jewelry shops are not as lavish as those in downtown Hong Kong, but they charge a much lower premium for workmanship, resulting in markedly lower prices for the finished piece. The price of the gold itself fluctuates with trading on the Hong Kong Gold Exchange, and each store will have an electronic display showing the current price of gold per *tael*, which is 1.2 troy ounces. Some counters display 14- and 18-karat jewelry, such as chains, earrings, pendants, brooches, rings, and bangles; however, the best-seller is 24-karat (pure) gold in the form of jewelry, coins, and tiny bars, which come with assays from a Swiss bank. Since prices for gold items are based on the established international price of gold plus a rate for workmanship and a small percentage profit, there is only limited scope for bargaining.

Some of the best-known shops are situated on the main street of Avenida Almeida Ribeiro, near the Largo do Senado. A wide selection of gold pieces can be found at **Chow Sang Sang** (✉ 360 Av. Almeida Ribeiro), where the salespeople are friendly, helpful, and speak English.

Wine

Because of Macau's long connection to Europe, wines—and little-known Portuguese wines in particular—are a real bargain. You can buy them everywhere, from the corner convenience store to the largest grocery, but the basement wine cellar at **Pavilions** (✉ 417–425 Av. da Praia Grande ☎ 374–026) has one of the best selections. And if you've developed a taste for port, consider loading up (just be aware that Hong Kong customs technically allows only one bottle per passenger); prices are much cheaper in Macau than anywhere else except Oporto itself.

MACAU A TO Z

To research prices, get advice from other travelers, and book travel arrangements, visit www.fodors.com.

AIR TRAVEL

East Asia Airlines runs helicopter service between the Macau Terminal and Shun Tak Centre in Hong Kong, with departures at 9:30 AM, and then every 30 minutes from 10:30 AM to 11 PM daily. The 20-minute flight costs HK$1,500 weekdays and HK$1,600 weekends each way, including taxes. Book through the Shun Tak Centre or the Macau Terminal.

The Macau International Airport opened before the handover and has established itself as a busy regional hub. Built on reclaimed land, the airport is 15 to 20 minutes by road from downtown Macau and the Chinese border. The handsome glass-clad passenger terminal is connected by the gracefully arched Friendship Bridge to the Ferry Terminal and the Chinese border. There are daily flights to and from Beijing, Shanghai, and Taiwan, with regular services from other Chinese cities, major capitals of Southeast Asia, and Japan, Korea, and Portugal. Air Macau is the local carrier. Departure tax for Chinese destinations is 80 patacas; otherwise it's 130 patacas.

🛈 **East Asia Airlines** ☎ 2108–9898 Shun Tak Centre, 727–288 Macau Terminal ⊕ www. helihongkong.com. **Macau International Airport** ⊠ Est. da Ponte da Cabrita ☎ 861–111 for airport information, 396–5555 for Air Macau reservations ⊕ www.macau-airport. gov.mo.

BOAT & FERRY TRAVEL

The Hong Kong–Macau route is one of the world's easiest border crossings. Ferries run every 15 minutes and take just under an hour, with no more than 5 minutes for immigration control on either side (be sure to bring your passport). Only on weekend evenings and major public holidays is it necessary to reserve in advance; at all other times, just show up and take the next boat. Of course, service can be disrupted when typhoons sweep in.

The majority of ships to Macau leave Hong Kong from the Macau Terminal in the Shun Tak Centre, which has its own marked exit from the Sheung Wan MTR station. From Macau, ferries use the modern three-story ferry terminal. There is also limited service to and from the China Hong Kong Terminal, on the Kowloon side of Hong Kong Harbour.

The Shun Tak Centre houses the Macau Government Tourist Office, booking offices for all shipping companies, and offices of most Macau hotels, travel agents, and excursions to China.

Following the merger of Far East Jetfoil Company and CTS-Parkview, there is now a unified service of turbojets, which run every 15 minutes around the clock, with slightly less frequent sailings from 3 AM to 6 AM. The turbojets are larger and more comfortable than the old jet foils and make the 64-km (40-mi) trip in about an hour. Beer, soft drinks, and snacks are available on board, as are duty-free cigarettes and Macau's instant-lottery tickets. There is no smoking on board. First-class seats are available for a small premium, but there is no discernible difference in quality save for a free box of unappetizing snacks.

There are three classes of tickets—economy, first, and super—as well as VIP cabins for four or six people. The prices, depending on class, are HK$130 to HK$232 on weekdays, HK$141 to HK$247 on weekends and holidays, and HK$161 to HK$260 at night (after 6 PM). The return trip from Macau is HK$1 more per ticket. Although boats are frequent, it's wise to book your return ticket if you visit on a weekend. Otherwise you'll be stuck back at the gambling tables or at a bar until the next available ferry.

First Ferry also runs service, with almost hourly round-trips daily from the China Terminal in Tsim Sha Tsui. Fares range from HK$140 on weekdays to HK$155 on weekend days, and HK$175 nights.

TICKETS Travel agents and most Hong Kong hotels can arrange tickets. Eleven of Hong Kong's major MTR stations have computer-booking outlets that sell turbojet tickets up to 28 days in advance. You can get your return ticket at the same time, though it's easy to get it in Macau except at very busy periods. If you decide to return earlier than the date on your ticket, you can sail standby at the terminal. Turbojet tickets can also be booked in Hong Kong by phone using American Express, Diners Club, and Visa credit cards, but they must be picked up at least a half hour before the boat leaves.

▪ **Ferry Reservations and Turbojet Tickets** ☎ 2859-3333 for schedules, 2921-6688 for bookings ⊕ www.turbojet.com.hk. **First Ferry** ⊠ Shun Tak Centre, 200 Connaught Rd., Sheung Wan, Hong Kong ☎ 2516-9581, 726-301 in Macau.

BUS TRAVEL IN MACAU
Public buses in Macau are cheap—2.50 patacas within the city limits—and convenient. Services from the terminal are most useful for visitors; itineraries are posted at bus stops. There are several services to Taipa, for 3.30 patacas, and Coloane, for 5 patacas. For 6 patacas, Minibus AP1 provides service between the airport, the Hotel Lisboa, and the ferry terminal. All other buses in town are chartered and are replicas of 1920s London buses, known as Tour Machines. Their depot is at the terminal, and you can hire one for a party of up to nine people for 300 to 380 patacas an hour depending on the time of day. Alternatively, you can join a city tour for two hours for 150 patacas. They're also often used to transfer groups to and from hotels.

CAR RENTAL
Macau is the land of counterintuitive directions, where roundabouts and detours often require you to turn left in order to go right, so you might think twice about driving yourself around. Still, you can rent *mokes*, little jeeplike vehicles that are fun to drive and ideal for touring. Unlike in Hong Kong, you drive on the *right* side of the road. International and most national driver's licenses are valid here. Rental rates are 350 patacas for 24 hours, plus a whopping 3,000-pataca deposit (credit cards accepted). The price includes third-party insurance, and the very nice

staff will often give a discount if asked. Hotel packages often include special moke-rental deals. Contact Happy Mokes for rental details. Along with mokes, Avis rents cars for 450 to 600 patacas weekdays and 500 to 650 patacas weekends. Book in advance and you'll receive a discount, but as always, you must ask for it. Avis also has 15% discounts for selected frequent-flyer programs.

🔲 Rental Agencies **Avis** ☎ 336–789 in Macau, 2576–6831 in Hong Kong. **Happy Mokes** ☎ 2523–5690 in Hong Kong, 831–212, 439–393 in Macau.

MONEY MATTERS

At this writing, one U.S. dollar is worth about 8.3 Macau patacas (sometimes denoted as MOP), making the pataca marginally weaker than the Hong Kong dollar, which is pegged at 7.75 to the U.S. dollar. You'll get roughly 5.5 patacas to the Canadian dollar and 12.8 patacas to the pound sterling. The Hong Kong dollar is accepted everywhere in Macau at parity with the pataca, so it is not really necessary to change money at all for short trips. No one in Hong Kong will accept patacas, however, so be sure to change any leftover patacas back into Hong Kong dollars back before you leave Macau.

PEDICABS

Tricycle-drawn two-seater carriages have been in business as long as Macau has had bicycles and paved roads. They cluster at the ferry terminal and near hotels around town, their drivers hustling for customers and usually offering to serve as guides. It used to be a pleasure to hire a pedicab, but heavy traffic and vast construction projects now detract from the experience. Macau's city center is not a congenial place for pedicabs, and the hilly districts are impossible. If you decide to take one, you'll have to haggle, but don't pay more than HK$30 for a trip to a nearby hotel.

TAXIS

Taxis are inexpensive and plentiful. The black cabs with cream-color roofs can be flagged on the street; the yellow cabs are radio taxis. All are metered, and most are air-conditioned and reasonably comfortable. Drivers often speak limited English and may not recognize English or Portuguese place names, so you're strongly advised to carry a bilingual map or name card for your destination in Chinese. The base charge is 10 patacas for the first 1¾ km (about 1¼ mi) and 1 pataca for each additional 250 meters. Drivers don't expect more than small change as a tip. Trips to Taipa incur a 5-pataca surcharge; trips to Coloane, 10 patacas. Expect to pay about 15 patacas for a trip from the terminal to downtown.

TOURS

Two basic tours of Macau are available. One covers mainland Macau, with stops at the Chinese border, Kun Iam Temple, St. Paul's, and Penha Hill; this lasts about 3½ hours. The other typical tour consists of a 2-hour trip across the bridge to the islands to see old Chinese villages, temples, beaches, the Jockey Club, and the international airport. Tours travel by bus or car, and prices vary between operators.

The most comfortable way to tour is by chauffeur-driven luxury car. A car with a maximum of four passengers goes for HK$200 an hour with Avis. You can also rent a regular taxi for touring, though few drivers speak English or know the place well enough to be good guides. Depending on your bargaining powers, the cost will be HK$60 or more per hour.

Most travelers going to Macau for the day book tours with travel agents in Hong Kong or before leaving home. If you prearrange in this way, you'll have transportation from Hong Kong to Macau all set, with your guide waiting in the arrival hall. There are many licensed tour operators in Macau; the ones we list focus on English-speaking visitors.

🚩 Tour Operators **Able Tours** also operates Grayline tours ⊠ Room 1015, Av. da Amizade, Ferry Terminal, Macau ☎ 725-813. **Estoril Tours** ⊠ Shop 333, Shun Tak Centre, 200 Connaught Rd., 3/F, Central, Hong Kong ☎ 2559-1028 🖷 2857-1830 ⊕ www.estoril-tours.com. **Sintra Tours** ⊠ Hotel Sintra, 58-62 Av. Dom João IV, Macau ☎ 710-361.

VISAS

No visa is required for Portuguese citizens or nationals of the United States, Canada, Australia, New Zealand, any European countries, and most Asian countries for visits of up to 20 days, or for Hong Kong residents for up to 90 days. Other nationals need visas, which can be obtained on arrival: these cost 100 patacas for individuals, 200 patacas for family groups, and 50 patacas for tour group members.

VISITOR INFORMATION

The Macau Government Tourist Office (MGTO) has an excellent Web site that provides information on the latest exhibitions and festivals, as well as cultural sights, restaurants, and hotels. The site also has an interactive city map. In 2003 the main office of the MGTO moved from the historic Largo do Senado to the modern Lam Van Lakes development area. There are information counters across Macau and at whichever location you find them at, the MGTO is exceptionally helpful and has brochures in a host of languages, on almost every aspect of Macau, as well as the usual maps and general information. They also have offices at the ferry and airport terminals.

Business visitors to Macau can get trade information from the Macau Trade and Investment Promotion Institute.

🚩 **Macau Government Tourist Office** (MGTO). ⊠ Macau Ferry Terminal, Macau ☎ 726-416 ⊕ www.macautourism.gov.mo ⊠ Macau International Airport, Arrival Hall ☎ 861-436 ⊠ Shun Tak Centre, 200 Connaught Rd., Sheung Wan, Hong Kong ☎ 2857-2287 🖷 2559-0698 ⊠ Hong Kong International Airport, Hong Kong ☎ 2769-7970 or 2382-7110 🖷 2261-2971. **Macau Trade and Investment Promotion Institute** ⊠ World Trade Centre, Av. da Amizade, 5/F, Macau ☎ 712-660 🖷 590-309 ⊕ www.ipim.gov.mo/pageen/home.asp.

SIDE TRIPS TO SOUTH CHINA

8

LUSCIOUS LINKS
Zhuhai Golden Gulf Golf Club,
the best course in South China ⇨*p.236*

RELAXING RETREAT
Zhong Shan Hot Spring Resort ⇨*p.233*

GUANGDONG'S FAVORITE SPORT
Shopping at Lowu Commercial City ⇨*p.244*

BEST CULTURAL PURSUIT
Guangdong Museum of Art ⇨*p.237*

BEST PLACE TO STROLL AND EXPLORE
Yuexiu Gongyuan ⇨*p.238*

BEST TRADITIONAL DINING
Banxi Restaurant ⇨*p.239*

LUXURY ON THE PEARL RIVER
White Swan Hotel ⇨*p.240*

Updated by
Sofia A.
Suárez

MAINLAND CHINA IS STILL a world apart from Hong Kong's glitz, high finance, and conspicuous consumerism. Hong Kong may be a part of China, but it's not until you cross the border into Guangzhou that you can say you've visited China proper.

Ever since the 7th century, foreign traders from Southeast Asia, India, and Arabia have come to the "tradesmen's entrance" at Guangzhou (Canton) at the mouth of the Pearl River delta. Because of the city's comparative isolation, local merchants didn't feel bound to obey the imperial ban on trade with Japan (according to the government, China needed nothing that any foreign "barbarian" had to offer). In the mid-16th century, when Portuguese trading adventurers arrived and offered to act as intermediaries between Guangzhou and the merchants of southern Japan (whose government had similarly banned trade with China), Cantonese businessmen were delighted to accept.

With Guangzhou's approval, the tiny peninsula of Macau was settled by the Portuguese and quickly became a great international port, eventually attracting traders from Europe and America. By the early 19th century, the Macau-based foreigners had gained a virtual monopoly on China's overseas trade.

Opium became the predominant commodity here, and the Chinese government's attempts to stamp it out only provoked the Opium War with Great Britain. Defeated by the British, the Chinese were forced to open up several coastal ports to Western merchants and cede to Britain nearby Hong Kong, which displaced Guangzhou as the mercantile hub of the delta.

In the 1980s China signed the agreements with Britain and Portugal that established the return to China of Hong Kong in 1997 and Macau in 1999. During the same period, investment poured across the borders into China as industrialists and property developers from Hong Kong and Macau transformed former farmland into booming new economic zones. History comes full circle: the fates of the two territories are once more bound up with that of South China.

Today, you'll find that South China's cities are developed, with luxury hotels, good restaurants, generally reliable transportation, and efficient communications. At the same time, this is an area in transition, with old buildings—however historic—succumbing to glass-and-steel skyscrapers, streets being dug up for new power lines, and growing industrial pollution that is quite visible.

So, what of the countryside, the "timeless China" promised in tour brochures? Sadly, a vast majority of the region has been converted into industrial suburbs, dormitory towns, and highways. You can still get an idea of the way it used to be, however, with glimpses of rural life off the main roads or in selected villages that are paid by the tour companies to preserve their traditional appearance and atmosphere.

A delta excursion is thus an opportunity to see China's past, present, and future at the same time. It's also a chance to experience Cantonese cuisine in Canton itself, and to visit the Shenzhen Bay theme parks that

8

Dining

When people outside China talk about Chinese food, they're usually referring to the cuisine of the Cantonese, who comprised the majority of migrants to the Americas, Australia, and Europe during the 19th and early 20th centuries. Forced to use their ingenuity to survive centuries of feudal repression and natural disasters, the Cantonese made use of roots, fungi, and every creature found on land and sea, developing what is arguably the most varied and imaginative cooking in the world. The results are at their most authentic in Guangdong, where eating is the favorite activity and restaurants are hubs of society. It's possible to have a Cantonese meal for 2 or 4 people, but ideally you'll have 12 or at least 8, so everyone can share the traditional 8 to 10 courses. The table is never bare, from opening courses of pickles, peanuts, and cold cuts to the fresh fruit signaling the end of the meal. Between the two you'll have mounds of steamed green vegetables (though vaguely identified, they will probably be Chinese cabbage, spinach, or kale), braised or minced pigeon, steamed or fried bean curd, luscious shrimp, mushrooms in countless forms, bird's nest soup (a delicacy made from the congealed saliva of sea swallows), egg-drop soup, fragrant pork or beef, and a large fish steamed in herbs, all accompanied by steamed rice, beer, soft drinks, and tea.

Golf

More affordable than the links at Hong Kong's prohibitively priced clubs, golf across the border is a big draw for Hong Kong residents. Since the 1980s, golf has become a popular elite sport in China, and that is true nowhere more than in the Pearl River delta, where dozens of full-service golf clubs with internationally recognized first-class courses have opened. Quite a few of them welcome nonmembers.

Shopping

If shopping is a sport in Hong Kong, it's an Olympic event in South China, where prices tend to be lower and bargaining is expected. You'll find clothing, copies of designer leather goods, souvenirs, and antiques. (But buy electronics at your own risk.) Expect to pay one-third to one-half of the asking price, so start low, and don't be afraid to walk away. They'll usually call you back. Many Hong Kongers, including the chief executive's wife, cross the border for tailoring services, which only require a few hours to a few days. Shenzhen is South China's shopping mecca, but quieter Zhuhai is gaining in popularity.

---

bring Chinese civilization into brilliant (if somewhat idealized) focus. Golfers can tee off at any one of the delta's many challenging courses, and shoppers can hunt for bargains, the main attractions for Hong Kong expats.

About the Restaurants

The restaurants of the Pearl River delta vary in atmosphere, but from the alleyway café to the banquet hall of a five-star hotel, many make use of only the freshest produce. Prices, of course, vary accordingly, but generally are much lower than in Hong Kong. Although price ranges are based on entrée prices, keep in mind that the Chinese style of dining is to order several dishes for a group and to share. A six-course meal in one of the hotels used by tour operators will cost the equivalent of US$15 per person (about HK$140), including unlimited beer and soft drinks. At top-ranked Guangzhou hotels the cost is about US$25 (HK$200).

WHAT IT COSTS In HK$				
	$$$$	$$$	$$	$	¢
AT DINNER	over 300	200–300	100–200	60–100	under 60

Prices are per person for a main course at dinner and do not include the customary 10% service charge.

About the Hotels

Tourists on arranged excursions to the Pearl River delta cannot always choose their own hotels, but those chosen are always among the best available. The growing number of independent travelers are usually businesspeople or golfers. If you are an independent traveler, be aware that although major hotels meet most international standards, staff members do not always speak English, so it's advisable to make reservations through a travel agent or hotel office in Hong Kong. In recent years there has been a large oversupply of rooms, and hotels have offered generous discounts. All the hotels we recommend have rooms with private baths. Restaurants in hotels and resorts are among the best in the region.

WHAT IT COSTS In HK$				
	$$$$	$$$	$$	$	¢
FOR 2 PEOPLE	over 3,000	2,100–3,000	1,100–2,100	700–1,100	under 700

Prices are for two people in a standard double room in high season.

ZHONGSHAN

Zhongshan, the county across the border from Macau, was originally known as Heungshan (Fragrant Mountain). The name was changed to Chung Shan (Central Mountain) in honor of Sun Yat-sen—Chung Shan was his pen name. Zhongshan is the pinyin transliteration of its name (pinyin is the system now most commonly used to romanize Chinese ideograms). The county covers 1,786 square km (689 square mi) of the fertile Pearl River delta and supports about 2.3 million people, many of whom are wealthy farmers who supply Macau with much of its fresh produce.

With substantial help from overseas Chinese investors, many new industries have been developed here in recent years. All those goods you purchase, from cheap commodities to high-tech electronics, that claim "Made in China" should probably more accurately read, "Made in the Pearl River delta." This region, comparable in size to Thailand, accounts annually for more than 30% of China's total trade. This productivity—and subsequent economic prosperity for all of those living here—contrasts starkly with Zhongshan's situation a century ago, when mandarins, or public officials, benefited from nature's bounty but the peasants who harvested it were kept in abject poverty. This was true in much of China, but in Zhongshan the downtrodden had a way out—crossing the border to Macau and taking a coolie ship to the railroads of California and the gold mines of Australia.

Tens of thousands of peasants left. Zhongshan's city fathers boast of the half million native sons now living in lands around the globe. Quite a number came back, though, either from a sense of patriotism or to show off their newly acquired wealth. Among these was Sun Yat-sen, born in Cuiheng, who went away to study medicine in Hawaii; he returned to China and led the movement to overthrow the Manchus, becoming known as the "Father of the Chinese Republic."

Cuiheng, where Sun Yat-sen was born in 1866, has a memorial park containing the town's attractions. The house that Sun built for his parents during a visit in 1892 is here, it's a fine example of China Coast architecture, with European-style verandas facing west. The **Sun Yat-sen Museum,** next to his parents' home, has rooms arranged around a patio with exhibits on Sun's life and times (labels are in English, Chinese, and Japanese). There are also videos about Sun and Zhongshan. ☎ 760/550–1691 ☞ Y20 ⊙ Daily 9–5.

Shiqi (formerly spelled Shekkei) is the capital of Zhongshan County and has been an important market center and inland port for 800 years. Today it's a convenient stopover on excursions to the delta. In the early 1990s, Shiqi was a picturesque port where a cantilever bridge over the Qi River was raised twice a day to allow small freighters to pass, but the old town has been all but obliterated by modern high-rises, and farms that once surrounded it are now covered with factories. Still, the **Sun Yat-sen Memorial Hall** and **Xishan Temple** are worth a visit—and the food here is exceptionally good.

Where to Stay

¢–$ 🏨 **Zhongshan International Hotel.** Topped with a revolving restaurant, this 20-story tower has become a landmark of downtown Shiqi. Rooms have unremarkable hotel furniture, but the suites, at least, are spacious. Breakfast is included, and the friendly staff will go out of their way to help you. ⊠ 142 Zhongshan Rd., Shiqi, Zhongshan 528400 ☎ 760/863–3388 🖶 760/863–3368 ⊕ www.zsih.com.cn ⇨ 358 rooms ♻ 3 restaurants, pool, hair salon, hot tub, massage, sauna, billiards, bowling, bar, dance club, video game room, laundry service ⊟ AE, MC, V ⓞ BP.

¢ 🏨 **Cuiheng Hotel.** Opposite the Sun Yat-sen Memorial Park, this hotel consists of low-rise wings and bungalows of an elegant contemporary design. There are gardens around the pool, a riding school next door, and a statue of Sun out front. ⊠ Cuiheng, Zhongshan 528454 ☎ 760/550–2668 🖶 760/550–3333 ⇨ 220 rooms ♻ 3 restaurants, pool, dance club ⊟ AE, V.

★ ¢ 🏨 **Zhong Shan Hot Spring Resort.** This vast complex consists of a charming compound of villas, which have pagoda roofs and Chinese antiques in some rooms. Villas are built around a traditional Chinese garden landscaped with classical pavilions and willow-screened ponds filled with

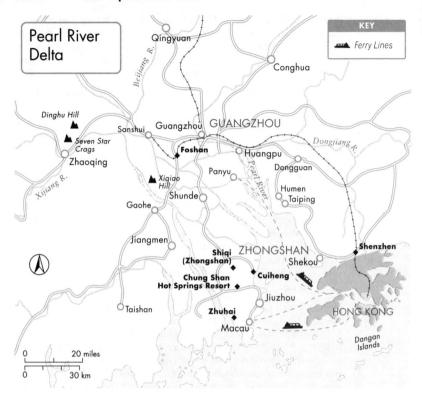

Pearl River Delta

KEY

⛴ Ferry Lines

Qingyuan

Conghua

Beijiang R.

Dinghu Hill ▲

▲ *Seven Star Crags*

○ *Zhaoqing*

Sanshui

Guangzhou **GUANGZHOU**

Dongjiang R.

Xijiang R.

▲ *Xiqiao Hill*

◆ **Foshan**

Huangpu

Panyu

Dongguan

Pearl River

Humen
Taiping

Gaohe

Shunde

Jiangmen

Shiqi (Zhongshan) ◆ **ZHONGSHAN**

Shekou

Shenzhen ◆

Shiqi (Zhongshan)

Cuiheng ◆

Chung Shan Hot Springs Resort ◆

Jiuzhou

HONG KONG

○ *Taishan*

Zhuhai ◆

Macau

Dangan Islands

0 ___ 20 miles

0 ___ 30 km

carp and lotus blossoms. The English-speaking staff is helpful, and there is a large Chinese restaurant (popular with tour groups) and a smaller Western restaurant. Outside, extensive grounds contain an impressive array of facilities, including the open-air hot springs, where you can take a soak. The hotel is 24 km (15 mi) from Macau, just outside Sanxiang. ⊠ *Macau–Shiqi Hwy., Sanxiang, Zhongshan 519015* ☎ *760/668–3888* 🖷 *760/668–3333* 🌐 *www.zshs.com* 🛏 *310 rooms* 👌 *2 restaurants, 2 18-hole golf courses, 4 tennis courts, pool, horseback riding, shops, Internet, business services* ⊟ *AE, MC, V.*

Sports & the Outdoors

GOLF ★ The **Chung Shan Hot Spring Golf Club** was the first course in China and is still considered one of the best. A half hour north of Macau, the par-71 course was designed by Arnold Palmer's company and opened in 1984, with Palmer among the first to try it out. A second 18-hole course of rolling hills and streams, designed by Jack Nicklaus, was added in 1993. The clubhouse, with gleaming mahogany paneling and elegant rattan furniture, has a bar, restaurant, sauna, and granite-walled pool, plus a pro shop with everything you'd expect to find in an American or Japanese club. Nonmembers are only allowed on weekdays, when they can enjoy a package rate of HK$600 that includes greens fees, caddy, locker rental, and lunch. Club rentals cost around HK$110 for 18 holes. Bookings, transport (via Macau or Jiuzhou), and visas can be arranged through the club's office in Hong Kong. ☒ *Sanxiang, Zhongshan* ☏ *Room 1403, 14/F, Tower 1, New World Tower, 18 Queen's Rd., Central, Hong Kong* ☎ *760/669–0055, 2521–0377 in Hong Kong* 📠 *760/ 668–3990, 2868–4642 in Hong Kong* ⊕ *www.cshsgc.com.cn.*

ZHUHAI

In 1980 Zhuhai was set up as one of China's first Special Economic Zones, which have special liberal economic laws to encourage foreign investment. The former agricultural town was rapidly developed and extended from 13 square km (5 square mi) to 121 square km (47 square mi), complete with a long coastline and many small offshore islands. It is now one of the cleanest and most congenial areas in China, thanks to its high-tech industrial base.

Zhuhai is made up of three main districts: Xiangzhou in the north, Jida in the east, and Gongbei, the main tourist area in the south. A walk or taxi ride from Macau, Zhuhai is a convenient entry point for China. Its shopping and restaurants have also made it an increasingly popular alternative to busy, dispersive Shenzhen for both Chinese and Western travelers. It's one of the best choices in South China for a day trip from Macau or Hong Kong.

Where to Stay

$–$$ 🏨 **Grand Bay View Hotel.** Sumptuously furnished, the rooms at this handsome hotel have soft beds and couches and a homier style—with colorful quilts and soft lighting—than you'll find in most South China hotels. It also has some of the zone's best nightlife and dining, as well as imaginative function areas that include a balcony overlooking the water and Macau. In addition to a disco, the Stargazer Nightclub has 20 private rooms for video karaoke. ☒ *Shui Wan Rd., Gongbei 519020* ☎ *756/887–7998* 📠 *756/887–8998* ⊕ *www.gbvh.com* 🛏 *273 rooms* ☖ *4 restaurants, in-room safes, minibars, cable TV with movies, pool, exercise equipment, gym, hot tub, massage, sauna, billiards, nightclub, Internet, business services* ▭ *AE, DC, MC, V.*

¢–$ 🏨 **Paradise Hill.** Looking like a belle epoque palace on the French Riviera, this hotel has a stunning white-and-cream stone facade, with balconies overlooking a garden that's terraced around fountains. A marble-clad atrium lobby and a grand marble staircase complete the rich touches. The rooms are tastefully decorated with glass-top coffee tables, potted flowers, and floor-to-ceiling windows. The health center is state-of-the-art. ☒ *193 Shi Ching Shan Rd., 519015* ☎ *756/333–7388* 📠 *756/333–3508, 853/552–739 Ext. 406 in Macau* ⊕ *www. paradisehillhotel.com* 🛏 *215 rooms* ☖ *7 restaurants, minibars, cable TV with movies, 2 tennis courts, 2 pools, gym, health club, hair salon, massage, sauna, business services* ▭ *AE, DC, MC, V.*

¢ 🏨 **Zhuhai Holiday Resort Hotel.** Expect modern, clean facilities in this resort set on a peaceful lake. Choose from regular hotel rooms or private villas, but whatever you choose, it will have an excellent water view. Service is attentive and friendly. ☒ *9 E. Shi Hua Rd., Ji Da 519015* ☎ *756/*

333–3838 🖶 *756/333–3311* ⊕ *www.zhuhai-holitel.com* ⤸ *500 rooms, 89 villas* ♨ *8 restaurants, 4 tennis courts, pool, massage, spa, bowling, Ping-Pong, bar, nightclub, video game room, shops, playground, dry cleaning, laundry service, business services, meeting rooms* ▭ *AE, DC, V.*

Sports & the Outdoors

GOLF   **Zhuhai Golden Gulf Golf Club,** one of Guangdong's newest, has an 18-hole
☺   and a 9-hole course designed by famous Scottish golfer Colin Montgomerie,
Fodor'sChoice   and ample practice facilities. The clubhouse has two restaurants, a pub,
★   locker rooms, and a pro shop. Even nongolfers and kids will enjoy the
country club, with pool, children's play area, juice bar, and spa. On-site
accommodations include a Thai-style golfer's lodge with 50 suites, and
villas scattered throughout the grounds. Greens fees inclusive of caddy,
cart, locker, and driving range are HK$762 on weekdays and HK$1,139
on weekends and holidays. ⊠ *Jinwan Ave., Golden Coast, Jinwan District* ☎ *756/763–1888, 2168–0691 in Hong Kong* 🖶 *756/763–1818, 2168–0822 in Hong Kong* ⊕ *www.zhggg.com.*

The lakeside **Zhuhai Wansheng Sports & Country Club** covers more than
700 acres with its shooting range, game farm, clubhouse, and challenging 18-hole golf course. The Moosehead Lounge occupies the main clubhouse along with a restaurant, a bar, a pool, and a health club. Most activities and amenities are priced individually. Other facilities include tennis (two courts), badminton, squash, boating, and fishing. ⊠ *Zhuhai Doumen County, Wushan Town, Sanli Village* ☎ *756/557–3888, 2827–0037 in Hong Kong* 🖶 *756/557–3388, 2827–7564 in Hong Kong.*

Shopping

One of China's antique-furniture restoration centers, Zhuhai has long been a destination for dealers and collectors. Now, more Hong Kong retailers are allowing customers to pick through their massive Zhuhai
★   warehouses, and will help arrange shipment. Some, like **Art Treasures Gallery** (⊠ G/F, 42 Hollywood Rd., Central, Hong Kong ☎ 2543–0430 🖶 2544–8365 ⊕ www.art-treasures-gallery.com), will even escort you from the Macau or Zhuhai border. Make an appointment through their Hong Kong showroom.

Near the Macau/Zhuhai border, the bustling **Gongbei Port Market** (⊠ Gongbei District) is a maze of shopping complexes and street stalls selling cheap clothing, fabrics, software (authenticity is not always guaranteed), ceramics, and antiques. Gongbei is a lively area worth a gander even for nonshoppers. It's open daily from 10 to 8.

GUANGZHOU

Guangzhou is still better known to foreigners as Canton, an English corruption of the Portuguese version of the Chinese name. The city has always benefited from its strategic location on the South China Coast, where it has been a major trading port for almost 2,000 years. Guangzhou received cargo from the Spice Islands (in what is now Indonesia), India, and the Middle East long before Europe knew that China existed, and it was the point of export for silk—centuries ago the city began holding semiannual fairs at which silk was bartered for spices, silver, and sandalwood. From the time the Portuguese settled Macau, Guangzhou was the prime meeting place of East and West. During the 19th century it was a business home for British, American, and European traders. Today, traders from all over the world flock to the Guangzhou Trade Fair twice a year, usually in April and October. Accommodations are usually scarce and most expensive during this period.

Guangzhou has long had a rebellious streak, and the Cantonese have frequently been at odds with the rulers in the north. Exposure to foreign ideas made them more independent, and it was no surprise that the 1911 revolution and the organization of the Chinese Communist Party both started here.

What to See

The **Chen Jia Ci** (Chen Family Institute) was built by the Chen clan late in the 19th century. It's an architectural masterpiece, with some magnificent porcelain friezes depicting the *Romance of Three Kingdoms* on the pavilion ridgepoles, and some intricately carved stone balustrades. ⊠ *7 Zhongshan Xi Lu* ☎ No phone ⊠ *Y10* ⊙ *Daily 8:30–5.*

★ Nestled among some of the city's splashiest condo complexes, northwest of Ersha Island, the **Guangdong Museum of Art** is billed as the largest museum of its kind in China. Specializing in contemporary Chinese art, the museum has 12 massive exhibition halls, including one devoted entirely to sculpture. The displays center on works of Chinese painters (working both here and overseas). ⊠ *13 Luhu Lu* ☎ *020/8735–1468* ⊠ *Y15* ⊙ *Tues.–Sun. 9–5.*

The 7th-century **Huaisheng Si Guang Ta** (Remember the Prophet Mosque) marks the site of the first mosque built in China. The current buildings were erected during the Qing dynasty. For centuries, the mosque's white-wall minaret was a beacon for ships. ⊠ *Guang Ta Lu* ☎ No phone ⊠ *Y12* ⊙ *Sat.–Thurs. 8–5, except holy days; no entry after 4:45* PM.

The Zen Buddhist **Liu Rong Si Hua Ta** (Temple of Six Banyans) was named for the trees that used to stand in its courtyard. Founded around AD 537, it is famous for its 184-foot pagoda, whose carved wooden roofs earned it the name "Flower Pagoda." ⊠ *Haizhu Bei Lu* ☎ No phone ⊠ *Y2* ⊙ *Daily 8–5.*

The **Nan Yue Wang Mu** (Museum and Tomb of the Southern Yue Kings) was uncovered in 1983 behind the China Hotel. Excavated treasures from the tomb include jade armor, pearl pillows, gem-encrusted crossbows, a bronze orchestra, and gold crowns buried with the king 2,000 years ago. ⊠ *867 Jiefang Bei Lu* ☎ *020/8666–4920* ⊠ *Y12* ⊙ *Daily 9:30–5:30.*

The **Nongmin Yundong Jiangxi Suo** (Peasant Movement Institute) is a monument to an early Communist organization. In 1924 Mao Zedong and his comrades set up a school in a Ming Dynasty Confucian Temple to teach their doctrine to peasant leaders from around the country. The classroom and Mao's spartan bedroom are preserved. ⊠ *42 Zhongshan Zi Lu* ☎ *020/8333–3936* ⊠ *Y2* ⊙ *Daily 10–6.*

Shamian (Sandbank Island) appeals to those who know something of its history: Western traders set up shop here when the island was a sand-bar in the Pearl River, linked to the city by bridges that closed at night. The traders built fine mansions, churches, and even a cricket field. Most buildings have been renovated to house government and business offices, hotels, and shops.

★ **Yuexiu Gongyuan** (Yuexiu Park) has man-made lakes, a swimming pool, Krupp cannons, and the 14th-century **Zhenhai Tower,** also known as the Five-Story Pagoda. The tower contains the **Guangzhou City Museum;** established in 1929, it's one of the oldest museums in China, showcasing the city's history from the neolithic period to the early 20th century. The legend regarding how goats were sent from heaven with gifts of cereals is depicted in the nearby **Statue of the Five Goats,** now a city symbol. Dr. Sun Yat-sen is, of course, honored in the city where he studied medicine and later celebrated the birth of the Chinese republic. The **Sun Zhong-shan Jinian Tang** (Sun Yat-sen Memorial Hall), built in 1931, contains a 5,000-seat auditorium. It stands at the foot of Yuexiu Mountain and is linked by stone steps with the Sun Yat-sen Monument at the top of the mountain. Records of Sun's political career are exhibited in a building complex to the west of the hall. ⊠ *Jiefang Bei Lu* ☎ *020/8354–1035 museum* 🚈 *Park Y6, museum Y10* ☉ *Park, daily 9–6; museum, daily 9–5.*

Where to Stay & Eat

The giant Guangzhou Trade Fair is held twice yearly, in April and October, attracting many visitors to the city from all over the world. Hotel occupancy and rates tend to go up accordingly—this is not the best time to visit the city for a leisure trip.

★ **$$–$$$** ✕ **The Connoisseur.** You could almost be in Regency France in the Garden Hotel's premier restaurant with its arched columns with gilded capitals, gold-framed mirrors, lustrous drapes, and immaculate table settings. And the food doesn't disappoint. A French chef is in charge, and the finest Continental fare is on the menu. ⊠ *Garden Hotel, 368 Huanshi Dong Lu* ☎ *020/8333–8989 Ext. 3962* ▭ *AE, DC, MC, V.*

$$–$$$ ✕ **Jewel of India.** This is Guangzhou's first Indian restaurant, and it serves some of the best curries you will find outside of Calcutta. The tandoori bread is made on the premises, and appetizers include the usual suspects from the south: samosas, pakoras, and some paneer (or cottage cheese–style dishes). And don't miss the kebabs, which range from lamb to vegetable. Their *chai,* or masala tea, is equally stupendous. ⊠ *30 Ti Yu Xi Lu* ☎ *020/8559–3882* ▭ *No credit cards.*

$$–$$$ ✕ **The Roof.** The China Hotel's fine-dining restaurant is tops in more than one sense: not only does it have wonderful food, but it also sits in understated splendor on the 18th floor, with panoramic views of night-time Guangzhou. The menu changes seasonally offering mostly Italian specialties, but there are also such staples as saddle of lamb marinated in mint and yogurt, fettuccine, scallops in saffron sauce, and prime cuts of U.S. beef. ⊠ *China Hotel, Liuhua Lu* ☎ *020/8666–6888 Ext. 71892* ▭ *AE, DC, MC, V* ☉ *Closed Sun. No lunch.*

$$–$$$ ✕ **Silk Road Grill Room.** As you'd expect from the superlative White Swan Hotel, the grill room is the ultimate in sophistication. It's furnished with brass fittings and big silver food covers, gleaming candlesticks, and crisp white linen. The service is impeccable, and the menu a fine selection of traditional French dishes. ⊠ *White Swan Hotel, 1 S. Shamian St., Shamian* ☎ *020/8188–6968* ▤ *AE, DC, MC, V* ☺ *No lunch.*

★ **$$** ✕ **Banxi Restaurant.** You may feel like you're entering a Taoist temple or private estate beautifully perched on the shore of Liwan Lake, but it's actually one of the city's most attractive traditional restaurants. Dining rooms of various sizes are spread out in rambling teahouses, one of them built on a floating houseboat. Between are landscaped gardens networked by zigzag paths over bridges, across ornamental lakes, and through bamboo groves. The food is just as good as the setting, with dishes such as scallop and crab soup, and quail eggs cooked with shrimp roe on a bed of green vegetables among the huge selection. ⊠ *151 Longjin Xi Lu* ☎ *020/8181–5718* ▤ *AE, MC, V.*

$$ ✕ **Guangzhou Restaurant.** This is probably the busiest Cantonese restaurant in town, serving a total of 10,000 diners a day. The setting is classic Chinese, with courtyards of flowery bushes surrounded by dining rooms of various sizes ranged along arcaded corridors. The house specialties include abalone sprinkled with 24-carat gold flakes, Eight Treasures (including game, chicken, ham, and mushrooms) served in winter melons carved to make a bowl, duck feet stuffed with shrimp, roast sliced goose, and Wenchang chicken (a stew made with chicken, chicken liver, and Chinese ham served with vegetables). Note that the restaurant closes at 9 PM. ⊠ *2 Wenchang Nan Lu* ☎ *020/8188–8388* ▤ *AE, DC, MC, V.*

$–$$ ✕ **Chiu Chou City.** One of the best places for authentic food from the Shantou area is this restaurant in the Landmark Hotel Shenzhen. It has a large main room and several private rooms, which are invariably packed for lunch and dinner. The house special is Chow goose, served as sliced meat or cooked in its own blood and dipped into a sauce of white vinegar and chopped garlic. ⊠ *Landmark Hotel Shenzhen, Qiao Guang Lu, Haizhu Sq.* ☎ *020/8335–5988* ▤ *AE, DC, MC, V.*

¢–$$ ✕ **Lai Wan Market.** This is a wonderful re-creation of the old Canton waterfront, with booths shaped like the flower boats that used to offer food, drink, opium, and girls, and small wooden stools at low counters. Lai Wan is known for its dim sum and two kinds of rice, one made with pork, beef, fish, and seafood, the other with fish, beef, and pork liver. ⊠ *Garden Hotel, 368 Huanshi Dong Lu* ☎ *020/8333–8989 Ext. 3923* ▤ *AE, DC, MC, V.*

¢–$ ✕ **Milano's Italian Restaurant.** A favored hangout of expatriates in town—and open until midnight every night—it's a relaxing place to visit. The bread is homemade, and you'll find the best pizzas in town here. The lasagna may well remind you of your mom's. ⊠ *103 Xin Chen Beijie, off Tian He Dong Lu* ☎ *020/3881–0594* ▤ *No credit cards.*

$$ ▦ **Dong Fang Hotel.** This luxury complex is across from Liuhua Park, which has the largest artificial lake in the city. The rooms, which were renovated in 2004, are modern and spacious, and include 12 deluxe rooms on a floor designed for women, and two executive floors. The elegant, golden-hue lobby has an interesting selection of Chinese antiques and carpets in its shopping concourse. The restaurants serve a variety of Chinese regional cuisines as well as Western and Southeast Asian dishes. ⊠ *120*

Liuhua Rd., 510016 ☎ *020/8666–9900, 2528–0555 in Hong Kong* 🖷 *020/8666–2775, 2510–0991 in Hong Kong* ⊕ *www.dongfanghotel-gz.com* 🖵 *911 rooms* ⚘ *8 restaurants, tennis court, pool, health club, hair salon, massage, sauna, recreation room, shops, Internet, business services, meeting rooms, travel services* ▭ *AE, DC, MC, V.*

★ $$ 🏨 **White Swan Hotel.** The first international hotel in town occupies a marvelous site on historic Shamian Island, beside the Pearl River. The luxury complex is surrounded by banyan trees and a landscaped pool with a jogging track nearby. Rooms have replicas of Chinese antique furniture and porcelain. Even if you don't stay here, pop into the lobby to see the spectacular indoor waterfall. The hotel also offers a Pearl River dinner cruise on Friday and Saturday nights for Y180. ⊠ *1 S. Shamian St., 510133* ☎ *020/8188–6968, 2524–0192 in Hong Kong* 🖷 *020/8186–1188, 2877–0811 in Hong Kong* ⊕ *www.whiteswanhotel.com* 🖵 *843 rooms* ⚘ *9 restaurants, refrigerators, cable TV, driving range, 10 tennis courts, 2 pools, gym, health club, hair salon, hot tub, massage, sauna, steam room, squash, bar, dance club, nightclub, shop, business services, meeting room, travel services* ▭ *AE, DC, MC, V.*

☊ $–$$ 🏨 **China Marriott Hotel.** This vast complex opposite the Trade Fair Exhibition Hall is favored by business travelers. It is conveniently located and has executive floors with business-center services, as well as plenty of entertainment options. The hotel also houses Guangzhou's Hard Rock Cafe, a hot spot for the city's night owls. ⊠ *Liuhua Lu, 510015* ☎ *020/8666–6888, 2724–4622 in Hong Kong* 🖷 *020/8667–7288, 2721–0741 in Hong Kong* ⊕ *www.marriott.com* 🖵 *1,013 rooms, 168 suites* ⚘ *4 restaurants, room service, in-room data ports, in-room safes, some kitchens, minibars, refrigerators, cable TV, pool, health club, hair salon, hot tub, sauna, bowling, theater, shops, playground, dry cleaning, laundry service, Internet, business services* ▭ *AE, DC, MC, V.*

$–$$ 🏨 **Garden Hotel.** In Guangzhou's upmarket northern section, this hotel has spectacular gardens, including an artificial hill with a waterfall and pavilions. Antiques and modern artwork decorate the complex, which also includes apartments, offices, and a convention center. The excellent Western and Eastern dining options include Carousel, a revolving restaurant on the 30th floor. ⊠ *368 Huanshi Dong Lu, 510064* ☎ *020/8333–8989* 🖷 *020/8335–0467* ⊕ *www.gardenhotel-guangzhou.com* 🖵 *1,057 rooms, 63 suites* ⚘ *11 restaurants, 2 tennis courts, pool, health club, hair salon, squash, dance club, shops, dry cleaning, laundry service, business services, travel services* ▭ *AE, DC, MC, V.*

$–$$ 🏨 **Guangdong International Hotel.** This urban landmark is a spectacular 80-story complex with a hotel on top—next to a complex with 14 restaurants and lounges, shops, and banquet halls. The rooms here have some of the best views in Guangzhou: obviously the higher you go the better the vista. There are extensive recreation facilities. ⊠ *339 Huanshi Dong Rd., 510098* ☎ *020/8331–1888* 🖷 *020/8331–1666* ⊕ *www.gitic.com.cn* 🖵 *420 rooms, 282 suites* ⚘ *5 restaurants, tennis court, pool, gym, health club, hot tub, sauna, steam room, bowling, bar, lobby lounge, shop, business services* ▭ *AE, DC, MC, V.*

¢–$$ 🏨 **Ramada Pearl Hotel.** In the eastern part of the city, on the Pearl River, the Ramada is a full-service Western-style hotel. Ask for a room overlooking the river. It benefits from its proximity (5 km [3 mi]) to the East Railway Station, a terminus for Hong Kong trains. ⊠ *9 Ming Yue Yi Rd., 510600* 🕾 *020/8737–2988* 🖷 *020/8737–7481* ⊕ *www. ramadainternational.com* 🛏 *330 rooms* ⟨ *3 restaurants, in-room safes, some kitchens, minibars, some refrigerators, cable TV, driving range, tennis court, pool, pub, dance club, babysitting, meeting room, travel services* ⊟ *AE, DC, MC, V.*

¢–$ 🏨 **Holiday Inn Guangzhou City Centre.** You'll feel at home in the familiar setting of the Holiday Inn, conveniently located in the financial district. The rooms are done in subdued neutral colors, with soft headboards, comfortable sitting areas, and wooden bureaus like those in Holiday Inns worldwide. There's an exhibition center and an 500-seat cinema in the same complex. ⊠ *28 Guang Ming Rd., Hanshi Dong, 510095* 🕾 *020/ 6128–6868* 🖷 *020/8775–3126* ⊕ *www.guangzhou.holiday-inn.com* 🛏 *430 rooms* ⟨ *4 restaurants, in-room data ports, in-room safes, refrigerators, cable TV, pool, gym, health club, hair salon, hot tub, massage, sauna, steam room, badminton, cinema, shops, babysitting, Internet, airport shuttle* ⊟ *AE, DC, MC, V.*

Sports & the Outdoors

GOLF The **Guangzhou Luhu Golf & Country Club** occupies 180 acres of Luhu Park. Forty minutes from the Guangzhou East train station and 20 minutes from Baiyun Airport, it's a convenient diversion for golfing visitors. The 6,820-yard, 72-par course was designed by Dave Thomas, and the club has a 75-bay driving range and fully equipped clubhouse. Members' guests and those from affiliated clubs pay HK$600 greens fees for 18 holes on weekdays, HK$1,200 on weekends. Nonmembers pay HK$800 to HK$1,400, respectively. The club is managed by Hong Kong–based CCA International and is a member of the International Associate Club network. ⊠ *Luijing Rd., Luhu Park* 🕾 *020/8350–7777, 2317–1933 in Hong Kong* 🖷 *020/8359–6698* ⊕ *www.luhugolf.com.*

About 60 minutes outside of Guangzhou, **Dongguan Hillview Golf Club** is worth visiting if only for the view of hills and lakes. Veteran Jim Engh designed both par-72, 18-hole courses, which are maintained to international standards. Greens fees are HK$500 on weekdays, and HK$1,000 on weekends and holidays, with an additional HK$110 for a caddy, HK$220 for a two-person cart, and HK$30 for a locker. The club is approximately the same distance from Shenzhen. ⊠ *Ying Bi Da Dao, Fucheng District* 🕾 *0769/220–9998, 2527–3613 in Hong Kong* 🖷 *0769/ 225–9998, 2866–9082 in Hong Kong* ⊕ *www.hillviewgolf.com.*

FOSHAN

Foshan (Buddha Hill), named for three Buddha statues excavated there in AD 628, holds historical significance as one of China's ancient cities. It was once a town of artisans—and you can still find ceramics shops and sculptors here—but the 30-minute drive along the expressway from Guangzhou is now lined with drab, Communist-style housing blocks and high-rise factories instead of handicrafts markets. Since it's so close to Guangzhou, which has some fine hotels, there is no compelling reason to stay overnight in Foshan.

Foshan might seem in danger of becoming a concrete extension of the great port, but happily the legacy of the past is preserved in the **Zu Miao** (Ancestral Temple), with its brilliantly decorated prayer halls and ridge-pole frieze containing thousands of figures, birds, animals, and tiny pavilions. The complex contains the **Wanfutai Chinese Opera** theater, which has the oldest surviving wooden stage in China. Figurines and other craft items are sold in the spacious courtyard. ⊠ *21 Zumiao Lu* ☎ *0757/229–3723* ⊙ *Daily 8:30–10:30.*

You can browse and buy crafts at the **Renshou Si** (Benevolent Longevity Temple). Part of this former Ming monastery has been preserved, while the **Foshan Folk Arts Center** occupies the rest of the complex. Intricate paper cutouts made by hand are sold at extremely reasonable prices, as are Chinese lanterns, fish-bone carvings, and other handicrafts. ⊠ *Renmin Lu* ☎ *No phone* ⊙ *Daily 8–6.*

SHENZHEN

Shenzhen (Shumchun in Cantonese) was just a farming village across the border from Hong Kong until it was designated a Special Economic Zone in the late 1970s and became the first "instant China" excursion for foreign travelers. As one of the fastest-growing towns in China, it jumped from a population of 20,000 in 1979 to well over 4 million today and is aspiring to become the next Hong Kong by 2010. It has its own stock exchange, one of the highest gross domestic products in China, and a tightly packed garden of skyscrapers—but it also has all the attendant pollution. Most visitors to Shenzhen are Hong Kong residents on business or family holidays, golfing, shopping, and relaxing in lavish but moderately priced resorts. The most popular sights are a series of theme parks near Shenzhen Bay.

What to See

Window of the World is Shenzhen's largest tourist attraction, where the world's most famous natural and man-made landmarks have been recreated in miniature (the pyramids of Egypt, the Grand Canyon, the Taj Mahal, the Sydney Opera House, etc.), with associated rides and performances. It's best seen at night, when everything is lighted up. ⊠ *Shenzhen Bay* ☎ *0755/2660–8000* ⊠ *Y100* ⊙ *Daily 8–10.*

Jin Xiu Zhong Hua (Splendid China) replicates the major historical and geographical sights of China on a scale of 1:15. Elaborate and slightly tacky sculpted scenery peopled by 50,000 pottery figures is laid out along winding paths. ⊠ *Shenzhen Bay* ☎ *0755/2660–0626* ⊠ *Y70* ⊙ *Daily 8:30–5:30.*

Adjoining Splendid China is **Zhong Hua Minzu Wen Hua Cun** (China Folk Culture Villages), where China's different ethnic minorities are represented by people in traditional costumes making local crafts and performing songs and dances. There is a grand stage show and parade at night. ⊠ *Shenzhen Bay* ⊠ *Y70* ⊙ *Daily 8–5.*

Where to Stay & Eat

$$–$$$ ✕ **Jin Guan Cheng.** The specialty at this Szechuan restaurant is *huoguo*, or hot pot, which seems to contain everything but the kitchen sink—

from pig's brain to pork liver to duck tongue. If you're adventurous, it's worth trying since most of the ingredients come from Szechuan, which is one reason why transplants hailing from the Western province flock to the restaurant. Beware: Szechuan food is quite spicy. The restaurant is cozy, with blond-wood paneling and basketwork lanterns. Two large stone murals of the Chengdu region grace the walls. Note that reservations, which are recommended, should be made via fax. ⊠ *2/F, Hong-gui Bldg., 2068 Honggui Rd.* ☎⊟ *0755/2586–5666* ⊟ *No credit cards.*

¢–$$ ✕ **Muslim Restaurant.** The proprietor of this interesting restaurant hails from Ningxia, one of China's autonomous Muslim regions. Most of the main-course options include lamb; a favorite is *shouzhua yangrou,* or baby lamb poached in water and served with a dish of rock salt. If you give the restaurant a day's notice, the chef will prepare a roasted whole lamb, which serves six. All of the meals are prepared in accordance to halal standards. ⊠ *2013 Wenjin South Rd.* ☎ *0755/8223–5467, or 0755/ 8222–8207* ⊟ *No credit cards.*

¢–$ ✕ **Long Ji Guilin Mifen.** This inexpensive noodle joint near the Landmark Hotel Shenzhen is an authentic look at how the 1.3 billion Chinese citizens usually dine. The menu is only in Chinese—your safest bet is to point at a neighbor's meal and nod your head in approval. ⊠ *3010 Nanhu Rd.* ☎ *No phone* ⊟ *No credit cards.*

★ $–$$ 🏨 **Shangri-La Hotel.** Next to the train station, in the busiest section of Shenzhen, this is the plushest hotel in town. The rooms are large, with comfortable beds and subtle lighting. The restaurants are some of the best in town; Hong Kong shoppers break for the buffet lunch at Tiara (Y188 excluding drinks), while Henry J. Bean's Bar & Grill is a hangout for homesick Western expatriates. ⊠ *East Side Railway Station, 1002 Jianshe Rd., 518001* ☎ *0755/8233–0888, 2331–6688 in Hong Kong* 🖷 *0755/8233–9878, 2331–6699 in Hong Kong* ⊕ *www.shangri-la. com* ⇋ *553 rooms* ♻ *6 restaurants, room service, some in-room data ports, in-room safes, minibars, cable TV with movies, pool, gym, hair salon, hot tub, massage, sauna, steam room, bar, shops, dry cleaning, laundry service, concierge floor, Internet, business services, meeting rooms* ⊟ *AE, DC, MC, V.*

¢ 🏨 **Holiday Inn Donghua Shenzhen.** A good choice if you're catching a flight at Shenzhen's busy international airport or want reasonable lodging, the hotel is about 40 minutes from the border, within minutes of the Shekou Ferry Pier and high-tech zone. Book a room with a bay view in the 28-story shiny glass tower. ⊠ *Nanyou Rd., Nanshan District, 518054* ☎ *0755/2641–6688, 800/965–888 in Hong Kong* 🖷 *0755/2664–5282* ⊕ *www.ichotelsgroup.com* ⇋ *231 rooms, 62 suites* ♻ *2 restaurants, coffee shop, in-room safes, minibars, refrigerators, cable TV with movies, indoor pool, gym, health club, hair salon, hot tub, massage, sauna, steam room, billiards, bar, pub, babysitting, laundry facilities, Internet, business services, travel services, no-smoking rooms* ⊟ *AE, DC, MC, V.*

¢ 🏨 **Landmark Hotel Shenzhen.** Close to the train station, the Landmark is popular with Hong Kong business travelers. The four-story atrium gives the lobby a spacious, opulent feeling typical of China's flashiest hotels. The Chinese restaurants are particularly good. The hotel's nightspot, Hollywood, is a glitzy combination of a pub, a disco, and a karaoke lounge. ⊠ *3018 Nanhu Rd., 518001* ☎ *0755/8217–2288, 2375–6580 in Hong Kong* 🖷 *0755/8229–0473, 2730–6871 in Hong Kong* ⊕ *www.szlandmark.com.cn* ⇌ *351 rooms* ⚲ *3 restaurants, in-room safes, minibars, cable TV, pool, exercise equipment, gym, hair salon, hot tub, massage, sauna, steam room, bar, nightclub, shops* ▭ *AE, DC, MC, V.*

Sports & the Outdoors

GOLF **Mission Hills Golf Club** is Asia's largest golf resort, with 10 18-hole courses, all designed by well-known professional players. It has already hosted the World Cup of Golf, and drew crowds again for the Tiger Woods's Mission Hills China Challenge. Adjoining the clubhouse are basketball, tennis, and squash courts, a variety of restaurants, and an indoor-outdoor pool. For nonmembers, greens fees are HK$1,100 on weekdays and HK$1,650 on weekends. Caddies are HK$110 and carts cost HK$220. For more details contact the club's Hong Kong office. ⊠ *Mission Hills Rd., Guanlan Town* ⌖ *29/F, 9 Queen's Rd., Central, Hong Kong* ☎ *2973–0303, 2826–0288 for reservations* 🖷 *2869–9632* ⊕ *www.missionhillsgroup.com.*

Just across the border between Hong Kong and Shenzhen, the **Sand River Golf Club** can be the quickest golf course to reach from Hong Kong if there's no delay at immigration. Next door to the Window of the World park, it has courses designed by Gary Player, one of which has 9 holes and is floodlighted. It also has a large driving range, a fishing lake, and various resort facilities. Greens fees for visitors are HK$400 weekdays and HK$600 weekends for 9 holes, HK$800 weekdays and HK$1,200 weekends for 18 holes. ⊠ *1 Bai Shi Rd., Nanshan District* ⌖ *19/F, SPA Centre, 55 Lockhart Rd., Wanchai, Hong Kong* ☎ *800/938–079* 🖷 *800/938–080* ⊕ *www.sandrivergolfclub.com.*

Shopping

Shopping in Shenzhen, just 40 minutes away by train from Hong Kong, is immensely popular. A series of pedestrian bridges near the train station will take you straight into **Luohu Shangye Cheng** (Lowu Commercial City), the place for tailors, fabrics, bags, shoes, jewelry, home furnishings, souvenirs, and more. Although Shenzhen now has many other shopping hubs, this is still the best one-stop shop. Visit the tailor first, then rest your feet while you wait at one of the many restaurants inside the building that serve delicious Cantonese cuisine, including fresh dim sum. You can even treat yourself to a massage or pedicure, all under the same roof. Be wary of pickpockets, as you would be in any major city. ⊠ *East Side Railway Station* ☉ *Daily 10:30–8:30.*

SOUTH CHINA A TO Z

To research prices, get advice from other travelers, and book travel arrangements, visit www.fodors.com.

AIR TRAVEL

China Southern has five daily flights between Hong Kong and Guangzhou's Baiyun Airport; the trip takes about 40 minutes, and the round-trip fare is about HK$1,360 (plus a departure tax of HK$120 from Hong Kong, Y90 from Guangzhou).

☒ Carrier China Southern Airlines ☎ 2973-3733 ⊕ www.cs-air.com.

BOAT TRAVEL

CKS (Chu Kong Passenger Transport Co.) catamarans make seven round-trips daily between the China Ferry Terminal in Kowloon and Zhongshan Harbor, close to Shiqi, between 8 AM and 8 PM. The last boat of the day, which departs Zhongshan at 8 PM, arrives at the Macau Ferry Terminal on Hong Kong Island. The trip takes 75 to 90 minutes and costs HK$189 for economy, HK$199 for first class, or HK$219 for VIP class (a cabin with four to six people).

CKS schedules about 14 round-trips per day to the Jiuzhou Harbor near Zhuhai. Its fast, modern catamaran ferries depart regularly daily from the China Ferry Terminal in Kowloon between 7:30 AM and 5:30 PM, and from the Macau Ferry Terminal on Hong Kong Island between 8:40 AM and 9:30 PM. The last boat departs Jiuzhou at 9:30 PM. A one-way ticket costs HK$165 to HK$205 depending on class, and the trip takes about 70 minutes.

TurboJet ferries for Guangzhou depart from the China Ferry Terminal in Kowloon daily at 7:30 AM and 2 PM. Return ferries depart from the East River Guangzhou Ferry Terminal daily at 10:30 AM and 4:30 PM. The journey takes about two hours and costs HK$198 for economy, HK$293 for first class, or HK$1,758 for a VIP cabin (six seats) each way.

TurboJet ferries also make a pleasant, one-hour trip to Fuyong Ferry Terminal, near Shenzhen Airport, nine times daily with departures between 7:30 AM and 5:30 PM from both the Macau Ferry Terminal on Hong Kong Island and the Hong Kong China Ferry Terminal in Kowloon. The last return TurboJet leaves Shenzhen at 7:45 PM; fares are HK$189, HK$289, or HK$1,734 each way depending on class. For fractionally less, jet cat ferries depart frequently for Shekou from both sides of the harbor.

☒ Ferry Companies Chu Kong Passenger Transport Co. (CKS) ☎ 2857-6625 ⊕ www.cksp.com.hk **TurboJet** ☎ 2859-3333 for information, 2921-6688 for bookings ⊕ www.turbojet.com.hk

☒ Ferry Terminals Hong Kong China Ferry Terminal ✉ 140 Canton Rd., Tsim Sha Tsui, Hong Kong. **Macau Ferry Terminal** ✉ 3/F, Shun Tak Centre, 202 Connaught Rd. Central, Sheung Wan, Hong Kong ☎ 2547-5265.

BUS TRAVEL

China Travel Service (CTS) makes numerous round-trips daily, servicing Hong Kong and South China. Major hotels are usually pickup/drop-off points. Costs tend to be below HK$200 each way.

If you want something a bit more adventurous than a hotel car or tour bus, minibuses headed for the Foshan stop at Guangzhou's major bus stations, and only cost Y8 to Y12.

☒ China Travel Service (CTS) ☎ 2789-5401 ⊕ www.chinatravelone.com.

MONEY MATTERS

Units of Chinese renminbi (RMB) are known as yuan (Y) and may also be referred to as *kuài* (kwye). You can easily change foreign currency at hotels and banks in Guangdong. Although the Hong Kong dollar is widely accepted as a second currency in South China, you will always receive change in RMB. The Hong Kong dollar is worth slightly more than the RMB. Hong Kongers will not accept RMB, so while it's not essential to spend all of your mainland currency before returning to Hong Kong, it's not a good idea to carry a lot of RMB back to Hong Kong since you'll only lose money to the banks changing it to Hong Kong dollars.

PASSPORTS & VISAS

You'll need a valid passport *and* tourist visa to visit mainland China (anything other than Hong Kong or Macau). Unless you are a U.K. citizen, you can get "border visas" on arrival in Shenzhen and Zhuhai, but the office is often overrun on weekends, so it may be easier to get a standard travel visa either in your home country before you leave for Asia or to get the visa in Hong Kong. At the Lowu border in Shenzhen, everyone *except* people carrying U.K. passports can get visas on arrival. Such visas are valid for five days and restrict travel to Shenzhen. They cost HK$150, and a photo is not necessary. The office is on the second floor of the train station. Ask a police officer for directions as it's not well marked.

The cost for a standard visa for travel to China depends on how quickly you have it issued. A single-entry visa costs HK$210 with a three-day processing time, HK$360 with a two-day wait, or HK$480 for pickup in one working day. Visas are available in Hong Kong from the CTS and from most travel agents (expect a service charge), and require one passport-size photo. FYI: the Chinese, as a rule, are quite wary of anyone who is a journalist or works in publishing or the media. Most Americans and Canadians traveling for pleasure who work in these professions often enter "teacher" under "Occupation" on their visa permit.

TOUR PACKAGES

Although there is no shortage of transportation options in and out of Guangdong, you may have trouble finding travel operators who speak English. Ask your hotel concierge for the latest schedules and prices, or call the China Travel Service (CTS). CTS is the most convenient place to book tickets to China, though you'll pay a service charge. Bookings can also be made through their Web site.

The vast majority of travelers on side trips to other parts of South China take a guided tour of one or two days. The cost of these tours will include your visa, and CTS will make the arrangements, so it's necessary to book at least two or three days in advance to accommodate the waiting period to obtain a visa. Although transportation in the region has greatly improved, it is still much easier for foreigners to get around this part of China with a guide. Tours offered by CTS and Hong Kong travel agents are designed to fit into any reasonable schedule.

By far the most popular tour option for a quick trip into South China is Zhongshan, sometimes called a day trip to Lotus Mountain, a full and diverse (if rather tiring) day trip. All one-day Zhongshan tours begin with an early departure from Hong Kong to Macau and a bus transfer to the border at Gongbei, in the Zhuhai Special Economic Zone. From here itineraries vary, but all spend time in Cuiheng. A six-course lunch, with free beer and soft drinks, is taken in Shiqi, often at the Chung Shan Resort, or in one of the faux Ching Dynasty hotels of Zhuhai. Completing the itinerary is a visit to a "typical" farming village (kept traditional for tourists). Tours return to Hong Kong in the late afternoon via Zhongshan Harbor, taking about 10 hours total. The cost is around HK$1,240 per person.

Another well-established day trip takes in Shenzhen, immediately across the border from Hong Kong. This usually begins with a coach trip to Shenzhen and visits to the Splendid China theme park, the adjoining China Folk Culture Villages, a Hakka village, a kindergarten, and a market. The cost is HK$730 to HK$880.

🚩 **China Travel Service (CTS)** ✉ 1/F, Alpha House, 27-33 Nathan Rd., Tsim Sha Tsui, Hong Kong ☎ 2851-1700 for general enquiries, 2315-7188 for visa information ⊕ www. ctshk.com.

TRAIN TRAVEL

Ten intercity trains depart daily for Guangzhou from Hong Kong's Kowloon–Canton Railway (KCR) Station from 7:30 AM to 6:40 PM, calling at Dongguan, Guangzhou East, Foshan, and Zhaoqing. The Hong Kong–Guangzhou leg takes about 1 hour and 40 minutes, and the last train back to Hong Kong from Guangzhou leaves at 9 PM. Tickets cost HK$180 to HK$230 depending on the class, and are available from railroad stations, as well as at Mong Kok, Kowloon Tong, and Sha Tin MTR stations.

For trips to Shenzhen, the KCR's East Rail service runs from Kowloon Station to Lowu throughout the day (first train 5:30 AM, last train back to Hong Kong at 1 AM). The trip takes about 40 minutes. The fare is HK$66 first class and HK$33 economy, which is comfortable enough at nonpeak times. A word of warning: it can take up to 3 hours to go through immigration during Chinese holidays and on weekends. However, at nonholiday times it usually never takes more than an hour. Nonetheless, bring portable music and reading materials.

🚩 **Kowloon–Canton Railway (KCR)** ✉ Hung Hom Station, Hung Hom, Hong Kong ☎ 2929-3399 for information, 2947-7888 for Intercity Passenger Services Hotline ⊕ www.kcrc.com.

UNDERSTANDING
HONG KONG

Fast Facts

Name in local language: Xianggang
National anthem: *Yiyongjun Jinxingqu (Righteous and Brave Soldiers' Marching Tune)*
Type of government: Limited democracy
Administrative divisions: None, special administrative region of China
Constitution: Basic Law approved in March 1990 by China's National People's Congress is Hong Kong's "miniconstitution"
Legal system: Based on English common law
Suffrage: Direct election 18 years of age; universal for permanent residents living in the territory of Hong Kong for the past seven years; indirect election limited to about 100,000 members of functional constituencies and an 800-member election committee drawn from broad regional groupings, municipal organizations, and central government bodies
Legislature: Unicameral Legislative Council or LEGCO (60 seats; 30 indirectly elected by functional constituencies, 24 elected by popular vote, and 6 elected by an 800-member election committee; members serve four-year terms)
Population: 7.4 million
Population density: 18,393 people per square mi
Median age: Female 37.7, male 37.1
Life expectancy: Female: 82.8, male: 77.2
Infant mortality rate: 5.6 deaths per 1,000 live births
Literacy: 94%
Language: Chinese (Cantonese), English; both are official
Ethnic groups: Chinese 95%; other 5%
Religion: Mixture of local religions 90%; Christian 10%

By following the concept of "one country, two systems," you don't swallow me up nor I you.
—Deng Xiaoping, Chinese Premier

Geography & Environment

Land area: 1,042 square km (402 square mi), six times the size of Washington, DC
Coastline: 733 km (455 mi) in South China Sea
Terrain: Hilly to mountainous with steep slopes; lowlands in north; highest point: Tai Mo Shan 3,143 feet
Islands: More than 200
Natural resources: Deepwater harbor; feldspar
Natural hazards: Occasional typhoons
Environmental issues: Air and water pollution from rapid urbanization

Economy

Currency: Hong Kong dollar (HKD)
Exchange rate: HK$7.80 = $1
GDP: HK$1.5 trillion ($198.5 billion)
Per capita income: HK$193,027 ($24,750)
Inflation: -1.9%
Unemployment: 7.4%
Workforce: 3.5 million; wholesale and retail trade, restaurants, and hotels 31%; other 25%; financing, insurance, and real estate 13%; community and social services 12%; manufacturing 6%; transport and communications 6%; construction 5%

Debt: $49.5 billion
Major industries: Banking, clocks, clothing, electronics, plastics, shipping, textiles, tourism, toys, watches
Agricultural products: Fish, fresh vegetables, pork, poultry
Exports: $200.3 billion
Major export products: Apparel, electrical machinery and appliances, footwear, plastics, precious stones, textiles, toys, watches and clocks

Export partners: China 34%; United States 19.5%; United Kingdom 5.5%; Japan 4.8%
Imports: $208.1 billion
Major import products: Electrical equipment, foodstuffs, machinery, petroleum, plastics, transport equipment
Import partners: China 37.5%; Japan 12.2%; Taiwan 7.3%; United States 6.2%; Singapore 5.3%; South Korea 5%

Political Climate

China dissolved the legislature set up by the British and appointed a chief executive when it regained control over Hong Kong in 1997. In 1998 pro-democracy parties took a majority of the 20 directly elected seats in elections for a new legislature that is only partly democratically controlled. Beijing hasn't hesitated to act authoritatively however, nullifying Hong Kong court rulings and ignoring calls for universal suffrage. In the 2000 elections, pro-democracy parties won a majority of the directly elected legislative council seats again. Hong Kong's main political parties continue to be the pro-democracy Democratic Party, the pro-business Liberal Party, and the Beijing-oriented Democratic Alliance for the Betterment of Hong Kong.

The destiny of Hong Kong is now the same as the destiny of China. There is no escaping.

—T L Tsim

Did You Know?

• With 80,000 people living in an area measuring 1 square km (½ square mi), Ap Lei Chau, off the southwest side of Hong Kong Island is the most densely populated island in the world.

• With 1.8 mi of moving walkways, 14 acres of glass, and around 30 acres of carpeting, the international terminal at Hong Kong's Chek Lap Kok Airport is the world's largest. At $20 billion to build, it's also the world's most expensive airport.

• The city of Hong Kong is one of the greenest in Asia. Most of its residents live in high-rises in the densely populated Central district, surrounded by parkland and the acres of mountainous terrain that can't support buildings.

• The fastest rate of deflation worldwide is being experienced in Hong Kong, where prices fall by as much as 2% annually.

• One of the many things that didn't change when Hong Kong was returned to China were the rules of the road: People still drive on the left in the former British colony.

• Hong Kong is the watch and clock manufacturing capital of the world.

• The literal translation of Hong Kong is "fragrant harbor."

• When China reclaimed Hong Kong from Great Britain, locals lost the Queen's Birthday as an official holiday, but gained National Day (October 1) and Sino-Japanese War Victory Day (August 18).

FOOD & DRINK IN HONG KONG & MACAU

I F YOU ARE COMING to Hong Kong for the first time, you must leave certain misconceptions at home. Hong Kong does not, for example, have some of the best Chinese food in the world. It has *the* best Chinese food in the world.

Such a statement may not find immediate acceptance in Taiwan or the People's Republic of China, but, as they say in the West, the proof is in the pudding, and those Taiwanese and mainland Chinese who can afford it come to Hong Kong to eat. It is a historical fact that chefs were brought from Canton to Peking to serve in the Chinese emperors' kitchens, and that for many centuries the Cantonese were acknowledged as the Middle Kingdom's finest cooks.

An old Chinese maxim tells you where to find the prettiest girls, where to get married, where to die, where to eat, and so forth. The answer to "where to eat" is Canton (now called Guangzhou in the official romanization of Chinese names that also changed Peking to Beijing).

Hong Kong's more than 7 million population is 95% Chinese, of whom the vast majority are Cantonese. This includes a significant group of Chiu Chow people, whose families originated around the port city of Swatow. Food is a subject of overriding importance to the Cantonese, and it can be said, as it is of the French, that they live to eat rather than eat to live. Find out how true this is on a culinary tour of Hong Kong.

The Cantonese made an art out of a necessity, and in times of hardship they used every part of an animal, fish, or vegetable. Some dishes on a typical Hong Kong menu will sound strange, even unappetizing—goose webs, for example, or cockerels' testicles, cows' innards, snakes (in season), pigs' shanks, and other things that may not be served back home. But why

not succumb to new taste experiences? Who scorns the French for eating snails and frogs' legs, or the Japanese for eating raw fish?

There is no such thing, by the way, as a fortune cookie in a Hong Kong restaurant; the overseas Chinese came up with that novelty. Chop suey was invented abroad, too. Its exact origin is disputed: some say it began in the California goldfields; others give credit (or blame) to Australian gold miners.

Your first destination must be for *yum cha*, which literally means to drink tea. With your tea, you eat dim sum or dumplings. Served from before dawn to around 5 or 6 PM, these Cantonese daytime snacks are miniature works of art. There are about 2,000 kinds of dim sum in the Cantonese repertoire, and most dim sum restaurants prepare 100 varieties daily. Generally served steaming in bamboo baskets, the buns, crepes, and cakes are among the world's finest hors d'oeuvres. Many are minor engineering achievements—like a soup with prawns served in a translucent rice-pastry shell, or a thousand-layer cake, or the ubiquitous spring roll.

Hong Kong has hundreds of dim sum restaurants. The Hong Kong Tourist Board (HKTB) has color photos of some of the most popular dim sum (as well as other dishes) and "how-to" illustrations on chopsticks. (If you can't handle them, ask for a knife and fork; the object is to get the food to your mouth, not show off your dexterity.) The HKTB's *Official Dining, Entertainment and Shopping Directory* lists dozens of restaurants. Many of the top-rated Chinese restaurants in hotels and some of the better independent restaurants provide (somewhat incongruously) elegant settings for lunchtime dim sum, with bilingual check sheets, waiter service, and private tables. Such class costs about HK$15 or more per basket.

History-minded snackers will prefer, however, to visit the culinary shrine of the **Luk Yu Teahouse**, at 24–26 Stanley Street in Central, preferably with some Cantonese comrades. Luk Yu is more than a restaurant; it is one of Hong Kong's few historical monuments. It opened in the early 20th century as a wood-beamed, black-fanned, brass-edged place for Chinese gentlemen to partake of tea, dim sum, and gossip. When it was forced to relocate in the 1980s, everything was kept intact—marble-back chairs, floor spittoons, kettle warmers, brass coat hooks, and lockup liquor cabinets for regular patrons. Despite the addition of air-conditioning, fans still decorate a plain ceiling that looks down on elaborately framed scrolls, carved-wood booth partitions, and colored-glass panels. The ancient wooden staircase still creaks as Hong Kong's more traditional gentlemen ascend to the upper floors to discuss business and government.

Modernity has brought Luk Yu the English language, at least in the form of bilingual menus (though not for the individually served dim sum items), but you may have trouble making yourself understood.

As far as the Cantonese are concerned, anything that "keeps its back to heaven" is fit for cooking. Bird tastings in Hong Kong should include a feast of quails; smooth, salted chicken; sweet roasted chicken in lemon sauce; and minced pigeon served in lettuce-leaf "bowls" (rolled up with plum sauce). Pigeons appear on many menus, but **Han Lok Yuen**, on Lamma, specializes in roast pigeon and is a popular weekend pilgrimage spot for many Hong Kongers.

Fish is plentiful everywhere. Hong Kong is a major port with numerous fishing communities, a fact easily forgotten by the urbane traveler. Go to the islands—to **Lamma** especially, where the small village of Sok Kwu Wan has a waterfront lined

with restaurants offering fine seafood feasts.

Hong Kong's most famous dining experience is the **Jumbo Floating Restaurant,** at Aberdeen, which is moored to another floating seafood house covered with gaudy multicolor carvings and murals that form a sight in themselves. The Jumbo, a 2,000-seat three-decker, is a marvel of outrageous ostentatiousness. The excitement here is not about the food, which is average, but about the environment and, if you're lucky enough to have a table on the periphery, about the view. Many Hong Kong Harbour tours end their trips here.

✳ ✳ ✳

THERE IS NO SUCH thing as "Chinese" cooking in China. Every good "Chinese" chef has his (occasionally her) own repertoire, which will in turn reflect his clan's origin. Most Hong Kong restaurants are Cantonese; others prepare Pekingese or northern dishes, Shanghai specialties, or Szechuan (Sichuan) or Chiu Chow fare.

Crowds fill the new eating places in **Wanchai,** the fictional home of Suzie Wong and pretty much only known to foreigners for its girlie bars. Nowadays, the brothels are still there, but they stand shoulder to shoulder with restaurants and bars of every description. It's still the place where the boys go when they're looking for a good time, but it has also become respectable enough to draw young lovers, sophisticated couples, and even groups of girls who are out on the town for a fine dinner and a few drinks.

"Old" **Tsim Sha Tsui,** on both sides of Nathan Road from the Peninsula hotel up to the Jordan Road junction, has another batch of established restaurants. And the skyscrapers in Tsim Sha Tsui East burst with eateries, from grand Cantonese restaurants to cheerful little cafés. Here, as everywhere, you'll find not only Cantonese fare but Korean barbecues, Singaporean satays, Peking duck, Shanghainese breads and eel dishes, fine Western cuisine, and, of course, Western junk food.

The **Harbour City** complex, along Canton Road, has many fine restaurants tucked into shopping arcades or courtyards. **Central**, which once felt like a morgue at night, is now a bustling dining district with a warren of trendy bistros and good Indian restaurants up the hillside lanes on and off Wyndham Street and Lan Kwai Fong.

Another hip area is Hong Kong's own **SoHo** (South of Hollywood Road), accessed via the long outdoor escalator to Midlevels. Along the escalator are about 60 or 70 restaurants of just about every conceivable ethnic stripe.

Then there are the hotels, culinary competitors full of stylish salons—so stylish that it's now hard to find a simple, old-fashioned coffee shop. Travel away from the downtown districts and you find more temptations: every housing estate and community center now boasts at least one brass-and-chrome home of good Cantonese cuisine, often as chic as it is wholesome.

* * *

N SIMPLE TERMS, northern or Peking cuisine is designed to fill and warm—noodles, dumplings, and breads are more evident than rice. Mongolian or Manchurian hot pots (a sort of fonduecum-barbecue) are northern specialties, and firm flavors, such as garlic, ginger, and leek, are popular. Desserts, generally of little interest to the Cantonese, are heavy and sweet. Feasts have long been favored in the north, and not just by emperors holding weeklong banquets with elaborate centerpieces such as Peking duck (a three-course marvel of skin slices, sautéed meat, a rich soup of duck bones, and Tien Tsin cabbage). Beggar's chicken, about whose origins you'll hear varying legends, is another culinary ceremony, in which a stuffed, seasoned, lotus-leaf-wrapped, clay-baked bird releases heavenly aromas when its clay is cracked open.

Farther south, the Shanghai region (including Hangzhou) developed tastes similar to Peking's but with an oilier, sweeter style that favored preserved meats, fish, and vegetables. In Hong Kong the Shanghainese cafés are generally just that—unostentatious cafés with massive "buffet" displays of preserved or fresh snacks that are popular with late-nighters.

The phenomenal development of a Hong Kong middle class has prompted the appearance of grander, glitzier restaurants for Shanghainese and all other major regional cuisines. Those run by the Maxim's group are always reliable, moderately priced, and welcoming. Chiu Chow restaurants also come alive late at night, especially in the Chiu Chow areas of the Western District or in parts of western Kowloon. As with Shanghainese and Cantonese cuisine, the Chiu Chow repertoire emphasizes marine traditions, especially shellfish. The exotic-sounding "bird's nest" is the great Chiu Chow delicacy: it's the refined, congealed saliva of nest-building swallows (mainly gathered from nests built into Gulf of Siam cliffs). It may sound revolting to the uninitiated, but it's often exquisitely flavored—and, like many of China's most expensive foods, is said to be an aphrodisiac. A visit to any Chinese department store should include a (shocked) glance at the "medicine" counter's natural foods: the prices of top-grade bird's nest, shark's fins, deer horns, ginseng roots, and other time-tested fortifications are staggering representations of the law of supply and demand.

The food of the Szechuan region is known as the hottest and spiciest of all of China's cuisines. At first taste, the fiery chili dishes, somewhat akin to both Thai and Indian cuisines, can sear your tongue. Once your taste buds have blossomed again, the subtleties of Szechuan spices will be apparent—particularly in the classic smoked duck, where camphor-wood chips and red tea leaves add magical tinges to a finely seasoned duck that's been marinated for a full day.

Other regional variations, such as those of Hunan or the Hakka people, are not as distinctive as the major cuisines and are rare in Hong Kong. But other Chinese-influenced Asian cuisines are well represented. Even before the exodus of ethnic Chinese from Vietnam, that nation's exciting blend of native, French, and Chinese cooking styles was popular in Hong Kong. Now there are many cafés and a few smart restaurants specializing in prawns on sugarcane, mint-leaved meals, Vietnamese-style (labeled VN) salamis, omelets, and fondues. Look, too, for Burmese restaurants.

The most ubiquitous Asian cuisine is the multiethnic "Malaysian," a budget diner's culinary United Nations that includes native Malay, Indian, and Straits Chinese dishes, as well as "European" meals and the Sino-Malay culinary cross culture of *nonya* cooking.

Indian restaurants are also popular, and not just with Hong Kong's immigrant population from the subcontinent. The Indian kitchens usually concentrate on the northern Moghul styles of cooking, with reliable tandoori dishes; and vegetarians will find them a boon. Spicy Thai fare is readily available, as are the contrasting Indonesian and Vietnamese cuisines.

As for Northeast Asia, Hong Kong has some of the world's finest Japanese restaurants, which thrive on local seafood and still tempt big spenders with imports of the highly prized Kobe or Matsukaya beef (marbled slices with a fine flavor produced by beer-massaged and pampered steers). Smaller spenders welcome the many local Korean cafés, whose inexpensive *bulgogi* (barbecues) provide that country's distinctive garlicky, marinated meats and the minibuffet of preserved kimchi selections.

From Europe, Hong Kong has a wonderland of fine French restaurants (mostly in the top hotels), British pubs, German wining-and-dining havens, delis, and a sprinkling of pleasingly offbeat eating experiences—from Mexican and Californian to Austrian and Spanish-Filipino.

The Cantonese may be the world's finest cooks, but they're among the least polite servers. They're a proud people—some say arrogant—and their language has an abruptness that often translates poorly into English. Don't expect smiles or obsequiousness; Hong Kong is not Bangkok or Manila. It's friendly in its own way, and it's certainly efficient; so if you meet smiles as well, be fully appreciative and tip accordingly. Note that tips are not expected at local corner cafés and (the few remaining) roadside food stalls.

Wherever you eat, at the top or bottom end of the culinary scale, always check prices beforehand, especially for live fish, which is always expensive but becomes a serious luxury item when scarce. "Seasonal" prices apply to many dishes and can be steep, and some of the most prized Chinese delicacies—shark's fin, abalone, bird's nest, bamboo fungus—can cost an emperor's ransom. Although few Hong Kong restaurants set out to rip off tourists, waiters will of course try to "sell up."

Finally, don't settle for safe, touristy standbys. Sweet-and-sour pork, chop suey, and fried rice can be marvelous here, but the best dishes are not on the menu: they're seasonal specialties written in Chinese on table cards. Ask for translations, ask for interesting recommendations, try new items—show that you're adventurous and you'll get the respect and the food you deserve.

— Barry Girling

A food, travel, and entertainment columnist, Barry Girling has lived in Hong Kong since 1977.

BOOKS & MOVIES

Books

James Clavell's *Tai-Pan* and *Noble House* are blockbuster novels covering the early history of the British colony and the multifaceted culture of Hong Kong in the 1950s. Both books are insightful, if at times sensational. Robert S. Elegant's *Dynasty* is another epic novel, tracing the development of a powerful Eurasian family. It simplifies history a bit, but it does help reveal the Hong Kong worldview. Another best-seller set here is John Le Carre's *The Honorable Schoolboy*, a superb spy thriller. On a smaller scale is Han Suyin's *A Many Splendoured Thing*. Richard Mason's classic *The World of Suzie Wong*, written in 1957, depicts an American's adventures with a young woman in the Wanchai bar area during that era. Austin Coates's *Myself a Mandarin* is a lively and humorous account of a European magistrate handling Chinese society, and his *City of Broken Promises* is a rags-to-riches biography of an 18th-century woman from Macau. Derek Lambert's *Triad* will appeal to those who can't get enough of the street-gang movies on the subject.

Maurice Collis's beautifully written classic *Foreign Mud* covers the early opium trade and China wars. Colin N. Crisswell's *The Taipans: Hong Kong's Merchant Princes* describes the historical inspiration for novels exploring that era. G. B. Endicott's *History of Hong Kong* traces Hong Kong from its birth to the riot-wracked 1960s, but Frank Welsh's *A History of Hong Kong* is far more readable. Trea Wiltshire's *Hong Kong: Improbable Journey* is another readable history and has superb photographs. John Warner's compilation *Hong Kong Illustrated, Views & News 1840–1890* gives a marvelously detailed historical perspective.

Jan Morris's *Hong Kong: Social Life and Customs* and *Hong Kong: Xianggang* are primers on the region's daily interpersonal interactions. Younger readers might enjoy Nancy Durrell McKenna's *A Family in Hong Kong*, part of a series describing families all over the world. G. S. Heywood's *Rambles in Hong Kong* is a personal reflection. For an insightful read about local habits, check out Benny Constantine's *Let's Play Mahjong*. Books on the post-1997 future proliferate; a reading list might include Jamie Allen's *Seeing Red*, Mark Roberti's *The Fall of Hong Kong*, Robert Cottrell's *The End of Hong Kong*, Jonathan Dimbleby's *The Last Governor*, and Chris Patten's own *East and West*. Well-known local columnist and political analyst Stephen Vines's *Hong Kong: China's New Colony* looks at the situation well past the handover.

For businesspeople, the American Chamber of Commerce publishes *Living in Hong Kong*, *Doing Business in Hong Kong*, and *Establishing an Office in Hong Kong*, all of which are available to nonmembers. The *Far Eastern Economic Review Yearbook* and the *Hong Kong Government Yearbook* are essential reference books; the *Monthly Digest*, from the U.S. Census and Statistics Department, may also be useful. *Hong Kong Tax Planning* is useful in cutting through tax-related legalese. The China Phone Book Co. publishes a slew of useful publications on China in addition to its telephone and telex directories. The Hong Kong Trade Development Council publishes trade directories and has a good library. For a more cynical look at planning, check out Chinese University's *The Other Hong Kong Report*. And for handy, quick guides to local politics, you can't beat the comic books. Check out Larry Feign's *The World of Lily Wong* or *The Adventures of Superlily* for biting criticism of local life and politics in the late 1990s.

Films

Hong Kong is best known for its action films. Classic Hong Kong films are any that feature Bruce Lee, and more recently Jackie Chan, Jet Li, Chow Yun-Fat, Maggie Cheung, Brigitte Lin, Michelle Yeoh, Tony Leung, and the late Leslie Cheung. John Woo has been, perhaps, the most influential director since the late 1980s, and his action films—particularly those starring Chow Yun-Fat, have been quite popular. Many Hong Kong films are now available on DVD in either dubbed or subtitled versions. Some of John Woo's films include *A Bullet in the Head, The Killer,* the *A Better Tomorrow* series, and *Hard Boiled*; many of these star Chow Yun-Fat. You might want to check out the work of Wong Kar-wai, known as a director of more thoughtful, artistic films that have received much critical praise. His best works include *In the Mood For Love, Chungking Express, Happy Together,* and *Fallen Angels.* Other popular and recommendable films include the *Once Upon a Time in China* trilogy, which stars Jet Li; *The Bride with White Hair,* with Leslie Cheung and Brigitte Lin; the *Swordsman* films; *Chinese Ghost Story*; *Fist of Legend,* with Jet Li and Michelle Yeoh. Of course, you won't want to miss Ang Lee's *Crouching Tiger, Hidden Dragon* which stars Chow Yun-Fat and the venerable (and beautiful) Michelle Yeoh. Other classic Ang Lee films available on DVD and video include *The Wedding Banquet* and *Eat Drink Man Woman.* Even though it takes place in the mainland, you shouldn't miss the 1988 classic *The Last Emperor* for its insight into China. Amy Tan's *The Joy Luck Club* is also a useful insight into Chinese culture, albeit Chinese-American culture. Hong Kong films continue to be popular and influential, most notably for Quentin Tarantino, whose latest film *Kill Bill* shows obvious heavy influences from Hong Kong cinema. And the best Hong Kong actors often make films elsewhere in the world; Jackie Chan, Jet Li, and Chow Yun-Fat have all found some success in Hollywood, and Maggie Cheung won the best actress award at the 2004 Cannes Film Festival for her work in the film *Clean,* directed by Olivier Assayas.

INDEX